MOST SECRET
AND
CONFIDENTIAL

Horatio, Lord Nelson.

One of the most famous portraits of Nelson, done in 1798, by Lemuel Francis Abbott (1760–1803). Painted shortly after the Battle of the Nile, he is sitting in the regulation 1795 flag officers' undress uniform. In an age in which decorations and medals were rare, Nelson had an unusual number. The diamond-studded aigrette, or *chelengk,* on his hat is also a decoration; it was received from the sultan of Turkey in recognition of the Nile battle.

MOST SECRET
AND
CONFIDENTIAL

Intelligence in the Age of Nelson

Steven E. Maffeo

NAVAL INSTITUTE PRESS
Annapolis, Maryland

This book has been brought to publication by the generous assistance of
Marguerite and Gerry Lenfest.

Naval Institute Press
291 Wood Road
Annapolis, MD 21402

First Naval Institute Press paperback edition published in 2012.
ISBN: 978-1-59114-538-7

The Library of Congress has cataloged the hardcover edition as follows:
Maffeo, Steven E.
   Most secret and confidential: intelligence in the Age of Nelson/Steven E. Maffeo.
   p. cm.
   Includes bibliographical references and index
   ISBN: 1-55750-545-4
   1. Military intelligence—Great Britain—History—18th century. 2. Military intelligence—
Great Britain—History—19th century. 3. Great Britain. Royal Navy—History—18th century.
4. Great Britain. Royal Navy—History—19th century. 5. Nelson, Horatio Nelson, Viscount,
1758–1805. 6. France—History—Revolution, 1789–1799—Naval operations, British. 7.
Napoleonic Wars, 1800–1815—Naval operations, British. 8. France—History—Revolution,
1789–1799—Military intelligence—Great Britain. 9. Napoleonic Wars, 1800–1815—Military
intelligence—Great Britain. I. Title.

VB231.G7 M34 2000
327.12'41'09033—dc21   99-048837

∞ This paper meets the requirements of ANSI/NISO z39.48-1992 (Permanence of Paper).
   Printed in the United States of America.

20 19 18 17 16 15 14 13 12   9 8 7 6 5 4 3 2 1
                     First printing

   From *The Eyes of the Fleet: A Popular History of the Frigates and Frigate Captains 1793–1815* by
Anthony Price. © 1990 by Anthony Price. Selected excerpts reprinted by permission of A. P. Watt,
Ltd., Literary Agents, London, as well as W. W. Norton & Company, Inc., New York.
   From *Nelson the Commander* by Captain Geoffrey Bennett, RN. © 1972 by Geoffrey Bennett.
Selected excerpts reprinted with the permission of Scribner, a Division of Simon & Schuster, New
York, as well as the permission of the captain's heir, Mr. Rodney M. Bennett.
   From *The Great Gamble* by Dudley Pope. © 1972 by The Ramage Co., Ltd. Grateful acknowledg-
ment is given for the reprinting of selected excerpts.
   From *Dictionary of the Napoleonic Wars* by David G. Chandler. © 1979 by David G. Chandler.
Selected excerpts reprinted with the permission of Professor Chandler.
   From *The Post Office in the Eighteenth Century: A Study in Administrative History* by Kenneth Ellis.
© 1958 by The University of Durham. Selected excerpts reprinted with the permission of Oxford
University Press.
   From *Nelson and the Nile: The Naval War against Bonaparte 1798* by Brian Lavery. © 1998 by Brian
Lavery. Selected excerpts reprinted with the permission of Brian Lavery and the Naval Institute Press.
   From *Lord Nelson* by C. S. Forester. © 1929 by C. S. Forester; renewed 1957. Selected excerpts
reprinted with permission granted by Harold Matson, Co., Inc., as well as the permission of Peters
Fraser & Dunlop Group, Ltd., London, on behalf of the Estate of C. S. Forester.

To my grandmother Lucille and grandfather Carmine,
to my mother June and to my father Eugene,
to my wife Rhonda, to my son Micah,
and, inevitably, to C. S. Forester

What was scattered in many volumes, and observed at several times by eyewitnesses, with no cursory pains I laid together, to save the reader a far longer travail of wandering through so many desert authors.

John Milton, preface to *A Brief History of Muscovy,* 1632

CONTENTS

FOREWORDS

LIFE'S PLEASURABLE MOMENTS occur when we are requested to recognize an individual for superior performance. In this case, I am afforded the marvelous opportunity to introduce to you, the reader, a unique historical novel. The word "novel" was deliberately selected because this book reads like fascinating fiction, but factually stresses the principles of intelligence operations that are, historically and in contemporary times, critical to success.

That Cdr. Steven Maffeo's work, which emanated from a master's degree thesis, has been selected for publication by the editorial board of the prestigious U.S. Naval Institute is an honor indeed. In their wisdom that board identified for publication a book that is a "must read" for not only civilian and military intelligence personnel, and those individuals interested in matters of intelligence, but also—definitely—operators and warriors who must utilize intelligence to win in battle.

Maffeo's book focuses on a special period of history—Britain and Europe in land and maritime struggles from roughly the 1770s to 1815. The central theme explores the ingenious methods of collecting, analyzing, and disseminating intelligence by the British and how it was delivered to their sea forces. Even more important, he examines how the warriors executed both strategy and tactics by comprehending and utilizing intelligence information. Battles were won or lost on those factors alone.

Maffeo has thoroughly researched an amazing number of primary and secondary documents, has incorporated a zeal for accuracy and correctness, and brought a style of writing that compels continued interest.

He presents considerable information about Vice Adm. Lord Horatio Nelson, that formidable figure who stands astride this immense geographic panoply and who was the epitome of acquiring intelligence and making bold decisions as a result of his comprehension of the information. More important, the author allows us each to learn and grasp more of history that will assist us in making very important contemporary decisions.

Cdr. Steven Maffeo, USNR, has earned my highest compliments and congratulations for producing a splendid work. He has served each of us well in his endeavors.

So, reader, move ahead smartly—absorb, learn, enjoy!

REAR ADM. HOWARD ROOP (RET.)

IT WOULD BE INCONCEIVABLE for a modern naval commander to try operating without adequate access to accurate and timely intelligence. We take for granted the importance of good intelligence and its use in formulating our battle plans and all types of fleet operations and exercises—both in peace and in war. At the same time, we give little thought to the historical evolution of the use of intelligence. Most of us have small appreciation for the importance that good intelligence has played in successful military and naval operations throughout history.

Commander Maffeo's excellent and extremely well researched book helps us to understand how far we have come since the days of Vice Adm. Horatio Nelson and the great "age of fighting sail." As in all professions, a better understanding of history, and where we have come from, will give the true intelligence professional a firm foundation and understanding of the importance and use of good intelligence. That particular history is the basis for most of the operations within the present intelligence profession.

To my knowledge, this is the first definitive study of the use and development of intelligence and its evolution (beyond educated "guessing") in the days of fighting sailing ships. It is an excellent piece of research and analysis on one of the most important elements of naval conflict in one of history's most interesting times. It should become a standard reference and required reading for new naval intelligence officers, as well as other intelligence professionals who wish to understand and improve their professional knowledge in the art and science (as well as the prudent use) of intelligence.

Of particular interest are the historical examples and anecdotes throughout Commander Maffeo's book. These clearly illustrate the failure or success of a commander's intelligence awareness and his reaction to the available intelligence picture. The subsequent events and outcomes of battles—or avoidance thereof—which were defined in part by these intelligence perceptions (as well as the opposing commander's reaction to them) have truly shaped world history.

After reading this book, the intelligence professional cannot help but be better rooted in his or her sense of the past and the ever-increasing need for better, faster, and more accurate all-source intelligence. Clearly, the requirement for collection, analysis, and dissemination of pertinent intelligence to the war-fighter was as critical to Nelson and his colleagues in 1793 as it is today. However, we have tools Nelson did not; one can only wonder what the outcomes of his battles would have been had each of the combatants had the intelligence capabilities we have now. Because Lord Nelson, unlike too many of his peers, fundamentally believed in the value of good intelligence and worked extremely hard at obtaining and analyzing data, one cannot help but think that the results of his operations would have been much the same. It very often is, after all, the attitude of the war-fighter toward the value of intelligence that, in fact, makes it of value.

For this reason I also recommend this book to all who find themselves in command.

REAR ADM. BRUCE A. BLACK (RET.)

PREFACE

By "Intelligence" we mean every sort of information about the enemy and his country—the basis, in short, of our own plans and operations.

Gen. Karl Maria von Clausewitz

"Wot's wot?" repeated one of the buccaneers. "Ah, he'd be a lucky one as knowed that!"

Robert Louis Stevenson

IN EARLY 1792 the prime minister of Great Britain, the Rt. Hon. William Pitt, optimistically prophesied the peaceful closure of the eighteenth century and the opening of the nineteenth: "Unquestionably there never was a time in the history of this country when, from the situation in Europe, we might more reasonably expect fifteen years of peace than we may at the present moment."

It was not to be. Mr. Pitt's intelligence information, concerning the impending course of action of two foreign powers, was faulty. Twelve days after that speech Austrian emperor Leopold II died in Vienna. He was succeeded by the more reactionary Francis II, who promptly gave notice of his extreme unhappiness with the subversive revolutionists then on the rise in France.

In response to Francis, those French revolutionists opted for offensive action—and they did it in a remarkable way:

> Louis XVI, who was still a king, though only in name, entered the hall of the Legislative Assembly. The deputies rose and took off their hats. The King sat down; the deputies did the same. General Dumouriez read a report, detailing the grievances against Austria. Louis XVI followed the General with a speech for war.

> "The Assembly," replied the president of that body, "will take into
> consideration the proposition which you have made." Louis XVI
> gravely left the hall; the deputies shouted: *Vive le Roi!*
> In the same evening the Assembly declared war against Austria "as
> a just defence of a free people against the unjust aggression of a king."
> (Thompson and Padover, *Secret Diplomacy,* 181)

The ensuing war swept away Louis's already tottering throne, for five
months later the French monarchy was abolished and the republic was
proclaimed. The date of the declaration of war is significant: 20 April
1792. In effect it was the beginning of a world war that lasted, rarely
interrupted, for twenty-three years (ibid.).

Moreover, it heralded a sea change in the nature of war, for it was not
only a world war in terms of geographic scope and breadth, it was a
peoples' war in terms of the mass of numbers involved. Warfare, earlier
in eighteenth-century Europe, had evolved over time to something less
critical to governments and to the public than it was shortly going to be.
War had lost the significance it once had carried. It had become national
prestige that was at stake rather than national existence. Warfare that
actually threatened the life of the nation became almost unthinkable for
reasons of scope and sheer cost. As C.S. Forester notes, "Only when the
French Revolution came to make the existence of a government dependent upon military victory did war regain its overwhelming importance
in the scheme of things" (*Lord Nelson,* 56).

The recent American Revolutionary War had been, for the most part,
of this earlier nature and was thus "from the naval point of view one long
series of missed opportunities—more so, that is to say, even than the
general run of wars." For Horatio Nelson, a young British navy captain
during that war, "the realization of what was being missed was intense
and impressive. It is to these years that his later resolves of never to lose
an hour or waste a [favorable] wind can be traced" (ibid., 39–40).

In 1793, as Britain now faced France again, the new war was going to
be a strong unifying factor in a nation very divided by religion and class.
Victories—rare at first and at first only naval—were going to provide
unique opportunities for national celebration. People of all classes would

unite to shoot off fireworks and hold balls. Moreover, every intelligent citizen "knew that events in Bombay, Martinique, or the Cape of Good Hope could have an effect on his pocket, his standard of living and his national pride" (Lavery, *Nelson and the Nile,* 29).

King George III, much more perceptive than many people give him credit for being, immediately established a simple point of view, but it was one that clearly saw this war was not going to be business as usual. He firmly believed in fighting the French "until the Revolutionary government was overthrown and one based on anti-revolutionary principles was put in its place; this was the main purpose of the war and hence everything should be subordinated to it" (Barnes, *George III and William Pitt,* 321). This, incidentally, was Captain Nelson's view as well. A staunch monarchist, he hated republican—and, later, Napoleonic—France.

This is a good place to fully introduce Nelson—the famous naval figure who dominates this time period as well as this book. He was, of course, to become Sir Horatio Nelson, Vice Admiral of the White, Knight of the Bath, Baron and Viscount of the Nile and of Burnham Thorpe and Hillborough in the County of Norfolk, and Duke of Bronte (1758–1805). He was the British navy's most famous leader; a complex, multi-faceted genius. Arguably he was the greatest naval strategist and tactician that ever paced a deck, and in very many ways he was to prove a farsighted innovator, moving considerably away from eighteenth-century tradition. He saw things on a grand scale, wanting not only glorious victories but also the annihilation of the enemy. His idea was to do at sea what another visionary of the period—Napoleon Bonaparte—was going to do in land battles like Austerlitz and Ulm.

Like Bonaparte and many other practitioners of this more "total" way of warfare, Nelson was ruthless. More important, he had "the qualities of leadership. He had imagination. . . . He knew what he wanted. He knew what his men were thinking and he knew what the enemy would do. He had a deep knowledge of his profession, especially on the tactical side. He had the ability to organize and direct his forces. He had determination, a belief that the task would be accomplished, coupled with a gift for conveying his own confidence to the rest of his team" (Parkinson, *Britannia Rules,* 124).

Nelson was also a superb intelligence officer. He collected and used intelligence at a phenomenal rate, his mind constantly geared to seek out, analyze, and integrate intelligence information into his decision making. And he was not alone, for the British navy drew upon an enormous reserve of talent, no single officer able to replace Nelson—but some of them actually superior to him in specific ways. Indeed, Collingwood was "better as an administrator, Keats better as a seaman, Popham more original in some ways and Saumarez destined to gain a high reputation as a diplomatist. Nelson died with his reputation at its peak and it is not too easy to see him in the roles he would have had to fill in the years to come. He had made himself a heroic legend and that is what he has remained" (ibid., 125).

His legend has not previously highlighted, at least to any great extent, his skills as an intelligence officer. If that should come out in the following pages it can only further enhance his reputation. Moreover, "we must avoid the mistake of thinking that the war at sea ended with Nelson's death [at Trafalgar in 1805]. It did nothing of the kind. It continued for another ten years with plenty of incident" (ibid.), and it was during the ten years after Trafalgar that Britain's *maximum* naval effort in the age of sail occurred (Price, *Eyes of the Fleet,* 123).

In fact, this book is about much more than Horatio Nelson. There were many other officers and ministers, in Britain and other countries, who operated with heavy intelligence orientations and mastery of the various intelligence disciplines. This is very much their story as well.

THE PURPOSE of this book is to describe and analyze state of the art national and naval intelligence during, as the naval historian and novelist C. S. Forester popularized it, the "age of fighting sail." Many people also term this period the "age of Nelson," so called for its most prominent figure.

This great age of fighting sail, which is generally defined as the years between 1793 and 1815, is approximately the same twenty-three-year period of world war already described. It saw the technological peak of the sailing warship as well as the pinnacle of the Royal Navy's fame and glory. Also present, within the context of the French Revolutionary and Napoleonic Wars, were the fundamental characteristics of modern all-source intelligence available to—and used by—operational commanders. In fact, reasonably sophisticated national and naval intelligence existed during this time, lacking only the formal, institutionalized, and bureaucratic organizations that emerged in the late nineteenth century. These organizations, of course, evolved into the modern and extremely technical intelligence communities of today.

With a few exceptions, this book specifically focuses upon the British government and navy during this period. In so doing it attempts to analyze the impact of intelligence upon naval history during this extremely important era. Moreover, it attempts to investigate the effectiveness of command decision making relative to the commander's use, non-use, or misuse of intelligence, as well as the systems developed by governments and navies to gain effective use of intelligence. These are important issues to the naval historian as well as the student of practical intelligence application to modern naval warfare.

IN SOME FORM, the collection, organization, analysis, and dissemination of information always has been part of war. Countless secret-intelligence works seem to quote the Old Testament, referring to the Son of Nun sending two men to "go spy the land" of Jericho. Others find amusement in describing intelligence as the "second oldest profession." Yet a review of military- or naval-intelligence literature might well suggest that systems of intelligence have only existed since the later nineteenth century. In truth, it was then that modern technology, such as it was, began to shape intelligence collection and dissemination (Dennis Showalter, "Intelligence on the Eve of Transformation," in Hitchcock, *Intelligence Revolution,*

15). In fact, "the critical part played by intelligence in war and the establishment of immense intelligence bureaucracies began in earnest during the First World War" (Handel, *Masters of War,* 122).

Military intelligence, however, has existed for some thirty centuries. Naval intelligence existed long before "Magic" (the American World War II code name for the intelligence derived from breaking the Japanese diplomatic code "Purple" in 1940) and Midway and before "Ultra" (the British World War II code name for the immeasurably valuable intercepts obtained from the German Enigma cipher machine) and the Battle of the Atlantic. The history of warfare is the history of intelligence. Indeed, naval intelligence, in many ways as we know it today, has always existed to one degree or another.

Without doubt, a period of naval history—vital for its cataclysmic struggles in what were virtual world wars in terms of geographic scope —is the era of Nelson, or of fighting sail: "It was, after all, a *world war* that was then in progress—and, more than that, a world war in which the British sought to control and command the sea against all-comers in order to survive, let alone win" (Price, *Eyes of the Fleet,* 2). It was a period of enormous fleets and enormous naval establishments. In fact, according to the eminent naval historian Dr. N. A. M. Rodger, in the eighteenth century the British navy "was by far the largest and most complex of all government services, and indeed by a large margin, the largest industrial organization in the western world. It faced problems of management and control then quite unknown in even the greatest private firms" (Rodger, *Wooden World,* 29). This period encompassed the beginning of the French Revolutionary Wars to the closure of the Napoleonic Wars, and certainly included the American War of 1812; it saw the pinnacle of sailing-warship strategic deployment and fighting tactics and, again, the zenith of the Royal Navy's historical effectiveness and glory.

Also present, though generally ignored by military and particularly naval historians, was multisource naval intelligence available to operational commanders. Indeed, as the reader will shortly see, military- and naval-intelligence activity was considerable. The military and naval establishments were technologically primitive and thus significantly hampered, particularly in analysis and communications. This situation severely limited the rapid exploitation and dissemination of intelligence information that may otherwise have decisively influenced the outcome of many more significant battles and campaigns than it did (Gunther Rothenberg, "Military Intelligence Gathering in the Second Half of the Eighteenth Century, 1740–1792," in Neilson and McKercher, *Go Spy the Land*, 111). Nevertheless, though few records were kept, and though there were no true permanently established intelligence organizations, British strategic and operational intelligence can be shown to be reasonably effective.

The close of the eighteenth century saw tactical naval intelligence almost exclusively in the hands of the senior officer present at any given locale, for he often was the only one in place experienced enough, and fundamentally competent, to evaluate it. Moreover, he was the only one who was going to use it. In any event, he had no staff—competent or otherwise—to handle it on his behalf. In stark contrast, today's naval commanders have large staffs of highly trained and experienced experts in all fields, including intelligence.

Before this discussion goes any further, it might be useful to define more closely what is meant today when the word *intelligence* is used, and how it differs from the term *information*.

Information can be considered as unorganized, unrelated, unprocessed, and unanalyzed raw facts and data. It will include all documents or observations which may serve to throw light upon an actual or potential enemy or upon a theater of operations. Information will concern the enemy, the weather, the terrain, and any other data related to the military or diplomatic issues at hand. Information may be true or false, accurate or inaccurate, pertinent or irrelevant, positive or negative.

Intelligence is considered to be evaluated and interpreted information, including any conclusions based on this information. Information is analyzed and evaluated to determine the reliability of its source and its accuracy; it is then interpreted to determine its significance in light of what is already known. The conclusions drawn from this resulting intelligence may well include a deduction of the other side's capabilities and intentions.

Tactical intelligence (including *combat intelligence* and *combat information*) is essentially military intelligence which is often gathered and produced in the field during actual hostilities. Its initial and primary use is by a tactical commander for active operations. *Strategic intelligence* is the counterpart of tactical intelligence and differs from it primarily in its larger breadth of scope. It is produced in time of peace as well as in time of war. It might therefore include varied studies of many nations and many possible theaters of operations.

An *intelligence officer* is a person, civilian or military, accountable to a politician, diplomat, or commander for the collection of information. Such a person would also be responsible for production and dissemination of resulting intelligence, and for the receipt of processed intelligence from higher or parallel headquarters. Note that although many individuals in government functioned in this role, it was only as a secondary duty within their primary jobs. The concept of "intelligence officer" was effectively unknown at the turn of the nineteenth century, although there certainly was a considerable number of professional spies in the world! (There are countless experts and dozens of books which will give such definitions more or less in concurrence with these. These are essentially those of Lt. Col. Robert R. Glass and Lt. Col. Phillip B. Davidson in *Intelligence Is for Commanders,* with some modification from the U.S. Joint Chiefs of Staff (JCS) Joint Publication 2-0, *Joint Doctrine for Intelligence Support to Operations, 1995,* and the U.S. Naval Doctrine Command (NDC) Naval Doctrine Publication 2, *Naval Intelligence, 1994.*)

In the late eighteenth and early nineteenth centuries, the concise and precise definitions above did not really exist. Those few individuals who were in the business of intelligence work typically did not make such neat and clear discriminations in terminology. While these discrete ideas were neither unknown nor ignored in political and military thinking, *intelligence* was a very informal and a very loosely applied term. It is interesting to note, however, that only twenty-three years after the focus of this study closes, the great Swiss military thinker (and Napoleonic War veteran) Lt. Gen. Antoine Henri, Baron Jomini, published a relevant and comprehensive analysis of what intelligence should be. He wrote that intelligence should encompass a well-arranged system of espionage, reconnaissance by skillful officers, the questioning of prisoners of war, the forming of hypotheses of probabilities, and the observation (and perhaps interpretation of) signals (Jomini, *Art of War,* 269–74).

Nevertheless, the reality of intelligence in the period from 1793 to 1815 was fairly simple—essentially, any information that stimulated orders or changed plans was "intelligence" (Hoffman, U.S. Joint Military Intelligence College lecture, Washington, 15 September 1996). Perhaps, in the last analysis, this is a valid, though very broad and informal, definition even two hundred years later.

Looking at both diplomatic and operational issues, I have tried to develop, evaluate, and disclose the background and administration of British naval intelligence during this critical period. I specifically examine the sources of intelligence information on a national level and evaluate both the national Post Office and Lloyd's insurance marketing association as major sources of such intelligence. The book also discusses the Admiralty itself, searching for its various sources of both strategic and tactical intelligence, as well as the impact of signaling systems, message delivery, and other kinds of information transmission relative to intelligence utilization. I explore the use of frigates and other smaller ships— Nelson's "eyes of the fleet"—as intelligence collectors and transmitters, and analyze how the deployed senior officer, whether admiral in charge of a fleet or detached single-ship captain, was really his own intelligence officer and how he integrated this job with all of his other considerable responsibilities. Finally, I examine three historical, real-life naval-intelligence scenarios, which further helps to underscore the role of the on-scene commander as the ultimate intelligence collector, analyst, and user.

Before finally laying down this book, the reader might come to see that despite the somewhat haphazard, ad hoc, decentralized, and personality-driven eighteenth-century intelligence system, multisource intelligence was there for the commander to use—or not—sometimes to great significance. Moreover, the reader may grow to appreciate that radical differences exist over time in intelligence technology, collection, analysis, and dissemination. Finally, the reader might be persuaded to agree that, in the last analysis, the commander's possession and use of intelligence have been decisive in history, are decisive now, and will be decisive in the future.

THE STUDY OF naval intelligence in the late eighteenth century depends heavily on the researcher's ability to piece together a narrative from a wealth of disparate sources. A plethora of material exists if one is imaginative in exploring contemporary records of the period, as well as the abundance of excellent secondary sources. Usually the focuses of these works are not specific to intelligence.

From the traditional naval history approach, one cannot avoid the thirty-six-hundred-page treasure of primary-source material found in Nelson's own words—Sir Nicholas Nicolas's *Dispatches and Letters of Vice Admiral Lord Nelson* (as well as several other major Nelson collections). Additionally, the papers of many other significant actors—both naval and political—are reasonably available: First Secretary of the Admiralty Croker; Capt. Lord Cochrane; Vice Adm. Baron Collingwood; Adms. Earl St. Vincent, Baron Keith, and Baron Barham; Ambassador Sir William Hamilton; Secretary of State Viscount Castlereagh; and King George III, to name a few obvious ones. Military writer Robin Ranger correctly emphasizes that "to understand how the Anglo-French conflict looked to the naval commanders and governments fighting it, their own accounts [must] be sampled" (Robin Ranger, "Anglo-French Wars: 1689–1815," in Gray and Barnett, *Seapower and Strategy,* 185). These sources are where real keys to the topic are located; the letters, dispatches, memoranda, and diaries of contemporary leaders reveal their intelligence operations, procedures, and thinking—if any—in their own words. In addition, one cannot overlook the valuable material found in the press of the period; the *Naval Chronicle* and the *London Gazette* are somewhat difficult to locate, but microfilm collections of the *Times* of London are fairly widespread.

Most secondary sources do little more than touch on intelligence issues for this era. However, several specific volumes were crucial to this study because of their unusual emphases upon intelligence, communications, and commanders' responsibilities; indeed, of the wealth of secondary materials offering scattered nuggets of information, these several disclosed unusually rich veins of material. I have heavily stressed their findings in an effort to present the most comprehensive picture possible in this type of study, citing their sources whenever possible to reveal primary material unavailable other than through archival research in Britain. Finally, I have quoted them extensively to best share their valuable analyses and conclusions—and because to rephrase or paraphrase their words would be nothing short of hubris.

In fact, and as the reader will quickly observe, this book contains a large number of quotations and notes. Despite American general George S. Patton's belief—"To be a successful soldier you must know history . . . [and] how man reacts. Weapons change but man who uses them changes not at all"—the passage of many years really does precipitate change. The period from 1793 to 1815 was another time, another system, another navy, and, really, another world. Consequently, it seems reasonable to share quotations that give the flavor of the period and help the reader understand the issues within the context of the times. As Capt. Geoffrey Bennett, RN, author of the wonderful book *Nelson the Commander,* wrote, this is an era long gone from us and we are fundamentally able to recreate neither the environment, the emotions of the people, nor the *feel* of the time. The added information, found particularly in the fuller quotations, reveals and refines the flavor of the period and offers insights into the thinking of the actors. It also enriches "our understanding of the naval world that existed as the eighteenth century became the nineteenth" (Christopher McKee, in Pope, *Black Ship,* xvi).

Finally, there are two major aspects of this book I profoundly hope the reader will share with me. The first is the serious, documented historical information presented for study; with this I have tried to make a contribution to the common body of knowledge in existence about this fascinating topic and period. The other aspect, of no less importance, is purely entertainment. The activities and adventures of the real-life actors in this period—whether one focuses upon "wooden ships and iron men" or upon "secret intelligence"—are every bit as exciting as those in fiction. Indeed, Horatio Hornblower, Nicholas Ramage, Richard Bolitho, and Jack Aubrey really have nothing at all over Horatio Nelson, Lord St. Vincent, Nathaniel Dance, and Thomas Cochrane.

As a dedicated reader on the Age of Nelson myself (for over thirty-seven years), I have added to my own storehouse of information every time I have picked up a new book on any aspect of the subject. As others examine this book, I hope they will similarly add to their own storehouses and thereby enrich their understanding of those far-gone days, events, and people.

ACKNOWLEDGMENTS

I WOULD VERY MUCH LIKE to try to acknowledge everyone who assisted me in the development of this work. This kind of project is often done under extreme duress; so it was with mine, and I'm thus extremely grateful to those who eased my path. First and foremost, I need to thank C. S. Forester, Dudley Pope, and Alexander Kent for lighting the fire some thirty years ago—as well as Patrick O'Brian for somewhat recently infusing secret intelligence into the equation. Alexander Kent merits additional gratitude for his recent enthusiasm and warmth. Similarly, I'm extraordinarily beholden to Stephen Coonts for valuable advice and priceless encouragement. I can't overlook my cousin, Capt. Jack V. Roome, USN (Ret.), who first exposed me to naval intelligence. Past inspiration also comes from Midn. William J. Bartlett, USN, '74, who certainly underestimated the "threat," yet whose loss to the sea services was noteworthy none the less.

Key supporters in the U.S. Naval Reserve Intelligence Command were Yeoman 2d Class Traci T. King, Chief Intelligence Specialist Kristen Bright, Lt. Cdr. Kenneth R. Smith, Cdr. David K. Heller, and Capt. Bradley M. Inman; in particular were Rear Adm. Bruce A. Black, Capt. Timothy L. Kathka, and Capt. Michael L. Waldron. I also need to mention, from the U.S. Joint Military Intelligence College, Maj. Susan M. Horton, USAR, and Col. John K. Rowland, Ph.D., USAFR. I'm particularly indebted to Rear Adm. Howard Roop, Ed.D., USNR (Ret.), formerly commandant of the school when it was called the Defense Intelligence College.

Special thanks go to Lt. Cdr. David M. Keithly, Ph.D., USNR, who was my committee chairman for the thesis from which this book is derived and stood as a mentor as I braved the world of publishing. At the U.S. Air Force Academy I'm extremely indebted to my thesis reader,

Dr. Elizabeth A. Muenger, a wonderful friend whose contributions to this and other projects have been immeasurable, as well as the Director of Academy Libraries, Dr. Edward A. Scott, whose multifaceted support has been crucial and without which this project would not have reached fruition. Brig. Gen. Philip D. Caine, USAF (Ret.), supplied solid support and welcome criticism, as did distinguished visiting professor Dr. Frederick T. Kiley, formerly director of the National Defense University Press. Monica M. Scott was key to the organizational charts and translations from the French. From Annapolis I received encouragement and validation from Emeritus Professor Dr. John W. Huston. At the National Maritime Museum, Greenwich, Lindsey Macfarlane of the Picture Library put forth no little effort into helping me obtain most of the illustrations I wanted. Jon Wadick was instrumental in digitalizing the illustrations for publication. Barbara Luchte weighed in with prodigious word processing as I neared the intractable due date.

I can't overlook Cdrs. James Dargan, Daniel Butler, Jeffrey Subko, and Kurt Johnson; Lt. Cdr. Barry Zulauf, Ph.D; Iris McKenzie; Shaun Austin; Howard Wilson; Rodney Raleigh; Norma Cervone; and Gilda Baxter.

I have to admit to an enormous indebtedness to the librarians and staff of the U.S. Air Force Academy Academic Library, who have built a marvelous collection in a short forty years—a collection which supported this esoteric study remarkably well. Many thanks also go to the libraries of the Joint Military Intelligence College, Kansas State University, University of Colorado at Boulder, Auburn University, Rice University, Northern Arizona University, Creighton University, University of Denver, Metropolitan State University (Denver), University of Rochester, Arkansas State University, University of Maine at Orono, San Diego State University, Pittsburgh State University, Arizona State University, University of Kansas, University of South Carolina, Kent State University, Michigan State University, Flint (Michigan) Junior College, the Detroit Public Library, the U.S. Navy Library, and the New York Public Library, all of whose support, either personally or through interlibrary loan, was vital.

I'm very grateful to the panoply of naval, Nelson, and Napoleonic scholars who have worked so hard and written so extensively about this fascinating period, including C. S. Forester, Carola Oman, Brian Lavery, Anthony Price, Dudley Pope, Alexander Kent, Patrick O'Brian, Tom Pocock, Nicholas Rodger, David Howarth, Oliver Warner, Michael Lewis, Christopher Lloyd, Nicholas Tracy, Alfred Cobban, David Chandler, G. J. Marcus, Geoffrey Bennett, Julian Corbett, A. T. Mahan, Piers Mackesy, Arthur Bryant, C. Northcote Parkinson, Christopher Hibbert, and so many others.

My parents, Eugene and June Maffeo, both retired teachers, supplied tremendous enthusiasm and encouragement. Moreover, they were instrumental in proofreading my text and criticizing my grammar. If there remains anything wrong or less than elegant, it's because I've no doubt gone contrary to their judgments. (Indeed, my mother ultimately may well be responsible for this project, having bought for me a copy of *Captain Horatio Hornblower* when I was in the fourth grade.)

I thank my wife and son, Rhonda and Micah, for their patience while I was chasing the ghosts of Nelson and his associates, and for their understanding of my preoccupation. In addition, my wife's computer knowledge was truly invaluable. The editors and staff at the U.S. Naval Institute Press have been continuously helpful and encouraging. I am particularly indebted to my copy editor, Karin Kaufman, whose extra polish certainly enhanced the final product.

Finally, the greatest acknowledgments must go to Horatio Nelson, John Jervis, Thomas Cochrane, George III, Napoleon Bonaparte, Henry Dundas, Arthur Wellesley, the younger William Pitt, George Elphinstone, Charles Middleton, George Spencer, Home Popham, George Canning, James Harris, Alexander Scott, William Wickham, Philip d'Auvergne, Evan Nepean, Edward Pellew, Francis Willes, and countless other contemporary politicians, leaders, ministers, commanders, soldiers and sailors, whose involvement with intelligence and communications, so long ago, is the heart of this book.

MOST SECRET
AND
CONFIDENTIAL

1

The British National Intelligence Effort

One final impediment to strategic planning was . . . intelligence. In general in this crucial area Britain was very poorly served, particularly compared to Napoleon. There was no formal organization, either independent or attached to the armed forces, to acquire and assess information.

Prof. Christopher Hall

TODAY WE DEFINE STRATEGIC, NATIONAL INTELLIGENCE AS THE collection, analysis, processing, and dissemination of information aimed primarily to support the national command authorities. Perhaps less sharply articulated in the period from 1793 to 1815, secret intelligence of this nature would have been for the large-scale, strategic-level consumption of the prime minister, the secretary of state for the Foreign Office, the secretary of state for the Home Office, the secretary of state for War and the Colonies, the first lord of the Admiralty, and other top officials of the national-level military, naval, and political leadership—and certainly, during this period, this included the king. It might help the serious student of British history to note that the "home" and "foreign" offices had previously been "southern" and "northern," respectively. Either way, they both focused heavily on foreign affairs. For many purposes the Mediterranean and France generally fell into the domain of "home." (For a general organizational structure of the government, see Appendix 1; for a specific listing of the principal government officials of this period, see Appendix 2.)

Two hundred years ago intelligence was not clearly defined because political intelligence was the primary business of the state; intelligence was not a separate function. It was partially collected, and definitely analyzed, at the top of government, "by Napoleon, by Fouché for Napoleon, by their British adversary Pitt, by Lord Liverpool to a slightly lesser extent, by Canning to a greater extent, and certainly by Metternich." In the eighteenth century diplomacy had become bureaucratized and professionalized, "supplemented by the use of secret agents at the highest level of government. Kings resorted to what in France was called *secrets du roi,* the use of their own private, secret diplomatic agents."[1]

Having established that, and save for one unusual exception which will shortly be developed in detail, by and large there is very little evidence of organized, centralized, or bureaucratized intelligence offices operating in England in the late eighteenth century. In fact, the large view has to take into account other issues than just a specific focus upon intelligence, such as the parallel primitive state of national command and control, interservice cooperation, information dissemination, local commander or minister responsibility, and crisis-warning procedures. Essential lack of evidence will not necessarily prove anything decisively, one way or the other, as many scholars (such as Alfred Cobban) and novelists (such as Ian Fleming) will insist that the first priority of a secret service is to remain secret.[2] Indeed, this concept is cynically addressed by the British writer and intelligence officer Malcolm Muggeridge, who once wrote that "secrecy is as essential to Intelligence as vestments and incense to a mass, or darkness to a spiritual seance, and must at all costs be maintained, quite irrespective of whether or not it serves any purpose."[3]

Some years prior to the focus of this book, Gen. George Washington took the concept fairly seriously. During the American Revolution he wrote, "There is one evil that I dread, & that is [British] Spies. . . . I think it a matter of some importance to prevent them from obtaining Intelligence of our Situation." His famous letter on this subject, a copy of which is displayed in the office of the chief of modern Britain's Secret Intelligence Service, further addresses this issue, stating that "the necessity of procuring good intelligence is apparent & need not be further urged . . . [and you must] keep the whole matter as secret as possible. For upon Secrecy, success depends in most Enterprizes of this kind, & for want of it, they are generally defeated, however well planned."[4] In any event, whether or not total organizational secrecy ever really was a valid first priority, documentary evidence about such activity in this time period, while sparse, is available.

Unquestionably, secret services and secret-intelligence activities existed during this period. In fact, the origin of a secret-intelligence system (*espionage civile*) in England dates from around 1330, when King Edward III developed a great interest in foreign commerce and shipping.[5] The prominence and very existence of such systems radically varied, however, from era to era, king to king, and ministry to ministry. In fact, this is an aspect of history which has not received a great deal of attention. The diplomatic historian is not generally focused upon "what second secretaries are doing in lobbies and on the back-stairs. There are situations, however, in which such secret manoeuvres are the real heart of the diplomatic game, and to attempt to unearth them is the only way of discovering not only what happened but also why it happened."[6]

Until fairly recent times very little has been written (except in works of imagination) on the role of secret service activities in British diplomacy and wartime strategy; nowhere is this more true than the period of the French Revolution, the French Revolutionary Wars, and the Napoleonic Wars. Yet this was a period in which such activities developed to a significant degree.[7]

While there may be some truth to William Blake's warning that "nothing can be more contemptible than to suppose public records to be true," there are some records that give a few clues about this activity. Just as the scope of current intelligence operations essentially boils down to money, so it was in Britain two hundred years ago. Then as now, a government's money had a considerable amount of paperwork associated with it. After 1782 an act dealing with the Civil List identified specific conditions regulating secret service expenditures, such that "when it shall be deemed expedient by the Commissioners of his Majesty's Treasury, or the High Treasurer . . . to issue, or in any Manner to direct the Payment of any Sum or Sums of Money from the Civil List Revenues, for foreign Secret Service, the same shall be issued and paid to one of his Majesty's Principal Secretaries of State, or to the first Commissioner of the Admiralty: and [that official shall], within three years from the issuing the said Money, produce the receipt of his Majesty's Minister, Commissioner or Consul in Foreign Parts, or of any Commander in Chief or other Commander of his Majesty's Navy or Land Forces, to whom the said Money shall have been sent or given."[8]

A fairly detailed account of this funding does exist. For illustrative purposes, let us for a moment focus on British secret service operations in France in the nine years before the Revolution, 1784 to 1792. Of course, the amount of detail is relative; the existence and movement of secret funds were, by definition, intended to remain secret, so documentation is not extensive. What does exist is derived from analysis of parliamentary papers, Civil List accounts, treasury warrants and order books, Audit Office accounts and discharges, and Foreign Office registers. In 1786, the Civil List sum for foreign secret service was approximately twenty-five thousand pounds.[9] This was, in a round figure, the average yearly amount expended upon secret intelligence throughout the entire nine-year term mentioned above. Furthermore, most of this money passed through the hands of the Marquess of Carmarthen, secretary of state for the Foreign Office (1783–91), or one of the undersecretaries of the Home Office, Evan Nepean, who is also named in the Audit Office accounts—and who will continue to appear throughout this narrative.[10]

Nepean's superior for several of these key years (1791–94) was Henry Dundas, later Viscount Melville, then secretary of state for the Home Office and about whom we will continue to read as secretary of state for War and the Colonies as well as first lord of the Admiralty. Dundas and other holders of the office would, therefore, have certainly had oversight and direction concerning these funds.

Dundas, incidentally, always seemed to have a keen intelligence focus. In 1797 (probably the most grim of the war years) he caused a study of what we now call combined operations to be compiled and printed. Entitled *Report on Conjunct Expeditions* and written by John Bruce (librarian of the India Office), it was circulated only among the Cabinet. It "emphasized a number of lessons concerning the chain of command, the provision of landing craft and gunboats, the importance of 'a large marine corps,' [a sound system of supply, and] the need for up-to-date intelligence."[11]

In pre-Victorian times, the British Secret Service Fund was not intended to run an established "secret service." Instead, it was used to finance "British propaganda on the Continent, an assortment of part-time informants, a variety of secret operations by freelance agents, and an elaborate system of political and diplomatic bribery," as well as to finance the Secret Department of the Post Office (as will be developed later in this chapter).[12] Bribery could be large scale and extremely important; even as late as 1796–97 some of the French directors were open to bribes which allowed some opportunities to conduct secret peace negotiations.[13]

From 1792 to 1794, Dundas continued an existing policy of subsidizing friendly elements of the British press and clergy to help combat domestic radical movements. In fact, he was particularly favorable toward the Scottish Episcopalian and Roman Catholic churches: "Bills were passed in 1792 and 1793 relieving both of these of the religious disabilities under which they lay. Roman Catholic priests and seminaries [even] received money from the Secret Service Fund."[14] This is remarkable in a period when a Catholic could not be commissioned in the Royal Navy and when, six years later, Prime Minister Pitt had to resign his position when unable to persuade the king to relent on Irish Catholic enfranchisement.

Sometimes Secret Service Funds were used just to keep something secret—not directly intelligence nor espionage related—because the funds were immune from audit and disclosure. In the fall of 1804, for example, Mr. Pitt offered Sweden sixty thousand pounds in order to use Swedish Pomerania as a base for military operations, as well as for British merchants to establish a commercial depot at Stralsund. Since King Gustavas feared French reprisals, the subsequent treaty, signed in December, was kept secret, and therefore the subsidy was paid with secret service money.[15]

Similarly, in December 1807, foreign affairs secretary George Canning approved a Sicilian treaty with a significant change: "Parliament had never voted any money for the Sicilian subsidy in the past; it had been taken from the Secret Service Fund. Therefore, this article [was] made a secret provision and thus expunged from the text to be laid before Parliament."[16]

A final, and amazing, example was in 1803, when the British briefly entertained a suggestion that the family of Napoleon might persuade him to give up Malta—instead of fighting for it—in return for a "valuable consideration." On 17 March Lord Hawkesbury replied to Ambassador Lord Whitworth's "most secret and confidential" dispatch; he wrote, "I lose no time in informing you that if an arrangement could be concluded . . . by which [King George III] should retain the Island of Malta, the Sum of one Hundred thousand Pounds might be distributed as Secret Service."[17]

Though the Admiralty itself (through the first lord) also had the right of expending money for these same purposes, Admiralty records are sparse for this period. While there is some record of a number of naval officers being individually engaged in intelligence work in France, the only paper trail readily available leads to Nepean, the aforementioned undersecretary for the Home Office.[18]

In fact, twenty-five thousand pounds per annum, in late eighteenth-century terms, points to reasonably small activity—particularly when one considers that this appears to be the total of a secret service fund covering expenditure worldwide, not just for France or Europe. Moreover, the existing documentation indicates that secret service was a high-level affair, handled only by a principal secretary of state and two undersecretaries; clearly, there was no large scale of business when it could only cross the desks of three heavily burdened individuals who had many other duties and concerns with which they had to attend.[19] We can say heavily burdened because, in 1788, for example, the Foreign Office staff consisted of approximately twenty people, from "secretary of state" to "necessary woman" (maid). The corresponding French Affaires Étrangeres office had around seventy.[20] However, busy or not, these men had considerable oversight on their secret service activity and accounting; both the prime minister and the king were privy to, and interested in, this information. Indeed, the accounts could not be paid without their approval. Note this comment in a letter dated 1782 (of which a draft and fair copy exist in the king's handwriting) to Prime Minister Lord North: "I must express my astonishment at the Quarterly Account Books of the Secret Service being only made up to the 5th of April 1780, consequently that two years are as yet not stated. I cannot help saying it is a most shameful piece of neglect I ever knew. No business can ever be admitted as an excuse for not doing that; if every sum received had instantly been set down, as well as every article paid, this could not have happened."[21]

Throughout the Napoleonic Wars the secret service parliamentary vote came in at a little over £100,000 per year, peaking at £172,830 in 1805. After 1815 it rapidly fell to its pre-1793 levels.[22] The secret service expenditures for some of this period (1790–1800) look like this (amounts in pounds):

1790	3,165	1796	129,951
1791	3,299	1797	182,227
1792	9,794	1798	103,469
1793	21,165	1799	159,340
1794	29,334	1800	98,912
1795	90,232		

The actual spenders of these funds (for that same 1790–1800 period) are as follows, after the money first passed through Lord Grenville's hands as secretary of state for the Foreign Office (amounts in pounds):

Lord Grenville	16,000	George Canning	136,130
Evan Nepean	3,780	John Hookham Frere	119,425
James Bland Burges	64,541	George Hammond	100,597
Lord Auckland	12,984	Foreign ministers	377,807[23]

It is interesting to note that the new United States government immediately jumped into this business with a very similar arrangement. In fact, on 8 January 1790, in his first State of the Union address, President Washington asked for a "competent fund" to finance intelligence operations. Within six months Congress set up the Contingent Fund of Foreign Intercourse, or the Secret Service Fund "for spies, if the gentleman so pleases," as it was explained in the Senate. "For the first year, the fund was forty thousand dollars; by the third year, it had risen to over one million dollars, about 12 percent of the federal budget—a far higher proportion of the budget than the massive U.S. intelligence expenditure of the late twentieth century."[24]

In Britain, most money identified for foreign secret service was drawn by the Home Office and the Foreign Office, rather than the Admiralty. However, for all three offices the primary objective was heavily focused on information about French maritime affairs and the French navy.

Items of constant and specific interest—during peace and war—included French plans for action in the East Indies; exact terms of treaties in existence (or projected); presence of foreign warships in French ports;[25] the state and disposition of the French fleet; the defenses of the French coast; dispatches sent from Paris to India; the number and condition of ships at Brest, Rochefort, Toulon, Rochelle, St. Malo, Le Havre, Rotterdam, and Amsterdam; charts of the Normandy coast; the disposition of troops on the Atlantic and Channel coasts; and new port facilities under construction at Cherbourg.[26]

The sources of intelligence varied. Naturally, British diplomats posted around the world made constant observations, which they reported to

Whitehall; certainly this was the best and chief source of peacetime intelligence, and it of course continued after the war began. These reports were extremely valuable to the Cabinet for planning purposes. However, as the war progressed and French military prowess ticked off victory after victory, the number of friendly or neutral states from which diplomats could report steadily decreased. In fact, "by 1807 almost all of western Europe had been rendered hostile, and those countries like Portugal where diplomats might still work tended to be on the periphery of events and so of limited usefulness."[27]

Whitehall, loosely defined, refers to the executive nerve center of the British government. Just down from Charing Cross and up from Parliament, it was the site of the former royal Whitehall Palace, which was mostly destroyed by fire in 1698. It now housed the prime minister's residence, the Admiralty building (see fig. 1-1), the Horse Guards building (headquarters of the army), the Board of Trade, the Treasury buildings, and several other important offices.

Most funds earmarked for foreign secret service, however, were to pay informants. Not very much different from today's environment, candidates for such work were both men and women, most of relatively humble birth and economic means who became spies in return for payment. Others came from all backgrounds and all walks of life. Moreover, eighteenth-century Europe was a place for easy movement for those who had some money. A significant number of Britons, for example, had been educated in France and had lived for periods in other countries. Money and sufficient social standing opened many doors in London, Paris, Vienna, Rome, and elsewhere; indeed, an individual who possessed language skills, combined with local knowledge and key introductions, was a tremendous asset as an advisor or consultant—or more.[28] Informants went by many names: scouts, spies, informers, *espials,* intelligencers, and agents. Call them what you will, they generally transmitted their information to the local British minister, commissioner, or consul via "advices," "intelligences," or "letters of intelligence." This information would, in turn, be passed on to London.[29] While Whitehall dealt with

Fig. 1-1 *Old Admiralty Building, Whitehall.*
This rendition shows both the wind vane and the larger semaphore telegraph
mast installed in 1816, which replaced Lord Murray's "shutter" semaphore
system. This print is from the early nineteenth century and shows the 1722
façade designed by Thomas Ripley as well as the 1760 screen fronting the
courtyard, designed by Robert Adam.
© *National Maritime Museum, London*

some agents directly, notably the so-called Rotterdam Agency (the heyday
of which was earlier in the century),[30] most espionage was conducted
through British ministers abroad, who were allocated funds for the
purpose.[31]

Eighteenth-century high-level British diplomats were generally
expected to personally distribute bribes and pay secret informants. Some
—perhaps most—disliked it: "'I abhor this dirty work,' wrote Sir James
Harris (later Earl of Malmesbury) while minister at the Hague in 1785,
'but when one is employed to sweep chimneys one must black one's
fingers.' A few diplomats refused all direct contact with such 'dirty work.'
Sir Robert Keith claimed virtuously in 1792 that he had 'never charged

Fig. 1-2 *Admiralty Board Room, Whitehall.*
Note the pull-down maps to the right and the wind indicator above the globe
on the far end. Drawn c. 1800 by Rowlandson and Pugin.
© *National Maritime Museum, London*

[London] a *single shilling* for Secret Service' during his twenty-five year
diplomatic career.'"

Malmesbury may have disliked it, but he recognized its necessity, and
when John Hookham Frere entered the diplomatic service, the experienced Malmesbury gave him some good advice. He strongly recommended "the use of rascals in doing any dirty piece of work." Moreover,
it was very important "never to mix yourself in any such business," but
to leave such diplomatic dirty work to "foreign adventurers ready for
anything of the kind."[32] But sometimes it rubbed off anyway. During a
brief period of negotiations in 1796, Malmesbury personally was told to
leave Paris within forty-eight hours, partly because the Directory correctly suspected that he was in touch with agents and actively transmitting intelligence back to London.[33]

Some diplomats enjoyed the business and found they had considerable freedom in which to operate. The British envoy in Switzerland, William Wickham, discovered "his instructions 'so far as they relate to France . . . extremely general'; in fact he had none 'regularly drawn up.' The handling of agents and movements was left very much to his discretion."[34]

But even when a diplomat was enthusiastic and energetic in his secret activities the return was usually marginal. For example, Wickham saw little result from the considerable efforts and large sums he aimed toward French counterrevolution during the 1790s.[35] A primary example is the failed plot to assassinate Napoleon, in which Wickham had a hand to the extent of fifty thousand pounds.[36] Overall the odds may have been broadly miscalculated; France may not have been as ready for insurrection, nor the French resistance been as strong, as the British hoped.[37]

Diplomats abroad also gained valuable intelligence from other than paid agents and spies, since the nature of politics during this time was somewhat reflected by the willingness of highly placed individuals to provide information. Naturally, policy was "debated and discussed within each country [and] the debates about foreign policy were intertwined with struggles over power, patronage and domestic factional considerations, and this made it possible for foreign diplomats to find allies in divided courts and ministries."[38]

Parallel to the diplomats, "commanders in chief" and "other commanders of His Majesty's navy or land forces" were also funded by the principal secretaries of state or the first commissioner of the Admiralty for the payment of informants. It is interesting to note that after Lord Nelson's death in 1805, some persons of influence suggested that the Foreign Secret Service Fund be used to pay a pension to Nelson's mistress Lady Hamilton, as requested in his will. These unsuccessful arguments focused upon her diplomatic and translation services while she was the "ambassadress" at Naples, not for any overt acts of espionage.[39]

Before 1793 Nepean variously employed at least eight informants, most of whom were apparently inactive British naval officers. One of the most industrious was Richard Oakes, who, before being acquired by Nepean at the Home Office prior to 1782, was sending information to First Secretary Philip Stephens at the Admiralty. Oakes even corresponded directly with Prime Minister Pitt, forwarding his observations at the request of alternately Stephens and Nepean.[40] Another very effective agent was Philip d'Auvergne, who did considerable reconnoitering of the French coast between St. Malo and Le Havre during his active-duty frigate command during 1787–88. He later, in 1792, toured the French maritime provinces and established contacts in several French ports. He then began to operate as the chief organizer, under Nepean, of British agents in France; however, by 1806, there were complaints that the quality of intelligence supplied by now–Rear Adm. d'Auvergne was deficient.[41] Interestingly enough, in 1773 d'Auvergne had been one boy, of a very few, who was selected to sail on board the bomb (mortar) vessels *Racehorse* and *Carcass* during an ultimately unsuccessful North Pole expedition—another such boy being fifteen-year-old Horatio Nelson.[42]

Other "friendly" agents were constant contributors. In fact, "smugglers in particular were looked to for regular items of information, but such professional criminals were even more dubious than other sources and were just as likely to be double agents working for the French."[43] Some were deemed reliable, however; in 1798 both Pitt and Dundas hinged very high-level decision making on the reports of a smuggler named Johnstone.[44]

The results of these efforts, and of the money spent, were uneven. There were, as could be expected, great successes. In fact an unsigned 1796 letter, addressed to the French ministre des relations exterièrurs, remarks that the British government's information about the French navy was always very good, and that they never sent out a force without completely knowing the situation of the French fleet. The letter's author had conducted an investigation into information leaks from within the French admiralty.[45]

There were both large and small failures. For example, Lord Torrington, British minister at Brussels, once had to write the secretary of state

for the Foreign Office a letter of apology for employing a "useless" agent
—to whom had been going four hundred pounds per year in secret service payments: "I send your Lordship enclosed—the Expenses incurred
Last Quarter. Concerning the Chevalier Floyd—that affair is over. Sorry
I am to find! his Secret Intelligence has not proved so correct as Government expected."[46] Celebrations after the French victory of Austerlitz
were inaccurately reported to London as chaos in France in the wake of
defeats in Moravia.[47] After all, paid secret agents—smugglers, French
émigrés, or whomever—had to live; if there were no solid information
to sell there were other kinds which earned the same money.

On the other hand, sometimes money was very well spent. If the story
can be believed, the British achieved one of their most remarkable intelligence successes during the American Revolutionary War at the expense
of one Benjamin Franklin, then American ambassador to France: "Inside
this Embassy was a cell of British intelligence organized by [Doctor]
Edward Bancroft, Franklin's friend and chief assistant. . . . Not only did
Britain learn all the American secrets but many items of French intelligence as well, for the French trusted Franklin and gave him a great deal
of information. The kindest deduction one could make from all this was
that Franklin was duped by his assistant and, from a security point of
view, was utterly incompetent."[48]

Sometimes cabinet ministers just were not picky as to the quantity or
quality of intelligence they had to work with. As late as 1808, with an
expedition preparing to go to Sweden, the secretary of state for War and
the Colonies (Lord Castlereagh) admitted "an almost complete ignorance
of the region in which it was to operate. . . . His lack of knowledge including fundamental questions relating to the strength, positions and morale
of the Swedish, Norwegian and Russian armies."[49] Lord Nelson had not
been very impressed with Castlereagh upon meeting him in 1805.[50]

Bureaucratic disorganization contributed to potential intelligence failures as much as bad agents or unprepared and unorganized politicians.
The absence of organization, particularly in the Foreign Office, often
involved simple neglect of routine business. For example, Sir James Bland

Burges, when parliamentary undersecretary, wrote to his wife that the enormous "numbers of dispatches which come from and go to Foreign Courts are piled up in large presses, but no note of them is taken, nor is there even an index to them; so that, if anything is wanted, the whole year's accumulation must be rummaged over before it can be found. . . . As to the past, it would be an Herculean task to attempt to put things right, but it is my intention to take better care in future, and to enter the purport of every dispatch in a volume properly prepared for that purpose."[51]

It may have even been worse than Burges described. Intelligence historian Richard Deacon paints the Foreign Office as "so slothful, so inefficient that many intelligence reports went unread for years. When the Whigs formed a government in 1806 they found despatches of twenty years earlier still unopened."[52]

Diplomatic historians James W. Thompson and Saul K. Padover relate an amusing incident in which supposedly a Foreign Office official read a dispatch found in a pile on his desk, discovering an insult received from one of the Barbary states. After drafting orders to British naval units to respond with force, it was further discovered that the official "had not noticed the date of that despatch, nor the nature of the insult; the one was three years back, and the other had been apologized for and forgiven."[53]

The British, however, had nothing on the Austrian chancellor, Baron Franz M. Thugut. When he left his position in 1801 it was reported that there were 170 unopened reports and 2,000 unread letters found in his office.[54] This is in some contrast to the contemporary French practice, or at least French practice at the level of Napoleon: "In his eagerness to get things done he sometimes rose at 3 A.M. . . . He expected almost as much from his administrative aides. They were always ready to give him precise up-to-the-hour information on any matter . . . and he judged them by the accuracy, order, readiness, and adequacy of their reports. He did not consider his day finished until he had read the [many daily] memoranda and documents . . . from the various departments of his government. He was probably the best-informed ruler in history."[55] Of course, one must remember that Napoleonic France had six fully organized police systems, under the remarkable Joseph Fouché (effectively Napoleon's commander in chief of police), which contributed at least four daily bulletins to Bonaparte's reading load.[56]

Napoleon was an information-secure ruler, for while he was first consul—and then emperor—no country's agents, Britain's included, were particularly successful in "penetrating Bonaparte's deeper secrets." In fact, "no leakage of Napoleon's plans is known to have occurred . . . until the confusion of 'The Hundred Days' [in 1815]. Then information that the Emperor was moving on Brussels was sent to Wellington from a person in the *Ministère de la Guerre.*"[57]

There is one possible enormous contradiction to the above paragraph. It may well be that the timely sending of a British preemptive expedition to Copenhagen in 1807 (not to be confused with Nelson's attack on Copenhagen in 1801) was an intelligence coup rather than merely a diplomatic-military triumph. Somehow, Foreign Secretary George Canning learned of the key Russo-French agreement at Tilsit, with its section about forcing Denmark and Portugal to declare against Britain— and he learned in time to take decisive, effective action. Whether this information came from the strangely loyal-disloyal French foreign minister Talleyrand, from a British spy (on the raft in the river where Emperor Napoleon and Czar Alexander met), from a Mr. MacKenzie (confidant of the Russian army commander in chief), or a source totally unknown, this appears to have been a remarkable leakage of critical French war planning.[58]

In fact, by no means were the French always paragons in their intelligence operations. For example one story has Général Antoine-François Comte Andréossy, briefly ambassador to Britain in 1803, unskillfully and unsuccessfully offering the socially and politically eminent Georgiana Cavendish (duchess of Devonshire) a blatant and barefaced bribe of ten thousand pounds in return for Cabinet secrets.

In any event, British ministers abroad often felt neglected and ignored, with even dispatches of significance remaining unacknowledged for weeks and months. The British ambassador extraordinary to the Hague, Lord Auckland, addressed this issue in a 1792 letter to his brother, Morton Eden, who was envoy extraordinary and minister plenipotentiary to Prussia: "You seem to think it odd that you have so few official letters since your arrival in Berlin: but this is always the case [when nothing particularly] engages the anxieties of administration. . . . It sometime happens with respect to missions even of the first rank not to receive a syllable in six months."[59]

Capt. Lord Thomas Cochrane, who will be studied later in greater detail, had no respect for British strategic-level security, thinking that much more could be accomplished "if people at home would hold their tongues." In his autobiography he makes a particular note that "it is a curious fact, that there being no such thing as confidence or secrecy in official quarters in England, the French were as well advised as to our movements as were our own commanders, and were consequently prepared at all points."[60] Lord Nelson was of a similar mind, writing in 1805 that "the French know everything that passes in England."[61]

Historian and novelist Patrick O'Brian accurately underscores the problem when he has one of his leading characters, Dr. Stephen Maturin, wonder,

> How we shall ever win this war I cannot tell. In Whitehall . . . some fool must be prating. . . . We reinforce the Cape, and tell them [the French] so: they instantly reinforce the Ile de France, that is to say, Mauritius. And so it runs, all, all of a piece throughout: Mr. Congreve invents a military rocket with vast potentialities—we instantly inform the world, like a hen that has laid an egg, thus throwing away all the effect of surprise. The worthy Mr. Snodgrass finds out a way of rendering old ships serviceable in a short time and at little expense: without a moment's pause we publish his method in all the papers, together with drawings, lest some particular should escape our enemy's comprehension.[62]

O'Brian's other leading character, Capt. Jack Aubrey, airs his view on the subject by observing that "what I really cannot understand is that the

Ministry should expect me to take the [enemy] by surprise when our expedition has been advertised to the world in half a dozen daily sheets including *The Times*."[63]

The government was concerned about the problem. Note this secret "Order of Cabinet" dated 19 July 1797: "The King's servants . . . have agreed, not only that they will themselves hold themselves bound not to communicate to any persons whatever out of the Cabinet the particulars of what may pass between Lord Malmesbury and the French Ministers; but have resolved that all the papers upon the subject shall be . . . kept absolutely distinct and separate, and in such manner as to be accessible to no other persons whatever but the members of the Cabinet."[64]

Yet there was remarkable cabinet-level foolishness, too. Once Russian ambassador Vorontzov informed Home Secretary Lord Hawkesbury about a dangerous French spy active in London. When "sometime later the Russian envoy asked Hawkesbury whether the spy's paper[s] contained anything important, his lordship replied that he was sure he did not know, that it was the affair of the Alien Office."[65]

And, of course, poor security was more than a British affliction; other countries had similar problems. For example, Commodore Isaac Chauncey, commanding U.S. forces in the Great Lakes region during the War of 1812, felt obliged to write the following to his superiors on 24 September of that year: "Sir: As the place of my destination has been announced in the Publick papers, you may suppose that I have been imprudent in communicating it to my friends. In justice to my own character I assure you upon my honor that I have never communicated the subject to but five persons[,] . . . neither of which I am Confident has told it to a second person. The Subject was first published in a Philadelphia paper, (the *Democratic Press*) and copied into the Newyork papers."[66]

In any event, rewarded with a mixed bag of success and failure (prior to the French Revolution) the British government was busy funding routine, very restricted, and sporadic espionage in and about France.[67] After 1792 and after the outbreak of war this activity expanded, and the role of the infamous "English gold" in anti-French espionage, counter-espionage, underground warfare, subversive activity and covert operations rapidly developed and grew to large proportions as the struggle went on. The administrative structure, however, remained effectively unchanged.

IT MAY SEEM UNUSUAL to include a discussion of the British Post Office in a study of strategic or naval intelligence. Nevertheless, already over two hundred years old in the eighteenth century, its intelligence role cannot be overlooked—particularly the activities of its Private Office, its Secret Office, and its Decyphering Branch. Moreover, it seems to be the exception to the government's lack of bureaucratized intelligence mentioned at the beginning of this chapter.

In the eighteenth century the king remained the

> effective head of the government and director of the administrative system. Its purpose was to preserve law and order and defeat his enemies abroad. It depended on general support in Parliament, the principal source of supply and credit. It was managed by ministers responsible to the king and the courts of law. The king decided every important question of policy and patronage, controlling all departments either through the ministers in charge or the Secretaries of State who transmitted his formal commands. The ministers, sometimes making recommendations in the . . . Cabinet, executed his orders, handling routine business in accordance with traditional practice. . . . In the administrative sphere, the most important offices were those responsible for the [armed] forces, foreign policy, public order, and the revenue.[68]

Furthermore, although George II was the last English king to personally lead his troops in battle, George III remained in person head of the army and was actively involved in appointments, regimental affairs, the conduct, and the employment of his troops.[69]

Unlike the singular American official of the same title, there were several British secretaries of state, such as the secretary of state for War and the Colonies, the secretary of state for the Foreign Office, and the secretary of state for the Home Office. In addition, it is interesting to note that the modern British Cabinet has its origination in the "Committee of Intelligence" of the Privy Council, with which the king experimented, circa 1679–81.[70]

The revenue was managed by the Treasury Board, which oversaw various subordinate departments. While the Post Office was indeed one of those departments, it was much more than a branch concerned with revenue. We have established that the secretaries of state for the Foreign and Home Offices were particularly concerned with intelligence. We must now appreciate that the Post Office, in addition to all its other functions and services, employed "hundreds of officials, postmasters, and sailors; [and was] the centre of imperial communications, controlling a large fleet of packets [ships]; and a propaganda and intelligence organ, serving as the government's mouthpiece, eyes, and ears."[71]

Indeed, a primary example of the communications role was when Royal Mail coaches, rigged in laurel leaves, rolled out of London's Lombard Street late on 6 November 1805. This was the medium in which the news of the Battle of Trafalgar and the death of Lord Nelson— official, private, and commercial—was transmitted "through the length and breadth of the kingdom."[72]

As we have already seen, the British government fundamentally had no centralized intelligence agency. Instead, various offices in the bureaucracy participated in, and contributed to, what intelligence activity there actually was; the Post Office was the most important of these. The eighteenth-century British Post Office collected, processed, "finished," and transmitted intelligence.

"Although safe enough—apart from the occasional highwayman," notes Dudley Pope, "the post office was not secure from prying eyes and, *in particular,* no government was above having the mail watched and letters secretly opened."[73] With most departments located in London, Post Office staff maintained a wide scope of collection activities. In England, surveyors and county deputies reported on crime, civil disorders, economic conditions, and elections.[74] In Scotland, Ireland, and the colonies, deputy postmasters general, or their secretaries, reported on civil and military affairs. Postal agents gathered shipping news and information about suspicious persons or activities.[75] Finally, the captains of packet vessels collected shipping news and lists of passengers on board merchant ships; in addition, they were sometimes employed in the observation of enemy naval dispositions.[76]

The Post Office was also very much in the business of processing, or creating, "finished" intelligence. This was primarily accomplished in the arena of intercepting mail, opening it, copying it, analyzing it, and then sending either unedited full-text copies, or synthesized "interceptions," to the secretaries of state. An excerpt from a letter, dated 7 July 1772, from the secretary of state for the Southern Department to the king illustrates this methodology: "Lord Rochford who was gone a few miles out of Town did not see the last interceptions until this morning. . . . [He shall send off a messenger] as soon as your majesty has approved of the enclosed Draught, in which your Majesty will, it is hoped, think all the interceptions have been fully analyzed."[77]

This practice, dating back to the Tudor period, was legally validated several times by legislative acts. The Post Office Act of 1711 gave the activity unassailable legality, though it confined the right of ordering mail interception to the secretaries of state; sometimes, however, it was also exercised by other leading cabinet ministers—including the first lords of the Treasury and the Admiralty.[78]

Indeed, in 1730 the Sardinian envoy to London, one Ossorio, complained that "there was no remedy for the outrageous freedom that the English government takes in opening letters."[79] Twenty-five years later no less an espionage-sensitive ruler than Prussia's King Frederick the Great was similarly alarmed. He wrote Baron Knyphausen, his envoy in Paris, that "they are so well informed that they know my very phrases. . . . You are to press [French minister] Rouillé on the need for France to take better arrangements in order to ensure that secrecy is maintained. Tell him that unless this happens I will be unable to confide in France, as secrecy is crucial to me."[80] Frederick was extremely oriented toward operational security, once emphasizing the point by telling a subordinate that "if my nightcap knew what was in my head I would throw it into the fire."

Generally, the secretaries of state would send lists—actually warrants —to the Post Office for the interception of certain diplomatic, political, private, general, or suspicious correspondence.[81] Midcentury lists of foreign diplomats were replaced by a series of warrants which directed the copying of all diplomatic correspondence going through London;[82] such political warrants frequently ordered the copying of entire documents, or at least significant extracts, of specified mail without noticeable detention or delay of the originals.[83]

Methodology of interception varied with the correspondence's origin and termination localities. Generally, however, diplomatic or political letters were forwarded to London (if not actually intercepted in London) "to have the benefit of superior methods of opening available there."[84] Letters from the colonies were customarily opened by Post Office governors while in transit; or, in times of crisis they were seized in bulk on board ship and opened upon arrival at the Inland Office.[85]

In London, foreign correspondence was opened in a special office generally known as "the Secret Office." Various other descriptions were the Private Foreign Office, the Foreign Secretary's Office (not to be confused with the secretary of state for the Foreign Office), and the Secret Department. Having no "official" existence, the office actually had only three rooms physically adjoining the cabinet-level Foreign Office and was restricted to members of its own small staff and the postmasters general. Created in 1653, the Secret Office was funded variously by the Post Office—or with secret service money, issued to the Post Office, from surplus revenue legally controlled by Parliament.[86]

From 1793 to 1798 the Secret Office was required to increase interception of internal correspondence of various kinds.[87] However, in 1798 the office was refocused to concentrate on foreign, especially diplomatic, correspondence. By 1801 its annual cost was £5,060, including its staff of ten.[88]

The head of the office, entitled the Foreign Secretary, was responsible to the secretaries of state and the first lord of the Treasury.[89] Having the advantage of access, his recommendations were usually passed—or at least mentioned—to the king. The king, in turn, gave verbal directions frequently through the secretaries of state.[90] The Foreign Secretary's primary job was to oversee the opening and copying of foreign correspondence, and then send the interceptions—called "The Secrets"—to authorized officials marked "Private and Most Secret" or "Most Secret and Confidential."[91]

Interceptions that were uncoded, and that appeared to merit his attention, went straight to the king; those enciphered went to the "Decyphering Branch" and from there were forwarded to him. In fact, the one government office that really came the closest to being an unadulterated, professional intelligence service was the small Decyphering Branch, created in 1703. This was the invention of an Oxford don, the Rev. Edward Willes, who, by 1716 had virtually turned it into a family firm: "By the 1750s Willes, now Bishop of Bath and Wells, had three sons working with him. The Willes family were, however, only part-time intelligence officers who combined cryptanalysis with lives as squires and clerics, and did all their secret work in the comfort of their country homes."[92] Of course, by the later part of the century they were more fully employed in a Whitehall office.

Obviously, some ciphers were more difficult than others to break (in 1790, for example, the new Spanish "key" gave Sir Francis Willes considerable trouble);[93] but it was not unheard of that the king was reading interceptions within twenty-four hours of their posting, "frequently long before the intended recipient."[94] The king usually returned them or, more often, circulated them to senior ministers per his established distribution list; then, as they were classified as "private papers," they were not always kept on file.[95] A good example of King George exercising his routine control of information access was in January 1797, when he restricted the particulars of a specific operation, "knowledge of which is to be kept from all but the Duke of York (field marshal and second son of George III), Earl Spencer (first lord of the Admiralty), Mr. Pitt (prime minister), and

Mr. Nepean (first secretary of the Admiralty)."[96] This type of extreme compartmentalization is not unusual in secret intelligence; after all, the facts of the World War II Enigma-machine cipher were unknown to a majority of Churchill's ministers.[97]

At times the original documents were given to the senior ministers and the king for examination; in these cases there was a definite question of haste to get the papers back into the mail so as to not overly delay delivery and arouse suspicions. Note the following 11 February 1780 letter, to the king, from the first lord of the Admiralty: "Lord Sandwich has the honour & great satisfaction to send your Majesty an undoubted confirmation of Sir George Rodney's success [the relief of Gibraltar]. Your Majesty will observe that the letter is *not yet sent* to the person to whom it is addressed, therefore will have the goodness if possible to *return it as soon as may be convenient.*"[98]

His Majesty's Post Office, specifically the Foreign Secretary, was also very active in other intelligence special services, certainly including forgery and detection: "His office prepared 'plant' letters for foreign courts or agents, searched suspected letters with special 'liquors' for invisible ink, identified British reports to cover addresses, and occasionally facilitated contact between the government and enemy ministers."[99]

The importance of the Secret Office, and the regard given to the intelligence intercepted and/or produced by the office, "is reflected in the constant personal interest taken by the Hanoverian kings in the work of interception"[100] as well as the funding they channeled to the office—including encouraging talent with Royal Bounty money.[101] (While not the focus of our interest here, one cannot overlook the value of domestic interceptions either, particularly regarding the plans of disaffected subjects such as Lord Edward Fitzgerald, in Ireland, in the 1790s).[102] Moreover, the Hanoverian kings were sophisticated users of intercepts and other kinds of intelligence, and after years of experience were themselves fair analysts and discerning judges of the products. Note this closure, in a May 1778 letter, from George III to then–prime minister Lord North:

"Mr. Wentworth's intelligence *if confirmed by other quarters* will require [some formerly agreed upon orders] to be given to Vice Admiral Byron, *but it is not authentic enough to take any step whilst unsupported by corroborating circumstances.*"[103]

The value of postal intelligence to foreign-policy formulation and execution was immense, in peacetime as well as wartime, regarding the revelation of orders, plans, and outlooks of foreign heads of state and their governments.[104] However, there were four major limitations, or weaknesses, to the success of Post Office intelligence. First, any dispatches or correspondence sent by messenger totally avoided the system and, thereby, escaped examination. Second, for items caught within the system, the time needed for collection, deciphering (if necessary), analysis, and distribution all had the potential to reduce the value of any intelligence found. Third, the recalling of diplomats upon the outbreak of war (as well as their absence for the duration) drastically reduced the value of targeted mail when it would be of the greatest use.[105] Finally, general effectiveness degraded—and secrecy became much more difficult to preserve—as the volume of correspondence increased over time; the concomitant problem was the increasing difficulty in actually identifying and designating mail perceived as being most likely fruitful.[106]

Still, Prussian dispatches were read reasonably frequently from 1748 on, French from 1778, Russian occasionally after 1785, Austrian consistently from 1794, and Danish after 1801.[107] The British government, as a result, often had advance warning of impending hostilities as well as insights to the intrigues of foreign governments and their agents.[108]

In addition, the government of the German state of Hanover maintained a secret bureau, at Nienburg, which worked closely with its counterpart in London continuously helping to support British interceptions.[109] Intelligence against France was always a high priority—though in the 1790s so was that against the fractious United Irishmen.[110] The close relationship with Hanover makes perfect sense if one remembers that George III was the third British king of the Hanoverian line, and that he actually was the current "elector" of Hanover in title and reality. In fact, an outstanding example of this source concerns the ill-fated French expedition against Egypt in 1801 (which is fully developed later in this book). Upon his return to London from an extended stay in Scotland, Henry Dundas, then the secretary of state for War, received from King George a paper "obtained from Hanover." In a note to the king on 9 November, acknowledging the paper, Dundas wrote, "It is perfectly obvious that upon this document are founded all the ideas which have been floating in France for near a century past respecting the conquest of Egypt."[111]

The problems in Ireland, mentioned above, might be expanded a little —although not central to the theme of this book. The French Revolution in some ways precipitated the rise of the United Irishmen movement in 1791. While several threats of French invasion basically came to naught, in May 1798 a brief but violent indigenous rebellion was repressed by British forces. All through this time the British intelligence focus toward Ireland remained high, in many ways competing with resources aimed toward the French wars. Interestingly enough, out of this mess came one of the last known murder plots against the life of an English sovereign, the "Despard" plot. Arrested in London by several "Bow Street Runners" (the first formation of any kind of armed English police, who included counterintelligence and antisedition among their many duties), Lt. Col. Edward Marcus Despard was brought to trial for high treason at the Old Bailey in 1803. It is of minor interest to this study for two coincidental reasons. The intelligencer-diplomat William Wickham was involved in the prosecution as undersecretary of state (before going to Switzerland as envoy), and Vice Adm. Lord Nelson was the principal defense witness for Despard. Nelson gave him a strong character reference (although from twenty years earlier) as a brave officer and honorable man—to no avail, for he was found guilty. "Yesterday," wrote Nelson, "I was at Colonel Despard's trial, subpoenaed by him for a character. I think the plot deeper than was imagined."[112]

Returning to the subject, foreign governments often used seals, ciphers,

Fig. 1-3 *King George III,* by Sir William Beechey (1753–1839).
Ruling Britain for fifty-one years, George saw the American Revolution, the
French Revolution, and the Napoleonic Wars and was a very active ruler in
the great events of the time. He is shown here in general's uniform at Windsor
Castle.

cover addresses, and invisible ink—none of which was really adequate to defend successfully against the Post Office effort. (It may be of interest to note here that Nazi Germany operated seven communications-intelligence organizations before and through World War II, including the Forschungstelle [Research Post] of the Postal Ministry.)[113] The only effective guarantee against interception was to not use the mail at all and, instead, rely on private messages, messengers, and coaches. (But private messengers presented their own difficulties, and were in any event expensive.) Regardless, an adroit politician sent nothing by post that could not be read aloud from a soapbox at Hyde Park Corner.

Of course, British politicians were also wary of the French. Even in periods of peace they avoided the French post office, using instead continental banking houses if not their own diplomatic couriers. Moreover, they usually wrote in the form of business letters on continental paper, since English paper had a notably distinctive appearance.[114]

Lord Nelson was very aware of intercepted mail, even on a personal level. As a result, he and his mistress Lady Hamilton, expecting the birth of their daughter, invented another expecting couple so that by using other names they could write freely to each other and disguise the fact that they were referring to themselves.[115]

Still, while they might well have assumed it, most governments and individuals apparently had little hard evidence that His Majesty's government was reading their mail. The British certainly knew that good security was key to the volume and value of interceptions; their efficiency and technical skills were generally very high, particularly regarding diplomatic correspondence.[116] Opening and closing could be done without a trace with the help of meticulously engraved forgeries of seals, with special waxes, and the investment of infinite time, pains, and care. The typical dispatch from the king of Prussia required three hours to open and then reseal in this fashion.[117]

Of course, other countries were old hands in this business as well. Superb at it—the best in the second half of the eighteenth century—were the Austrians.[118] Their Black Cabinet (or *Manipulation*) worked day and night—even collecting against their allies during the 1815 Congress of Vienna—unsealing and copying mail (or *intercepta*). They were also specialists in wastepaper basket and fireplace scraps (*chiffons*), cleaning them out of diplomats' rooms, pasting them together, deciphering them, analyzing them, and copying them.[119] (It was the mistress of France's King Louis XV, Jeanne Antoinette Poisson, Marquise de Pompadour, who gave us the expression "black chamber" or "black cabinet." To facilitate Louis's interest in cryptology and cryptography, she set aside one of her rooms as an enciphering office, which she had called her *Chambre Noir*.)[120]

In fact, even from his relatively narrow experience, Lord Nelson was singularly impressed by the ruthless Austrian espionage and counter-intelligence system, headed by the cold Chancellor Thugut. He once wrote British ambassador Minto that "for the sake of the civilized world let us work together, and as the best act of our lives manage to hang Thugut. . . . As you are with Thugut, your penetrating mind will discover the villain in all his actions. . . . Pray keep an eye upon the rascal."[121]

In Britain, the compartmentalized, small staffs that were involved in this business (Private Office, Secret Branch, and Decyphering Branch), combined with short ultimate distribution lists, greatly helped restrict knowledge and lessen chances of leaks. At any given time only thirty people or less knew what diplomatic correspondence was being handled. It was larger during the later French wars, of course, but a snapshot look in 1774 would probably include no more than nine people at the Post Office, six among the secretary of states' staffs, three at the Treasury, three at the German Office, and the king.[122]

Post Office staff were generally zealously loyal and reticent, as were most knowledgeable politicians. Parliament, in the main, was similarly loyal. Moreover, Parliament was relatively unaware as to the full extent of interception and, in any event, was mainly content to allow the exercise of statutory powers.[123] In this period of study, the only major exception to this were incidents in 1786 and 1797, when parliamentary committees, searching for extravagance in Pitt's administration, published some secret names and salaries. Fortunately, there were no serious ramifications. As a matter of fact, the "best tribute to the standard of security came from foreign governments, diplomats, and private correspondents, continually trusting the Post Office and [thereby] providing the government with valuable intelligence."[124]

In addition to the Post Office, there was another remarkable institution heavily involved in the national-intelligence business. The huge international insurance-marketing association that today does business as "Lloyd's of London" existed in the eighteenth century. Called then "Lloyd's Coffee House" (for that is how it informally began, as early as 1688, established by Edward Lloyd), its membership of merchants, bankers, seafarers, ship owners, international traders, and insurance underwriters was extraordinarily knowledgeable about all aspects of British and worldwide maritime shipping and naval affairs. In fact, the news of the Battle of Trafalgar was posted at Lloyd's even before the London newspapers broke the story.[125] Initially the association involved a large committee, which received its global correspondence and met at Lloyd's Coffee House. Even then it was the greatest center of marine insurance in the world; in 1809 it covered risks approaching one hundred million pounds.[126]

In those days much social life in London revolved around coffee houses which were both cafés and clubs. Some, such as Lloyd's, had specialized clientele; city merchants went to Lloyd's, Garraways, or Jonathan's; booksellers went to Chapter; artists and foreigners went to Old Slaughter's;[127] and naval officers went to the coffee room in Fladong's Hotel, New Oxford Street. Lloyd's operated two coffee houses, two meeting rooms, and a "subscription" room within the Royal Exchange building between Threadneedle Street and Cornhill.[128]

While clearly not an arm of the government, the immense, detailed, and timely information in Lloyds' possession (via its own highly developed communications network) was often readily shared with Whitehall, either directly to the Admiralty or to other top-level ministries, depending upon the exact nature and relevance of the information. Note the following line from a memorandum, dated 2 April 1783, from the first lord of the Admiralty to the king: "Lord Howe has the honour to transmit for Your Majesty's information, a letter . . . from the Master of Lloyd's Coffee House respecting the arrival of Mons. [Admiral] Vaudrueil with the French Squadron under his direction, at Cape Francois."[129]

In fact, Lloyd's basically represented the shipping industry in its dealings with the Admiralty and the government—even more than the Society of Shipowners, which might more logically have had that role. Moreover, during the eighteenth century Lloyd's developed a unique system of maritime intelligence. On a worldwide basis intelligence of arrivals and departures, "together with other news of naval and military importance, from Lloyds' agents, was sent on immediately to the Admiralty; and the Admiralty in turn forwarded convoy and other useful information to Lloyd's."[130]

It is appropriate to include Lloyd's in any discussion of the Post Office, for Lloyd's was assisted by the Post Office in its supply of semiofficial maritime intelligence. From late in the seventeenth century, Lloyd's published *Lloyd's News,* later *Lloyd's List,* containing "Ship News" from various ports which it sometimes sent to the Admiralty. In 1790 they had around thirty-two port correspondents; to help expedite their communications they paid gratuities to the Post Office's secretary and to the controller of the Inland Office for franking privileges and immediate delivery. Such payments apparently ceased in 1793, but the assistance was continued nevertheless.[131]

While their information and help was generally freely given, this was a somewhat symbiotic relationship, and at times they expected some governmental help in return. Thus scenarios such as this came about every once in awhile: During the summer of 1809 a Danish privateer captured several merchant ships sailing from Archangel to England. As there were over one hundred more merchantmen scheduled for this run and similarly at risk, the Admiralty rapidly moved to provide strong protection in response to an urgent appeal from Lloyd's.[132]

Similarly, this May 1812 directive, to Lord Keith from first secretary of the Admiralty John Croker, shows the consistency of this arrangement: "My Lord, The Committee for the managing of affairs at Lloyd's Coffee House having represented to my Lords Commissioners of the Admiralty that there are still missing eighteen of the ships from Jamaica which parted from the *Dauntless* in long[itude] 56 on the 29th of last month, I am commanded by their Lordships to signify their direction to your Lordship to order out all cruisers for the purpose of looking out for and protecting into port the ships in question."[133]

As an aside, two centuries after the fact it is somewhat amusing to read that, during the War of 1812, an American privateer, Capt. Thomas Boyle (of the *Chasseur* of Baltimore), "cruised for three months off the coast of England, taking prize after prize, and in derision sent in, to be posted at Lloyd's, a proclamation of blockage of the sea-coast of the United Kingdom."[134]

It is very clear that the eighteenth-century British government was in the business of collecting, processing, evaluating, and disseminating intelligence information at the highest levels. Most of the information came from "friendly" courtiers, ministers, and diplomats—supplemented by espionage—as well as overt diplomatic, military, and naval observation. Indeed, the sources were extremely varied and widespread: paid spies in France working for the Home Office, observations of ministers in British embassies abroad, enciphered foreign diplomatic correspondence intercepted by the Post Office's Secret Office, and shipping movements reported by Lloyd's, to name but a few. As the secretary of state for War, the first lord of the Admiralty, and quite often the first secretary of the Admiralty were among these high-level ministers, the Royal Navy was continuously privy to this information.

How this national-level intelligence was integrated into the Navy's own intelligence, communications, and command processes is more the subject of the next chapter. Still, as we close this chapter it is appropriate to look at a relevant incident with enormous strategic ramifications.

This incident, Commodore Graham Moore's action off Cadiz, was fundamentally a strategic-intelligence occasion. Although the specific source is hard to identify, it was clearly national-level intelligence information that, after analysis, discussion, and decision in the highest offices, led to the Royal Navy's tasking to intercept a Spanish treasure fleet in 1804—the two nations not, at that time, in a state of war with each other. Convinced by secret intelligence from what remains an unidentified source, His Majesty's government determined that Spain intended to join with France in open hostilities against Britain. This information may have come from the British ambassador at Madrid (then Hookham Frere), who was at least partially aware of the terms of the Convention of 19 October 1803, wherein Spain had agreed to pay to Napoleon the yearly sum of seventy-two million francs (more than a third of the whole Spanish revenue).[135] Simultaneously aware, via secret intelligence, that hostilities were going to commence immediately following the arrival of this treasure fleet at the Spanish port of Cadiz (coming from Montevideo, Uruguay), the British determined to act. Since Spain was apparently going to become an active enemy regardless, it would be better if she did so minus four of the best frigates in her navy—not to mention 5,810,000 pieces of eight. The Cabinet, on 18 September 1804, discussed the situation at length and then resolved to intercept the treasure squadron—even though Lord Melville (Dundas) felt the policy of the act was doubtful and, it seems, was opposed to it.[136] Accordingly, the Admiralty stealthily formed a special squadron of four of its own frigates under Commodore Moore. This squadron, with foreknowledge of the Spanish place of departure, place of destination, time of departure, order of battle, and commander (Rear Adm. Don José Bustamente), intercepted, fought, and captured them on the high seas on 4 October 1804. (For very exciting and detailed [although fictionalized] descriptions of the operation, the reader may wish to look at Patrick O'Brian's *Post Captain,* as well as C. S. Forester's *Hornblower and the "Hotspur."*)

The operation went as smoothly as the planners could have possibly hoped, although Lord Nelson belatedly tried to send some ships of the line to create a clearly overwhelming force—so that Admiral Bustamente would have been justified in a bloodless (but honorable) surrender. The Spanish government was incensed of course, and Spain, as anticipated, declared war on Britain. That she did so—less four significant warships as well as less an enormous (approximately three million Spanish dollars) hard-cash treasure—was an enormous strategic victory for the British. This would have been impossible without the adroit use of national-level intelligence spliced into bold decision making—combined with efficient execution of naval planning and tactics.

2

The Admiralty

If anyone wishes to know the history of this war, I will tell them it is our Maritime superiority that gives me the power of maintaining my army while the enemy are unable to do so.

The Duke of Wellington

[Currently at the Admiralty] there is no method whatever observed in arranging or collecting information . . . which is of the utmost consequence in judging of the enemy's intentions; no time ought to be lost in adopting some plan for this purpose.

Admiral Middleton

THE KING, THE PRIME MINISTER, AND THE CABINET (PRIMARILY the secretaries of state) developed policy, rendered decisions, and issued instructions. These were in turn conveyed to the Royal Navy, as necessary, by the first lord of the Admiralty (a Cabinet member), who presided over the Lords Commissioners (or the Board) of the Admiralty. These men, and the central offices of the navy, were located in the seat of government at Whitehall. "The administration of the British Navy in the eighteenth century was," N. A. M. Rodger notes, "like the government as a whole, a haphazard collection of institutions whose responsibilities often overlapped and whose relations were not well defined. On paper the arrangements were chaotic, but they had evolved over a long time, they were familiar to those who operated them, and in intelligent hands they functioned much more efficiently than might have been expected."[1]

Actually, the Admiralty was much more than a service department; it was "a very ancient and peculiar corporation," as the *London Times* once called it, and it was enormously vital to the social structure, economy and, of course, the defense of Great Britain.[2] But it had a weak staff system—actually, hardly a staff or system existed at all.[3] And as alluded to above, the Admiralty followed the English tradition of independent agencies (certainly in regard to intelligence) with little or no communication between them.

During this time the Admiralty ran a number of operational commands. The Channel Fleet, based in Plymouth and Portsmouth, covered the Atlantic area, including the French and Spanish ports from Brest to Vigo to Ferrol. The Mediterranean Fleet is self-explanatory. The North Sea Fleet, based in the Thames, essentially watched Holland and Belgium, and the Baltic Fleet (when activated) was focused upon the Danes, Russians, and Swedes.[4] There were, of course, other stations and commands; of note were the Irish and Channel Island Squadrons, the East Indies station, the West Indies station, and the North American station.[5]

The Lords Commissioners' authority was extensive, including commissioning ships; appointing admirals, captains, and lieutenants; and issuing orders concerning the majority of ship movements. However, major decisions, including fleet movements and appointments of fleet commanders in chief, were often made at the Cabinet level; sometimes the decision (such as the appointment of Earl Howe as commander in chief of the Channel Fleet in 1793) was made by the king himself.[6] Moreover, there is no doubt that the king was instrumental in Nelson's selection to command Adm. Lord St. Vincent's detached squadron, in 1798, in preference to senior officers already present in the Mediterranean. A December 1798 letter from Sir Edward Berry to Lord Nelson confirms this: "The Duke of Clarence desired I would tell you from him that it was the *King that sent you* with the Squadron up the Mediterranean, and formed the whole plan."[7]

While some first lords were, or had been, seamen, most were appointed politicians. In fact, of the ten listed in Appendix 2, only Jervis and Middleton had been seamen; John Pitt (the prime minister's elder brother) and Henry Phipps were high-ranking soldiers. The tasks of the subordinate professional (later the "sea") lords varied over the years, depending upon the desires of the first lord as well as upon the initiative of the individuals concerned. The first professional lord, during the tenure of Lord Barham (Adm. Sir Charles Middleton, quoted at the beginning of the chapter) as first lord, had several significant roles, including responsibility for ship movement, personnel, promotion, and equipment, as well as "taking upon himself the general superintendence and arrangement of the whole. . . . His duty will also be to attend to the correspondence of the day, but more particularly to that of the ports and all *secret services.*"[8]

The second professional lord oversaw transport, victualling, the Sick-and-Hurt Boards, and Greenwich Hospital. The third professional lord worked with the first primarily upon the appointment of officers and other personnel issues. From two to three civil lords (civilian appointees) focused on daily paperwork.[9]

A key position in the Admiralty—perhaps *the* key, which will be developed later—was the first (or principal) secretary to the Board. In order to effectively handle the Admiralty's voluminous correspondence, he was aided by an assistant secretary, in turn assisted by the chief clerk, "the Senior Clerks (who had 'Esq.' after their names), the Junior Clerks (no 'Esq.'), the extra clerks, the Supernumeraries, the First Lord's private secretary, and the Keeper of the Records and Papers."[10] The overall staff was very small; it included less than sixty people in 1801,[11] compared to

Fig. 2-1 *Charles Middleton, Lord Barham.*
Barham was a great naval administrator; under him staff work at the Admiralty probably reached its highest level of efficiency during the war. Originally drawn by I. Downman.
© *National Maritime Museum, London*

eighty-eight in 1830, eight hundred in 1924, and around eight thousand in 1964.[12]

It is interesting to note that, prior to Lord Barham's reorganization, the duties of the Board could be confusing or at least somewhat nebulous; even if a given first lord knew what he wanted each of his immediate subordinates to be doing, it was not always clear to others, including commanders at sea. Consider the following, from Nelson to First Secretary William Marsden: "There is [a] little alteration I wish for; and if I

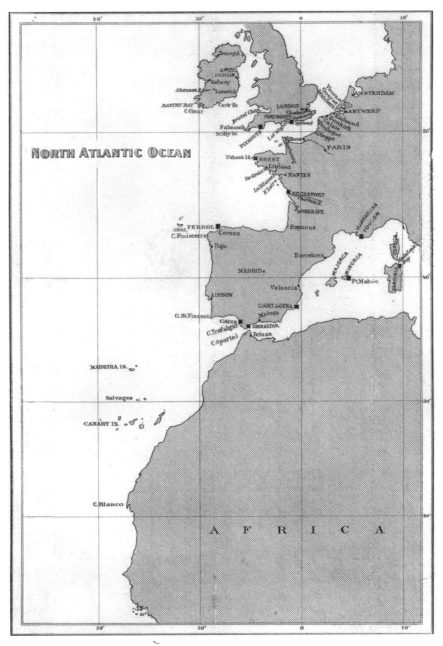

Map 2-1 The North Atlantic Ocean
Mahan, Life of Nelson

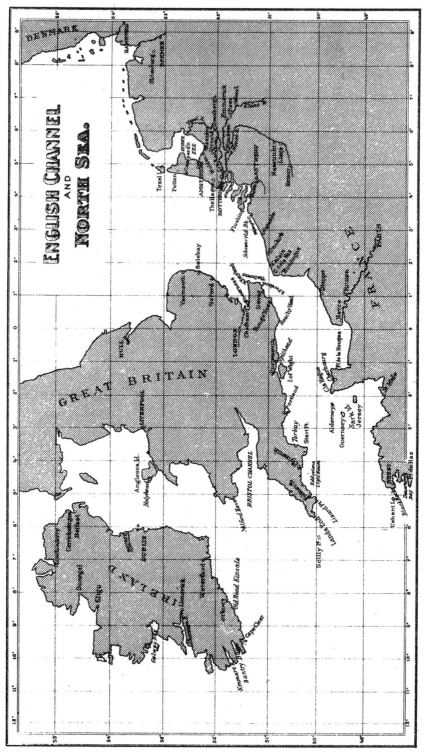

Map 2-2 The English Channel and North Sea
Mahan, Life of Nelson

knew the particular Lord of the Admiralty that managed this business, I would take the liberty of writing him."[13]

Generally, after the first lord received instructions from the Cabinet, the Board of the Admiralty would meet and draft orders. "It had no system of delegation or of sifting out less important items by means of sub-committees and executive officers."[14] Specific orders were written by the first lord or the first professional lord; however, the specificity was relative. Certainly the main decision, general sense of instruction, and any pertinent or supporting information (including intelligence) was enclosed to the relevant admiral (or detached captain). "The Admiralty," Brian Lavery notes, "preferred to do its business by formal letter whenever possible, and these were laboriously copied out by its staff of sixteen clerks."[15] As a rule, very detailed direction was omitted; specific decisions were left to the commander "on the scene" because in this era of very slow communications there really was no viable nor practical alternative. Moreover, most commanders were sensitive to Admiralty "interference" in their spheres of influence and with their rights and prerogatives.

It might be worth developing this issue for a moment. Lord Nelson, for one, was certainly not hesitant to disagree with the Admiralty, particularly when he had reached the vice admiral rank and had won several dramatic victories. For example, in February 1804, as commander in chief, Mediterranean, he was very clear about his unhappiness with the Admiralty's different view of how to manage convoys, writing, "If I form plans for the sending home our Convoys, and the clearing the different parts of the station from Privateers, and the . . . Admiralty in some respects makes [other] arrangements, *we must clash.*"[16]

He was even more upset over some of the circumstances involved in Commodore Moore's action, which was described at the end of chapter 1. Nelson initially countermanded the orders given to Captain Gore, commander of one of the involved frigates, for he was offended that other flag officers and the Admiralty were giving orders to one of his subordinates; he felt this was no way to be treating the commander in chief of the Mediterranean Fleet. However, he had another reason as well. He felt that the decision to seize the Spanish treasure fleet was an overreaction of the government to Spanish breaches of neutrality—with which he was intimate as the on-scene commander. He felt it was wrong to "molest the lawful commerce of Spain." The reader will recall that Dundas was uncomfortable, at the Cabinet level, about this issue as well. Nelson's assessment was that the seizure of this treasure, on which the Spanish economy was hugely dependent, would without question provoke the Spanish into a declaration of active warfare. He did not believe that Spain's reentry into the war was inevitable. Moreover, for Nelson, whose resources were already desperately strained, Spain's active hostility right then would present a very unwelcome additional tasking vis-à-vis containing the five Spanish ships of the line in Cartagena. If those vessels should join with French Admiral Villeneuve's fleet—Nelson's current primary focus—they would form a force significantly superior to his own.[17]

Such things were probably inevitable in a world war. Nevertheless, and as a general rule, the Admiralty tried not to cross the convinced opinions of (capable) local commanders; usually such commanders were allowed considerable freedom in how they executed their Admiralty directives: "The Admiralty was very much like a board of directors of a large company who make the broad and important decisions but leave others to fill in the details. The 'important decisions' were limited to three main areas—which men were to be in command of fleets and ships; how these fleets and ships were allocated; and what tasks the fleets, and sometimes individual ships, were to carry out."[18]

The way the Lords Commissioners passed formal directions to the fleet is interesting. This order to an admiral is a typical example of a format that was used for decades:

> The Rt. Hon. Lord Hobart, one of H.M. Principal Secretaries of State, having acquainted us that information has been received that the Batavian Republic has been called upon by the French Government to furnish a considerable number of boats and vessels with a view to the execution of a plan of invasion against this country, and signified to us H.M. pleasure that instructions should forthwith be given for the purpose of bringing into port all hoys and fishing boats belonging to the

French and Batavian Republics, or to the citizens of either, and to detain the crews of such vessels until further orders; you are hereby required and directed to give immediate orders to the Captains and Commanders of H.M. ships and vessels under your command to seize and bring into port all French and Batavian fishing boats, hoys and vessels of every description employed in the fisheries they may happen to fall in with.

Given 18 June 1803.

St. Vincent, P. Stephens, T. Troubridge[19]

The Admiralty was a primary recipient of intelligence information from national-level resources, and this information was then integrated into the navy's own intelligence, communications, and command process. The further evaluation, transmission, and dissemination of this intelligence was at the discretion of the first lord or first secretary, both of whom corresponded directly and frequently with government ministers, diplomats posted abroad, fleet commanders in chief, squadron commanders, and, not infrequently, individual ship commanding officers.

The navy was always hugely interested in timely operational and tactical intelligence. Thus, even during times of peace "the Admiralty sent fast ships . . . to 'look' into French and Spanish ports, to count the ships, and to evaluate their likely ability to sortie."[20] As well as their own reconnaissance missions, the Admiralty focused on Spanish and French naval bases for early warning of mobilization through several other sources—including, of course, London-controlled agents, embassy and consular networks, and the debriefing of merchant-ship captains returning from overseas. Incidentally, "this British system for reporting selected foreign movements survived late into the Cold War."[21]

But there was no real structure to naval intelligence—or to military intelligence, for that matter. In 1803, the British army's quarter master general established the Depot of Military Knowledge to collect, mostly from overt sources, maps and information on the military resources and topography of foreign powers. But during the forty years of comparative European peace which followed the defeat of Napoleon at Waterloo in 1815, the Depot, like much else in the British army, withered away.[22]

Indeed, an official army intelligence establishment did not reappear until 1873 with the founding of the War Office Intelligence Branch. Only then did the Admiralty follow their lead; they created a Foreign Intelligence Committee. The first British War Office and Admiralty Directors of Intelligence (DMI and DNI, respectively) were appointed in 1887,[23] (several years after the establishment of the U.S. Office of Naval Intelligence, by the way).

Regardless, at the end of the eighteenth century the Admiralty first lord and first secretary were, in fact, the main brokers for intelligence analysis and distribution to the operating forces. Indeed, Lord Sandwich (first lord during the earlier period, 1771–82) took deliberate pains to assure the king of this in a letter dated 13 September 1778, when he told him that "all intelligence that comes to the Admiralty is regularly sent to Admiral Keppell."[24]

Lord Sandwich was, moreover, very active in passing intelligence wherever it was needed—including directly to the king—and he wanted the king to be confident of that as well: "Your Majesty may be assured that every express from Plymouth, or anything else that deserves your attention is sent the moment it comes to hand."[25] Another note, written a month later from Portsmouth, promised that "if your Majesty chuses [*sic*] to be troubled with [this] sort of detail while Ld S: remains at Portsmouth, he will continue to send every observation he makes, and all the intelligence he procures."[26]

Lord Sandwich was not the best speller of the time period, even granting the lack of uniformity present in the mid-eighteenth century; however, he was keenly aware of, and a knowledgeable user of, intelligence information in the critical position of first lord. Cognizant that there were political and diplomatic aspects to foreign intelligence, he decided that "it did no harm for a First Lord of the Admiralty to develop his own private sources, independent of the Secretaries [of State and of the Post Office], and Sandwich did not hesitate to do so."[27]

Without doubt, some first lords were not particularly interested in intelligence, nor did they take much initiative in collecting and relaying intelligence to subordinates. One who was very proactive and intelligence-oriented was Adm. (later Admiral of the Fleet) John Jervis, the Earl of St. Vincent, who was first lord from 1801 to 1804. St. Vincent (1735–1823) was arguably Britain's greatest admiral, after Nelson, during this period. An extraordinary operator and administrator, he earned his earldom at the Battle of Cape St. Vincent in February 1797 (mostly due to then–Commodore Nelson's combat initiative). He became first lord of the Admiralty under Prime Minister Addington, planning the 1801 Copenhagen campaign, working hard (and making many enemies) to accomplish administrative reform, and planning coastal defense against the French threat of a large-scale cross-Channel invasion. St. Vincent's intelligence awareness and activity were considerable, both as a commander at sea as well as head of the Admiralty. His correspondence is packed with examples; a few from 1801, quoted below, are illustrative.

In regard to the French invasion mentioned above, one should pause for a moment to reflect that the Admiralty was not obsessed with the threat of invasion: "The main threat, as seen at Whitehall, was still what it had always been; the danger to British commerce. . . . What ministers feared was the capture of a whole East India or West India convoy. . . . It was Britain's good fortune that Napoleon never fully understood the importance of commerce or its relation to sea-power. . . . The truth was that the military invasion, without sea-power, was more or less impossible. Given sea-power, on the other hand, it was not even necessary."[28]

Nevertheless, Whitehall was faced with renewed large-scale public worry of a cross-Channel invasion in July 1801. St. Vincent wrote to his commanders in The Downs (the roadstead and anchorage formed by the shifting sands at the northern end of the Strait of Dover) that "the state of the enemy's preparations, on different parts of the coast . . . [are] beginning to wear a very serious appearance, and all the intelligence [agrees] that a descent is actually intended."[29] He continued with a note the next day to Adm. Archibald Dixon in the North Sea: "Our intelligence touching the . . . number of French troops in Holland is very different [from yours], for we are told from various quarters that the French have not less than 40,000 men in the United Provinces: probably this is a little exaggerated."[30]

Several days later, on 31 July 1801, addressing Nelson (who had just been appointed to take charge of all measures for "frustrating the enemy's designs" regarding the invasion), St. Vincent wrote that "we are certainly very defective in local intelligence: the French newspapers inform us that Carnot has lately made the tour of the coast of Flanders, with a view to preparations for invasion, and, as he is the great adviser of all military measures of importance, I place some reliance upon the newspaper account, and will endeavor to obtain more precise information thereon."[31] It is interesting to note that this Général Lazare, Comte Carnot (1753–1823), had been imprisoned earlier in his career for the "unauthorized publication of a military document."

Subsequently, on 10 August, St. Vincent wrote Nelson that "our advices from Paris say that the First Consul [Napoleon] has declared himself Generalissimo of the Army of Invasion, and that we are to look to Flanders for the grand effort."[32]

Then, by 14 August, a letter from St. Vincent to Nelson announced, "Our intelligence received this day indicates that Ireland is the great object of descent, but that it will be accompanied by demonstrations from Boulogne and Dunkirk or Ostend."[33] This was followed on 17 August: "The intelligence lately received . . . gives reason to believe that Dunkirk is the rendezvous of the Dutch and Flemish flotilla, and the principal embarkation will probably be made from thence."[34] On 26 August 1801 he wrote Nelson again that "our intelligence from Holland and Hamburg states that the expedition preparing in Holland is destined for the north coast: Newcastle, Berwick and Leith are named as points of attack; and it is asserted that the squadrons from Cadiz and Rochefort are intended for Ireland."[35]

On 5 September St. Vincent gave Nelson the benefit of his operational analysis of the enemy, writing, "I have observed during the last eighteen months that it has been the practice of the enemy to put to sea on the cessation of a gale of wind, and that our cruisers have been very tardy in leaving port after being driven in by the stress of weather, by which much mischief has happened."[36]

St. Vincent had written earlier to Admiral Cornwallis, on 7 March 1801, showing his considered willingness to rely on French sources—at least for some information: "The French Papers state authentically that [French vice admiral] Ganteaume was off Cape de Gatte on the 13th February and has captured the *Success, Incendiary,* and *Sprightly,* cutter."[37] Adm. Sir William Cornwallis (1744–1819), "Billy Blue," a longtime friend of Nelson, had been commander in chief in the East Indies in 1789, and then commanded the Channel Fleet in 1801, and again from 1803 to 1806.

Also in March, writing to the Duke of Northumberland, St. Vincent showed great concern for French false intelligence: "A thousand thanks for your obliging communication touching the Brazils. A prepossession in favour of that idea in narrow Lisbon politics has already done us irreparable injury, and [Napoleon's brother] Lucien Bonaparte[38] has shown much address in imposing false intelligence on the Government of Portugal."[39]

Of course, while St. Vincent was unusually active, by no means was he the only first lord to be very intelligence-minded. In an internal Admiralty memorandum dated May 1804, for example, Lord Barham listed some of his requirements concerning the type of person needed to provide for secret services:

> He should be a perfect master of arrangement. Without this, he must be in continual perplexity, misemploy and lose the force which is put under his direction. . . . I mention forethought and preparation as the pivot on which every kind of success must depend. . . . Both in the last and in the American war, the greatest part of our misfortunes proceeded from a want of these qualities in those who directed the war. No hurry nor activity can make up for the want of these essentials; and whoever possesses them must succeed.
>
> In all business that *requires secrecy,* he must communicate with the comptroller of the navy, in that *great line of the service.*[40]

In June 1808, on a matter of great importance, Barham wrote Vice Adm. Lord Collingwood, "It is probable his Holiness the Pope may endeavor to effect his escape from the States of the Church recently usurped by Bonaparte. . . . Station such frigates as [you] may be able to spare at such points on the coast of Italy as, from intelligence [you] may receive of his Holiness' movements, are most likely to facilitate the object in view; with directions to their captains to receive him and his followers on board, and convey him to such place of destination as he shall point out, paying every possible attention to him during his continuance on board."[41]

Of course, Lord Barham was also in constant communication with the prime minister regarding intelligence issues. For example, in December 1805 Pitt wrote that he wished "Lord Barham to consider whether it might not be expedient to direct Sir J. Warren to proceed to the Cape Verd. . . . This suggestion arises out of the intelligence received from the Cape, of . . . the expectation that a body of French troops was expected there."[42]

St. Vincent often corresponded with the prime minister as well, even if the intelligence was unconfirmed from unconventional sources. Addressing Addington on 27 July 1801, St. Vincent wrote that by the "accounts in the French newspapers, [our] ships under the orders of Sir James Saumarez have suffered to such a degree that I am very apprehensive we have not means at Gibraltar to put them into an efficient state."[43]

Likewise intelligence minded, on 15 April 1806, First Lord Charles Grey, Viscount Howick, wrote to Adm. Lord Keith (commanding in the North Sea):

> We have received indisputable evidence that . . . there is a constant communication kept up between Harwich [England] and the little fishing town of Katwijk;[44] that the Dutch Government employ between 10 and 12 fishing smacks appropriate to this service; and that despatches received in this manner are constantly forwarded by express to the Hague.
>
> It is thought necessary to stop this communication, and as the best means of doing this, as well as of discovering the sources of the enemy's intelligence, I am to request your Lordship to select some intelligent and confidential officer, to whom you will give strict orders to stop these smacks as if by mistake; to observe carefully if any packets are

Fig. 2-2 *The Rt. Hon. William Pitt (the Younger),*
Prime minister of Great Britain from 1783 to 1801 and 1803 to 1806.
Shown here by J. Hoppner (engraved by J. Thomson).

thrown overboard, and to search very narrowly both vessels and crew,
and to send any papers he may find to your Lordship, which you will
forward immediately under a cover marked "secret."[45]

First Lord George, second Earl Spencer, cannot be discounted as an
intelligence-oriented leader. In an April 1798 memorandum to the
Cabinet, he concluded that

all the intelligence received from time to time has constantly been circulated for the information of the Cabinet, and it is all entered in books
(now forming a pretty voluminous collection) kept on purpose.

A précis of the latest intelligence last received may easily be made
out, and shall immediately be prepared if it is required;

but no very great stress can be laid upon the inspection of any such
partial extract, because it cannot always be known what degree of
reliance should be placed on any particular piece of information, and
it is only from a general view and comparison of the whole that anything like a tolerable judgement of it can be formed.[46]

Incidentally, although not extensively quoted in this chapter, some further comment on Lord Spencer is warranted, for even with no particular
naval background he "by his energy, zeal, and whole-hearted devotion
to the business of the Navy, had become one of the ablest and most successful First Lords ever to preside over the Admiralty. . . . The debt
owed to Spencer by his country during these years of peril is almost
incalculable. It was he who successively chose for their high commands
Jervis, Duncan, and Nelson."[47]

Finally, Henry Dundas, mentioned in chapter 1, was of course very
intelligence-oriented in whatever position he held. So was his son Robert,
who succeeded him as Viscount Melville and also later held office as the
first lord of the Admiralty. As a second coincidence, Henry had been
joined at the Admiralty by his former assistant—in secret service as well
as other things—Evan Nepean, who became his first secretary ("the
aide of his old associate in the public service would add much to Lord
Melville's comfort and confidence in the arduous task [first lord] he has
undertaken").[48]

Even without Nepean's support, Robert Dundas was himself an intelligence broker; note his letter to Lord Keith of 27 June 1815: "Reports . . .
[indicate] that in the event of adverse fortune it was the intention of
Bonaparte to escape to America. If there is any truth in these statements
he will in all probability make the attempt now. . . . It is desirable that
you should take every precaution in your power with a view to his seizure
and detention should he endeavour to quit France by sea." This was sec-
onded three days later by J. W. Croker, Robert Dundas's first secretary,
who further wrote Lord Keith, "We have fresh reports every hour of
Bonaparte's intention to escape—he pretends for England, we think for

Fig. 2-3 *George, Lord Spencer.*
Under the leadership of the second Earl Spencer, the Royal Navy saw some
of its greatest achievements during this era. This likeness was painted by J. S.
Copley and engraved by B. Holl.

America. It is of great consequence to intercept him and we reckon on
your vigilance."[49]

Several years earlier, in September 1803, First Secretary Nepean had
passed similar intelligence to the same Lord Keith about the movements
of Napoleon's brother. He sent him an "extract of a letter from New
York stating that Jerome Bonaparte had sailed from Baltimore on July
28 in the *President,* a Swedish ship under American colours bound for
Amsterdam. . . . [Please] give orders to your cruisers in the event of their

falling in with the said ship to detain her and bring her into port in case any person who answers to the description therein contained shall be found on board her."[50]

Perhaps the key official in the Admiralty was this first, or principal, secretary to the Lords Commissioners. In fact, depending upon who the individual was and what year it was, this man was "the confidential servant of the Board in principle, but in practice an official of greater consequence in both the naval and political worlds than several of the Lords Commissioners."[51] Included among the enormous scope of his duties was the control of almost all correspondence between the Admiralty and commanders around the world—both outgoing and incoming. As a result, this individual was critical in the passing of information in and out of the "nerve center" of the Admiralty, on all subjects, which certainly included intelligence. The men who held this position during this period of study were Sir Philip Stephens, Sir Evan Nepean, William Marsden, William Pole, and John W. Croker.

Leaving this post in 1795, Stephens had held it for a little over thirty years, during which time he frequently handled secret intelligence and secret service money. Earlier in his career he had actively supported the earl of Sandwich—clearly a very intelligence-minded first lord. Indeed, one French scholar found Stephens (and his position) so much involved that he actually called him "the head of the intelligence service":

> In [a modest Admiralty room] on tables covered with a constant flow of papers and documents, is decided the actual fate of England. . . .
>
> From there come the orders which move simple pawns on the chessboard of seas of the flotillas of the Antilles, of America, of the Indies, or of the North Sea. That is where are stored the hurried [writing] of the English admirals from all the seas, the reports of even the lowest commander of a [warship], the coded information transmitted by blockade runners. . . .
>
> Inside these four walls is found the man who holds in his hands the responsibility of the Navy and, therefore, that of the kingdom. This man is not the minister responsible before the king and before Parliament. . . . This is not the First Lord of the Admiralty. . . . No, the

man who gladly carries the crushing weight of the enormous Naval machinery of England is none other than Mr. Philippe Stephens, Secretary of the Admiralty. . . .

The secretary of the Admiralty is not . . . the machine that [merely records] the decisions of the lords of the Admiralty and transmits them for execution; it is not the passive role of secretary of a naval committee, controller of orders issued, simple organ of transmission or of signature or of receiving [copies of orders].

In fact, the activity of [this civil servant] is immense, covering all the domains of British naval power since the head of the naval administration is none other than he. He centralizes all correspondence (incoming and outgoing) and countersigns all the essential acts (laws) of the ministry. Nothing is hidden from him and nothing . . . escapes [his notice].[52]

Perhaps "head of the Secret Service" is an exaggeration in discussing the Admiralty secretary;[53] however, more than one expert agrees that the Admiralty's intelligence "network"—such as it was—specifically functioned as the secretary's project.[54]

Regardless of exactly who controlled it, this might be a good point at which to discuss two remarkable incidents of supposed British naval intelligence activity. The first one involves an "agent" named John Barnett, who worked in the eastern Mediterranean area against Napoleon subsequent to the 1798 Battle of the Nile.

While based on board HMS *Lion,* cruising off the coast of Egypt, he is reported to have organized a network of spies—using considerable "English gold"—among the Egyptian servants and guides supporting the French army occupying Cairo. Moreover, he further learned that Napoleon had made an amorous conquest of the wife of one of his officers, a Madame Fourès. From French clerks, whom he had also bribed, Barnett also found out that Bonaparte had sent the officer back to Paris on an important "mission," so as to get rid of him. The *Lion* intercepted the sloop in which Fourès was embarked and Barnett told him the situation. Fourès begged to be allowed to return to Egypt and "avenge his honor," so the British smuggled him back to Cairo hoping he would confront Bonaparte and assassinate him. Caution may have superseded anger, or patriotism may have outweighed personal emotion, but as it turned out, Fourès made no known attempt to kill Napoleon.[55]

The second incident, in 1808, involves a patriotic Catholic priest named Rev. James Robertson. He had spent considerable time in the Scottish Benedictine abbey in Ratisbon (Regensburg) and was fluent in German. Posing as a German commercial traveler named Adam Rorauer, he made a number of trips among various Danish islands looking for some Spanish troops serving Napoleon—a force of around eighteen thousand men. Enlisting the help of a Catholic Spanish army chaplain, Robertson learned where all the troops were scattered, as well as the location of their commander, Gen. Pedro Caro y Sureda, Marquis de la Romana (who, interestingly enough, had previously been a naval officer—commanding a Spanish frigate—before transferring to the army). Staying in disguise, Robertson moved to Copenhagen and then to the island of Fyn, where Romana was effectively kept in isolation without recourse to letters. He was able to gain Romana's trust by reminding him of a dinner the general had had with British ambassador Hookham Frere in Toledo, where they had admired a picture of Saints Peter and John by the neoclassic artist Anton Mengs. When Romana was apprised of the changed political situation in Spain (Napoleon's elder brother Joseph had been installed as king of Spain against the Spanish national will), he decided his relationship with the French was over. Robertson was then able to make arrangements for around nine thousand men of the Spanish force to be taken on board British ships cruising in the Great Belt.

The importance of this operation was twofold. Romana's forces were going to be used as a large part of a French effort to invade Sweden from Denmark; the invasion was forestalled by Robertson's coup—as well as the arrival of a detachment of the British North Sea Fleet off Zealand. In addition, Romana's troops were returned to Spain to throw their considerable weight toward the national uprising against Bonaparte. (Readers of Patrick O'Brian's novels will recognize much of this scenario in *The Surgeon's Mate,* in which Dr. Maturin looks like the Rev. Robertson, and Maturin's godfather (Colonel Ramon d'Ullastret i Casademon) resembles the Marquis de la Romana.)[56]

Not all British naval intelligence operations ended well. The outstanding example remains the perhaps too–active agent Cdr. John Wesley Wright, who was caught, imprisoned, and almost certainly murdered in 1805 by Napoleon's police.[57] Wright was an officer whose name makes frequent appearances in the literature. He apparently was the chief British agent in the Royalist plot of 1803 led by Generals Cadoudal and Pichegru. According to what Bonaparte said later while imprisoned on St. Helena, "on different nights [between August 1803 and January 1804] Wright landed Cadoudal, Pichegru, Rivière etc. at Biville near Dieppe." But Napoleon realized something was amiss, and in March 1804 he arrested and had shot the young Duc D'Enghien for complicity in the plot. Of the genuine conspirators, Cadoudal and eight others were shot, while Pichegru committed suicide in his cell. On 8 May, Wright was captured when his brig ran aground on the coast of Brittany; his solitary confinement ended in November 1805 when (at least according to Napoleon) he committed suicide before he could be brought to trial.[58]

In March 1804, Lord St. Vincent may have had an idea that all was not well, writing to Adm. Lord Keith:

> Secret [and] Private Captain Wright has [reportedly] made nine attempts to land on the opposite Coast, but found the surf so high he could not succeed—not a word of which I believe. . . . Should the Secret Service be continued, I will propose that Captain Wright shall be authorized to engage vessels for the purpose at Dover.
>
> Lord Hawkesbury has desired that the Lively Revenue-Cutter may be placed under [Wright's] Orders [but] I believe Your Lordship's suspicions of the late Secret Operation having been disclosed to the Enemy, and all the correspondence intercepted and afterwards conveyed to the parties, are too well founded.[59]

In any event, Wright's demise caught the British attention. It certainly worried C. S. Forester's fictitious Capt. Horatio Hornblower, captured after the loss of HMS Sutherland. He speculated that he, too, would never return as he was transported toward Paris: "Wright . . . was said to have committed suicide in prison in Paris. Everyone in England believed that Bonaparte had had him murdered—they would believe the same in [Hornblower's] case."[60]

Whoever truly was in charge of the above operations, the first secretary frequently analyzed and passed on intelligence in lieu of the first lord. Flag officers in receipt of such information would in turn pass it along to subordinate commanders, as did Lord Keith in this letter to a junior rear admiral in August 1805: "Sir, I herewith transmit a copy of a note of intelligence which I have received from the Secretary of the Admiralty, and as it appears that the enemy may be contemplating movements to the eastward I desire that you will take particular care that the whole squadron, as well off Boulogne as in the Downs, is kept in constant readiness."[61]

Similarly, many years later First Secretary Croker passed intelligence and orders to this same Lord Keith, on 13 August 1813: Per an account "of H.M.S. *Alexandria* and sloop *Spitfire* having . . . fallen in with the American frigate *President* off the North Cape, [you must] endeavour to keep two ships together always, as the force of the *President* is reported to be as follows: Main deck—30 24-pounders long guns. Quarter deck and forecastle—4 24-pounders long guns and 22 42-pounders carronades. Main and fore top—4 4-pounders in each. Mizen top—2 3-pounders."

Furthermore, recaptured British prisoners of war reported that Commodore Rodgers, commanding the *President,* intended to attack the Archangel convoy, and that the American officers hoped to encounter a British seventy-four-gun ship of the line by itself as they felt sure they could beat one. Finally, "the *President* fights under two large white flags with black letters, one expressing '*No impressment,*' and the other '*This is the haughty* President, *how do you like her?*'"[62]

On 21 December 1812 Croker also sent this interesting item to Lord Keith:

> My dear Lord, It has been discovered at the Board of Trade that a very clever forgery of British licenses has been made in France or Holland

under cover of which many ships have passed our cruisers unmolested and unsuspected. . . . The most prominent mark of detection is the Secretary of State's seal, which the forgers have not accurately copied.

Your Lordship will see the great advantage of communicating this information with all possible celerity to all your cruisers . . . and your Lordship will also I think agree with me that the discovery should be kept a profound secret.[63]

Secretary Nepean sent this unusual intelligence to a flag officer on 19 June 1803: "The Admiralty having been informed that a plan has been concerted by Mr. Fulton, an American resident at Paris . . . for destroying the maritime forces of [Britain with a submarine vessel], I am commanded by their Lordships to send you herewith the substance of the information they have received relative thereto."[64]

The communication of intelligence was a two-way path, of course. Flag officers and detached captains, around the world, passed intelligence to the Admiralty as well as received it. Note this letter, dated 1 August 1803, from Lord Nelson to Secretary Nepean:

Sir, You will please to acquaint the Lords Commissioners of the Admiralty, that by the last information of the Enemy's force at Toulon, there are seven Sail of the Line, five or six Frigates, and six or seven Corvettes, in all eighteen Sail, apparently perfectly ready for sea: a Frigate and three Corvettes have been three times out of the harbour, but returned again. At Genoa there are three Genoese Vessels of War ready for sea, about forty sail of French Merchant Ships, and three Dutch Merchantmen; and at Marseilles, from reports of Vessels spoke, they are putting in requisition eighty or ninety Sail of Vessels, about forty tons each, to be fitted as Gun-boats, and to proceed by the Canal of Languedoc to Bordeaux; but I believe, if they are really fitting out, that they are destined to protect the movements of their Army in the Heel of Italy.[65]

Sometimes flag officers wrote directly to the first lord, bypassing the convention of addressing their letters to (or through) the first secretary. Here we find a younger Nelson who, as a junior flag officer in the middle of the Nile campaign, was at first timid to do this when writing to Earl

Spencer in June 1798: "Not having received orders from my Commander-in-Chief to correspond with the . . . Admiralty, I do not feel myself at perfect liberty to do it, unless on extraordinary occasions."[66]

His hesitation soon wore off, however; from this point on he started to feel much more at liberty and for the rest of his life maintained a frequent correspondence with the first secretary, the first lord, various ambassadors, various politicians, and a good number of highly placed ministers, including the secretaries of state and, indeed, the prime minister himself. In fact, his letter to Prime Minister Addington, on 28 June 1803, containing insightful military, naval, and political analyses of Gibraltar, Algiers, Malta, Sicily, Sardinia, Rome, Tuscany, Genoa, and the Morea, was extremely valued in Whitehall. His analysis was found so useful that, as a result, he was requested in the future to direct any observations he might have on *any* political subject immediately to the secretary of state for the War Department.[67]

Nelson became so comfortable with this arrangement that he encouraged other officers to do the same under certain circumstances. Just before he was killed at Trafalgar, he ordered Rear Adm. John Knight to "inform Rear-Admiral Sir Richard Bickerton of your proceedings, from time to time, during my absence from the Mediterranean. . . . And you will also, when it may be necessary, communicate with the Admiralty direct, as it might very much retard your correspondence to send your letters through the Rear-Admiral; but you will, as early after as possible, transmit Sir Richard copies thereof."[68]

WHETHER TRANSMITTING national-level intelligence down to the fleet or relaying intelligence garnered by the fleet up to the secretaries of state, it is clear that the Admiralty was significantly involved in collecting, processing, evaluating, and disseminating intelligence information. Paralleling the relatively small-scale, noncentralized intelligence apparatus of the overall government, there was neither a specific office of naval intelligence nor a naval intelligence bureau. Indeed, the extent that intelligence was emphasized—or left unexploited and uncommunicated—was directly proportional to the personal inclination and interests of the key navy officials in office from year to year. Those officials were the senior political minister (the first lord), the senior professional officer (just beginning to be called the first sea lord), and the senior civil servant (the first secretary).

How intelligence was gathered, utilized, communicated, received, and generally integrated into the operating naval forces are the subjects of the next several chapters—all leading to a focus upon the ultimate "intelligence officer"—the at-sea commander.

3

Signals and Information Transmission

Communications dominate war; broadly considered, they are the most important single element in strategy, political or military.

Rear Adm. A. T. Mahan, USN

Communication across the sea has been the principal concern of the Royal Navy for nearly 1,000 years. . . . [I know] a book on eighteenth-century naval warfare that was in fact a book about signaling systems: the two were inseparable.

Prof. J. R. Hill

AS STATED IN THE PREFACE, THE MILITARY AND NAVAL ESTABLISHMENTS were significantly hampered by their technologically primitive communications. This severely limited the rapid analysis and exploitation of information that may otherwise have decisively influenced the outcome of many significant campaigns.

In the time period of this study, the common system of strategic communications was essentially based upon the hand-written letter, with concomitant delays of transportation. As a result, the lords of the Admiralty could usually give only very general orders, instructions, and directives due to the expectation that these letters would take days, weeks, and months to get to their addressees. This meant that close, let alone detailed, management was impossible. Close control had to be left to the admiral or detached captain in receipt of the general guidance; that guidance presumably conveyed the intentions of the government as passed by the Admiralty. The man-at-the-scene therefore had great flexibility in his actions, which was often very advantageous. Also advantageous was that the extremely general nature of most Admiralty orders, combined with the slowness of communications, enabled the Admiralty to direct literally worldwide naval operations from a very small board room with a very small staff.[1]

At times, however, the system was disadvantageous, as on-scene commanders could undertake activity contrary to the wishes of the government. Witness Rear Adm. Sir Home Popham, who, after capturing the Cape of Good Hope, decided it would be strategically consistent, good initiative, and generally officerlike to sail across the South Atlantic and to attack and capture Buenos Aires. Unfortunately, unknown to him, the British government was very interested in establishing and maintaining friendly relations with the Spanish American colonies as they struggled for independence against Spain, and Popham's adventure did not help those relations at all.[2] As it turned out, "the invasion failed dismally, ending in capitulation, the cashiering of Lt. Gen. John Whitelocke [the senior army officer] and a . . . court-martial reprimand for Popham."[3]

SURFACE MAIL traveled reasonably quickly and cheaply through England at the turn of the nineteenth century. (In addition to the mail, in Britain the Admiralty could send communications via "king's messengers," men employed by the government for just this task. Occasionally such officers traveled abroad, but this was more the exception than the rule.) External mail took some time; a letter from London took "a week to [a ship] in the Baltic, two weeks or more to one in the Mediterranean, and [at the very least] a month to one in the West Indies." Of course, dispatches from deployed ships were similarly delayed in transit to Whitehall.[4]

Overall, slow communications to and from the operating forces were a significant problem. Lord Nelson was always bothered by this, and during the Trafalgar campaign particularly so. Writing to Lord St. Vincent from the Mediterranean in September 1803, for example, he observed that "it is now near three months since my last letters were dated from England; and but for a French newspaper, which hitherto we have procured through Spain from Paris, we should not have known how the world went on."[5]

A year later, on 8 July 1804, he wrote, "I have had nothing from England since April 5th; and if we did not get the French [news]papers, we should be left in total ignorance."[6] In November 1804 he complained, "I am to this moment ignorant, except by the French papers, of what is passing in Spain. *What can be expected from such communications to a Naval Commander-in-Chief?*"[7] This was followed in December with "It is now ninety days since I have heard from England; it is rather long at these critical times."[8]

Interestingly enough, intelligence from newspapers continued to be a significant source for commanders—much as cable television is today. Almost 140 years after Nelson's time, American admiral Kimmel (during his testimony after the Pearl Harbor attack) mentioned that he had been dependent upon newspapers for information regarding the state of negotiations, and that he obtained a major portion of "his diplomatic information from the newspapers."[9]

The Post Office's packet ships, which it used to transport mail around the world, were often also used by the navy for communications—excluding the most urgent dispatches. Some officers disliked the lack of control and the parliamentary politics that influenced packet schedules and operations. St. Vincent once wrote that he could not "but lament most exceedingly that Borough influence should ever be exercised in such very important concerns as the navigation of Packets. No wonder that so many of them have failed in their duty."[10]

Even Gen. Lord Wellington spared time from his land campaign with worries about the safety of such "unofficial" ships. In early August 1812 he wrote from Madrid, "I have heard of war being declared by America, and I beg to draw your Lordship's attention to our communications by the packets. We may depend upon it that the mouth of the Channel and the coasts of Portugal will swarm with [American] privateers."[11]

Nevertheless, the packet service was particularly useful in communicating with the Americas. Sailing every two weeks from Falmouth, England, the Post Office ran a regular nine-ship relay between Britain and its American and West Indies stations,[12]

> averaging forty-five days to Jamaica after calling at several of the Windward and Leeward Islands. Port Royal, Jamaica, was the last port of call before sailing for Falmouth, usually a 35-day passage. . . . Duplicates of all letters went by the next packet and third copies were often sent in a convoy.
>
> The whole system . . . could, however, be halted if the French captured the packets, and there were periods when privateers had great success—at one time four homeward-bound packets were taken within four weeks. Not only were original letters lost but the duplicates were lost as well.[13]

Because of the great distance, communications to the East Indies required considerably more time. In fact, the East Indies station was the regional area of operation that gave its commander in chief the greatest power and widest discretion: "To send a despatch . . . [via] the Cape of Good Hope and St Helena, took about six months, so that a reply could not be looked for inside a year; and unless the [return] despatch from Admiralty was very peremptory, *another* year might well elapse before the C-in-C had to alter his plans."[14]

In lieu of Post Office packets, the navy had to rely on its own smaller vessels for communication. That is not to say that privately owned ships were not used when convenient. The ships of the British East India Company certainly helped in this arena. Moreover, in various parts of the world, a naval commander might encounter a merchant or whaling ship with which he could entrust official and ship's company's personal mail. O'Brian's Capt. Jack Aubrey used this method, even if it was a surprise to his friend Dr. Maturin: apprised of Aubrey's intention to finish and copy an official letter, he asks, "Why are you in haste? Whitehall is half the world away or even more for all love." Aubrey replies, "Because in these waters we may meet with a homeward-bound whaler any day."[15] However, neither fictitious nor real captains could count on this method, for the truth was that "even a single sail in mid-ocean was something of an event; Jack had often traveled five thousand miles in quite frequented sea-lanes without seeing another ship."[16]

Admirals almost never had enough dispatch vessels, such as real-life Lord Gambier talking to fictitious Capt. Horatio Hornblower—who had just recaptured a cutter from the French: "'*Witch of Endor* can carry the despatches,' he said. As with every admiral the world over, his most irritating and continuous problem was how to collect and disseminate information without weakening his main body by detachments; it must have been an immense relief to him to have the cutter drop from the clouds, as it were, to carry these despatches."[17] Lord Nelson often suffered from this problem, as evidenced by this apology to Sir Alexander Ball in January 1804: "I have nothing in the shape of a small Vessel, or your letters for Egypt should have been sent from the fleet."[18] When a naval ship was used for dispatches, the sending admiral (or the Admiralty itself) tried to ensure its efficiency. When challenged by another British vessel, such a ship would signal 'carrying dispatches,' which meant that a ship must neither stop nor be stopped even for a moment.[19] In fact, "a ship carrying them was excused from all ordinary decencies or politeness; forbidden indeed to delay for even a minute."[20]

Lord Nelson was careful not to rely on custom to ensure the noninterference of his dispatches. Note the two memoranda below:

TO THE CAPTAIN OR COMMANDER OF ANY OF HIS MAJESTY'S SHIPS OR VESSELS WHO MAY FALL IN WITH HIS MAJESTY'S SLOOP CAMELEON: You are hereby required and directed on no account to interfere with Captain Staines, or to demand a sight of his Orders, which are *most secret,* unless from particular circumstances it may be judged necessary, in which case you are to keep them most inviolably secret.[21]

Private Instructions from Lord Nelson to Captain Parker: Bring to for nothing. . . . Hoist the signal of Quarantine, and that you are "Charged with dispatches." If you are forced to speak by a Superior Officer, show him only my order for his not interfering with you; and, unless he is an Admiral superior to me, you will obey my orders instead of [his].[22]

When using Post Office packets, or naval vessels, commanders prepared multiple copies of dispatches to help ensure delivery. For example, after the Battle of the Nile, Nelson sent his official reports with Captains Berry and Thompson in HMS *Leander.* But, "lest Berry might meet with an accident, he decided to send his signal lieutenant, Capel . . . to Naples in the *Mutine,* with duplicates."[23] This was fortunate, for the *Leander*—and Nelson's original dispatches—were subsequently captured after a bloody duel with a French ship of the line.

Duplicates notwithstanding, sometimes the message never got through. A commander who had this happen to him—neither receiving original nor duplicate—was Rear Adm. Sir Charles Vinicombe Penrose, operating in the Mediterranean in 1816. He was to have joined forces with Lord Exmouth (Adm. Sir Edward Pellew) in order to jointly attack the Dey of Algiers. Having received no such order, Penrose and his ships made no effort to rendezvous. Wondering where they were, Exmouth was forced to proceed without them; fortunately, he was nevertheless successful in the last great action of the period.[24]

Slow communications were an enormous disadvantage, in many other ways, for overseas naval and military commanders. Ships at sea found it very difficult to gain information regarding declarations of war. The country first declaring war could give advance information to its commanding officers, but other than rumor the ships on the receiving end usually had to *wait until actually attacked* to know for sure.[25] Novelist Alexander Kent's Capt. Richard Bolitho knew this very well: "Every ship under a foreign flag was suspect; without fresh intelligence he knew nothing of greater affairs in Europe. A Spanish or Dutch flag might now be an ally, a Portuguese perhaps hostile."[26]

C. S. Forester's Commander Hornblower faced this dilemma as a French frigate approached HMS *Hotspur:*

> "Sir," said Bush. "Mr. Wise is asking on behalf of the hands, sir. Are we at war?" Yes or no. "The Frogs know, and we don't—yet, Mr. Wise." There was no harm in a captain admitting ignorance when the reason for it should be perfectly clear.
>
> . . . There was a sudden shriek overhead. . . . A [lucky shot] had passed over the *Hotspur* twenty feet above her deck.
>
> "Mr. Wise!" yelled Hornblower. . . . "Get that halliard re-rove." "Aye aye, sir." The spirit of mischief asserted itself in Hornblower's mind. . . . "And Mr. Wise! If you think proper you can tell the hands we're at war."[27]

In fiction or reality, this was a real problem for captains and admirals. Lord Nelson, for instance, was very worried about being caught off guard by the Spanish in the fall of 1803, and thus wrote Ambassador Frere that recent Spanish behavior, he supposed, indicated a state of war: "I have therefore earnestly to request, that you will send me immediate notice of such an event, that I may . . . act upon it myself. If your news of War passes [to me] *through England,* it will be two or three months before I shall know it officially."[28]

He continued this concern through October 1804, warning Capt. Henry Richardson of HMS *Juno: "Most Secret.* Whereas, from the recent conduct of the Spaniards at Ferrol, the greatest circumspection becomes necessary . . . in communicating with the Spanish Ports, or on falling in with any of their Ships or Vessels of War. . . . To do so with the utmost caution, taking care to anchor . . . well out of reach of shot from their Forts or Batteries, and always to be on your guard against surprise."[29]

Vice Adm. Sir Herbert Sawyer, commanding British naval forces at Halifax, commenced operations against the United States in 1812, but without solid information lost the courage of his convictions. He had taken some American prizes, but "still not sure that a state of war existed, released them and actually sent one of his precious sloops under flag of truce to ask for explanations." Simultaneously, however, American commodore John Rodgers, more knowledgeable than Sawyer, surprised HMS *Belvidera;* but the real "importance of the incident lay in the exasperation of the British seamen and officers at what they tended to look upon as a treacherous attack, or at least as one made in ungentlemanly fashion. Rodgers' behavior had been correct enough . . . but . . . it might have been well had it occurred to Rodgers to give *Belvidera* some definite warning of the outbreak of war before he opened fire. A gesture—unnecessarily chivalrous—would have cost nothing."[30]

Indeed, when one reflects on the relative need for quick communications vis-à-vis diplomatic, naval, and military affairs, state of the art then was absolutely primitive compared to the multimedia, high-volume, instantaneous, clear, and encrypted systems at our disposal today. Fortunately for the British, all nations operated under the same conditions. Having said that, it was the French who developed a methodology that revolutionized the land-based part of this equation.

Communications on land in those days, especially "before the British had copied the brilliant new French invention of the semaphore signal system (which increased the speed of message transmission, on line-of-sight, from days to 200 mph on a few vital routes), was agonizingly slow."[31] As Capt. Geoffrey Bennett explains in his book *Nelson the Commander,* "Following up an idea suggested by [an Englishman], Claude Chappe erected a chain of 116 'aerial *telegraph*' stations in 1794, linking Paris with Lyons, each comprising a tower surmounted by a mast to which were affixed a pair of rotating arms, given the name *semaphore.* This initial chain was subsequently extended to a network of over 500 stations serving 29 towns in more of Europe than France itself, because Napoleon found this speedy visual method of signaling messages of [great] value for controlling his armies."[32]

Capt. E. W. C. Owen, in HMS *Clyde,* reported on this system in June 1806, writing that a telegraph line he had previously identified he now observed extending from Calais to Étaples. Moreover, he was certain that it had replaced an older flag system used along that coast. "This telegraph seems so simple and at the same time so comprehensive," he wrote, "that I take the liberty of forwarding your Lordship a sketch thereof for the information of My Lords of the Admiralty."[33]

Lord Collingwood, whose officers could read the enemy's semaphore (thanks to code books captured by Capt. Lord Cochrane), sent the following intelligence report to Whitehall in July 1809 (it concerned a British army attack against islands in the Bay of Naples): "Yesterday the French Signal Posts telegraphed that a Fleet of Transports were anchored to the southward of Port Especia and Transports landed—the Ships of War standing into the Bay. . . . I have not heard from Admiral Martin & Lieutenant General Sir John Stuart that they were about to make this movement."[34]

In 1796 the British Admiralty fielded its own version of this system, as envisioned by the Rev. Lord George Murray, which was a mechanically operated shutter system. In England, Murray's shutter system was later replaced by a mechanical rotating-arm system in 1816, which survived until the development of the electric telegraph around 1846. Slow, clumsy, and useless at night or in fog, these systems were still a quantum leap in naval-communications capability. Indeed, "the Plymouth telegraph, which began in July 1806, could send a message to the Admiralty and receive an answer in less than thirty minutes. A short message would receive an answer in ten minutes."[35]

In fact, the Admiralty semaphore system was very quick, as Capt. Lord Cochrane could testify. On 19 March 1809 he came into Plymouth on board HMS *Imperieuse;* via telegraph the Admiralty learned of his arrival and sent him an order to attend at Whitehall, which he received within an hour of anchoring.[36]

Interestingly, Waterloo hero Prussian field marshal Gebhard Leberecht von Blücher, visiting London in 1816 after the war was finally over, showed a particular interest in the workings of the Admiralty telegraph.[37] It was mounted on the Admiralty's roof, and had

Fig. 3-1 *Cuthbert, Lord Collingwood.*
Nelson's longtime friend. He assumed command of the Mediterranean Fleet upon Nelson's death, dying himself in that capacity in 1810 (probably of stomach cancer). This posthumous painting shows him in full dress uniform. The original portrait is by Henry Howard (1769–1847).

© National Martime Museum, London

repeating structures on hill-tops and church towers at intervals of about ten miles, all the way to Portsmouth in the south-west, Chatham in the south-east and, later on, Harwich in the north-east. It worked on a kind of blackboard divided into six ports. Combinations of ports, opened or closed, denoted the letters of the alphabet" [see fig. 3-2].

Details of the Harwich line seem to be lost, but the "Chatham line" went: (1) the roof of Admiralty House; (2) Number 36, West Square, Southwark; (3) New Cross Gate, Nunhead (now called Telegraph Hill); (4) Shooter's Hill; (5) Swanscombe; (6) Gad's Hill, Shorne; (7) Chatham Dockyard.

And to Portsmouth: (1) Admiralty House; (2) Royal Hospital, Chelsea; (3) "The Highland," Putney; (4) Netley Heath; (5) Hascombe; (6) Blackdown; (7) Beacon Hill, Harting; (8) Portsdown Hill; (9) The Glacis, Portsmouth.

In the 1790s metropolitan citizens and sleepy-hollow rustics alike ... took comfort, perhaps, from the thought that at least one Government department remained abreast of science and alive to the perils of invasion. It signified everything that was new, startling, efficient or supernaturally swift; by association, the British public got it into its head that the Admiralty was all of these things.[38]

Of course, neither the Admiralty nor the system was perfect. As late as 4 August 1815 Lord Keith wrote a note to the Admiralty, complaining that a "telegraphic message [was only] partially and indistinctly received last night."[39]

Other countries were not left out of the race to develop semaphore telegraph systems. The Danes had a system operational at least in time for the Battle of Copenhagen in 1801. On 29 January the *Times* of London told Britain that a semaphoric "telegraph has been already erected on one of the Towers of [Kronborg Castle]; to carry on a correſpondence along the coaſts, as far as Gillelilge, on one ſide, and Copenhagen on the other."[40] In addition, there exist several pictorial illustrations made at the time that give us a visual portrayal of the Danish system—which used neither the British shutter nor the French rotating arm methodologies.

Robinson Kittoe, who was the secretary to Rear Adm. Thomas Graves (Nelson's second in command at Copenhagen), was also a talented drafts-man and made a number of heavily annotated drawings during the

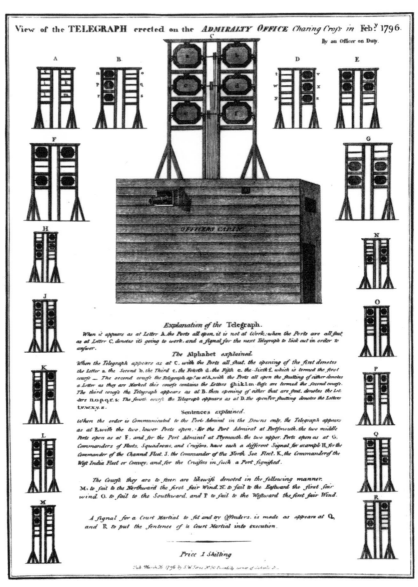

Fig. 3-2 *Admiralty semaphore telegraph, 1796.*

This contemporary print shows the station erected at Charing Cross, London, as part of the overall relay system from 1796 to 1816. The illustration shows how the letters A to R were signaled by different arrangements of the six shutters.

campaign.[41] Among these include a view of the British fleet, passing through the sound, under fire from Kronborg Castle. Kittoe's drawing shows a semaphore mast on top of the left-hand tower of the castle, and, in fact, Kittoe was so impressed by this device that he redrew the mast in larger detail on the top right of his main illustration. This same mast, with four crossed yards looking very much like a ship's mast, can also be identified in several other contemporary drawings and paintings; moreover, another such device can be readily seen in a drawing of the Battle of Copenhagen (view from Amager, looking northward across Nyeholm) beside the Sixtus Battery, with the mast standing out against the smoke of the battery's guns (see fig. 9-1).

British frigate captain Lord Cochrane was particularly aggressive about destroying French signal stations, realizing how important this invention truly was. After a cruise full of just such activity, on 28 September 1808 he reported to Vice Adm. Lord Collingwood that "with varying opposition, but with unvaried success, the newly constructed semaphoric telegraphs . . . at Bourdique, La Pinede, St. Maguire, Frontignan, Canet, and Fay, have been blown up and completely demolished, together with their telegraph houses."[42] For a realistic and graphic, though fictionalized, account of the destruction of a telegraph station and battery—and the dangers involved—see C. S. Forester's *Hornblower and the Hotspur.*

Communications at sea were equally appalling as those on land—generally worse—and remarkably cumbersome, relying on speaking trumpet, boat messages, line-of-sight flag signaling, and ship-borne dispatches.

It was not until the First Dutch War (1652–54) that the British developed any sort of code signaling using flags, and this system was restricted to a few, very limited, preestablished tactical directions. While the French, again taking the lead, had created a system of flag vocabulary as early as 1693, it was 1776 before Adm. Lord Richard Howe generated a signal book for his West Indies fleet that really started the British down this same path.

Sir Charles Middleton (later Adm. Lord Barham) was another officer always keenly interested in signals. His 1779 correspondence with Capt. Richard Kempenfelt included:

> Signals pointed out by numbers . . . I have been long acquainted with. They don't require many flags; however there must be three of each sort, or you can't express a number which consists of three figures of the same rank.
>
> However, I think all these objections may be obviated; and in my opinion, the signals used by numbers, or those by a superior flag, as used by D'Orvilliers the last two summers, are by much superior to any method we have.[43]

In 1781 Middleton and Kempenfelt were still studying the French: "*Project for Signals.* Signals should be simple, clear, and easily discernible. I don't know any more perfect than those invented by M. de la Bourdonnais. He made use of broad pennants as more readily fixed to any part than flags. He fixes a number for each pennant; and that several pennants, each designating a particular number and, put one above the another, serve as cyphers. . . . With this arrangement an infinite number of signals may be made."[44] In 1788, reviewing Vice Adm. Lord Hood's signal proposals, Middleton dared write that "the night and fog signals are amongst the worst I ever saw and would be productive of certain separation [of ships]."[45]

Again borrowing from the French, Rear Admiral Kempenfelt next developed a *Primer of Speech for Fighting Ships.*[46] Kempenfelt was a pioneer in many areas, though signaling remained one of his favorites. He maintained that even in the crisis of battle most naval officers worked well "with their heads," but they nevertheless sometimes failed "because they could not transfer their thoughts beyond the bulwarks of their own ship."[47]

Adopted by Lord Howe (who remained extremely interested in the subject), Kempenfelt's system had increased the capability to 256 predetermined meanings using sixteen different flags. In 1790 Howe then produced a *Signal Book for Ships of War,* which reduced the number of flags to ten, but increased the number of meanings to 9,999. Middleton's comment at that point was more circumspect: "I understand that there has been an examination of Lord Howe's and Lord Hood's plans of signals by some flag officers convened for that purpose, and that their decision has been in favour of Lord Howe's."[48]

Nelson used the last system to advantage; in fact, he acknowledged Howe's contribution in a letter to him on 8 January 1799. After the Battle of the Nile, he wrote, "I was enabled to throw what force I pleased on a few Ships. This plan my friends readily conceived by the signals [I made]—(for which we are principally, if not entirely indebted to your Lordship)."[49]

The final breakthrough to virtual freedom of speech via flag signaling occurred in 1801; indeed, it only became reasonably efficient around 1810, with the development and widespread use of Capt. Sir Home Popham's system. Popham had served in the first Copenhagen campaign, and had worked at transmitting messages between the fleet and the negotiators on shore. From that point on he became extremely interested in the navy's signaling system, and over the next ten years substantially contributed to the improvement of the methodology.[50]

Sir Home published his ideas in his *Telegraphic Signals or Marine Vocabulary,* which not only allowed for an enormous flexibility in predetermined signals and commonly used words but also simply identified all numbers and letters so that any word could be easily spelled out. Popham was very modest as he started to promote his system; on 30 June 1801 he wrote to Adm. Lord Keith, "I take the liberty of sending you a vocabulary or marine telegraph. . . . I have found it of particular use in receiving intelligence . . . from . . . detached ships. . . . For every proper name and word not in the vocabulary can be spelt. . . . I conceive the advantage to be not only a saving of time and trouble, but of boats. . . . Instead of making signals for [lieutenants to come to the flagship to take a message] the intent might be directly communicated."[51]

Nelson, always concerned with communications, tactics, and tactical control, instantly saw the huge advantages afforded by Popham and aggressively ensured that all ships in the Mediterranean Fleet were supplied with Popham's book and the required flags. In fact, he twice personally went to the Admiralty, working with Second Secretary John

Barrow, to make this happen. Barrow later wrote that Lord Nelson had been with him "at the Admiralty in the morning, anxiously inquiring and expressing his hopes about a code of signals just then improved and enlarged. . . . I pledged . . . that he might rely on their being at Portsmouth the following morning."[52]

It is significant to note that at these various times the systems discussed were available but not required. Like so many things, commanders incorporated them at their own discretion (and, quite often, own expense).

Night and fog signaling were primitive; there were, especially after 1800, some codified signals involving the use of fireworks, guns, horns, bells, and arrangements of lanterns hoisted in frames to the mastheads, but this was very limited; there were only seventy night signals and twenty fog signals available.[53] Sometimes, when poor conditions ruled, or when other circumstances dictated, admirals could make a simple signal for a junior officer to come fetch letters or documents from the flagship. For example, right before the Battle of Copenhagen in 1801, "the *Elephant*'s log recorded, 'At 8 the *London* made our signal for a midshipman and at ½ past 11 the general signal for lieutenants'" to repair on board the flag.[54]

By the way, fog and night were not the only conditions affecting flag signaling; one cannot overlook the intense smoke generated by black-powder cannon. For example, at Trafalgar, "'the smoke was so thick in the action,' wrote a midshipman of the *Royal Sovereign,* 'we could hardly make out the French from the English.'. . . For want of a breeze to carry it off, the murky powder-smoke from hundreds of guns rolled in an ever-thickening cloud over the rear of the Combined Fleet, increasing the confusion into which it had fallen."[55] Obviously, visibility in general became a problem, to say nothing of seeing small, colored flags.

In fact, "seeing" is the key to this entire issue. After all, it was the human eye—aided by a basic telescope—that was the primary tool, and it was extremely limited. If swimming in the ocean (assuming he could swim; few knew the skill), a sailor's "horizon was a mere 1.1 miles away.

But climbing to the maintop—about 100 feet above the water on a 74-gun ship—extended the distance he could see to nearly 12 miles. . . . Perched in the rigging of a large ship, a loo kout might see the sails of another large ship at 20 miles. . . . Height was the key. Yet a person's range of view could be affected by many circumstances, such as fog or even loud distractions on deck. At long distances, the atmosphere could create strange refractions, causing mirages."[56]

There were different kinds of telescopes to address different conditions. For example, there were "night glasses" to try to compensate for low light, and there were "come-up glasses," having "a lens half way along divided into two, so that it gives you two images. When they separate the ship is moving from you; when they overlap she is coming nearer."[57] Still, the limitations were significant; thus one finds Nelson's last word on the subject, focused upon signaling at the time of battle: "But, in case signals can neither be seen or perfectly understood, no captain can do very wrong if he places his ship alongside that of the enemy."

Admirals and captains were quick to seize upon Home Popham's new system, recognizing its importance and reveling in its detail and flexibility. Capt. Henry Blackwood, of HMS *Euryalus* (who would physically bring England after-action details from Trafalgar), wrote to his wife just prior to that battle, "At this moment we are within four miles of the enemy and talking to Lord Nelson by means of Sir Home Popham's signals."[58] And, of course, it was this system that enabled Nelson, after completing his tactical communications three weeks later, to "amuse the fleet" by making his immortal signal, "England expects that every man will do his duty."

Captain Blackwood was to exercise all of his (and his ship's) signaling skills in earnest the night before Trafalgar. Shadowing the French and Spanish fleets throughout the night, Blackwood "constantly informed the Admiral of their position by means of guns, blue lights, and rockets, as did also the other look-out frigates." According to one of Blackwood's midshipmen, "For two days there was not a movement that we did not communicate, till I thought that Blackwood, who gave the orders, and

Bruce, our signal midshipman, and Soper, our signal man, who executed them, must have died of it."

Of course, the French admiral was in no way oblivious of this activity, which told him that battle was imminent. Villeneuve, when "apprised of the rockets and signal-guns that had been seen and heard ahead, at about 7.30 P.M. ordered the Combined Fleet, which had been sailing in three columns, to form a single line of battle."[59]

A few details about flag signaling would be useful at this point:

> In a flagship, the flag lieutenant was in charge of signals, but on [other ships] the job usually fell to a midshipman. . . . A flagship needed many halyards to hoist signals, and [typically] had fifteen on each side.
> [The flagship's] halyards needed 973 fathoms of rope, and allowed many positions for hoisting signals, so that they could be seen from any desired angle. [Other ships of the line] needed to make fewer signals, and had 339 fathoms of halyards. To help spread the message, repeating frigates were stationed on one side of a fleet in line of battle, to show the signals being made by the admiral.[60]

It is interesting to note that the flagship's signals officer was the "flag lieutenant." While such an officer may have also acted as the flag officer's aide—as in modern usage—the title in Nelson's day accurately described the intense focus on signaling.

As with the land telegraph system, error was frequent even regarding simple instructions. Observe this note from Lord Nelson to the captain of HMS *Active,* who had done something other than his admiral intended: "My dear Sir, I believe you mistook our signal this morning—it was to reconnoitre Toulon."[61]

Security was an issue. Ships, upon meeting each other, challenged each other by flying their individual "recognition" numbers and then a "private signal." The private signals "were issued by individual commanders-in-chief. They were changed as soon as it was known that the enemy might have captured them." Lord Hood directed his commanding officers that "the signals were to be kept 'with sufficient weight affixed to them to insure their being sunk if it should be found necessary to throw them overboard,' and he added that, 'As a consequence of the most dangerous nature to His majesty's Fleet' resulting from the enemy getting hold of them, any officer who let that happen 'will certainly be made to answer for his disobedience at a court martial.'"[62]

Nelson addressed this problem in June 1804, writing to the Admiralty secretary that "as there is doubt that the late Private Signals, established for . . . this station . . . were taken [captured] in the *Swift* Cutter, I herewith transmit you a Sheet of Signals altered on the 10th instant, and issued to the different Ships under my command, which you will please to lay before the Lords Commissioners of the Admiralty."[63] He had been concerned with a related security issue six months earlier, writing this memo to all of his ships in the Mediterranean: "And their lordships having reason to apprehend that Officers under the rank of 'commanders' have . . . obtained, copies of the Signals described in the Day and Night Signal-Books above mentioned, direct me to give the strictest injunctions that such improper proceedings may not take place in future, and that you recall such copies of the said Signal-Books as may be in the possession of the Officers for whom they are not intended."[64]

Lord St. Vincent wrote Rear Adm. Saumarez, in June 1801, regarding a similar situation: "The Portuguese squadron is in possession of the day and night signals, but I see many and strong objections to supplying any ship of that ally with the private signals; it will therefore be necessary to establish a distinct set of signals."[65]

Security of the signaling system itself was always of concern, although the main use of the system was to facilitate tactical directions to fleet units; obviously, if flag signaling had been capable of, or designed to, transmit critical pieces of sensitive information security would have been much more important. Still, officers were usually very careful to keep their signal books from being captured. Most such books were bound in leaden covers, promoting the obvious method of throwing them overboard if capture were imminent.

Over time various signaling systems of the rival navies were compromised by specific captures of signal books. In fact, signals were captured during the very first naval battle of the war between ships of equal force. Capt. Edward Pellew's *Nymphe* took the French national frigate *Cléopâtre* in June 1793; after a brief but fierce struggle the British boarded and "on the quarterdeck they found the heroic Captain Mullon mortally wounded. . . . He had in his pocket a list of private coast-signals, and as he lay in his death-throes he pulled a paper from his pocket, bit it to pieces and was trying to swallow it when he died. In fact the paper he destroyed was his Captain's commission, and the signals fell into British hands; but no mistake could dim his heroic devotion to duty."[66]

In February 1804, Lord Keith had possession of other captured French signals, and he was determined to use them and ensure no one knew he was using them:

> Sir, I herewith transmit two sets of signals, supposed to be at present in use on the French coast . . . in order that you and Captain Owen of the *Immortalité* . . . may have the chance of availing yourselves of a knowledge of the enemy's intended movements; and it will be very important that, by a minute attention to the signal station, you ascertain yourself how far the code herewith sent is that which is actually in use or not.
>
> And as it is of the greatest importance that the possession of these signals by us should be most completely concealed, you will use the most cautious measures for preventing the existence in the minds of any of the officers in the other ships or your own of any suspicion that these signals are in your hands.[67]

Having made the point that officers were usually very careful to destroy their important documents prior to surrendering their ships, it is surprising how often no mention was made of doing this in after-action reports. For example, none of the six captains involved—victors or vanquished —in the first three great frigate duels of the War of 1812 refer to the capture or destruction of such materials.[68]

Nelson was aggressive in instructing his officers to think in these terms, as this letter to Lt. Kortwright, commanding HM Cutter *John Bull,* indicates: "You are to keep a proper weight constantly affixed to the . . . dispatches, and, in case of falling in with an Enemy of superior force, and seeing no probability of escaping capture, you are to throw them overboard, and sink them."[69]

Fictitious Capt. Jack Aubrey was always ready. He had an "iron box in his locker—pierced iron, weighted with lead, for documents that must not be taken, that must sink on being thrown overboard, sunk at once, beyond recovery: signals, codes, official letters."[70] (Ironically, sometimes one had to go to extremes to keep a dispatch from getting wet and ruined, as "indeed it is blowing so hard at present that I am under the necessity of putting this letter into a keg, in order to convey it on board the lugger.")[71]

One cannot quit a discussion of communications security without observing that contemporary officers knew that many letters and codes were compromised—regardless of media and of location. Lord Nelson constantly tried to ensure thorough security, but was also resigned to losses. For example, he wrote Ambassador Frere, in October 1803, that "as probably this letter will be read before it gets to you, I can only tell the reader, that a British Fleet never was in higher order, health, and good humour, than the one I have the happiness to command."[72] On 12 August 1803, Nelson wrote his friend Alexander Ball that the latter's letter from "the *Redbridge,* I fear the French are reading, for I dare say he [the captain] never threw his dispatches over-board, although it has not been for want of caution on my part, for I charged him, when he was with me off Naples, always to have lead or plenty of shot tied to his dispatches."[73]

Regarding a similar problem, in 1799 Capt. Thomas Troubridge became convinced that the queen of Naples had her secret agents reading Nelson's letters—including those written by Troubridge—and then passing them on. Troubridge informed Nelson that he believed "some person about [Ambassador] Sir William Hamilton's house sends accounts here, as I have frequently heard things which I knew your Lordship meant to keep secret."[74]

After a dispatch vessel was captured in April 1805, Nelson wrote to his mistress, "I find, my dearest Emma, that your picture is very much admired by the French Consul at Barcelona; and that he has not sent it to be admired—which, I am sure, it would be—by Buonaparte. . . . I wish I had [it, but it is] gone as irretrievably as the dispatches. . . . But, from us, what can they find out? That I love you most dearly; and hate the French most damnably."[75]

Nevertheless, for the most part such holes in communications security yielded no significant intelligence triumphs nor meaningful strategic advantages.

THIS IS A GOOD PLACE to more fully develop the subject of cryptography. Loosely defined, cryptography is the enciphering and deciphering of messages in secret codes or ciphers. Technically, a *code* is based on the substitution of complete words or phrases for others, whereas a *cipher* works on the principle of replacing single letters.[76] While historically small scale in comparison to his experience, statesmen had known for centuries what Winston Churchill wrote in 1924: "I attach more importance to [the decrypts] as a means of forming a true judgement . . . than to any other source of knowledge at the disposal of the state."[77] Churchill was speaking of intelligence gathered during the First World War; however, even by the mid–eighteenth century, European countries "had skillfully developed . . . complicated and efficient cipher and code systems. Moreover, their skill in intercepting dispatches and breaking cryptographic designs became famous as they employed bright code clerks and shrewd administrators."[78]

Diplomats abroad often were their own "bright code clerks"; sometimes they employed whatever local talent they could find. It is interesting to note that British ambassador to Naples Sir William Hamilton used his wife Emma (later to be Nelson's mistress) in this role. A superb example (not reproduced here) is Item 259 of the *Hamilton and Nelson Papers,* a partial transcription of an eleven–page 1795 enciphered letter, in Italian, in Lady Hamilton's handwriting, from Sir William to the Neapolitan foreign minister.[79]

Another interesting example, which will bear upon this book's analysis of the Battle of Copenhagen, is a letter from British envoy to Denmark William Drummond to Secretary of State for the Foreign Office Lord Grenville, just prior to the 1801 Copenhagen campaign. Deciphered by one of the Willes family (the "decypherers of letters" mentioned in chapter 1), it begins (showing both deciphered meaning as well as the cipher itself),

Your Lordship will have

209 227 1913 241

seen that the Danish Ministry has

at length avowed its intention

3365 3357 345 1417 3269

with respect to the Armed Neutrality,

2368 3874 345 779 132

I believe however I can safely

1447 1662 1447 1924 3755

assure your Lordship that (there?)

1353 2076 1377 266 2498

prevailed upon this subject

345 2695 4175 3315 1070

considerable difference of opinion

in the cabinet. Count Bernstorff

631 39 132 3749 2253

does not even affect to conceal

529 2360 1268 2201 3356

his alarm and inquietude.[80]

Most encryption and enciphering was at the diplomatic level within the Home and Foreign Offices. The military and naval forces generally did not use such techniques and essentially gambled that their correspondence would not be captured or otherwise intercepted.

Lord Nelson was irritated by his lack of ability in this area—"Every *Jack* in Diplomatic affairs is intrusted with a cipher, but an Admiral Commander–in–Chief *is not.*" He always maintained an interest in cryptography, as his letters occasionally show. Note this remark in June 1804: "I send you some intercepted papers from Egypt; I cannot make out the ciphers. . . . When read, pray take a copy of them . . . and let me know the cipher if you can make it out."[81]

Nelson did occasionally use some codes and ciphers belonging to certain Mediterranean kingdoms. For example, on 22 December 1803, he wrote "to the Pasha [of Yannina] *in his cipher,* to say that Captain Cracraft [the senior British officer in the Adriatic] was gone to Panormo, if he wished to have any conversation with him."[82]

Nevertheless, Nelson had no access to official British systems. Admirals did not have, or were not allowed to employ, official encryption. He was constantly concerned for the security of his own official and private communications—as well he should have been, for the small vessels (in lieu of frigates) commonly used to carry dispatches were constantly being taken by the enemy. He therefore repeatedly complained that unenciphered information was doubly at risk, for he felt that if documents had to be captured at least they did not have to be in plain English. For example, Nelson was particularly irritated by the April 1804 capture of the cutter *Swift:* "She was taken the 5th, and all our dispatches, letters, &c. &c., are gone to Paris."[83] He further wrote to Lord St. Vincent, "I only hope that no dispatches of any consequence were entrusted in such a Vessel. Whatever they are, they are this day before Buonaparte."[84]

Lord St. Vincent maintained an interest in cryptography, though this particular letter in 1802 might make one think he equated the use of codes and concealment as prima facie guilt: *"Private.* I was at Gibraltar when Lord Henry Paulet brought [a seized ship] in, and upon the discovery of concealed papers in cypher, under the most suspicious circumstances, I sent the Master and Supercargo to America as State Prisoners, and acquainted the Secretary of State therewith, sending him a copy of the papers so found."[85]

It is worth noting that even as late as 1812 naval cryptography was still ad hoc and ad lib among most powers. Among the instructions given to American Commo. Isaac Chauncey by Secretary of the Navy

Fig. 3-3 *John Jervis, Lord St. Vincent.*
Shown here as a rear admiral by Sir William Beechey, St. Vincent was perhaps
the greatest admiral—along with Nelson—of the period.
© *National Maritime Museum, London*

Paul Hamilton, when ordering him to command U.S. naval forces at
Lakes Ontario and Erie, was for him to personally *"establish a cipher,* by
which when necessary, you will correspond with the [local American
army] commanding officer, and . . . you may establish with the army a
telegraphic communication—by which means you may be able to ascertain their movements and to communicate your own, with celerity and
Secrecy."[86]

Both cryptography and cryptology were to gain emphasis as the nineteenth century wore on. After all, the widespread use of flag hoists—and particularly the growing use of shore–based semaphore telegraph systems —essentially made government and military communications open to the public.

Of course, encoding required decoding even among those whom the communications were meant, and encoding always meant the greater likelihood of error. Note this letter from Dundas to Lord Spencer in 1799: "We had been led to hope from the telegraph communication . . . that the loss on our part had been five killed and wounded, and on the part of the enemy fifteen killed and wounded. In short, either from an original mistake or from an inaccuracy in decyphering the communication at Deal, the oo in both instances were omitted."[87]

THIS BOOK is particularly concerned with an admiral commanding a fleet, squadron, or station with no superior officer in the area, and with a captain, commanding a ship detached on an independent mission or cruise—again with no superior officer in the area. An admiral (probably a vice or rear admiral) closely subordinate to a superior officer, as well as a captain in the same circumstances, were tasked much differently—a prime example being ships making up part of a large fleet blockading an enemy port. When a superior was in close proximity, to include most certainly visual proximity, the subordinate was limited to the most routine activities and thoughts. In a fleet at sea, cruising or blockading, almost all communications were handled, and decisions were made, by the senior officer present, including course, speed, when to tack, when to wear, what sails to carry, when to mess, *what to do!* A commander's talents and burdens of responsibility were extraordinarily minimized under such circumstances. Only when the commander was himself the senior officer present (admiral or captain) was his plate full and his burden heavy. Moreover, C. S. Forester would add that officers in command "in those days of poor communications had some strange responsibilities thrust upon them,"[88] a subject which will be fully developed in chapter 6.

Historian/espionage writer Anthony Price develops the real import of communications to intelligence and operations in general, particularly relative to such senior officers present:

> Consider the enormous burden placed on commanders in the days before radio. . . . Of the [perils facing a] commander, battle was the least[,] . . . with rock, tempest, and fire preceding. But to these hazards might very reasonably be added the stress factor, to which admirals at sea and captains on detached duties . . . were particularly exposed for prolonged periods. With the fate of the country perhaps at stake, and certainly their own lives and professional reputations, lone commanders had to make decisions on the basis of information which might not only be sparse and imprecise, but also often days, weeks, or even months old.[89]

The modern commander has to sympathize with Capt. William Hoste (one of Nelson's favorites) when he wrote to the Admiralty (his admiral perhaps a fortnight away, and London a month away, at best) from HMS *Bacchante* in 1813, "Sir—I have acted without any precise orders from my admiral . . . [but] upon motives which at the time I considered as best calculated . . . for the interest of Great Britain."[90]

One cannot leave any discussion of effective and timely intelligence transmission without observing that in 1797 Britain had been barely saved from disaster. She was saved "by [an enormous] failure of French intelligence to learn of the 'Great Mutiny' (the widespread fleet mutiny at the major anchorages of Spithead and the Nore) in time to gain any advantage of it."[91] This was relative to a second attempt at an invasion of Ireland by the Irish rebel Wolfe Tone and the French general Louis Lazare Hoche.[92] The failure to discern the paralysis of the Royal Navy, followed by a failure to quickly transmit the information to France, is likely "a failure as gross as that of German intelligence during the French Army mutinies" of World War I for the exact same reasons.[93] The Great Mutiny effectively lasted from 15 April to 12 June 1797; Britain was virtually defenseless for about two months.[94]

Bemoaning the lost opportunity, Tone later complained that for eight weeks the English fleet was "paralyzed by mutinies at Portsmouth, Plymouth, and the Nore. The sea was open and nothing to prevent both the Dutch and French fleets to put to sea. Well, nothing was ready; that precious opportunity, which we can never expect to return, was lost; and now that at last we are ready here, the wind is against us, the mutiny is quelled and we are sure to be attacked by a superior force."[95] In fact, the expedition failed to get ashore at Bantry Bay and was abandoned.

The ultimate issue, regarding timely information transmission, must surely be the relay of the most important piece of intelligence of all: the event that makes hostilities unnecessary, or the news that peace has been signed and, therefore, hostilities are over. Two major incidents during this time period immediately come to mind. One, which will be studied in greater detail later in this work, concerns the former. The second great victory of Nelson's career was, of course, the 1801 Battle of Copenhagen. Very briefly, the campaign was pursued because Britain felt compelled to force Denmark to accede to neutrality issues viewed as critical to Britain's national existence; Denmark refused to cooperate, fearing the eccentric Russian czar's enormous armies at a time when Czar Paul was raging particularly anglophobic. Unfortunately for the two thousand Britons and Danes killed and wounded at Copenhagen, the czar was assassinated on 12 March 1801, causing a total reversal of Russian foreign policy. Had this information been passed to the west more quickly than the technology of the time permitted, Danish foreign policy would have altered significantly in favor of Britain, and the battle would have been avoided. Nelson's anguished exclamation underscores the tragedy: "Good God! why did I not know that event eight days sooner?"[96]

The second incident concerns ignorance of the closure of hostilities. One of the most famous land battles of this period, with horrific consequences for the British army, was the Battle of New Orleans (8 January 1815) at the end of the War of 1812. In this case a treaty (the Treaty of Ghent) had been signed between the two belligerents on 24 December 1814. Again, had it been possible to transmit this critical information more quickly across the Atlantic and then down through the American continent, over two thousand British soldiers (including their commanding officer, Gen. Sir Edward Pakenham) would have escaped death or injury in a major battle that happened literally after the war was over.

4

Frigates: The Eyes of the Fleet

So far as is necessary to enable the battle-fleet to secure the control, we have to furnish it with eyes from our cruiser force.

Sir Julian Corbett

Was I to die this moment, "Want of Frigates" would be found stamped on my heart.

Lord Nelson

DURING THE AGE OF FIGHTING SAIL, ONE CLASS OF VESSEL WAS THE frigate—a small, fast warship, large enough to rate a full captain as its commanding officer but too small to lie in the line of battle and contest the ultimate control of the sea with the enemy's battle fleet. That was left to the ships of the line of battle, or as we more commonly know them today, battleships. Nevertheless, the frigate—also widely known by the term "cruiser"—was a considerable tool with the potential for significant flexibility and versatility in its employment. In fact, the frigate was the key workhorse relative to naval intelligence.

It is important to specifically define the designation *frigate* as understood during this time. Again, smaller than the ships of the line, frigates were nevertheless the busiest and most aggressive warships: "Rarely in port except for refit or damage sustained in action, they were the Navy's light cavalry, scouting, patrolling, protecting, capturing—and . . . fighting."[1]

A wonderful example of the frigate's versatility—showing also that British and American ships had no corner on the market—is the following operation executed by the small French frigate *Brune*. In late 1795 the French gained intelligence that an Austrian commissary was spending a night at an inn in Voltri, Italy (about nine miles east of Genoa) and that he had almost ten thousand pounds sterling in pay for the Austrian troops operating in that area. So, on a bitter winter's night "a landing party of about three hundred from *La Brune* took the neutral post[,] . . . robbed the commissary, and seized the corn and flour magazines. Next day, flushed with triumph and rich in booty, their captain was publicly enlisting men for [the French army] in the streets of Genoa."[2]

In any event, the classic wooden sailing frigate was a descendent of the 1757 *Pallas* (and the French *Aurore* of the same period).[3] They were basically single-gun-deck warships which functioned as scouts and as cruiser/escort vessels. Of the fifth and sixth "rates," in naval establishment description, these ships had from twenty-two to forty-four "great" guns (cannon).[4] Essentially built for speed, they nevertheless outmatched everything else afloat except the enormous ships of the line.

Despite the relatively slow evolution of technology in that time, there was notable development of the frigate class in the last half of the eighteenth century. Soon after the launching of the thirty-six-gun seven-hundred-ton *Pallas* (and her related sisters in the sixth rate of twenty-eight and thirty-two guns), skillful French and Spanish designers brought forth thirty-eight- and forty-gun ships (mounting 18-pounder cannon versus the common British 12s). By the time that the pioneering Capt. Edward Pellew (later Sir Edward and ultimately Adm. Viscount Exmouth) deployed with his 12-pounder thirty-six-gun *Nymphe* in 1793,

Fig. 4-1 HMS *Triton.*
A British thirty-two-gun frigate, the *Triton* was built in 1796. Shown here
hove-to, it presents the appearance of the typical, if small, frigate operational
in the Age of Nelson. Prior to the familiar black-and-yellow striping pattern,
which began to appear (and then became standard) in the years after 1800,
most ships displayed one dominant color with various contrasting trim colors.
Paint schemes were basically at the captain's discretion, though anything
much beyond the dockyard minimum would come out of the captain's purse.
This marvelous illustration was done by one of the foremost marine artists of
the day, Nicholas Pocock (1740–1821).
© *National Maritime Museum, London*

the French were producing forty-gun, 1,000-ton frigates—quickly followed by forty-four-gun 1,240-tonners (often carrying 24-pounders). This
rapid evolution more or less ended, at least for this era, with the creation
of Joshua Humphrey's American *super*frigates circa 1797—though no
real notice was taken of these until the USS *Constitution* (the famous, still
commissioned, and still afloat "Old Ironsides") and her sisters played
havoc with the Royal Navy in 1812–13.

Indeed, any discussion of naval intelligence during this period must spend time on the frigate's two most important and very closely related jobs—sea control and reconnaissance—which were the keys to the operability of fleets two hundred years ago. However, any discussion of frigates and their employment opens the debate among authorities as to which function was the more vital.

On one side is sea control. This is essentially focused upon aspects removed from the role of the main battle fleets, including hunting and patrolling, convoy and shipping protection, blockading, attacks on enemy coastlines, commerce raiding and otherwise taking "prizes," ship-to-ship combat, conveying communications, and shadowing enemy fleets. Frigates were all-purpose cruisers, sweeping the seas of enemy frigates, privateers, and merchant ships, not to mention conducting special operations, escorting convoys, and blockading. Some of this work fell to small brigs and sloops. However, "unable as they were to take on enemy frigates, such vessels were essentially auxiliaries: the Navy's cutting edge was always its frigates—and it was they, above all, which were consequently always in short supply."[5]

Today we might use the modern term C^3 (command, control, and communications) to encompass—at least obliquely—most of these activities. As the eminent British naval strategist, historian, and theoretician Sir Julian Corbett notes, "If the object of naval warfare is to control communications, then the fundamental requirement is [a] means of exercising that control."[6] The frigate was the ideal means for the task; in fact, Sir Julian insisted that this was the principal duty of the frigate class—not reconnaissance:

> On no . . . communication theory, can we regard the primary function of cruisers as being to scout for a battle-fleet. [Even in] Nelson's practice [the frigate's] paramount function was to exercise the control which he was securing with his battle-squadron. . . . He was so deeply convinced of their true function that he used them to exercise control to an extent which sometimes reduced his [scouting] cruisers below the limit of bare necessity. . . . If he found that he had not a sufficient number of cruisers to exercise that control and to furnish eyes for his battle-fleet as well, it was the battle-fleet that was made to suffer.[7]

The critical subtask of shipping protection and convoy duty—which many considered the cruiser's true priority, must not be underplayed. Lord Nelson certainly believed it important. Consider the opening of this letter to Capt. Benjamin Hallowell of HMS *Argo:* "Whereas I consider the protection of our Trade the most essential service that can be performed . . ."[8] Nelson also was very concerned with the frigates' reconnaissance and signals-transmission support to the fleet in combat, as expressed in a letter to Sir Alexander Ball in August 1804: "I am keeping as many Frigates as possible round [my flagship]; for I know the value of them on the day of Battle: and compared with that day, what signifies any Prizes they might take?"[9]

Importantly, the lure of prize money—the proceeds of the sale of a captured vessel and its cargo, paid by the government and distributed among the officers, crew, and admiral of the ship making the capture— was extremely motivating to most officers: "Patronage, promotion, and prize-money have been described as the three masts of the Royal Navy. It would be illiberal to assert that prize-money was by any means the most important, but . . . it was certainly the subject still most frequently discussed."[10]

All that aside, the other overall frigate role, which this chapter will tend to focus on a little more sharply when discussing intelligence, is the one of scouting, reconnaissance, and general gathering of information. It must be stressed that sources of intelligence are far different today than in 1800; the modern fleet commander can rely on national-level satellite imagery and communications interceptions, tactical communications interception, and radar, sonar, and aerial reconnaissance to help him find the enemy or acquire other important information—and all of it is virtually instantaneous. In great contrast, Nelson and his colleagues fundamentally had only the eyes of a human being—albeit enhanced by a telescope—on board their ships. Moreover, these ships had no radios to communicate their information, and their ability to move, in order to physically bring any gathered information to the commander (or a political minister), was entirely dependent upon the vagaries of wind, tide and current. Nevertheless, for the purpose of this discussion, the basic *scouting* function may, when added to the above sea-control notion, let us loosely appropriate the equally modern term of C^3I (command, control, communications, and intelligence) to cover the whole concept.

In fact, a key raison d'àtre for the frigate was to be the "eyes" of the fleet, trying to identify where the enemy was, what they were doing, and then communicating that information to larger fleet units. (Of course, even though ships are referred to as "she," they are, after all, inanimate things; it was the men on board, and most specifically the commanders, who really were the fleet's eyes. It is the commander's collection, processing, and dissemination of intelligence information that is central to this book.)[11] And even though one might consider "cruisers as the eyes of the fleet, their purpose is almost equally to blindfold the enemy. Their duty is not only to disclose the movements of the enemy, but also to act as a screen to conceal our own" by preventing "our" movements and strength from being scouted by enemy cruisers.[12]

With respect to Sir Julian and his supporters, the "eyes of the fleet" aspect was at the core of frigate utilization. Reconnaissance and communications were inseparable for this model, and after highlighting this concept it is possible to proceed with the discussion.

IN 1798 THE ROYAL NAVY had approximately two hundred frigates. Yet this number was significantly short of operational necessity. Nelson's often-quoted (and misquoted) lament, from a letter to Lord Spencer on 9 August 1798, forcefully articulates this problem, which plagued him and most other fleet commanders for the entire war: "Was I to die this moment, 'Want of Frigates' would be found stamped on my heart. No words of mine can express what I have, and am suffering for want of them."[13]

He understood the problem, even if he did not like it. After all, he knew perfectly well that the demands on warship distribution were staggering, for at "the tail-end of the eighteenth century, the blockade of

France had to be maintained, the approaches to the British Isles patrolled, and dozens of convoys escorted somehow."[14]

Nelson was so short of frigates that after the Battle of the Nile, in which he annihilated a French fleet in the first of the three great victories of his career, he was obliged to send off his dispatches in a small ship of the line as he had no other suitable smaller vessel—nor any other means of message transmission. (Nelson's messenger was HMS *Leander*, which was unfortunately caught and captured by the French *Généreux* while on this mission.) Moreover, Nelson's need was even more acute prior to the battle, as he unsuccessfully attempted to search the Mediterranean in an effort to intercept France's huge Egyptian expeditionary-invasion force —including Napoleon himself (see chapter 10).

This lack of frigates (as well as other, smaller vessels, such as sloops and brigs) to act as scouts and conveyers of information was a continual problem for intelligence-minded fleet commanders all through the war. Nelson's letters, for over eight years and at least three campaigns, are full of this concern. While literally dozens of his complaints exist, a handful here will illustrate his frustration:

> To Sir William Hamilton, Ambassador to Naples, on 20 and 23 July 1798: "The destruction of the Enemy . . . would have fallen to me if I had had Frigates. . . . What a situation am I placed in! As yet, I can learn nothing of the Enemy. . . . I have no Frigate, nor a sign of one."[15]

> To Prime Minister Addington, 27 July 1803: "From Cape St. Vincent . . . to the Head of the Adriatic, I have only eight frigates; which, with the service of watching Toulon, and the necessary Frigates with the Fleet, are absolutely not one half enough. I mean this as no complaint, for I am confident the Admiralty are hard pressed, and will send me more when the Service will admit it."[16]

> To Capt. Sir Alexander Ball, governor of Malta, 7 November 1803: "I am too often with only five Frigates. . . . Lord St. Vincent's words are, 'We can send you neither Ships or Men, and *with the resources of your mind, you will do without them very well.*' Bravo, my Lord!"[17]

To Sir Alexander, again, 11 February 1804: "The loss of the *Raven* is very great, and the Admiralty seem determined not to increase my force. I, at this moment, want ten Frigates or Sloops. . . . —It is shameful: Lord St. Vincent was not treated so."[18] And again, 10 November 1804: "The Admiralty have directed me to keep a Frigate with the King of Sardinia . . . and to place a Naval Force [there]. Sometimes I smile, sometimes I am angry; for in the same packet, Lord Melville says, 'We can send you nothing [no additional ships].' "[19]

To Viscount Castlereagh, secretary of state for War and the Colonies, 5 October 1805: "I have only two Frigates to watch them. . . . I am most exceedingly anxious for more *eyes,* and hope the Admiralty are hastening them to me. *The last Fleet was lost to me for want of Frigates; God forbid this should.*"[20]

To Mr. Marsden, secretary of the Admiralty, 5 October 1805: "I am sorry ever to trouble their Lordships with anything like a complaint of a want of Frigates and Sloops. . . . I am taking all Frigates about me I possibly can; for if I were an Angel, and attending to all the other points of my Command, [if I] let the Enemy escape for want of the eyes of the Fleet, I should consider myself as most highly reprehensible. Never less than eight Frigates, and three good fast-sailing Brigs, should always be with the Fleet to watch Cadiz; and to carry Transports in and out to refit it, would take at least ten and four Brigs, to do that service well. At present I have only been able to collect two, which makes me very uneasy."[21]

To the Rt. Hon. George Rose, vice president of the Board of Trade, on 6 October 1805: "I think, not for myself, but for the Country, therefore I hope the Admiralty will send . . . Frigates, and Sloops of War, for I am very destitute. . . . *Therefore, if* [Prime Minister] *Mr. Pitt would hint to [Admiralty First Lord] Barham, that he shall be anxious until I get the force proposed, and plenty of Frigates and Sloops* in order to watch them closely, it may be advantageous to the Country: you are at liberty to mention this to Mr. Pitt, but I would not wish it to go farther."[22]

Clearly, as commander in chief of the Mediterranean Fleet, Nelson was constantly in friction with Whitehall regarding his difficulties in making do with the small force under his command. The small numbers of frigates and dispatch vessels were the main problem. Adequate disposition to the east meant losses of merchant ships to the enemy in the west; shifting of frigates back to the west resulted in losses in the east—with strong complaints made to the Admiralty.

Nelson wrote the Admiralty, begging for frigates, until they stopped answering those parts of his letters. "It was only by the most persevering and ingenious economy in the employment of his small craft that Nelson was able to struggle along at all," Forester explains. Dispatches were not sent, nor ships sent to dock, unless those ships could simultaneously convoy merchantmen. Frigates gathering intelligence were also searching for enemy privateers. All ship movements were planned weeks and months ahead. Nelson's considerable skills at organization and his incredible attention to detail allowed this system to work—barely: "He kept his scanty forces on the move ceaselessly, round and round the Mediterranean, and once or twice ill-advised orders from London, over his head, upset the whole precarious arrangement and annoyed Nelson exceedingly, although he realized that the Admiralty had not appreciated how delicate were the workings with which they were interfering."[23]

Two hundred frigates in the fleet seems a large number, by eighteenth- or twentieth-century standards, and it was certainly the greatest cruiser force ever seen in history. But "more than half of it was always under repair, fitting out or otherwise non-operational. Not until the last years of the next round of this war, when there were some 250 of such ships in commission and France's frigates had been almost driven from the oceans and seas would there be British frigates to spare."

Of course, other commanders had this same problem; it certainly was no eccentricity of Admiral Nelson. Another such commander was Lord St. Vincent. Hard pressed to handle French vice admiral Eustache Bruix, who was "descending upon him, St. Vincent warned Spencer and Nepean on May 10, 1799, that he had no frigates with which to track down Bruix, and that he could no longer protect convoys."[24]

Lord Keith observed repeatedly that the number of cruisers at the disposal of a commander in chief was extremely limited; this was particularly true later on as the navy was stretched to the limit by the outbreak of further war with the United States.[25] Lord Collingwood was as short of frigates, from 1805 to 1810, as Nelson ever was when operating as Mediterranean commander in chief.

Even as late as 6 July 1815, Rear Adm. Henry Hotham, writing from Quiberon Bay to Lord Keith, brings up this same lament: "As I am quite alone, if your Lordship can send me any vessel for communications I should be thankful; of those named [by] your Lordship . . . the *Helicon, Telegraph* and *Nimble* are absent on voyages to England."[26]

What exactly were frigates tasked to do with regard to gathering intelligence? The different circumstances provide a wide range of examples. As a fleet commander, Nelson frequently operated in this pattern: "Leaving a frigate or some smaller cruiser at the appointed rendezvous, with intelligence as to where the flagship was to be found at any time, and dispersing his cruisers at various strategic points to keep watch for the enemy, Nelson sailed to and fro across a wide stretch of sea . . . through which the [enemy] fleet, wherever bound, would be obliged to pass."[27]

The order below, written by Nelson on board HMS *Victory* to the captain of HMS *Active* on 5 December 1803, is typical of dozens of similar assignments in his letters:

> *Secret.* Whereas it is of the utmost importance that the Enemy's Squadron in Toulon should be most strictly watched, and that I should be made acquainted with their sailing and route with all dispatch, should they put to sea, You are therefore hereby required and directed to employ his Majesty's Ship *Active,* under your command, on the above service. . . . Should the Enemy's Squadron, or any part of it, put to sea in the meantime, or you obtain any intelligence necessary for my immediate information, you are to dispatch a Frigate to St. Pierres, near the Island of Sardinia, with an account thereof. . . . You are to continue on this service until relieved, or you receive my orders for your further proceedings.[28]

Another order directed Capt. Thomas Staines of HMS *Cameleon* to seek intelligence from merchant ships: "Whereas, it is probable, from the information I have received, that the Enemy's Fleet may be at Sea, or that some of their Frigates, with Transports, having Troops on board, may be coming this way, You are therefore hereby required . . . to speak every Merchant-Vessel which you may be able to fall in with, for the purpose of gaining intelligence of any of the Enemy's Ships or Vessels."[29]

This order tasked Capt. Ross Donnelly of HMS *Narcissus* to actually contact people on shore in order to find out what was current; he was to proceed "into the Bay of Rosas, and endeavour to communicate with the shore, for the purpose of obtaining the latest and most correct information of what is passing in France."[30] This one directed Capt. Richard Moubray, of HMS *Active,* to execute a quick patrol through an area for information in the company of HMS *Seahorse:* "Proceed immediately to the head of the Gulf of Lyons, where you will take a sweep for the space of forty-eight hours, in order to obtain intelligence of the Enemy's intended movements at Toulon."[31]

Actually, large-scale sweeping was utilized as well. When Nelson briefly returned to England in the summer of 1805, "the whole system of cruiser control was carefully overhauled and reorganized by Barham and Nelson with a view to securing more efficient communications and protection of commerce. A line of frigates was directed to cruise between Cape Clear and Finisterre, and between Finisterre and St. Vincent, for the dual purpose of intelligence and trade protection. To the same end the telegraphic signal code of Sir Home Popham was issued to frigates as well as to battleships."[32] Sir Julian Corbett confirms that these new lines were primarily intelligence patrols.[33]

It must be observed that the presence of frigates, as intelligence-gathering sensors, did not always equate to successful operations. As an example, sighting no British blockaders in mid-January 1805, French vice admiral Pierre Charles Jean Baptiste Sylvestre de Villeneuve sortied from Toulon on the seventeenth. He was hopeful of combining with Adm. Edouard Thomas de Burgues, Comte de Missiessy, who had left

Rochefort on 11 January. Missiessy had five ships of the line, three frigates, and thirty-five hundred embarked troops; he was successful in eluding the blockading forces of Rear Adm. Sir Thomas Graves. Villeneuve intended to join Missiessy with eleven ships of the line and seven frigates in an expedition to the West Indies. However, HM frigates *Active* and *Seahorse* were just over the horizon and shortly sighted the French fleet. After shadowing them for two days and, presumably, ascertaining their course, they broke contact to carry the news to Nelson at Agincourt Bay. Nelson's diary reads that in the morning they had very heavy "squalls from the West-ward; *Seahorse* in sight coming down. At half-past nine, she made the signal that she had been chased by the Enemy's Frigates; and at ten, that she had 'Intelligence to communicate.'"[34] Within two hours Nelson's fleet was under way in hot pursuit.

This became an intelligence failure, however, for the French changed course after the British frigates broke contact. Only able to signal key information at very limited range, they had to choose between maintaining contact with the enemy and reporting their intelligence to the principal officer who needed it. Reporting required them to come almost into physical contact with Nelson, who then could only estimate, from the last sighting, where the French were bound. While his analysis was very sound, given the information available, as it turned out he guessed wrong and totally lost the trail. Fortunately, in this instance anyway, no real harm was done; the French had run into a gale and sustained significant damage to masts and rigging. Deciding they could not go on, the majority of the fleet returned to Toulon.[35]

One cannot leave the topic of frigates—as well as other small vessels —acting as the fleet's eyes without the observation that the duty was not entirely safe. The enemy certainly was not happy about being observed, and when the opportunity presented itself to attack such a scout they were not very shy. Nelson comments on such an incident in a 10 August 1803 letter to Lady Hamilton, writing that "a Schooner belonging to me, put her nose into Toulon, and four Frigates popped out, and have taken her. . . . However, I hope to have an opportunity, very soon, of paying them the debt, with interest."[36] Two days later he instructed the captain of HMS *Active,* Richard Moubray, on such hazards: "It is not my intention to close watch Toulon, *even with Frigates;* for I see the gentlemen want one of *our* Frigates. . . . I beg you will not keep too close to Sepet or Sicie in the night."[37]

Even if the enemy did not always pose a threat, the dangers of trying to handle large sailing ships in tight quarters and varying sea conditions always did. For example, the distinguished and experienced frigate captain Jahleel Brenton wrecked HMS *Minerve,* shortly after the war resumed in 1803, while scouting the approaches to Cherbourg. He was captured with his entire crew.[38]

MANY TYPES OF VESSELS were used by the navy for scouting, reconnaissance, and information transmission including sloops, brigs, cutters, schooners—and, of course, Post Office packets. However, it was the cruiser class known as frigates that played the key role relative to gathering, transmitting, and disseminating intelligence information. They were fast (though some finely designed French and Spanish ships of the line were faster!), they were formidable (carrying considerable armament, crews, and marine detachments), and they were versatile (capable of multiple simultaneous missions).

In a low-technology era, they were basic gatherers of intelligence for the fleet, continually working to identify the enemy's location and what the enemy was doing, and then communicating that information back to the larger fleet concentrations. Although the navy owned many of them, they were always in short supply because of the heavy all-around demands present during a world war. Moreover, it took many units to cover the seven seas when the main sensor was the line-of-sight human eye. It is of some interest to speculate how things might have been different had there been more frigates operational earlier in the war.

5

Deception

Though fraud in other activities be detestable, in the management of war it is laudable and glorious, and he who overcomes an enemy by fraud is as much to be praised as he who does so by force.

Machiavelli

All warfare is based on deception.

Sun Tzu

WHILE DECEPTION MAY NOT BE AN INTELLIGENCE ISSUE PER SE, it cannot be divorced from the study of intelligence. Indeed, in the words of Sir Michael Howard, "deception is rooted in the influencing of an enemy's moves while concealing one's own and, thus, demands not only good security, but also good intelligence."[1] On the deceiver's side, it fundamentally involves the deliberate attempt to make reality appear other than it is; on the other side, it involves the efforts of the potentially deceived to see through the deception and discover the reality.

Today we define deception as the ability to "provide misleading or false information in order to achieve the element of surprise; those measures designed to mislead [others] by manipulation, distortion, or falsification of evidence to induce a reaction that is prejudicial to [their own interests]; and the practice of employing various ruses to disguise real intentions and true capabilities." Some subsets of deception are camouflage, misinformation, diversions, feints, and fabrications.[2]

The art and science of military and naval deception, as well as the counter art and science to uncover deception, were fairly rudimentary at the close of the eighteenth century. This is in particular contrast to the very sophisticated and highly technical deception and counterdeception capabilities available to today's commanders. In addition, a number of eighteenth-century officers retained a subconscious (or even conscious) perception that deception—like outright lying—was dishonest, unchivalrous, dishonorable, and generally unofficerlike. Many felt that preparation, training, initiative, skill, bravery, and audacity were the proper tools for military and naval commanders, and that victory or defeat should effectively hang on those qualities alone. (The concept that spying, torture, and many other forms of intelligence activities were morally reprehensible, to many eighteenth-century officers and gentlemen, is also discussed in chapter 7).

The majority of officers, however, acknowledged a legitimacy to *ruses de guerre* even if they retained a discomfort in relation to dishonorable things such as bribery, espionage, and torture. As a result, active deception, mostly at the tactical level, was reasonably common—as was the concomitant realization that one needed to be constantly on the lookout for such activity employed against one's own forces.

Indeed, some officers became "specialists" in deception. As mentioned earlier, Lord Cochrane was, perhaps, the most famous captain of the time. Even as early as 1806, while he was still a young frigate commander, no less of a personage than Napoleon himself bestowed upon Cochrane the sobriquet *Le loup des mers,* "the Sea Wolf." Moreover, reflecting many years later in exile on St. Helena, Napoleon added more to his original thought: "The French admiral was an *imbécile,* but yours was just as bad [at the action off the Basque Roads]. I assure you that, if Cochrane had been supported, he would have taken every one of [our] ships."[3]

Cochrane particularly liked to destroy French coastal signal stations.[4] As his career progressed, he refined his technique; during the summer of 1808, while cruising in command of HMS *Imperieuse,* he spent considerable effort against French batteries, coastal trading vessels, and signal stations. He later wrote that

> the precaution of obtaining their signal books before destroying the semaphores was adopted; and in order to make the enemy believe that the books also were destroyed, all the papers found were scattered about in a half burnt condition. The trick was successful, and the French authorities, considering that the signal books had been destroyed also, did not deem it necessary to alter their signals, which were forwarded by me to Lord Collingwood, who was thus informed by the French semaphores when re-established of all the movements of their own ships, as well as of the British ships from the promontory of Italy northward![5]

During his first command, Cochrane, knowing the enemy had published a description of his ship, "had the *Speedy* painted in imitation of the Danish brig *Clomer,*" a well-known vessel which traded up and down the Spanish Mediterranean coast. In addition, he had embarked a native Danish-speaking quartermaster equipped with a Danish officer's uniform, all of which he used to great effect.[6]

American officers could play this game too. During the War of 1812, David Porter, captain of the U.S. frigate *Essex,* captured the British naval sloop *Alert* by luring her close while posing as a merchant ship.[7] However, the trained eyes of Americans were just as likely to be deceived by the similarities found in ship design. In 1814 Commo. Sir George Collier was cruising off the American coast with two superfrigates, HM ships *Leander* and *Newcastle,* which were on station trying to cope with the U.S. Navy's huge frigates (the *Constitution, United States,* and *President*). Collier was successful in passing off his ships as an American squadron

—at least to one Yankee skipper, who came aboard the *Leander* and addressed Collier

> as Commodore Decatur, that he knew his ship to be the *President* the moment he saw her, and Nick himself would not deceive him. When asked what ship the *Newcastle* was, he did not know, but accepted that she was the *Constitution,* saying only that she was not painted as she used to be. Having been pumped by Sir George, and communicating the pious hope that his squadron would do "a tarnation share of mischief to the damned English sarpents, and play the devil's game with their rag of a flag," the Yankee took his leave with great apparent satisfaction; but when about to quit, the first lieutenant told him the truth of his situation, and on seeing Sir George come up in his uniform coat, he became almost frantic.[8]

One can see that tactical deception was reasonably easy during this time period, when there was great similarity in the design of both warships and merchant ships. In fact, it needs to be strongly emphasized that ship identification was always extremely difficult. There were remarkable similarities in the appearance of ships around the world, regardless of mission or function. Most ships were designed to deal efficiently with the physical requirements of wind and water within the technical limitations of the era. This was the dominant theme of design, not the specific mission of the ship. Just as today we see more and more automobiles closely resemble each other as designers around the world grapple with the same issues of materials application, aerodynamics, and fuel efficiency, so it was then with shipbuilders.

Standard "classes" of ships effectively did not exist. Rarely were more than two or three ships built from the same design. Ship mission requirements, in fact, did not demand great variance in design. A large merchant ship might need to be deep and wide to carry heavy cargoes, but so did a large warship to carry lots of heavy artillery. Further, even within a given nation's navy, there were no standard paint schemes. In fact, standardization only began to appear after 1805. In addition, many navies and merchant marines were full of foreign-built ships.

Finally, because it was so easy to alter the appearance of ships, many merchant and naval captains frequently did so for various operational reasons. Of course, a ship's lookout and/or captain had to differentiate between merchantmen and warships; but, there were even greater challenges. First of all, there were merchantmen trying to look like the large ships of various nations' East India companies. Then "there were Indiamen trying to look like men-of-war. There were Indiamen armed as men-of-war. There were men-of-war that had once been Indiamen. There were men-of-war trying to look like Indiamen. And, to complete the circle, there were men-of-war trying to look like ordinary merchantmen."[9]

Novelist Patrick O'Brian's fictional Capt. Jack Aubrey is a master of ship disguise. At one point he alters his ship, the crack HMS *Surprise* (which truly existed, by the way), so it appeared that "an old tired shabby whaler, with a crow's nest aloft, trying-out gear and general filth on deck and deeply squalid sides stood into Pabay . . . under a single blue-patched foretopsail. In her crow's nest stood her even shabbier master in a black-guardly round hat [Aubrey], crammed up against his unshaven mate [Lt. Pullings]."[10]

Other things one could do to foster the nonnaval appearance of a ship were displaying overly patched sails, lots of Irish pennants, "fag ends" of rope everywhere, filthy heads, general disarray on deck, rope yarns hanging in the rigging, loose reef points, and sails loosely furled with gaskets all "ahoo."[11]

Lord Nelson thought the altering of ships' appearance a sound tactic. For example, on 1 September 1804 we find him writing Capt. Thomas Staines, of the appropriately named *Cameleon,* "I am led to hope from your disguising the *Cameleon* . . . that your present visit to the Adriatic will clear that place of the Privateers before alluded to."[12]

Deception could go both ways, however; the cagey Cochrane was not beyond being fooled himself, as when sighting a large ship which had "all the appearance of a well-laden merchantman, we forthwith gave chase. On nearing her she raised her ports, which had been closed to deceive us, the act discovering a heavy broadside, a clear demonstration that we had fallen into the jaws of a formidable Spanish frigate now crowded with men, who had before remained concealed below."[13] In fact, "in this connection it is interesting to note that what in our own day was to become known as the 'Q-ship' stratagem (but was then called 'disguise' or 'deception') was often resorted to by [all] sides" in this period.[14]

Lord Cochrane's passing off of his tiny naval sloop for a Danish coastal trading vessel is nothing, however, to the successes the British East India Company enjoyed against the French navy in the Indian Ocean. Examples are legion; however, the greatest instance, with considerable strategic ramifications, occurred in February 1804 (see the analysis of the Battle of Pulo-Aur in chapter 8).

A standard *ruse de guerre* was for a ship to hoist flag signals to a nonexistent allied ship (or fleet) when in visual proximity to an enemy force. Knowing full well that it could be a trick, the enemy commander nevertheless was placed on the horns of a dilemma. Were there additional hostile ships over the horizon, receiving these signals, or were there not? This deception was often attempted by a lone ship or a small, inferior force being pursued by a larger force. A classic example was the occasion in 1797, when, toward the end of the major British fleet mutiny at the Nore (in the Thames estuary), Adm. Adam Duncan, with only two loyal ships in the North Sea, deceived a larger Dutch force by sending signals to imaginary British ships over the horizon. The Dutch, unwilling to call the bluff, and believing themselves fully blockaded, abandoned ideas of pursuit or escape.[15] (Duncan, a Scot, was coincidentally a nephew-in-law of our previous acquaintance, Henry Dundas, Lord Melville.)[16]

Another instance was on 17 June 1795, when a British force under Vice Adm. Sir William Cornwallis was retiring from a strong French squadron under Vice Adm. Louis Thomas, Comte Villaret-Joyeuse. The French were coming up very fast on both quarters of Cornwallis's squadron, and at this point the frigate *Phaeton,* "which was detached several miles ahead of the British force, pretended to be in communication with an imaginary fleet over the horizon. The *Phaeton* continued

Fig. 5-1 *Henry Dundas, Lord Melville.*
Dundas was a major figure during this period, serving as treasurer of the navy,
secretary of state for War and the Colonies, and first lord of the Admiralty.
© *National Maritime Museum, London*

making these signals throughout the day." According to the great naval historian William James, this ploy eventually caused Villaret-Joyeuse to break off the action.[17]

Some extremely bold captains in such a situation would, after signaling to non-existent support, turn and aggressively close with the pursuing enemy—which is what a small force might very well do to begin an action that would be finished by oncoming reinforcements. Lacking any other source of intelligence to confirm or deny the reality of potential enemy forces just out of sight, most prudent commanders would abandon pursuit in the face of such tactics.

One might also briefly observe that flying false colors was a standard ruse during this time—a deceptive ploy used by all and recognized by all as internationally legitimate and legal. (Of course, in international law and custom your true colors needed to be flying *prior* to the commencement of gunfire.) This simple deception tactic often bore fruit in causing an enemy to hesitate, and sometimes even momentary hesitation would be of great significance in a given situation.

Even as a young captain, during the American Revolutionary War, Nelson happily used the technique; in the spring of 1783 he cruised HMS *Albemarle* off Curaçao, while under French colors, trying to locate the forces of Admiral De Vaudreuil for Lord Hood. While so doing he captured a Spanish launch, which, "being hailed in French, came unsuspectingly alongside, and answered every necessary question as to the number and force of the squadron in Puerto Cabello."[18]

In 1801 Lord Cochrane was particularly fond of this ruse. Flying the American Stars and Stripes, he maneuvered to attack the Spanish *El Gamo* (thirty-two guns) with his *Speedy* (fourteen guns). Prior to that he had been flying the Danish *Dannebrog,* as he cruised the Mediterranean, capturing over fifty Spanish and French prizes.[19]

Because the use of false colors was so prevalent, most countries also employed "private" signals to which, presumably, the enemy would not be privy. Knowing this, a strange sail hoping to continue a ruse, might pretend to have blocked signal halliards, which would prolong confusion; after all, failure to show the proper recognition signal because of a mechanical malfunction could happen to a friendly ship. O'Brian's fictional Captain Aubrey loves this trick and uses it frequently: "Jack, old in deception, replied with a vague hoist that went up and down, the halliard constantly jammed, wasting irreplaceable minutes."[20] A general appearance of bungling and the hauling down of the hoist before the flags actually flew clear were all part of the trick.

To further a false-color deception, a vessel might hoist a third country's flag, making the concept of private signals moot. Both tricks were played against Lt. William M. Crane, commanding the U.S. brig *Nautilus,* by the ships of Commo. Philip Broke's British squadron on 15 July 1812. As Crane reported the incident, which led to the *Nautilus*'s capture, the unidentified ships displayed

> signals which were not understood and hoisted American colours. I also hoisted my private signal and ensign which not being answered, continued to carry a press of sail to the Westward. . . . At 10 the Squadron hoisted French colours and we saw they neared us fast. . . . There was not no chance of escape if the chasing vessels were enemies, which we were not certain of as they still kept French colours flying at ½ past 12 I consulted with my principal officers all were of opinion, that, everything had been done to preserve the vessel, and, that no hopes of escape were left. . . . The chaseing ship put her helm up hoisted a broad pendant and English colours and ranged under my lee quarter—unable to resist I was compelled to strike the Flag of the United States.[21]

Flying internationally recognized flags signifying contagious disease, or otherwise signaling to a pursuer that one had fever or plague on board, was also an effective tactic of deception used by Cochrane and others. Only a bold or foolhardy commander would, with the primitive medical scenario of the day and lacking any other means to ascertain the truth, risk his crew to prove wrong a possible bluff. Cochrane tells us that he once "ran the quarantine flag up to the fore, calculating on the Spanish horror of the plague. . . . On the boat coming within hail,—for the yellow flag effectually repressed the enemy's desire to board us—our mock [Danish] officer informed the Spaniards that we were two days from Algiers, where at the time the plague was violently raging. This was enough. The boat returned to the frigate, which, wishing us a good voyage, filled, and made sail, whilst we did the same."[22] In fact, note Nelson's letter, of 13 June 1805, to Hugh Elliott: "There has been much pains taken to make Europe believe that we were all dying of the fever. General Fox is arrived at Gibraltar, and the Rock was considered in *pratique,* and the yellow flag struck upon January 1st."[23]

A number of authors, of history and fiction (as well as Nelson himself in his letters), refer to the yellow or "Q" flag used for this role when flown by itself. However, the Q flag was originally designed (particularly when entering a port) to state "my vessel is healthy and I request [a certificate of good health]". Evidence of such use dates to 1806 in the log of HMS *Superb.*[24]

Returning to Lord Cochrane for a moment, in his battle with the vastly superior *El Gamo,* one needs to appreciate one more piece of inspired tactical deception. At the deciding point of the struggle, when his 50 men had boarded the enemy and were facing 250, Cochrane shouted down (in Spanish?) into his essentially empty ship for 50 more reinforcements. Disorganized, confused, and now expecting a new wave of desperate British boarders, the Spanish crew on deck surrendered. ("Time and again, whenever a ship was actually boarded, the capture of her upper deck—or her foredeck or quarterdeck—decided the fight.")[25] Quickly seizing upon this incredible break—caused by his bluff as much as anything—Cochrane took a number of steps to secure the capture and, thereby, the beginnings of his widespread fame both within and without the navy.

Cochrane was a master. In one operation, when commanding the frigate *Pallas,* most of his men were ashore or in boats away from the ship. Suddenly, three French corvettes appeared and rapidly closed on him. He faced the enemy's fifty guns and three hundred men with only forty men of his own: "I immediately set the few hands we had to fasten the furled sails with rope yarns; the object being to cut the yarns all at once, let fall the sails, and thus impress the enemy with an idea that from such celerity in making sail we had a numerous and highly disciplined crew. . . . The manoeuvre succeeded to a marvel." The three corvettes turned about and fled. The *Pallas* pursued, firing its bow chasers (effectively the only guns it could man). The corvettes, one after another, ran themselves ashore to allow their men to escape the frigate. Cochrane noted that "the chase of these corvettes forms one of my most singular recollections. . . . Had any one of the three known our real condition, or had we not put a bold face on the matter, we might have been taken."[26]

Another time while commanding the frigate *Imperieuse,* and in company with HMS *Spartan* (Capt. Jahleel Brenton), Cochrane attacked Port Vendre along the French coast near the Spanish frontier. In order to draw off the French troops who awaited his attack, Cochrane "assembled the ship's boys from the *Imperieuse* and the *Spartan* and . . . ordered them to dress in the scarlet uniforms of [the] marines. They were then put into boats and rowed towards the Spanish side of the town. . . . The French cavalry . . . charged through the quiet streets . . . in order to reach the place and repel the invaders. . . . Cochrane then put ashore his real marines [at the center of the town] and presently there came the first sounds of a French shore-battery being demolished."[27] "It is hardly to be denied," notes Anthony Price, "that . . . Cochrane . . . was the greatest frigate captain of them all, and the greatest and most daring fighting *captain* (with Nelson the greatest fighting *admiral*)."[28]

O'Brian's Jack Aubrey—whose career bears an astonishing resemblance to Cochrane's—is adept at simulating ship damage in order to lure in the enemy. These methods include making yards fall to resemble damage from shot, false fires—"Mr Stourton, a fire in the waist would do no harm: plenty of smoke. One of the coppers filled with slush and tow might answer. Let there be some turmoil"[29]—and dragging a sail under water behind the ship to slow it artificially, making an observer believe the ship is much slower and less capable than it really is: "'Nothing obvious, you understand me. And the old number three foretopsail is to be bent to a hawser and veered out of the lee sternport.' . . . A few moments later the frigate's speed began to slacken [though appearing under full sail]; and as the strain came on to the drag-sail, opening like a parachute beneath the surface, it dropped further still."[30]

Cochrane can also be used to illustrate another old trick, utilized by commanders long before and after him. In 1805, while commanding the *Pallas,* he fell in with three French ships of the line. Being particularly fine examples of French naval architecture (which, along with Spanish design, was generally exceedingly fine) these large vessels were actually faster than the *Pallas.* Fortunately, making the most of foul weather and a well-drilled crew, Cochrane was able to evade them until nightfall, and "when quite dark, we lowered a ballasted cask overboard with a lantern, to induce them to believe that we had altered our course, though we held on in the same direction during the whole night."[31]

Following this "stern light" during the night, the French were chagrined to discover at dawn that they had been pursuing not the *Pallas,* but the cask. What direction the darkened British frigate had gone they could only surmise. "Let's see if the Frenchies will follow that red herring" was Cochrane's comment as the cask was set adrift.[32] In fact, this was merely a reprise of a trick he had pulled before, in the tiny *Speedy* on 18 March 1801, when pursued by a large French frigate off Port Mahon. "After dark," Cochrane later wrote, "we lowered a tub overboard with a light in it, and altering our course thus fortunately evaded her."[33]

Another clever commander was Commo. William Bainbridge, USN. In 1812, while commanding the frigate *Constitution,* he planned to rendezvous with Capt. David Porter (USS *Essex*) at Fernando de Noronha— in the desolate Portuguese islands two hundred miles off the Brazilian coast. Deciding not to waste time waiting when he could be hunting British shipping, Bainbridge visited the Portuguese penal authorities on the islands and passed himself off as the captain of the British frigate *Acasta.* The Portuguese bought the ruse and accepted from Bainbridge a letter addressed to Captain Yeo, of HMS *Southhampton,* and agreed to deliver it when summoned. The letter had orders written in secret ink for a further rendezvous for the *Essex,* and Captain Porter, who later successfully posed as Yeo, collected the letter and deciphered it.[34]

Late in 1797, Capt. Edward Cooke of HM frigate *Sybille,* and Capt. Pulteney Malcolm of HM frigate *Fox,* decided to reconnoiter Manila while waiting to convoy an East India Company fleet from Macao. As both captains could speak French, they decided their frigates would pose as the French national ships *Seine* and *Prudente* of Rear Admiral Sercey's squadron and enter Manila Bay. After looking into Cavite Harbor and observing the ships there, they were approached by a Spanish guard boat. Accepting their French identity, the Spanish navy captain and his boat's crew were invited on board and, after considerable drinking and disclosing of information, were taken prisoner.

Then, two large Spanish boats approached, bringing an aide of Admiral Alaba (commanding at Cavite) and the governor's nephew. These officers and crews were also seized. A large party of British seamen, now disguised in Spanish clothes, used the Spanish boats to capture three large gunboats lying off the city. Subsequently, a fourth Spanish boat approached the British frigates bearing the captain of the port, who wanted to know what was going on. He and his boat crew were also captured, and now since it was dinner time, the British and their two hundred prisoners consumed a good meal and considerable liquor, after which the prisoners were allowed to take their small boats and depart. The *Sybille* and the *Fox* then left, towing the three fine gunboats they had captured. Moreover, they had also acquired a considerable amount of valuable information. A remarkable day's work, with no one killed or wounded on either side, all originating with two daring, deception-minded, and French-speaking officers.[35]

Some deception was larger in its scope—perhaps more strategic than tactical. For instance, one might consider the simple effort of Lord Nelson to conceal his fleet's strength in the fall of 1805: withdrawing the main body of his offshore force fifty miles out into the Atlantic allowed him to both fool the enemy and control more sea area.[36] Or it could be

MOST SECRET AND CONFIDENTIAL

more complex activity, such as another 1805 deception that intimidated the French. On 15 August Admiral Villeneuve dashed any remaining hope of an invasion of England when he "picked up from a Danish merchantman a cock-and-bull story, carefully planted by a British officer, of an English fleet of 25 ships of the line advancing upon him. That night, without checking this story, Villeneuve turned south to run to Cadiz."[37]

It also could be very complicated, such as the 1799 plan of French vice admiral Bruix to move his fleet from Brest into the Mediterranean. Hoping to deceive the British into believing they were going to invade Ireland, the French established an elaborate cover plan, facilitated by a recent "rebellion which had actually taken place in Ireland. Irish representatives were assured that help was on the way and troop movements gave the same impression, reinforced by press reports and instigated rumors. Dutch ships were prepared for sea and French troops sent to Holland. The stroke of genius was to allow the schooner *Rebecca* to fall into British hands with fake despatches aboard."[38]

Completely eluding the forces of Adm. Lord Bridport on 25 April, Bruix had no problems getting safely to sea on a dark and foggy night, ultimately reaching the Mediterranean without major incident. One has to wonder if all the deception plans were even necessary, for such was the inefficiency of Bridport's blockade that "the lugger which was sent to mislead the British with false dispatches had to cruise for several days before she discovered a frigate obliging enough to capture her."[39]

The method of planting false information meant to be captured was not uncommon—and therefore captors were sometimes suspicious. Note these remarks to Lord Spencer concerning Admiral Bruix's cruise: "Relative to the French dispatches [Lieutenant Nicholson] had secured in a *chasse marée* which he captured off the French coast. . . . I rather suspect they are not coming to these coasts [Ireland]; and am the more inclined to this opinion from the circumstance of the French dispatches being found in the cabin, though the *chasse marée* had been chased four hours, and from the *lame excuses* of the French officers who have been examined, and appears to have been sent out purposely to be taken and to deceive us."[40]

One cannot leave the concept of deception without reference to an unusual incident in November 1812. Interestingly enough, although Britain and the United States were at war, the British had a desperate need for supplies (particularly grain, flour, and naval stores) as they fought toward the finish of the Napoleonic Wars. As a result, they promoted trade with those Americans willing to continue supplying British forces in Spain and Portugal. Consulates issued trading licenses to protect such ships; of course, U.S. naval officers took a dim view of such activity and took steps to seize those vessels whenever possible. With that as background, note the following report from Henry Denison, an American prize master, as he used a captured British license to avoid being taken by two British warships: "I arrived here last evening in the Ship *Ariadne* of Boston . . . with a cargo of above 5,000 barrels of flour. . . . The U.S. Brig *Argus* fell in with her on the 15th Ulto . . . & by boarding under British colours obtained possession of her passport [detaining her for being under British license]. I was ordered to take charge of her and bring her into the first port I could make in the United States. On the passage I fell in with two British cruisers, Viz. The Sloop of War *Tartarus* & Brig *Colibri,* & was strictly examined by each, but by making use of the *license* and a little *finesse,* we escaped capture."[41]

OVERCOMING THE gentleman's dislike of falsehood, most eighteenth-century naval officers embraced the concept of deception—or the *ruse de guerre.* While not specifically an intelligence issue itself, deception nevertheless requires the employment of good information collection and intelligence disciplines to see through the illusion and discover the reality. Indeed, many officers, such as Cochrane, became deception specialists. The disguising of ships was extremely common; moreover, the ability to penetrate these disguises was made very difficult by the great similarity of ship design—even between merchantmen and men-of-war. The flying of false signals and of false colors was very prevalent, very effective, and very legal. In the final analysis, tactical naval deception was a widely practiced art; indeed, ship lookouts and, ultimately, ship captains were sharply challenged. It was never an easy task to gather enough information, and then analyze some very subtle nuances, in order to penetrate such deceptions and discover the enemy's true intentions and activities.

As Nelson wrote in June 1805, "I shall guide my movements according to the best of my judgement, for I have too often, unfortunately, been deceived by false intelligence."[42]

6

The Commander:
Jack and Master of All Trades

None other than a Gentleman, as well as a Seaman both in Theory and Practice is qualified to support the Character of a Commission Officer in the Navy.

John Paul Jones (attributed)

When I follow my own head, I am, in general, much more correct in my judgement, than following the opinion of others.

Lord Nelson

THE REALITY OF LATE-EIGHTEENTH–CENTURY NAVAL INTELLIGENCE was that deployed (detached) ship captains and fleet commanders were their own intelligence officers. Two areas of analysis draw forth this concept. First, there was a significant amount of intelligence activity appearing at all levels of governmental and naval operations. Second, there were no naval-intelligence officers, no naval-intelligence staffs, nor even good staffing in general available to the commander.

Indeed, it is very clear that the commander had an enormous breadth of specific responsibility, with virtually no direct officer or enlisted support at his level. While there certainly were other capable commissioned and warrant officers present, they were themselves generalists absorbed by their own demanding duties.

This was well before any great specialization among officers or any established specialized career patterns. Of course, what we now refer to as "staff" officers existed—including physicians, surgeons, chaplains, pursers (ship-level supply)—holding warrants from the Navy Board. "Sea" officers were homogeneous, however. To use modern U.S. Navy parlance, all "line" officers were "unrestricted" in the broadest sense. Holding commissions from the Admiralty, their career training ran mostly to navigation, seamanship, gunnery, and command. Furthermore, every sea officer was just that; with the exception of port admirals, dockyard commanders, a handful of flag officers and captains on specific boards, and a few lieutenants in shore-impressment and signal-station billets, no naval officers served ashore. "In particular," Capt. Geoffrey Bennett writes, "all commanders-in-chief flew their flags afloat."[1]

In any event, every admiral (and every captain, *en petit*) had to wear many hats concurrently. Depending upon the proximity of his next superior, by default he was to one degree or another his own strategist, diplomat, interpreter, tactician, administrator, disciplinarian, recruiter, personnel manager, communications officer, meteorologist, hydrographer, maintenance officer, engineer, logistician, provisioner, paymaster, and intelligence officer. And not "intelligence officer" by name, of course; the point being that there were no naval intelligence officers in those days. Of the captain's forty-eight duties, specified by regulation, the closest reference is the one that required him to "keep secret the private signals."[2] Intelligence, even as of 1815, had "not yet really extended to intelligence for wars, and it was not a staff specialty. It was still the case, as with Napoleon, that the chiefs of armies [and fleets] tended to be their own intelligence officers."[3]

Truly, the captain (admiral) had to be jack of all trades and, in reality, master of all as well.

THE COMMANDER, above all else in the age of sail, had to be a skillful sailor. It might seem as if that would go without saying; however, it really cannot be emphasized enough. Seafaring was a dangerous profession, and sea life was hard; most sailors would have concurred with the officer who "after eight days and nights of struggle against a gale, eating raw meat for want of fire, exclaimed that 'a man had better be a fish than a sailor, excepting the little time he is on shore.' He that would go to sea for pleasure, the proverb had it, would go to hell for a pastime."[4]

The commander had to spend an enormous amount of time and effort on seamanship and navigation, for in this era these were by far his greatest challenges. Not only was the acceptable performance of his ship (or fleet) constantly on the line, but more often than not the very survival of the ship(s).[5]

In our age of powerful nautical engines, tug boats, weather satellites, global-positioning satellites, radar, sonar, and so on, we can be somewhat forgiven if we overlook this point. But the commander of a "powerless" sailing ship (or fleet of sailing ships) had to be, through-and-through, a seaman. Moreover, that seaman was dependent upon three heartless, uncompromising and unforgiving agents—the wind, the tide, and the current, "and over them he has no positive control; he must take them as they come and be ready with his resources."[6]

Novelist Patrick O'Brian sums up the problem of the wind very clearly, as Capt. Jack Aubrey harangues his friend Dr. Maturin: "Sometimes I wonder whether you have really grasped that it is the wind alone that moves us. You have often suggested that we should charge to the right or the left as the case may be, just as though we were *flaming cavalry,* and could go where we chose. . . . You must understand that everything, *everything* at sea depends on the wind."[7]

One has to understand very clearly that at sea, particularly during this period, nothing whatsoever could be guaranteed: "The sea is a stealthy, implacable enemy that gives no quarter."[8] From 1793 to 1805 the Royal Navy lost five ships to enemy action and nineteen to "hazards of the sea." One of those hazards was running aground on England itself; in 1780 there were only twenty-five lighthouses in Britain, whereas by 1980 there were over twenty-five hundred.[9]

After all, even when totally calm, the sea has a substantial presence that must be acknowledged. The Atlantic Ocean covers an area of 31.8 million square miles, with an average depth of thirteen thousand feet; and while the Baltic Sea is only 163,000 square miles (and only averages two hundred feet in depth), the Mediterranean Sea is 1.2 million square miles and averages five thousand feet in depth.

The following forcefully illustrates one aspect of the problem. Most readers will know William Bligh as the captain of the *Bounty,* against whom the famous mutiny occurred in 1789. Whatever the truth may be regarding his leadership skills and general personality, he is universally recognized as an outstanding navigator and a peerless seaman. Yet at the beginning of his doomed voyage in the *Bounty,* even this master mariner was completely at the mercy of a contrary wind: it took him twenty days until the wind allowed him to move from Deptford to Spithead (approximately two hundred miles along the English coast), and then it was an additional twenty-nine days (after receiving his sailing orders) before a fair wind allowed him to leave Spithead and proceed down the English Channel—"On the 24th [of November] I received from Lord Hood, who commanded at Spithead, my final orders. The wind, which for several days before had been favourable, was now turned directly against us. . . . We made different unsuccessful attempts to get down Channel, but contrary winds and bad weather constantly forced us back to St. Helen's, or Spithead, until Sunday the 23rd of December, when we sailed with a fair wind."[10]

All seamen faced this constant problem. Here are two relevant comments, in 1805, from Lord Nelson: "We crawled thirty-three miles the last twenty-four hours; my only hope is, that the Enemy's Fleet are near us, and in the same situation,"[11] and, from three months earlier, "I cannot get a fair wind, or even a side-wind. Dead foul!—dead foul!"[12]

Back to 1789. Lieutenant Bligh went on to make a comment about his official clock—issued by the Board of Longitude—that was critical for navigation: "On the 19th of December, the last time of its being examined on shore, it was 1' 52", 5 too fast for mean time, and then losing at the rate of 1", 1 per day; and at this rate I estimate its going when we sailed."[13] Many captains bought one or two more high-quality clocks out of their own pockets, so that they might have a chance at knowing the correct time after months at sea, so that they might have a chance at knowing their correct positions!

Modern navigators, with radar, sonar, and inexpensive global-positioning instruments, may not give this much thought. But navigation, in an era of handmade mechanical time pieces and handmade, hand-held optical devices, was a very imprecise science with its own very difficult challenges. The following interlude between Patrick O'Brian's characters is indicative, though Captain Aubrey makes light of the subject. When told by Aubrey that two recent lunar sightings allowed him to know where they were, Dr. Maturin exclaimed,

> "You will never tell me, for all love, that you have been careering over this stormy ocean like a mad bull day and night without knowing where you were? And if you had run violently upon an island . . . where would you have been then, your soul to the Devil?"
> "There is dead reckoning, you know," said Jack mildly.

Many military men, as well as politicians of the time (Napoleon himself being one of the greatest offenders), could not or would not appreciate this issue; so if it is also hard for us two hundred years later, perhaps we can be forgiven. Yet the great Duke of Marlborough, a hundred years earlier, understood the issue very well, "having fought at sea as a young officer onboard the British flagship at the battle of Sole Bay (1672). [He] was wise enough to rebuke those who would have him interfere with the conduct of naval operations in the War of the Spanish Succession, with these words: 'The Sea Service is not so easily arranged as that of land, there are many more precautions to take, and you and I are not capable of judging them.'"[14]

The Admiralty board room had a spectacular wind indicator (seen

Fig. 6-1 *Napoleon Bonaparte.*
This engraving shows the future emperor as a young general and may indi-
cate his appearance at the time of the Nile campaign.
© *National Maritime Museum, London*

clearly in fig. 1-2), which was there for practicality as the lords commissioners drafted orders. It served another purpose, however, for its very
presence "reminded even the least seamanlike politician that everything
depended on natural forces, that no officer on active service could neglect
the wind strength and direction for a moment."[15]

The reminder did not always work, for many officers felt their orders had been written with no thought whatsoever for the forces of nature. C. S. Forester's Captain Hornblower certainly had that concern as his ship made landfall on the Pacific coast of Central America: "Only a landsman would have given those opening orders to sail to the Gulf of Fonseca without sighting other land in the Pacific—only a succession of miracles (Hornblower gave himself no credit for sound judgment and good seamanship) had permitted it being carried out."[16] On another occasion, O'Brian's Jack Aubrey was even more sharp: "It may seem wicked, even blasphemous, to say that my orders might have been written by a parcel of landsmen, accustomed to the regularity of travelling by stage-coach, or by navigation on an inland canal: yet on the other hand some of the Lords *are* mere landborne politicians . . . who may never [have] been afloat at all—but all that to one side. I have received orders that make no account of wind or tide before this, and so have all other sea-officers. I do not complain."[17]

Some Admiralty lords may well have been inexperienced appointees, but the professional sea officers of the Royal Navy were decidedly not: "The quality which above all determined an officer's fortunes in the Navy, and marked it out from other professions, was his practical ability as a seaman. The capacity, not merely to command and to navigate, but to hand, reef and steer, was the basic requirement for an officer. . . . Other attainments were highly desirable, but this alone was indispensable."[18]

Unlike the army and the civil service, where commissions were purchased and political appointments made routine, the navy—facing the perils of the sea in addition to the aggression of the enemy—needed particularly competent people. Skill and experience always headed the list of qualities by which naval officers were judged—criteria not always used ashore: "As late as 1797 . . . a Commissioner of Stamps was appointed because he was the nephew of a duke, and because 'a natural, constitutional indolence governed him with irresistible sway,' disabling him from other employment. It is easy to see how dangerous this charitable spirit" would have been in the sea service.[19] It cannot be said that politics and "influence" had no role in naval appointments and promotion. In fact, "the decencies of the day required peers to be treated with due deference[,] . . . but the reality was that civilian politicians" and aristocrats were able to exercise only slight control of the system.[20]

Regardless of how he was promoted, the commander's skill and flexibility were constantly on call. His responsibility ranged from the very continued existence of his ship to deriving the greatest performance from his ship given any tactical and weather conditions.

THOUGH NOT AS vitally important as seamanship, a number of the other virtues—enumerated at the beginning of this chapter—need to be recognized and developed in a little more detail. Some have a markedly intertwined relationship with intelligence.

A business of commanders, related to both seamanship and intelligence, was that of hydrography and its ancillary arts. Today we take for granted the incredibly detailed knowledge we have of (almost) all parts of the earth, but two hundred years ago accurate information regarding the world's seas, coasts, winds, weather, and the like was very incomplete. This lack of data was one reason that naval commanders and other mariners were so heavily dependent upon "pilots," who were men with heavy, practical experience and knowledge of specific geographic areas.

It was only in 1795 that the British Admiralty formally established a Hydrographic Department. Prior to then, it truly was a hit-and-miss business regarding the collection and collation of such information. Horatio Hornblower certainly knew the problem as he approached Central America; he could not depend upon his charts. After all, they had been copied from ones Lord Anson had captured sixty years before, "and everyone knew about Dago charts—and Dago charts submitted to the revision of useless Admiralty draftsmen might be completely unreliable."[21]

The navy was always extremely dependent upon individual officers compiling such data from around the world, and then sending it in to London:

At one time, accurate sea and coastal charts were so hard-won and so valuable that they were considered by some nations to be state secrets. During the seventeenth and eighteenth centuries, however, private Dutch and English engravers published atlases and charts for use at sea.

Following the lead of the French Navy, which established its *Depôt des Cartes et Plans* in 1720, the Admiralty created the Hydrography Department in 1795 to carry out surveys at sea, to collate authoritative information for its own use and for chart publishers, and to publish its own charts. . . . In 1800 the Hydrography Department published the first Admiralty charts.[22]

The Admiralty also commissioned a number of surveys. These included Commander Broughton in Japanese and Korean waters, 1795–98; Graeme Spence around the southern coast of England in 1800; Captain Flinders in Australia, 1801–3; Francis Beaufort at the River Plate (between Argentina and Uruguay) in 1807 and at the southern coast of Turkey in 1811–12; and William Smyth in the Adriatic starting in 1811.

But even with an established Hydrographic Department the input from individual officers continued to be critical: "Just as Bligh, even during his desperate open-boat voyage, accurately surveyed parts of the coast of Australia[,] . . . many other hydrographer-seamen contributed valuable small-scale surveys to the mass of information compiled by the Hydrography Department."[23] Thus, many commanders spent considerable effort in collecting this type of "natural" intelligence. The Hydrographic Department often asked for specific help from operational commanders. The following 1805 letter shows a Mr. Dalrymple, first head of the department, asking assistance from the Admiralty secretary: "Sir, Be pleased to lay before their Lordships the chart herewith sent, on which a comparison is made of Captain Bligh's chart of Dungeness with that by Captain Johnstone. The differences are so great and so important that it seems indispensably necessary to ascertain which is wrong, 'shallow water' being expressed in Captain Johnstone's chart where 7 fathoms are marked in Captain Bligh's."[24]

Jack Aubrey absolutely loved this type of work. During one voyage he and his clerk carried out "a chain of observations, always made at stated intervals: wind direction and strength, estimated current, barometrical pressure, compass variations, humidity, temperature of the air (both wet bulb and dry) and of the sea at given depths together with the salinity at those depths, and the blueness of the sky, a series that was to be carried round the world and communicated to Mr. Humboldt on the one hand and the Royal Society on the other."[25]

Lord Nelson always maintained a great interest in this type of work. In 1801 after the Battle of Copenhagen, he sent a coastal plan to Lord St. Vincent that had been drawn by his associate, Lieutenant Colonel Stewart. He wrote that Stewart "is an excellent and indefatigable young man and, depend on it, the rising hope of our Army. As there is no other plan in existence, perhaps you will direct a copy to be lodged in the Hydrographer's Office."[26]

On 19 August 1803, Nelson tasked Capt. John Stuary, in HMS *Kent,* to the effect that "you will furnish me (for the information of the Lords Commissioners of the Admiralty) with a particular account of your taking the sounding of some Spanish Ports in these seas during the time you commanded the *Termagant.*"[27] In October 1804, Nelson directed Thomas Atkinson, sailing master of the *Victory,* to proceed "to the Island of Cabrera . . . for the purpose of ascertaining correctly the soundings and bearings, &c. of the Shoal Rock, which his Majesty's Ship *Excellent* struck upon in May last. . . . Survey the said Shoal, taking the most correct soundings on every part of it, and between that and the Isle of Biche, its bearings, and every particular remark necessary to prevent any accident to his Majesty's Ships in future."[28]

And despite the unfortunate personal link Nelson often faced between writing and seasickness, he felt individually committed to such data collection—even as a vice admiral. There are preserved two small books in which he daily entered "in his own hand, the state of the Barometer, Weather, and Wind twice, three times, and occasionally four, five, and even six times in every twenty-four hours, from the 24th of October 1803, to the 13th of May 1805."[29]

THE COMMANDER had to be a serious disciplinarian. Whether as a ship's captain or as an admiral, the discipline of the service was always of major concern. Captains had much more authority than they do now, able to direct a wide range of punishments—including the dreaded flogging—for an equally wide range of offenses.

Famous as a harsh disciplinarian (a flogging captain and a hanging admiral) was Lord St. Vincent. In fact, as a strict officer, St. Vincent had viewed the great fleet mutinies at Spithead and the Nore with even more alarm than he did the French threat. Upon assuming command of the Channel Fleet in 1800, he worked very hard to stamp out anything left from the mutiny using a variety of very effective methods. One method he did not implement, but suggested, was that the Post Office might include in its letter-interception program all mail to and from his ships' lower decks.[30]

Nelson hated punishing his men, and particularly detested flogging. However, it was a hard service and he was hard enough to lead it. Note this November 1803 memorandum to all his commanding officers, which he directed be read to all hands in the fleet:

> Lord Nelson is very sorry to find that notwithstanding his forgiveness of the men who deserted in Spain, it has failed to have its proper effect.
> Therefore Lord Nelson desires that it may be perfectly understood, that if any man be so infamous as to desert from the Service in future, he will not only be brought to a Court-Martial, but that if the sentence should be Death, it will be most assuredly carried into execution.[31]

Neither captains nor admirals could personally direct capital punishment. However, an admiral could convene a court martial (if he had several captains present to act as judges), the sentences from which could be death—and there was no appeal, as Nelson implies above.

THE COMMANDER'S SKILL as a strategist (here more pertaining to an admiral than a captain) was critical in the days before the radio enabled politicians in a nation's capital to direct worldwide strategy. Two hundred years ago, with the dismal contemporary communications that have been described in chapter 3, admirals serving overseas "had to have a clear understanding of how sea power should be used to further the conduct of a war so that the final victory might be gained on land; how best to employ their ships for the protection of their country's and its allies' maritime trade and in support of their armies, *and* to prevent the enemy from using the sea for either of these vital purposes."[32]

In fact, appalling slowness of communications, between the Admiralty and fleet commanders in chief, rivaled those of the foreign office to diplomats posted abroad. Nelson's papers are filled with complaints on this issue, not only relative to direct correspondence but also in regard to basic information and general news. All too often, whatever the situation was before the commander left Britain, it had become worse by the time he reached the scene—or if not worse at least far different than when his orders were written.

This certainly was not unique to Nelson. Some five years after Trafalgar, Vice Adm. Lord Collingwood, Nelson's successor in command of the Mediterranean Fleet, wrote his wife (from his flagship *Ocean*), "I so seldom hear from England now, that I scarcely know what is going on in the world. I conclude every body is so occupied with Spanish affairs, that they can think of only them."[33]

The commander, at all levels, had to be a skillful tactician—a role less dependent upon timely communications with the government. He had to "know not only how to manoeuvre and fight his [ship or] fleet, but how to engage, or avoid action with, the enemy in circumstances that are most favourable to his own [ship or] fleet."[34]

FINALLY, THE COMMANDER had to be a diplomat. In overseas stations, admirals as well as detached captains (of whom their were many) often had to

> work in harmony with kings and statesmen, governors and generals, of his own country and of its allies. He must negotiate with those of neutral powers; sometimes with those of the enemy. He should know when to threaten, when to plead, when to show the iron hand, when

to wear the velvet glove, when to be tolerant of weakness, when to defy a bully's strength. And in all this he operates in waters more dangerous than those in which his [ship] sails, a sea in which he is more likely to founder. For whilst the successful . . . commander is the man who follows Danton's advice, "*De l'audace, et encore de l'audace, et toujours l'audace,*" the diplomatist must remember Talleyrand's[35] counsel, "*N'ayez pas de zèle.*"[36]

A remarkable example was Adm. Sir James, Baron de Saumarez (1757–1836), who was a significant contributor to Britain's ultimate victory when, during his command in the Baltic Sea, from 1808 to 1812, "he not only cleared the Baltic of a hostile Russian fleet, but maintained such amicable relations with Sweden that her ports remained open to British shipping, even though *force majeure* compelled her to join France's allies."[37]

In fact, after Sweden had to declare war, and the British diplomats had to leave Stockholm, Saumarez effectively became the regional director of political affairs. His flagship (the venerable *Victory*) became a headquarters of northern resistance to France, "and the skilful diplomacy and personal popularity of the Admiral were a major contributory factor in the development of the alliance against Napoleon in 1812."[38]

Sometimes a commander translated his diplomatic analyses directly into naval decisions. For instance, and as previously discussed in chapter 2, with his on-scene knowledge Lord Nelson was amazed at his government's plan to intercept the Spanish treasure fleet. Note this letter from Nelson to John Gore, captain of HMS *Medusa,* in October 1804:

> Last night I received . . . a copy of Captain Graham Moore's orders from Admiral Cornwallis, which has filled me with astonishment; but without presuming to set myself in opposition to the Honourable Admiral's orders, there is a duty which I owe my Country that, although I risk the most precious thing to me in the world—my Commission,—I feel it my duty to give you my full opinion of the line of conduct you ought to pursue on this most extraordinary occasion;
>
> I [cannot] think that England has any wish to go to War unnecessarily with Spain. Therefore, unless you have much *weightier reasons*

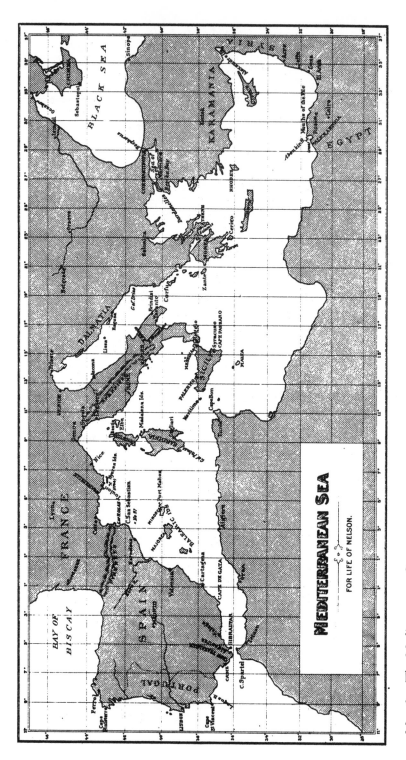

Map 6-1 The Mediterranean Sea
Mahan, *Life of Nelson*

than the order of Admiral Cornwallis, or that you receive orders from the Admiralty, it is my most positive directions that neither you, or any Ship under your orders, do molest or interrupt in any manner the lawful commerce of Spain, with whom we are at perfect peace and amity.[39]

In addition, Nelson's attempt to walk a very narrow line between the bashaw of Tripoli and the United States is interesting. This letter was written to Lord Hobart, secretary of state for War:

I send you my correspondence with the Bashaw. . . . He is, as usual, most friendly disposed towards us. During the time of Buonaparte's greatest success in Egypt, [he] gave up to me, as prisoners, the French Consul, and every Frenchman in his Dominions, [and] his Arsenal was always open for the supply of our Ships.

I have not thought it, however, proper to notice the indirect application for gunpowder and grape-shot, on account of his War with the Americans. . . . It might give cause for a discontent on the part of the Americans, which it must be our wish to avoid.[40]

At other times a commander could become too much a politician and too little a naval officer, degrading his primary role to the detriment of his profession. For example in 1799, while recovering from his wound after the Battle of the Nile, Nelson became overly involved in Neapolitan politics, including seizing and executing persons in rebellion against the Neapolitan government. Moreover, he was formally appointed one of the Neapolitan king's advisors. "The presence of an officer of a belligerent state on the council of a neutral one was a little odd," notes Forester, "but Nelson never seemed to appreciate the oddness."[41]

Still, as with everything else, the commander was usually totally on his own, making judgments and forming plans in a vacuum. It was often better to be too active than too passive, and British officers for the most part acquitted themselves judiciously, certainly including Nelson. In fact, while 1799 may not have been Nelson's best year in this regard, his tenure as Mediterranean commander in chief (1803–5) joins Collingwood's Mediterranean command (1805–10)—and Saumarez's Baltic command—as examples of extraordinary diplomatic responsibilities being exceptionally well executed. After all, no one knew better than Nelson that "political courage in an Officer abroad is as highly necessary as military courage."[42]

Of course, diplomatic activity always meant language and translation problems. Very often the commander had a practical need for personal fluency in at least one foreign language. But all too often, particularly for ship captains, there was no personal fluency, and it was virtually left to chance in that there may or may not be anyone on board with the particular skill required. Nelson was quite aware of this; as a young commander, after the close of the American Revolutionary War, he decided to take advantage of the peace to try to learn French. Writing to Admiralty secretary Philip Stephens on 8 October 1783, he requested that "you will be pleased to move their Lordships to grant me six months' leave of absence, to go to Lisle, in France, on my private occasions."[43] Indeed, he had no doubt witnessed too many of the awkward scenarios when a British ship, "commanded by an officer who knew no language but his own, captured a prize. ('Boatswain's mate, pass the word for *any* man who can speak French to come aft on the quarter-deck.') It was even worse when the papers of a foreign vessel needed examination, for a seaman who had picked up some French or Spanish very likely could not read it. Besides, French was an accomplishment expected in high society."[44]

However, even after a very earnest start to the project ("He bought *Chambaud's Grammar of the French Tongue,* on the title page of which he wrote neatly, 'Horatio Nelson began to learn the French Language on the first of November, 1783'"),[45] Nelson returned to London, for professional and personal reasons, several months later. He never succeeded in learning the language, and was therefore dependent upon interpreters —wherever he could find them—for the rest of his life.

An admiral's translation problems were more significant and generally required better advance preparation. Often a secretary, chaplain, or even flag lieutenant was selected at least partially on the basis of lan-

guages in order to supplement whatever skills (if any) the admiral personally boasted. Sir Hyde Parker's chaplain in the West Indies and at
Copenhagen ("Sir Hyde's parson-secretary"), the Rev. Alexander John
Scott, served the country admirably with remarkable language skills
(though Parker acquired his services oblivious to this aspect of his knowledge). Scott also later served Nelson in the Mediterranean as chaplain
and secretary; however, Nelson was very aware of Scott's useful language
skills and was always deeply appreciative of his tremendous contributions to both diplomatic and intelligence situations: "Languages were
his prey, and to [Nelson], who never attained proficiency in a single
one, there was fascination in presenting [him] with a captured French
despatch, letter, pamphlet, or foreign newspaper, out of which they would
together tear the heart in a few minutes. . . . [Scott] modestly claimed
master of no more than eight [languages], and admitted that elementary
Danish had taken him three days, and Russian several weeks."[46]

One of Patrick O'Brian's fictional Mediterranean commanders in
chief discussed his translation problem: "In principle the Navy writes to
foreigners in English; but where I want things done quick I send them
unofficial copies in a language they can understand whenever I can. . . .
We have clerks for Arabic and Greek: French we can manage for ourselves, and that answers for most other purposes; but. . . . I should give a
great deal for a really reliable Turkish translator."[47]

For most of his early, shore-based Mediterranean operations as a flag
officer, Nelson was dependent upon (his mistress to be) Lady Emma
Hamilton and her husband, Ambassador Sir William. In fact, on one
occasion shortly after the Battle of the Nile, the ambassador "acted as
interpreter during the early stages of an interview which soon degener-
ated into an altercation, and when he retired, worn out, Lady Hamilton
took his place. How difficult their task may be judged from the fact that
when the admiral spoke of 'the rebels' and [Cardinal Ruffo] spoke of
'the patriots,' they were referring to the same body of men."[48]

Some commanders, of course, could personally speak other languages
and were thus less dependent upon translators. One whose abilities vastly

Fig. 6-2 *Sir Hyde Parker.*
This illustration was done by James Northcote (artist) and H. R. Cook
(engraver) and was published on 30 November 1808 by Joyce Gold.
© *National Maritime Museum, London*

aided his job was Sir James Saumarez, who, like many Channel Islands
people, was actually bilingual, speaking both English and French.

WHILE THE ROLE of the commander's secretary will also be more fully
developed in the next chapter, the concept of the commander as administrator is appropriate here. Even in a simpler time, the administration of
a ship (or a fleet) required a prodigious amount of paperwork. Captains
and admirals were aided by staffs basically either non-existent or, at best,
tiny by modern standards.

Lord Nelson's staff can well serve as an example. In mid-1805, Nelson led the Mediterranean Fleet including thirty-three ships of the line and containing over seventeen thousand men,[49] exercising the full authority of a commander in chief. His staff consisted of exactly three people, two of whom had to devote at least some of their time to other duties on board the flagship, HMS *Victory*. These men were Lt. John Pasco, his flag lieutenant; the previously mentioned Rev. A. J. Scott, his private secretary (who also had collateral responsibility as the ship's chaplain); and John Scott, secretary (who likewise had collateral responsibilities in the ship's purser's office). To further underscore the point, Vice Adm. Lord Collingwood, Nelson's second in command on board HMS *Royal Sovereign,* had no staff support at all other than that which was available to him from the ship's company.[50] Rear Adm. the Earl of Northesk and Rear Adm. Thomas Louis, Nelson's third and fourth in command, were similarly ill served—although the *Britannia*'s chaplain, Rev. Laurence Halloran, performed some collateral duties as Northesk's secretary.[51] As a result, one cannot be overly surprised to learn that, on 1 October 1805, Nelson noted, "I had been writing seven hours yesterday."[52]

Indeed, Nelson was an extraordinarily hard-working administrator. While he never neglected his other duties, and was "generally on deck six or seven hours in the day,"[53] he was a phenomenal desk worker and an elegant writer—even though C. S. Forester felt that Nelson's "letters and orders might have benefited from a fuller formal education; while precise and unequivocal, they lack the literal clarity of Wellington and the exacting vigor of Napoleon's early writing."[54]

Most captains' and admirals' correspondence had to be at least workmanlike, if not elegant, though it certainly came to some more naturally than others: "the desk," said an admiring brother officer of Capt. Sir Thomas Hardy, "was *not* his *forte*."[55] Actually, it is somewhat of a marvel that any of them were any good at all; most left whatever early schooling they may have had to go to sea, and many (like Nelson) went to sea at twelve or thirteen. Regardless, the desk *was* Nelson's forte, among so many other important things, and "he displayed . . . a gift for administration such as is seldom possessed by men of imagination, a combination which did much to enable such commanders as Caesar and Napoleon to achieve immortal fame."[56]

Nelson crowded in considerable desk and deck time, typically working very long days, usually beginning at 5:30 A.M. and "till after 8 o'clock at night, I never relax from business."[57] In this regard he was more balanced than his friend Collingwood, who perhaps focused on administrative issues to the detriment of operational ones. Professor G. J. Marcus was of this opinion, writing that Collingwood's meticulous attention to detail became obsessive. He once remarked that he very much liked his flagship, the *Ville de Paris,* "but all ships that sail well and are strong are alike to me; I see little of them, seldom moving from my desk." "I am ceaselessly writing," he observed on another occasion, "and the day is not long enough for me to get through my business."[58]

The problem of the remarkably small staff is in enormous contrast to the situation 134 years later. In 1939 the Royal Navy's Mediterranean Fleet commander in chief, full admiral Andrew Cunningham, led eleven capital ships and some fifty smaller vessels, containing about 15,500 men. However, counting neither junior officers nor clerical support, nor his attached flag officers (a vice admiral and three rear admirals), his staff included a commodore, two captains, and four commanders. Although he went on to several assignments much larger than the Mediterranean Fleet, eventually becoming an admiral of the fleet and a viscount, Cunningham valued the support of these men so profoundly that he later dedicated his huge autobiography "to my staff in the Mediterranean to whom I owe so much."[59]

Rightfully so, Nelson was always impressed by his own workload— even before he became a commander in chief: "My public correspondence besides the business of sixteen Sail-of-the-Line, and all our commerce, is with Petersburg, Constantinople, the Consuls at Smyrna, Egypt, the Turkish and Russian Admirals, Trieste, Vienna, Minorca, Earl St. Vincent and Lord Spencer. This over, what time can I have for private correspondence?"[60]

Unfortunately for Nelson, his constant desk work took a toll on his fragile constitution, to say nothing of generally aggravating the seasickness to which he was always prone. At one point his friend Captain Ball expressed concern, writing, "I wish he could be prevailed upon to write less, because I am very apprehensive he impairs his health."[61] Right before his Copenhagen campaign he was actually forced to stop writing for a brief period; his "good" eye (the other having lost sight from an earlier wound) "was giving him such trouble that he had been driven to consult the physician to the fleet, who prescribed an operation as soon as possible, meanwhile, no writing, and green shades."[62] Nelson certainly was not alone, either in doing considerable personal writing or suffering because of it. Note this 1797 apology from Lord St. Vincent to Lord Spencer: "My Lord,—A violent inflammation in my eyes and head compels me to make use of the pen of my secretary."[63]

Nelson was not a robust person; the workload continuously wore away at his overall health, reaching a crisis during the Trafalgar campaign. In the spring and summer of 1804, Nelson found that the prodigious, incessant desk work he had to do began to erode his physical health and his personal optimism. In fact, after fifteen months in command he began to solicit Whitehall for an interval of leave.

Seven years earlier, Sir Hyde Parker was similarly overloaded—if not quite worn out. As commander in chief of the West Indies station, and with a tiny clerical staff, "Sir Hyde was always kept busy with a great deal of paperwork. . . . There were always many official letters to write —to the Admiralty, Navy Board, Sick and Hurt Board, Pay Office and Victualling Office, among many others. Surveys and reports had to be made on sick ships and sick men; details of prizes captured, requisitions for shot, powder, provisions, masts and spars, rigging and paint—all these had to go through the commander-in-chief."[64] Indeed, on Sunday, 12 February 1797, "Sir Hyde spent the whole day—after Divine Service on board his flagship—dictating and writing letters 'to the Admiralty and other naval Boards.'"[65]

It is significant to note that Lord Collingwood, ultimately, was overwhelmed by his work. During the five years he commanded the Mediterranean Fleet, with all the associated responsibilities of that terribly important command, he effectively wore out. He requested to be relieved several times, to no avail, and he literally died on board his flagship. He saw it coming, writing to his sister-in-law, "my fear, my only fear, is that my strength of body, impaired by length of days and weight of years, should unfit me for the arduous duties I have to fulfil. Fourteen or sixteen hours of every day I am employed."[66]

It is perhaps useful here to expand the several specific references to writing, for at this time all writing was by hand with pen and ink. Nelson, St. Vincent, and Collingwood all literally meant, in the quotations above, that they personally wrote for several hours per day above and beyond whatever their secretaries might have been doing.

In this time, when one wrote, one used a quill (usually from goose feathers) pen dipped every few strokes into an ink bottle—state of the art since 200 B.C. The metal-dip pen was only developed in 1815, the year this study closes; the fountain pen in 1880; the ball-point pen in 1940 (the ball-point pen was really invented in 1888, but was not broadly used until World War II);[67] and the roller-ball pen in 1980. Though an early form of carbon paper was in use as early as 1808, the typewriter was not invented until 1869 (to say nothing of the mimeograph machine, the photocopier, or the word processor!).

As a result, whether you were the king, a secretary of state, an admiral, a captain, or a ship's clerk, the quality and clarity of your handwriting became a key factor in the efficiency and accuracy of your transmission of information. After the loss of his right arm (courtesy of grapeshot at Tenerife in 1797), and having been right-handed, Nelson's neatly scripted handwriting became horrendous. Ironically, Nelson himself did not think much of *Napoleon*'s handwriting. Some of Bonaparte's letters were captured after the Battle of the Nile; Nelson commented on this to Lord Spencer in a letter dated 9 August 1798: "I send you a pacquet of intercepted Letters[,] . . . in particular, one from Bounaparte to his brother.

He writes such a scrawl, no one not used to it can read; but luckily, we have got a man who has wrote in his Office, to decipher it."[68]

Indeed, as one reads the logs of ships or the correspondence of officials which have been transcribed and published, *"unintelligible"* is a frequent notation in the texts as editors, holding the original documents, have had trouble deciphering them. In fact, King George's off-and-on relationship with Henry Dundas, who among other things was secretary of state for War from 1794 to 1801, apparently was partially due to Dundas's penmanship. Sir James Bland Burges, undersecretary of state for Foreign Affairs, claimed that George felt "a mortal antipathy to [Dundas's] handwriting, which I have heard him, and with great truth, declare to be the worst and most ungentlemanlike he had ever met with. This, by the way, was a curious particularity of our good King; but it was one which operated forcibly on more occasions than one that have fallen within my own observation, to add to the dislike which he might have preconceived against an individual." King George must have disliked many of his officers and ministers, for clear writing was the exception during this time.[69]

For the embarked admiral·or captain, desk work was complicated by the fact that one generally had no real office in which to work. As a rear admiral during the Nile campaign, Nelson lived in HMS *Vanguard's* quarterdeck accommodation: "At night there would only be a thin wooden partition between him and the steering wheel. He would hear the shouted orders of the officer of the watch, the warnings of the lookouts, and be instantly aware of any crisis in the sailing of the ship. It is not surprising that he got little sleep at crucial stages in the campaign."[70] The stern cabin, almost thirty feet across at the widest point, "would be his home, office and headquarters for the next few months. . . . It was divided into three separate cabins, one for sleeping, one as a lobby and *perhaps an office* and the largest, well-illuminated by the stern windows, where he would dine, receive guests and perhaps relax."[71]

Years later, in the *Victory,* he would work beside the stern windows at

Fig. 6-3 *Nelson's "Office."*
Painted by Charles Lucy and engraved by C. W. Sharp, this portrait shows
Nelson before Trafalgar. One can clearly see the small, cluttered desk in the
corner of the cabin by the stern windows. It is not much of an office.
© *National Maritime Museum, London*

a very small desk, without the benefit of drawers, filing cabinets, or book shelves (see fig. 6-3). It is a wonder, to the modern reader, that such enormous administrative requirements could be handled with no dedicated office spaces.

But it was done, and Nelson—with no right eye, no right arm, no significant staff, and no office—was one of the best. In fact, when Lord Castlereagh once told him that he did not believe he had in his possession some of Nelson's earlier dispatches, Lord Nelson offered, if they could not be found, to provide the whole series immediately. He had kept duplicates, with an index.[72]

Admirals did have one particular benefit in regard to staff work. After 1795, a "captain of the fleet" was authorized for fleets of fifteen ships or more when the Lords of the Admiralty felt it advisable. When authorized and present this officer, also called the "first captain," above and beyond the flagship's captain,[73] was in some ways the admiral's chief of staff and acted as a main advisor, particularly in helping regulate the administrative and disciplinary details of the fleet.[74] It was a demanding position; Nelson once commented that "the situation of First Captain is certainly a very unthankful office."[75] In contrast, the flagship's captain, called the "second," or flag captain, "was generally newly promoted and less experienced than the captains of smaller ships, so custom permitted . . . the admiral to interfere a good deal in the internal management of his flagship."[76]

Nelson had Rear Adm. George Murray as his captain of the fleet from May 1803 to August 1805. However, when he returned to the Mediterranean command after leave (in late August 1805), until his death, he was operating without one. In any event, Nelson always remained immersed in the details. Note this line, written to a ship's captain, in summer 1804: "Your log and weekly account have been delivered me by the Captain of the Fleet. Let them in future be transmitted [directly] to me."[77]

Clearly, even when a captain of the fleet was present, an admiral had precious little staff support—neither at the routine, clerical level nor at the senior advisor level. This was an army problem as well—though the army was often better staffed than the navy. As late as 1812, Lt. Gen. the Marquess of Wellington was commanding the bulk of the British Army in the Iberian Peninsula, fighting a series of successful campaigns while simultaneously "acting as his own paymaster general, economic advisor, chief-of-staff, and commissary general."[78]

The captain of the fleet was generally "free to make suggestions, put .forward plans, and generally offer advice to the admiral."[79] This was the exception for a subordinate, not the rule. The commander was very, very much a "man alone," isolated from his superiors by geography and from his subordinates by status. C. S. Forester underscored this concept in his fictional writing, particularly in *Captain Horatio Hornblower.* In fact, there probably "is no one in the modern world that can appreciate the burden" of this isolation.[80] A captain led

> a solitary existence: although surrounded night and day by scores of men, he lived the life of a recluse. Because of the rigid bulkhead of discipline and tradition he was isolated from his own officers, entertaining them occasionally at his table but otherwise remaining socially aloof.
>
> In addition to this unnatural and enforced solitude the captain bore the sole responsibility for the fighting efficiency, safety and welfare of upwards of seven-score men, and for the ship herself. Combined with the knowledge that one error of judgment or navigation by himself or his officers could wreck his ship and possibly his career, it imposed a great strain on every type of captain.[81]

Moreover, the customs of the period and of the service were such that commanders could very rarely seek (or even accept) advice or discussion from their subordinates.[82] Rank and position demanded more distance and respect than we are used to today. Admirals experienced an even greater solitude than did captains: "The majority of the great admirals were by nature stern and sombre men and for the most part unapproachable to subordinates."[83] Most commanders were very solitary, authoritarian figures working, living, and dining in dignified solitude.[84]

Indeed, most flag officers wanted active command at sea, particularly overseas, with its significant opportunities and independence. But independence also meant enormous responsibility: "There was no chance to consult one's superiors, to weigh the advice of wiser and more experienced heads. Issues of war and diplomacy, of life and death turned on an admiral's unaided decisions, and if there were any who took them lightly, they did so no more after the death of Admiral Byng, shot in 1757 for failure in action."[85]

In addition, based upon position, education, experience, and social station, captains and admirals were expected to know all. Indeed, they could hardly *not* know a great deal, because "to command a frigate needed a minimum of eight to ten years' training; the captain of a sail of the line needed ten to fifteen. An admiral, even a clever man of the most junior rank, needed several more years. Nelson, unique among them all, went to sea at thirteen and was thirty-nine when he became a rear admiral."[86] While this idea of the senior officer being the most knowledgeable is not a foreign concept in today's armed forces, it was much more tangible in that era.

In that time—very unlike today—it was possible for the captain to be the most knowledgeable individual on board in all areas of expertise. For one thing, it is an "undeniable fact that in those days a naval officer had less to learn in the technique of his profession than he would have nowadays."[87] (These were also times, however, where many captains felt a strong responsibility, if not absolute duty, to thoroughly know all their men, including names, divisions, watches, ratings, abilities and history.)

Most commanders, including the sometimes liberally minded Nelson, disdained anything resembling a "council of war" as a weakness.[88] Actually, Nelson did call one during the Nile campaign—even though he disliked such councils, for he felt they promoted indecision. As he was to comment on another occasion, "If a man consults whether he is to fight, when he has the power in his own hands, *it is certain that his opinion is against fighting.*"[89]

O'Brian's Capt. Jack Aubrey, even more conservative than Nelson, is

comfortable with this aspect of solitude: "It was not usual for him to discuss his orders with anyone."[90] In fact, "he had always been a silent captain in the matter of strategy, tactics and the right course of action, and
this was not from any theory but because it seemed to him evident that a
commander was there to command rather than to ask advice or preside
over a committee. He had known captains and admirals call a council of
war, and the result had nearly always been a prudent retreat or at any
rate an absence of decisive action."[91]

All in all, the commander was profoundly alone on board his ship,
needing to be jack and master of all trades—as well as the final authority, in all subjects, to all of his subordinates.

Novelist Alexander Kent's Vice Admiral Broughton would agree,
once asking his flag captain to "remind that officer that if I am in such
dire distress as to require an opinion of no value, he will be the first to be
told."[92] Even the relatively sensitive Horatio Hornblower was of this
mold, at one time sparing not even his first lieutenant—who was also his
best friend: "Mr. Bush," said Hornblower spitefully, "I can judge of the
situation without the assistance of your comments, profound though
they be."[93]

Fictional officers aside, real-life Capt. Edward Hamilton of HMS
Surprise, famous for retaking HMS *Hermione* from the Spanish in 1799,
was certainly as much of a loner as any: "Hamilton did not discuss his
plan with his officers, and that night . . . [he worked alone] in his cabin
with the watch and quarter-bills—which listed the name and various
tasks of every man in the ship[,] . . . and then wrote out six different sets
of instructions."[94] And, of course, Nelson was ever the man alone, writing during the Trafalgar campaign, "I have consulted no man, therefore
the whole blame of ignorance in forming my judgement must rest with
me. I would allow no man to take from me an atom of my glory, had I
fallen in with the French Fleet, nor do I desire any man to partake of any
of the responsibility—all is mine, right or wrong."[95]

It is not that commanders did not feel loneliness; indeed, after going
back to sea and resuming command Nelson once wrote that "to tell you

how dreary and uncomfortable the *Vanguard* appears, is only telling you what it is to go from the pleasantest society to a solitary cell, or from the dearest friends to no friends. I am now perfectly *the great man*—not a creature near me. From my heart I wish myself the little man again!"[96]

EACH OF THE FACTORS developed so far in this chapter come strikingly into play as we consider Lord Nelson as British Mediterranean Fleet commander in chief from 1803 to 1805. In this role his task was to blockade or destroy the French and Spanish fleets based at Toulon and Cadiz, to control the sea for the protection of commerce, and to assist the continental allies on shore in the struggle against French hegemony. Additionally, he had to maintain diplomatic relations in and among the many coastal states in his area, detail ships to convoy British trade, maintain close communications with local British diplomats as well as with Whitehall, support friendly forces of various pedigrees in the region, and —of course—gather, analyze, act upon, and/or relay all available intelligence, whether pertinent locally or for ultimate digestion in London.

The Mediterranean situation—for the entire war—was particularly complex. In 1803 Nelson was required to oversee the safety of Malta; work toward the destruction of the French fleet at Toulon; try to protect Naples, Egypt, and Corfu against the French; monitor naval preparations in Spanish ports; try to prevent a junction of French, Spanish, and Dutch ships; protect British, Neapolitan, and Turkish commerce; intercept French ships expected from the West Indies; and monitor French naval activity in Genoa, Leghorn, and other Italian ports.[97]

His supply and general logistics problems were immense, with virtually no support from Britain. Nelson was always very personally engaged in this business. One may truly consider him his own commissary officer, as evidenced by this letter to Rear Admiral Knight at Gibraltar, from the *Victory,* on 22 July 1805: "Be so good as to allow the Gun-Brig to bring over to Tetuan 3000 lbs. of onions, which I have desired Mr. Cutforth to put on board her for the Pursers, as I find we shall get no onions for the [crew's] broth at Tetuan."[98]

As commander in chief, Nelson personally handled large quantities of cash—in gold, as a rule—principally to buy food for the fleet in every nook and cranny all around the western Mediterranean. (Of course, he also used cash to pay agents who supplied him with all sorts of political and military information.)[99]

Nelson's logistical problems were even more complex than they might have been, because he really had no useful base: "Genoa and Leghorn were in enemy hands; Minorca had reverted to Spain; Naples and Palermo, not to mention Malta and Gibraltar, were too far from Toulon." Determined to keep his fleet continuously at sea, he wrote, "I have made up my mind never to go into port till after the battle, if they [the French] make me wait a year." To bring this about, "he organized storeships to bring supplies from Gibraltar and Malta, from the Two Sicilies and Sardinia whose rulers were benevolently neutral to Britain, and from ports in Spain where British gold spoke louder than Madrid's preoccupation with placating Bonaparte's demands."[100]

Nelson was determined to keep his ships well supplied and on station. Thus, he certainly contributed his share of organization and innovation to a concept of efficient victualling which had been first introduced by Hawke in 1759. This had been recently reestablished by Jervis, Duncan, Cornwallis, and Keith, enabling large fleets to remain on station throughout years of blockade.[101]

He was further determined to keep his men healthy, which added urgency to his supply challenges. He was personally involved in victualling, for "you will agree with me that it is easier for an Officer to keep men healthy, than for a Physician to cure them." "Acting on this belief," Carola Oman notes in her biography of Nelson, "he sent to Malta for sweet oranges and deputed his second-in-command to discover on the spot why all the bread from this quarter should arrive infested with weevils. He wrote to Gibraltar to order more cheese, cocoa, and sugar and less rice. To his chagrin, ship's companies in general did not much like rice or . . . macaroni."[102]

And note the following memorandum, from December 1803, sent to all British ships in the Mediterranean, from "chief medical officer" Lord Nelson: "As a preventive against the effects of disease which the men are subject to . . . a dose of Peruvian-bark, in a preparation of good sound wine or spirits, [should] be given to each man in the morning, previous to his going on shore [to get wood or water], and the same in the evening after his return on board. . . . And on the Ship's being completed in wood and water, an account of the quantity of wine or spirits issued to the men as above in addition to their allowance, is to be sent to me for my information."[103]

THE CHALLENGES present for the at-sea eighteenth-century commander were remarkable. First and foremost, he was very isolated, from both his superiors and his subordinates. Partly because of the remoteness of higher headquarters, and partly because of the relative simplicity of the age, the commander had an incredibly wide range of tasks. He certainly had to be eclectic in his expertise, and he had to be in many ways the most knowledgeable and skillful officer in his command. The variety of duties was amazing, and with little staff support the commanding officer was often the one to handle them. For example, note this remarkably unusual assignment, in September 1804, from Nelson to Capt. Charles M. Schomberg of HMS *Madras:* "*Lord Elgin* having requested . . . that I would allow a Ship to call at Cerigo, to bring from thence to Malta some *marble antiquities,* and as I am perfectly disposed to meet his Lordship's wishes on this occasion, I am to desire you will send a small Transport to Cerigo . . . for the purpose of receiving the antiquities before-mentioned on board."[104]

Above all, a commander had to be decisive, clear-headed, calm, "and equally competent whether manoeuvring his own [ship or fleet] or a foreign diplomat. A skillfully turned phrase might have more effect than a thousand skillfully aimed broadsides."[105] Indeed, commanders had to be, of course, active, meritorious, and bold, but most important, judicious. Perhaps this latter characteristic was really the key, for "meritorious officers were two-a-penny, insanely-brave ones the norm and competent seamanship the result of years of experience at sea." But there was a real "premium on judgement in complex situations, tact in handling foreigners (allied or neutral) and superiors, and even real diplomatic skills requiring an understanding of higher policy."[106]

Finally, the commander had to be a master of his art, for there was truly more art than science to being a naval officer two hundred years ago. This was, of course, always dependent upon "the vagaries of wind and sea and the seamanship, courage and ability of individual captains." It also depended upon a serious knowledge and understanding of the enemy's potential, intentions, "strength and weakness in ships, tactics, seamanship, leadership, and courage."[107] And that is the subject of the next chapter.

7

The Commander as
Intelligence Officer

Until the mid-nineteenth century . . . controlling [intelligence] collection and evaluating the results were integral parts of . . . military command.

Prof. Michael Herman

Washington [was] his own intelligence clearinghouse, consolidating information from his infantry regimental commanders and passing along intelligence to them in return.

Prof. Christopher Hibbert

Napoleon, like Wellington, interpreted intelligence data himself.

Prof. Martin Van Creveld

THE CLOSE OF THE EIGHTEENTH CENTURY SAW NAVAL INTELLIGENCE almost exclusively in the hands of the deployed senior officer. For good or bad, commanders, whether ship captains or fleet commanders in chief, were their own intelligence officers. Information presented in the preceding pages notwithstanding, this can be shown by exploring two routes of investigation. First, there was considerable intelligence activity appearing in the fleets of the day; second, there were virtually no other personnel qualified and available, other than commanders, to do the intelligence work.

Organization and staffing are key issues in a discussion of naval intelligence during this period. The reality is that, whether one focuses primarily upon the British or any other navy, there really was no intelligence organization at any level—ship, squadron, fleet, or Admiralty. Commanders, at whatever level, had to collect all the information they could. This was done in a variety of ways:

> They questioned deserters, prisoners of war, fishermen and such neutrals as still came and went from enemy's harbours. When they could, they introduced their own agents or suborned disaffected persons in key places ashore. Somehow they managed to acquire the enemy's newspapers pretty frequently; and they studied his signal code in order to read the messages he passed over his semaphore telegraph. Occasionally, too, they had the luck to intercept secret letters of the enemy's high command.
>
> Wherever possible one of their most important tasks was to make regular and direct inspections of what was going on inside the enemy's harbours. This, of course, was not possible at a place like Antwerp which lay far up a well-defended river, and no clear view could be had of the dock-yards in Venice either. But Brest, Rochefort, Toulon, Genoa and Naples were all regularly examined by sloop or frigate commanders who climbed to the masthead with telescopes after sailing as close in as possible.
>
> From all these sources British admirals compiled the reports on the enemy's progress which they were required to send the Admiralty.[1]

In fact, the transmission of intelligence occupied commanders considerably. Captains passed information to admirals, as here Cdr. Charles Marshall Gregory, of HMS *Beaver,* communicated with Lord Keith in September 1805: "The French have withdrawn their troops from all places they lately occupied on the banks of the Rivers Elbe and Weser. They quitted them on the 23rd inst. . . . Having considered that the above information might at this moment be of importance to H.M.

Government, I have despatched Lieut. Brompton in a Prussian galliot bound for England for the purpose of giving your Lordship the earliest intelligence."[2]

Sometimes naval officers even shared information with the army, though interservice cooperation was not common in that age. For example, early in the ground war in Spain, one naval lieutenant from HMS *Barfleur* found himself commanding gunboats supporting the army: "This officer perceived, on the 5th of March [1810], that the French had broken up from Santarem [Spain], and had fled in disorder. He immediately crossed the river and gave the intelligence to Lord Wellington."[3]

As a captain, Nelson was adroit at collection and transmission. For example in mid-1796, while commanding HMS *Agamemnon*, his job "was to forward to his admiral news of uninterrupted French successes in Italy. He reported Buonaparte's defeat of the Allies at the battle of Montenotte on April 12, in the gorges of Millesimo, at the village of Dego, and at the bridge of Lodi. Sardinia had made peace; Naples was preparing to desert; Spain was getting ready; Genoa had begun to be openly insolent ('Commodore Nelson is very much surprised that, whenever he approaches any Town belonging to the Genoese Government, they fire shot at him')."[4]

He was able, however, to also report a personal, operational, and intelligence success, because his squadron captured a siege train en route to Bonaparte at Mantua. "I have got," he wrote happily, "the charts of Italy sent by the Directory to Buonaparte, also Maillebois's *Wars in Italy,* Vauban's *Attack and Defence of Places,* and Prince Eugene's *History.* If Buonaparte is ignorant, the Directory, it would appear, wish to instruct him; pray God, he may remain ignorant."[5]

Admirals forwarded intelligence reports to each other, as well as to Whitehall. The following is an excellent example, from Sir John Borlase Warren to Lord Keith (number of guns follow ships' names):

> I have forwarded to your Lordship Captain Hallowell's reports of the enemy's force with other intelligence which he had been enabled to collect during his continuance at Toulon. . . .

List of French Men of War in the Mediterranean at Toulon

In the	L'Indivisible	80
outer road	Jean Bart	74
	Constitution	74
	Le Dix Aout	74
	Swiftsure	74
	La Creole	40
	Le Abeille brig	18
In the	La Badine	30
inner road	La Fauvette	20
	Le Lodi	16

With Rear Admiral Linois

Le Formidable	80
L'Indomptable	80
Le Desaix	74
Le Minion	40

In France they talk seriously of invading England. All the private letters from Paris speak decidedly on that subject. Bonaparte has appointed himself Commander in Chief of the Army and has named the four following Generals of Divisions to command under him— Massena, Augereau, St. Cyr and Bernadotte.[6]

At times, of course, admirals did not receive reports from captains in the timeframe or format they desired. Lord Keith thus chastised Commo. Sir William Sidney Smith in November 1805, "Sir, I am again without your weekly returns, which are the only ones that do not reach me regularly on Fridays. I am also without reports from off Boulogne for these eight or ten days."[7] Keith actually had a number of procedural troubles with Smith: "Sir, Having discovered in the hands of Mr. John Robb two papers . . . having marginal answers written upon them stated by Robb to have been sent to him by some branch of H.M. Government *through you,* I desire that you will be pleased to . . . explain to me how it happens that any communications of this kind are carried on by you without my knowledge."[8]

Similarly, Vice Adm. Sir Alexander Cochrane had considerable trouble, with one of his subordinates, in America during the War of 1812. Cochrane, a very intelligence-oriented commander, was particularly irritated with his general lack of intelligence information and constantly encouraged his subordinates to develop networks of agents to facilitate this problem. However, on this issue he could never get the attention or cooperation of Rear Adm. George Cockburn, who seemed to spend all of his time ashore on hit-and-run raiding.[9]

However, admirals generally cooperated with one another, as evidenced by this July 1814 note from Vice Adm. William Dommett to Lord Keith: "I beg leave to transmit to your Lordship a copy of certain intelligence received of the depredations committed by the United States ship of war *Wasp,* which I am sorry to say has extended to the capture of H.M. sloop *Reindeer.*"[10] Admirals certainly transmitted intelligence down to their captains. Here Lord Keith sent a memorandum to all his frigate commanding officers on 15 July 1813: "The Admiralty [has] informed me that all American frigates are at sea, and that they do not conceive that any of H.M. frigates should engage single-handed the larger class of American ships, which, though they may be called frigates, are of a size, complement and weight of metal much beyond that class, and more resembling line-of-battle ships."[11]

As an aside, much more so then than today, captains and admirals totally controlled all communications from their ships or squadrons, and therefore very personally and tightly regulated what was passed on and what was not. Thus, in 1794, Captain Nelson could—by his own later confession—withhold some of the information in his possession from his commander in chief (then Lord Hood) regarding the strength of the enemy. His object was to "help" Hood make the decision Nelson wanted (which was to lay siege against the garrison of Bastia).[12]

Some commanders—certainly not all—were very sensitive to issues of communications and operational security as they engaged in intelligence activities. Nelson always wanted his own movements to be invisible to the enemy, such as when he wrote to Rear Adm. John Knight, at

Gibraltar, in July 1805, that he wished "the probability of the Fleet's anchoring at Gibraltar to be kept as secret as possible, for everything which is known on the Rock gets into Spain."[13] On 30 September he wrote to Lt. Gen. Henry Edward Fox, governor of Gibraltar, requesting him to forbid the publisher of the *Gibraltar Gazette* from mentioning the force of the fleet, much less the names and strength of the ships, concluding, "For I much fear, that if the Enemy know of our increased numbers, we shall never see them [come] out of Cadiz. If my arrival is necessary to be mentioned, the Ships with me need not; and it may be inserted that an equal number, or some Ships of Admiral Collingwood's, are ordered home."[14]

Five days earlier he had written Collingwood to "request that if you are in sight of Cadiz, that not only no salute may take place, but also that no Colours may be hoisted, for it is as well not to proclaim to the Enemy every Ship which may join the Fleet. . . . P.S.: I would not have any salute even if you are out of sight of land."[15]

On 19 October 1804, Nelson tantalized Capt. Courtnay Boyle, of HMS *Seahorse,* without actually revealing anything; his secret was the probability of war with Spain: "(*A hint: most secret.*) My dear Boyle, If you knew what I *could* tell you, you would think every moment an age till you joined me." Captain Nelson, ten years earlier, was not as careful. In May 1794 he wrote a letter to his wife containing secret information he had about the approaching fall of Bastia.[16]

However, shortly before his death, in 1805, Nelson had become very choosy in whom he would confide—even at Whitehall. On 30 July he wrote Lord Barham that "it was not until my return to the Mediterranean, that I knew who was appointed First Lord of the Admiralty, in the room of Lord Melville, or I should have wrote you whenever opportunities offered for sending letters. . . . There must be, your Lordship well knows, many things which may be said to the First Lord, which would be improper to address to a . . . Board."[17]

"HUMAN" INTELLIGENCE—which included, among other sources, prisoners of war, returning prisoners of war, deserters, neutrals, paid spies, and "friendly" enemy nationals—was always a major factor.

Information from prisoners of war was never a very significant source —barring any obvious details or what little a prisoner freely wanted to offer. By and large, most countries did not put prisoners or other captives to any sort of serious interrogation, duress, or torture. Officers, who may have held useful knowledge, were rigidly bound by the prevalent eighteenth-century concept of honor and would instinctively guard any such information. Conversely, captors, having the same views of honor, really expected nothing and would generally have been surprised by any free admissions of substance by any captive.

Indeed, when the USS *Constitution* defeated and captured HMS *Java* on 29 December 1812, the *Java*'s officers did not even feel obliged to acquaint their captors with the basic number of men in their crew, forcing the Americans to figure it out themselves. Far from reacting harshly or even being particularly irritated, the Americans took it in stride. Note Commo. William Bainbridge's dry comment that "the number she had on board at the commencement of the Action, *The officers have not candour to say;* from the different papers we collected, such as a muster book, Watch List and Quarter Bills, she must have had upwards of 400 souls."[18]

Moreover, the very ideas of utilizing aggressive interrogation, duress, or of inflicting torture would have struck most as dishonorable conduct in itself. One needs to pause for a moment and reflect that espionage and most other forms of intelligence collection were, by and large, morally reprehensible to many eighteenth-century officers and gentlemen. Tactical and strategic reconnaissance, in uniform, was totally acceptable as was mild, cursory questioning of prisoners; however, espionage, letter opening, secret ink, use of informers, and sneaking around in disguise was generally considered repugnant. Our more modern sense that the arts of intelligence are necessary, practical, prudent, appropriate, routine—

and even dashing and glamorous—was not widespread. Many officers considered the arts of intelligence, and those who practiced them, as unsavory. Even Gen. Robert E. Lee, during the much-later American Civil War, refused critical information at Gettysburg because of his extreme distaste for such sources.

This is not to say that the desire for information never carried a captor beyond the acceptable. In fact, the breaking of many established norms in revolutionary and Napoleonic France could well have spread into this arena; it was no doubt an unpleasant experience to fall into the clutches of Minister Joseph Fouché's secret police. And, no matter where or what nationality, even honorable, humane, and unselfish men can occasionally be ruthless for patriotic causes. Still, it is reasonably safe to write that the grilling of prisoners, as an intelligence-gathering tool, was not a significant factor during this period.

Sometimes seamen of belligerent countries deserted their flags and willingly brought over useful intelligence. Note this memorandum from now–Vice Adm. Philip d'Auvergne, to First Secretary Croker, in September 1811: "Three French Sailors and one Spaniard . . . deserted a week since from the *Eylau,* the Flag Ship at L'Orient bearing Allemand's flag. . . . The following information, which is corroborated by neutrals lately arrived at Guernsey from those ports, has been obtained from them. . . . One of them (very intelligent) left Rochefort in the last week of August, says there were 10 Line of Battle Ships, one of which was a Three-Decker, ready for sea in the Charrentee."[19]

As one might expect, after several years of war both sides had captured large numbers of prisoners (the British kept their prisoners of war either in floating hulks or in several new specially built prisons, among them Dartmoor), and now and then exchanges took place:

> Occasionally prisoners were exchanged on a strict one-for-one basis, and the only French subject living in England as a representative of the French Government was M. Otto, the agent for the exchange of prisoners. As soon as the French Government was ready, Otto informed the Board of Transport in London and a cartel ship would sail from England for Cherbourg or Le Havre under a flag of truce with an

agreed number of French prisoners, who would be released—in return for appropriate receipts—and a similar number of freed Britons would be taken on board.

The cartel ships were hired merchantmen—it was part of the arrangement with the French that a ship of war was not used.[20]

Whenever a cartel came in there was usually good information to be obtained. Note the following from Lord Keith, in early October 1796, reporting on the results of an exchange in the Indian Ocean:

> Captain Campbell being just arrived in the cartel ship *Glasgow* with prisoners exchanged at the Isle of France; you will be pleased immediately on your junction with Capt. Losack to communicate the following intelligence obtained by the said Captain Campbell to him.
>
> The French Frigates now at sea and cruising in the vicinity of the Isle of France are: *La Forte* 46, *La Vertu* 40, *La Regeneire* 44, *La Seyne* 44, *La Cybele* 44, *La Prudente* 40, A Schooner 12 Guns. Remain in harbour *La Preneuse* 40.
>
> You will be pleased to make known also to Capt. Losack that off Fort Louis there is very good anchorage without the reach of the cannon ashore.[21]

Of course, occasionally prisoners of war—on both sides—escaped and returned home with good intelligence. While Britain was an impossible place from which to escape in the twentieth century, two hundred years ago escape was very possible for a Frenchman who was willing to break his parole and bribe a smuggler to cross the channel—and republican and imperial France condoned parole breaking, while conservative Britain punished such dishonorable activity by British officers. Thus, between 1809 and 1812 alone, 464 Frenchmen escaped from Britain to France.[22]

British naval officers who managed to escape typically did it the hard way; having generally been given no parole, they broke none. They "schemed and dared, and climbed and risked, and talked and walked and fought their way back to sea." Numerically, they may have totaled around one hundred during the entire war. Strangely enough, this was in spite of the fact that the "escapees' favorite ploy of passing themselves off as Americans rarely seems to have deceived French policemen."

British prisoners usually had to make their way from incarceration at Verdun-sur-Meuse, France, although unruly prisoners and habitual escapers (often recaptured) were eventually put in the high-security penal fortress at Bitche, in the northern Vosges Mountains.[23]

Regardless of whether a man escaped from Bitche, Verdun, or from a coastal city, he generally could bring back useful information as well as himself. Note the following three memoranda as examples. The first is from Sidney Smith to Lord Keith in early 1804:

> I beg leave to transmit for your Lordship's information the substance of intelligence I have received from Mr. Dalyell, one of the two midshipmen of the *Antelope* taken with Mr. Hanchett. They have both found their way back safely through Holland . . . in a neutral vessel from Emden.
>
> *Summary of intelligence report:* At the Hague 3,000 troops; all fishing vessels bought up by the French; 5 sail of the line ready in the Maas; 50 vessels in harbour at Flushing; loyal fisherman might be employed as spies.[24]

This next one was from Gen. Sir David Dundas (brother of minister Henry Dundas) to Lord Keith, in September 1803, disclosing naval intelligence brought back by an army officer:

> On the other side is an extract from a letter of a Major McKenzie, 85th Regt., who has just made his escape from France. It is not very distinct, but I suppose he has given a clearer account where it was essential.
>
> *Enclosure.*—In a moment of despair I determined to attempt an escape from France . . . and have happily succeeded. I left Paris this day fortnight, traveled through France by way of Valenciennes and Antwerp to Holland, embarked at Rotterdam and arrived at Gravesend last night. I saw preparations for the invasion in the neighbourhood of Paris and at Rotterdam; in both places they have not more than 20 covered boats finished, which may carry each about 100 men; these are of the largest class and carry each 2 six-pounders in the bows; they have about 20 more of the above description on the stocks, and about 30 open boats which may each carry 20 or 30 men.[25]

This last one is a report from a seaman who escaped in 1809:

Declaration of Ralph Dunlop, Seaman . . . who escaped from Rochefort in a Neutral Vessel, on the 1st of August last.

He declares that having been taken prisoner about six years ago, he had been detained at Givet till the 10th of last November, when . . . he with several others agreed to engage in the French Service, in the hopes of being brought to the Coasts, to find an opportunity to escape. . . . That on the day they were ordered out to Basque Roads, the Ship *Jean Bart,* of 74 Guns, ran aground and was wrecked, and most of the stores saved; that on the 12th of April the four following Ships were destroyed by the English fleet, viz., *La Ville de Varsovie, Le Tonnerre, L'Aquilon, Le Calcutta,* and the Frigate *L'Indienne,* burnt by the French.

The *Triomphant* of 74 Guns, *La Hortense* Frigate, *La Pallas* Frigate, and *L'Elbe* Frigate, were in the Charente, with a Corvette from Bordeaux, name not known, and *L'Epervier* Brig of 18 Guns.[26]

In addition to prisoners of war, solid and useful intelligence was very often obtained from neutrals. For instance, Adm. Sir John Jervis (not yet Lord St. Vincent in March 1797) reported to Lord Spencer that a French cartel with "Portuguese prisoners is this moment come in, eleven days from Brest; and an intelligent captain of a Brazilian [ship] reports that there were not more than fourteen line-of-battle ships in any state of forwardness, and that much desertion had taken place, and a general aversion to invasion shewed by all the persons employed there, both by sea and land, and a tumultuous joy expressed by all, on hearing of the defeat of the Spanish fleet."[27]

Capt. Thomas Lemprière sent this report to Lord Keith on 7 June 1800:

My Lord, I beg leave to enclose the declaration of Gabriel Reyas, a Minorquin who belonged to the *Bellone* French vessel captured by H.M. ship *Success.* . . .

Enclosure: Declaration made by a Mahonese . . . upon the oath to the undersigned and was released at the request of the Lieutenant Governor and by directions of the Senior Officer—viz.

That he had resided at Malta for two months and the place where he was quartered was in Valetta.

Question	Answer
What is the strength of the Garrison?	Five thousand men including seamen.
Do you think that force sufficient to garrison the place?	No, not half.
How many months provisions have they?	Four.
At what allowance of bread?	One pound per diem.
Have they any meat or vegetables?	Neither.
How many ships are there in Port, what force?	A Maltese ship of 64 guns and two frigates of 36 ready to sail and two other vessels but so old not fit for sea.
What place of fort do you think most accessible?	La Cotonera.

He further declares that behind the walls of La Cotonera there are a great quantity of shells loaded[,] ... all laid up in heaps, so that if any of our shells were thrown to that part, it would set fire to the whole, and most likely make a breach. . . . It is always guarded by 1,200 or 1,500 men. After being taken, the remaining part of the batteries would easily surrender.[28]

During 1803 Lord Nelson received a stream of valuable information, from inside Spain, via a Quaker merchant at Rosas Bay, "which he transmitted to Nelson's officers when they called to water and provision."[29]

Note this interesting memorandum, written by Capt. F. W. Ricketts of HMS *Liffey,* concerned with the results of the Battle of Waterloo:

Intelligence received from the Captain of the American Ship Cora, boarded by the Liffey the evening of June 19, 1815—

Left Brest this morning at daylight. A boat was sent to him from the French frigate *Flore* . . . to communicate that a telegraphic message had arrived last evening stating that Bonaparte had defeated Lord Wellington. Does not believe it, as the weather was so thick yesterday that the telegraph could not work.

The French frigate *Hortense,* reported the fastest sailor in the French Navy, has received sudden orders to prepare for sea. . . . The people say she is intended to take off Bonaparte in the event of defeat and the further success of the Royalists in the south, who are increasing in numbers rapidly.[30]

Of course, the enemy also profited by intelligence from neutrals. For example, in June 1805, Admiral Villeneuve "learned from a passing American schooner of a British convoy homeward bound to the NNE. He immediately gave chase. . . . Before nightfall he had not only captured fifteen prizes but learned of Nelson's [location]."[31]

Fishermen, regardless of nationality, were always a help and a hindrance. In fact, in the fall of 1800 St. Vincent mentioned to Spencer, "Your Lordship is aware that the Dutch and Flemish fishermen are better acquainted with our sands than we are."[32]

On at least one occasion, Alexander Kent's Capt. Richard Bolitho worried that a fishing boat was under his stern trying to catch more than fish. He "sat down on the bench seat below the stern windows and watched a fishing boat sculling below the two-decker's counter. The fisherman glanced up at him without expression. Probably in the pay of the Spanish commandant across the water in Algeciras, he thought. Taking the names of the ships. Tit-bits of information which might convey something in return for a few coins."[33]

A classic example of "friendly" enemy nationals were the French fishermen that Capt. Sir Edward Pellew relied upon in 1796, when an antirepublican Breton fisherman told him of French troops embarking in Brest for an attempt to invade Ireland: "Friendly Breton fishermen were a major source of British intelligence during the period; Pellew . . . had even acquired a royalist Breton to help him navigate those treacherous waters."[34]

Some years later Pellew's fictional protégé, Cdr. Horatio Hornblower, also gained considerable intelligence from Breton fishermen, particularly when he broke out some strong navy rum: "The Breton captain . . . did nothing to conceal either the smouldering Breton resentment against the atheist regime now ruling France or the contempt of a professional user of the sea for the blundering policies of the Republican Navy. Hornblower had only to nurse his glass and listen, his faculties at full stretch to catch all the implications of a conversation in a foreign language."[35]

In 1812, however, Commo. Sir Horatio Hornblower was not at all pleased with some *English* fishermen, who were to row him out to his flagship. With his "most secret" orders safe in a leather portfolio, Hornblower was addressed as he boarded the boat:

> "Morning, Captain. . . . All the breeze anyone wants today. Still, you'll be able to weather the Goodwins, Captain, even with those unweatherly bombs [ships] of yours. Wind's fair for the Skaw once you're clear of The Downs."
>
> So that was military secrecy in this England; this Deal hoveller knew just what force he had and whither he was bound—and tomorrow, as likely as not, he would have a rendezvous in mid-Channel with a French *chasse-marée,* exchanging tobacco for brandy and news for news. In three days Bonaparte in Paris would know that Hornblower had sailed for the Baltic—with a ship of the line and a flotilla.[36]

Fishermen aside, commanders quite often developed their own sources of intelligence in their areas of operation. Reflecting, in some ways, the lack of formal organization at the national level, admirals in particular established unofficial and improvised organizations, largely based on personal contact.

Lord Nelson was adept at this throughout his career, and his correspondence is full of references to private sources—which he often fails to identify even to his friends. Sometimes, however, he did mention names, as in this letter of 25 February 1804: "You are hereby required and directed to proceed immediately . . . to the Bay of Rosas, and communicate with Mr. Edward Gayner . . . for the purpose of obtaining any intelligence of the Enemy's Fleet at Toulon, or of the line of conduct which Spain is likely to pursue, with any other information . . . and join me with an account thereof . . . with the utmost dispatch, bringing with you any letters, &c., which Mr. Gayner may have for me."[37]

Captain Elphinstone (later Lord Keith) had developed such sources as far back as the American Revolutionary War: "*Secret Intelligence, No. 1:* On the 30th October an express arrived at Cape Français . . . and has brought orders from the Court of France to prepare for the reception of 10,000 men under the command of the Marquis de Bouille, who are immediately to sail with a convoy of fifteen sail of the line for the Cape; it may be depended upon that the object of this armament is to unite with the Spanish at Cape Français, and to proceed immediately for the attack of Jamaica."[38]

Elphinstone would occasionally admit to names as well, as when writing in his journal that the "*Orpheus* Indiaman, Capt. Bowen arrived, with Mr. Pringle the Company's *Secret Agent* on board from St. Helena with good news." Often he was more discreet, even when writing to a full general in 1795: "One of the batteries to the south of this bay has been deserted and the guns spiked; from private information of which I have some, it may be expected that another of five guns will be abandoned in the night."[39]

Nelson, in particular, developed a private organization when he took control of the Mediterranean Fleet in 1803. He immediately recognized that he had enormous intelligence requirements, and that information from London would be terribly insufficient. Therefore, he effectively did what Adm. Jackie Fisher (famous as the "father" of the *Dreadnought*) had to do almost one hundred years later when he was Mediterranean commander in chief. As he had "little faith in the . . . government's sources of information [he] built up an intelligence network *of his own* among the consuls in the Mediterranean seaports, among . . . businesspeople and among friends and acquaintances of all nationalities."[40]

Despite his continual need for information, Nelson was not particularly enamored with true, professional "spies": "I have read the account of the Marquis Dasserto. I never intended to hold any communication with him. I considered him as a French spy. . . . I can be told nothing of any consequence to me; but a copy of the French Admiral's orders, when he is to put to sea, and where he is destined to, is the only useful information I can care about. I can see the number and force at Toulon any day I please, and as for the names of the Captains or Admirals, I care not what they are called."[41]

I⅃ ᴛᴏᴏᴋ ᴀ ʟᴏᴛ of money (usually in gold) to fund intelligence operations. Commanders in chief could, of course, draw upon London for the myriad expenses that remote operations would demand—including some for intelligence. Nelson certainly knew the requirement: "Information upon these points is so important, to enable me to form a probable guess at the destination of the Toulon Fleet, that no *money* or *trouble* ought to be spared to obtain it." For security reasons, expenditures for intelligence were not generally supported with the usual kinds of vouchers; however, the Admiralty and the Foreign Office did expect reasonable accountability. It is interesting to note that Rear Adm. George Rodney's accounts were held up in 1775, relative to his tenure as commander in chief of the Leeward Islands Station, for lack of acceptable documentation for fifteen hundred pounds allegedly spent on intelligence.[42]

In fact, ultimately, the accountability of money caused the downfall of Lord Melville (Henry Dundas). While he was never an operational commander, of course, as secretary of state for War and the Colonies—and as first lord of the Admiralty—he handled considerable secret-service funds. In 1804 he was impeached by his political enemies for improper financial stewardship; before it was over he was forced to resign all offices, and the case almost brought down his friend William Pitt's entire administration. He protested that "first, when he resigned the position of Treasurer of the Navy [he] subsequently destroyed papers which he felt were of no value; and, second . . . he held other confidential offices in the government and sometimes he found it necessary to use funds from the Navy for delicate transactions in other branches of government of such a confidential nature that they could not be revealed to the public. Melville obviously referred to money used for Secret Service."[43] In fact, he underscored that "If I had materials to make up such an account as you require, I could not do it without disclosing delicate and confidential transactions of government, which my duty to the public must have restrained me from revealing."[44]

This may have been a red herring. There is the probability that Melville was guilty as charged, and it probably had nothing to do with the secret-service funds. Still, it is not entirely clear, and it is possible that had he been able to disclose everything he may have been able to successfully defend himself.

Accountability of large funds was generally the problem of ministers and admirals. Captains were more operationally tasked. Again, during this period the most active British captain, when it came to intelligence awareness, was Lord Cochrane. Indeed, his activities truly covered the full range, from the most basic (ferrying Mediterranean Fleet dispatches in 1801) to the most sophisticated (in-shore commando-type special operations). With reference to the dispatch-ferrying duty, although he was commanding then a very small ship, and therefore could likely expect some of this type of vital, if unglamorous duty, one cannot ignore the fact that he drew this duty after an exchange of acrimonious letters with the Earl of St. Vincent—the first lord of the Admiralty.

Cochrane was always interested in obtaining enemy documents and dispatches, hoping not only to deprive the enemy of his communications but also to obtain the same for British analysis. For example, on 17 December 1807, he captured dispatches from "a brig bound from Trieste . . . announcing that Russia had declared hostilities against England. This intelligence was fortunate, as there were several Russian ships of war in the Gulf." As Cochrane writes in his autobiography, "I never knew what was in the letters we rescued, as they were sent to Lord Collingwood; but no doubt they contained important intelligence for the French squadron then in the Archipelago, and, coming from a Russian source, there was little question as to the nature of their contents."[45]

In another example, in September 1808, Cochrane was operating in the Gulf of Foz on the French coast. On

> this excursion we had perceived a new telegraph station. . . . We set fire to the building, but the destruction not being fully accomplished,

the boats were again sent on shore to blow it up, which was done in the presence of about a hundred troops assembled for its protection. A shot from the ship was so well aimed that it fell right amongst the party, killing one man and wounding several. A few more shots completely dispersed them in such haste as to compel them to relinquish their dead comrade. . . .

It occurred to me that [the abandoned body] might have papers about him which would prove useful. In order to secure them, if there were any, the frigate's barge was again despatched on shore. . . . The boat's crew . . . found it to be that of an officer, as I had conjectured, the poor fellow been nearly cut in two by a round shot. As no papers of any consequence were found, our men wrapped him in a sheet . . . and again returned on board.[46]

Cochrane fundamentally enjoyed disrupting communications (he called it "effecting mischief") and thought it extremely important to interfere with enemy land communications and operations as much as possible. Writing of his activities in early summer 1808, he adds a further role not previously listed to the eclectic duties of British commanders: "The next two days were employed in blowing down rocks, and otherwise destroying roads in every direction which the French were likely to take. . . . In short, I had taken on myself the duties of an engineer officer, though occupation of this kind was, perhaps, out of my sphere as commander of a frigate. Having effected all the mischief possible, we weighed for Mangat, ten miles from Barcelona, and anchored off the place at sunset."[47]

LACK OF OTHER STAFF notwithstanding, every captain and certainly all admirals had secretaries to help handle the huge paperwork load—and the load was formidable. The correspondence involved in running a ship, let alone a fleet, was extensive. For example, during a three-month period in 1793, Lord Hood issued an average of 1.5 new officer commissions per day on top of all other business. And, on one June day of 1807, Lord Collingwood executed the following range of letters: "To the Foreign Secretary relating to the Barbary States. To the Secretary of the Admiralty on the same subject, acknowledging receipt and in reply to their lordships secret order of 2nd June with intelligence received from the *Bittern* from Sicily and Egypt. . . . To the ambassador at Lisbon. . . . To the governor of Gibraltar. . . . To the several public officers at Gibraltar . . . and to the senior officer to hasten ships out."[48]

Clearly, a secretary was key to such an effort. In fact, an admiral's secretary was "the business manager of the squadron. He controlled, drafted, and sometimes even signed the admiral's correspondence; he was heavily involved in victualling. . . . He was usually the admiral's prize agent and often the squadron's as well. This was big business, and it demanded ability and experience. A secretary needed extensive connections and good credit in the world of business and finance, and he needed to move easily among senior officers afloat and great men ashore."[49]

The secretary was often assisted by one or more "writers," or actually "copiers," for in the absence of carbon paper or photocopiers their sole jobs were to literally hand copy everything, such as orders into the order books and letters into the letter books.[50]

In addition to business management, the secretary—an admiral's secretary in particular—was sometimes needed to support the commander in the areas of politics and intelligence. It was not unusual to have a political advisor in the secretarial role. In fact, most secretaries to admirals with important commands were discreet, capable men, thoroughly used to dealing with diplomatic and official correspondence and with matters to do with intelligence. For example, Vice Adm. Sir Alexander Cochrane (uncle of Capt. Lord Thomas Cochrane), when commanding the North American station during the War of 1812, relied on a political-intelligence expert named James Stewart, who had formerly been British vice consul at New London.[51]

The year 1812 also saw Commodore Hornblower, when tasked to operate in the Baltic, assigned a secretary intended to help him in these areas. Born a Finn, this Mr. Braun spoke Finnish, English, Russian, Swedish, Polish, German, French, Lithuanian, and Estonian. Hornblower's Admiralty orders "enjoined him to pay the closest attention to the advice and information which he would receive from Braun, 'a gentleman whose acquaintance with the Baltic countries is both extensive and intimate.'"[52]

Sometimes secretaries were assigned to admirals by the Foreign Office itself, as was Vice Adm. Sir James Saumarez's Baltic political adviser, who possessed a singular grasp of detail as well as a flair for intelligence. And prior to Trafalgar, a Dr. Lambton Este was designated "one of six secretaries with commissions from the Foreign Office to be carried in the *Victory,*" who were to assist in the "arduous political negotiations which [Admiral Nelson] anticipated."[53]

The Rev. Alexander John Scott, introduced in the previous chapter, remains perhaps the most interesting of the admirals' secretaries. As already shown, he was a master linguist, and as Lord Nelson's chaplain and private secretary during the Trafalgar campaign he proved himself invaluable. Moreover, he brought some other important skills to the job. Scott's services are properly most associated with Nelson, but earlier in his career he also worked for several other noted officers, including Sir John Jervis, Sir Hyde Parker, and Sir John Thomas Duckworth.

Some brief passages from his biography, written by his daughter and son-in-law, are useful to examine for their remarkable account of Scott's activity as a naval "secretary-intelligencer":

> Mr. Scott . . . accepted in May 1795, the invitation of Admiral Sir Hyde Parker, to join him as chaplain of the *St. George* of 98 guns [for service in the West Indies station]. . . .
>
> "Sir John Jervis has employed me [later in 1795] in translating his Italian papers, some of which are of the most material consequence. . . ."
>
> [In 1801 Scott joined HMS *London,* before the Battle of Copenhagen, as] chaplain to the ship, and interpreter and translator of languages to the expedition, by a warrant from the commander-in-chief; . . .
>
> It was not merely a linguist that was wanted, but a diplomatist of skill and tact, and experienced in the negociation of delicate public business. . . . Scott "maintained a correspondence with great honour and credit to himself, with the Crown Prince of Denmark; and that he acted as the confidential friend and adviser of both Sir Hyde Parker and Lord Nelson. . . ."

Admiral Duckworth [found] in Mr. Scott, in addition to his perfect knowledge of the French language, and dexterity in negociation, the [ideal agent, in 1802] for the avowed object of complimenting [French] General Le Clerc, on his presence in the West Indies, [and finding] out in conversation with the French officers, what was really intended by so large a force. . . .

[In 1803 the Peace of] Amiens was dissolved, war was declared anew with France, and Lord Nelson, at a day's notice, was put in command of the Mediterranean fleet, with unusual powers. He instantly desired Mr. Scott to accompany him as chaplain, and his foreign and confidential secretary. . . .

[Nelson was] intrusted with almost unlimited powers. Every English ambassador, envoy, or consul in the Mediterranean was directed to forward to him duplicate despatches, and to receive and obey all orders from him. . . .

The examination of all papers and letters found on board the prizes, as well as of the captains of the vessels, was one of his occupations, and the utmost resources of his readiness in languages, were on some of these occasions called upon, as the vessels came from almost every quarter of the civilized globe. . . .

Lord Nelson made it a point of etiquette, to accompany all his original English letters to foreign courts with translations in their respective languages, and preparing these was an office that occupied much of Dr. Scott's attention; as, besides constant communications with the royal families of Naples and Sardinia, a correspondence was carried on, at intervals, during the greater part of the blockade of Toulon, with the Dey of Algiers. . . .

Besides the graver employments above, Dr. Scott was in the habit of reading to his chief all the French, Italian, Spanish and other foreign newspapers, which were sent regularly to the fleet, and these were ransacked as well for the amusement, as the information they contained. Dr. Scott had also to wade through numberless ephemeral foreign pamphlets, which a mind less investigating than Lord Nelson's would have discarded as totally unworthy of notice; . . .

[Nelson's] quickness in detecting the drift of an author was perfectly marvelous . . . and nothing was too trivial for the attention of this great man's mind, when there existed a possibility of its being the means of obtaining information. . . .

Day after day might be seen the admiral in his cabin, closely employed with his secretary over their interminable papers. They occupied two black leathern armchairs, into the roomy pockets of which, Scott, weary of translating, would occasionally stuff away a score or two of unopened private letters, found in prize ships, although the untiring activity of Nelson grudged leaving one such document unexamined. . . .

[Nelson] spoke of him as "the doctor," for after they became intimate in the *Victory,* he always addressed him as either Doctor or Scott, although he had not yet taken his D.D. degree. . . .

The use derived from [Scott's] abilities as an agent on shore, was even greater than from his employment as foreign secretary. As a confidential agent he was exactly the man required—full of observation —agreeable where-ever he went—able to understand all he heard and saw—whilst his condition as an invalid, and his pursuits as a scholar, facilitated his opportunities. Often, therefore, as he was sent into Spain, to Naples, &c. &c., *apparently* for his pleasure or for the benefit of his health, it was never without some special purpose. . . . The object of those missions was known to himself and the admiral alone at the time they occurred, the business being kept so strictly secret that there is no mention even in the diary, of what took place on any one occasion; a precaution which may also have been dictated by common prudence, as he was constantly liable to fall into the hands of the French faction. . . .

There can be no doubt that the risks he ran were considerable, and . . . when Dr. Scott was absent on these services, Lord Nelson was in a state of the most restless uneasiness and anxiety on his account; and when the few days' absence was over, "was always more pleased to see Dr. Scott safe back, than at the success of his missions" [Readers of O'Brian's novels may well see a parallel here between Nelson/Scott and Aubrey/Maturin]. . . .

It may be stated generally of his employments in Spain, that he was gaining information throughout Catalonia, (which, as a province adjoining France, was overrun by French influence,) and establishing every possible quick means of communication between Madrid, Barcelona, and the fleet.[54]

Both captains and admirals had to be able to analyze the information in their hands, either for their own operational use, or for transmission to their superiors. Otherwise they would be in a pitiable condition, as described by Prof. Michael Handel, for a commander "unable to estimate his capabilities . . . will advance in a stumbling and hesitant manner, looking anxiously first to his right and then to his left, and be unable to produce a plan. Credulous, he will place confidence in unreliable reports, believing at one moment this and at another that."[55]

Lord St. Vincent was always a sharp analyst, never credulous, and always careful. Note this early 1803 letter to Sir Evan Nepean at Whitehall: "The paper of intelligence you have sent me carries strong marks of having been fabricated in London, although it may have come from Paris last. Those who have been accustomed to the Channel can alone judge of the importance to be given to it. Before the ships now preparing for the Mediterranean are dispatched it may be wise to probe this paper of intelligence to the quick."[56]

Here, in March 1801, he criticizes the analyses and actions of others, writing to the Rt. Hon. William Windham:

> The infatuation under which all our engines, civil and military, at Lisbon have acted touching the destination of Ganteaume's Squadron is incomprehensible, for after receiving the best possible evidence of its being actually seen between Tetuan Bay and Marabella, they determined that it was gone to the southward; nor does it appear that any advice boat was sent after Sir Robert Calder to Madeira or Teneriffe after more positive intelligence was received of the enemy being seen off Cartagena.[57]

At times, however, he could believe that the opportunity for collection and analysis was over, and that only action remained. Note the opening of the Battle of St. Vincent, on 14 February 1797—the victory that won him an earldom:

> The fleets . . . were most unevenly matched, a fact which was not confirmed to Sir John Jervis until the dense morning mists clinging to the waters began to part. Amongst the many scraps of conversation recorded of that eventful day, none is more characteristic than that which opened between him and the first captain of the *Victory* at 10:49 A.M.:

"There are eight sail of the line, Sir John."

"Very well, sir."

"There are twenty sail of the line, Sir John."

"Very well, sir."

"There are twenty-seven sail of the line, Sir John; nearly double our own!"

"Enough of that, sir! If there are fifty sail, I will go through them. England badly needs a victory at present."[58]

Adm. Adam Duncan shrewdly analyzed the activity of his Dutch opponent in August 1797. Writing to Lord Spencer, he reported that "since I last did myself the honour to write your lordship we have a little more intercourse with Admiral de Winter by a flag of truce. . . . My own idea it was a frivolous excuse to see our force, and rather think they saw nothing very agreeable."[59]

Lord Keith's abilities as an analyst were so highly respected that he was continuously solicited by Whitehall for his opinions. In February 1806 he replied to the first lord's inquiry, giving his ideas, which he thought

> may prove acceptable to you in forming your arrangements for the protection of the country and its commerce.
>
> As reports vary very considerably respecting the extent of the enemy's invading force, and consequently of the means which it will afford for the conveyance of troops, I subjoin two distinct computations of it—one taken high, the other low; but from either of which it will appear that they have collected a very extensive force for threatening, if not attacking, the coasts of His Majesty's dominions.[60]

Six months earlier, Prime Minister Pitt had written to him directly, asking for his analysis of Mediterranean conditions: "My dear Lord, Some circumstances have arisen which make me very desirous of comparing the opinions of persons acquainted with the subject, on the utility of the different naval stations in the Mediterranean, and I should feel greatly obliged to your Lordship if, from your peculiar knowledge of that part of the world, you would give me without reserve the benefit of your opinion on this important point."[61]

If these examples appear overly simplistic, it is certainly well to note that not all commanders were competent analysts of intelligence or operational issues. If they were, for example, then the assumption that Spanish soldiers would show no more fight than Spanish seamen would not have led to a bloody repulse at Tenerife, and the loss of Rear Admiral Nelson's right arm.[62] Moreover, why were British captains (and admirals), who had had fourteen years to watch, examine, and visit the USS *Constitution* and her sisters, as shocked by their spectacular performances —in the War of 1812—as if they had been new secret weapons? And, finally, how could a Dutch admiral, on 20 January 1795, neither analyze his vulnerability nor assess the enemy's potential and thus allow French cavalry and horse gunners to charge across the ice and capture his entire frozen-in fleet?

As with so many other things, Horatio Nelson's analytic abilities were formidable, and he was seldom shy about sharing his analyses. Like St. Vincent, he analyzed not only information but also sources. For example, as he prepared to meet the threatened French invasion in 1802, the "opinion . . . of old Yawkins, an ex-smuggler, 'a knowing one,' now master of the *King George* cutter, weighed more with him than that of Captain Owen, whose zeal, [Nelson] suspected, had caused him to overlook such *trifles* as tides and sandbanks."[63]

In 1805 Nelson wisely trusted the information given him by Rear Adm. Donald Campbell, of the Portuguese navy, that the French fleet had left the Mediterranean and sailed for the West Indies (for which unneutral act Campbell was subsequently dismissed from his command at the instigation of the French ambassador at Lisbon).[64] A few weeks later, however, and against his better judgment, he erred: "All his instinct told him to seek the enemy at Martinique, but when, at Barbados, he received substantial intelligence from General Brereton, commanding the troops at St. Lucia, that 'it was apparently clear that the enemy had gone south' to attack Trinidad and Tobago, he felt compelled to pursue them there. Not until he arrived off Trinidad on 7 June did he learn that he had been mislead. . . . 'O General Brereton! General Brereton! But for his damned information.'"[65]

Nelson frequently provided analysis for the Admiralty, such as this note from HMS *Victory* on 10 January 1804: "From the information I have received, there is every reason to believe that the Enemy intend sending a force from Corsica, to take possession of the Madalena Islands, with a view to prevent us from using that place as an anchorage."[66]

He also often wrote to the secretaries of state, such as with this analysis of Sardinia: "Such is its present state, that an offer will generally be made of it to the French, if we will not take it, by treaty, or some other way. . . . If France possesses it, Sicily is not safe an hour; and the passage to the Levant is completely blocked up. Pardon me, my Lord, for bringing this important subject again before you: but I really think that I should not do my duty to my Country if I did not."[67]

Upon occasion he appeared to slide into the modern intelligence specialist's narrow focus upon the enemy, rather than upon his own forces —but perhaps this was more jest than reality. Once, at a social affair in London before Trafalgar, he told the company that he "reckoned that France and Spain together had a hundred ships of the line at their disposal. Someone asked, 'How many have *we* in all?' but the baffling reply of an admiral in great good humour was, 'Oh! I do not count *our* Ships.' "[68]

Finally, it must be noted that Nelson's analytical abilities ranged from the broadest strategic issues to the smallest tactical details. A remarkable example of his focus upon detail follows.

In early August 1805, Nelson's fleet was returning from the West Indies, where he had chased Admiral Villeneuve and from where he was now pursuing him back to Europe. A British frigate encountered an American merchant ship; the American had earlier discovered a dismasted, abandoned British privateer, which had apparently been attacked by another ship and partially burned. A log book and other items were taken by the frigate, which ultimately passed them on to the flagship. Lord Nelson was immediately approached, and he quickly worked to explain the mystery to his officers—as well as glean any useful intelligence that he could:

After an attentive examination, he said, "I can unravel the whole: this Privateer had been chased and taken by the two Ships that were seen in the WNW. The Prize master, who had been put on board in a hurry, omitted to take with him his reckoning; there is none in the Log-book: and this dirty scrap of paper, which none of you could make anything of, contains his work for the number of days since the Privateer last set Corvo, with an unaccounted-for run, which I take to have been the chase, in his endeavour to find out his situation by back-reckonings."

"The [seamen's] jackets I find to be the manufacture of France, which prove the Enemy was in possession of the Privateer; and I con-clude, by some mismanagement she was run on board of afterwards by one of them, and dismasted. Not liking delay (for I am satisfied those two Ships [remarked in the log book] were the advanced ones of the French Squadron), and fancying we were close at their heels, they set fire to the Vessel, and abandoned her in a hurry."

"If my explanation, gentlemen, be correct, I infer from it they are gone more to the Northward, and more to the Northward I will look for them."

Subsequent information confirmed that Nelson's analysis was correct in every way.[69]

THERE IS NO DOUBT that intelligence matters, secret information, oper-ational security, and secure communications were constant and important issues for naval commanders during this period. Moreover, the comman-der needed to handle these and all his major responsibilities, plus count-less other details, effectively by himself.

Strategy and diplomacy demanded his attention, particularly in his isolation from higher headquarters due to the abysmally slow commu-nications of the age. Quite often the commander had to use great initia-tive in developing his own local sources of general and intelligence information for, even though there were such items coming to him from his superiors, they were relatively infrequent and insufficient.

In fact, clear communications were a constant problem, due to the vicissitudes of document delivery, but even as much due to the primitive writing technology then available. The clear transmission of information, intelligence or otherwise, varied directly with the speed and clarity with which the commander (and perhaps his secretary) could pass a quill over paper.

The commander, in order to be a successful intelligence officer, had to want to be such. He had to have a frame of mind geared toward intelligence. Many, frankly, did not. As Clausewitz said, a commander in time of war "is constantly bombarded by reports both true and false; by errors arising from fear or negligence or hastiness; by disobedience born of right or wrong interpretations; of ill will; of a proper or mistaken sense of duty; of laziness; or of exhaustion; and by accident that nobody could have foreseen. In short, he is exposed to countless impressions, most of them disturbing, few of them encouraging. . . . If a man were to yield to these pressures, he would never complete an operation."[70]

Some commanders handled these issues very well, constantly analyzing, and constantly thinking ahead:

> "We're not far enough east yet for the Gulf Stream to set us to the nor'rard." said Hornblower.
> "Didn't you say you'd never navigated these waters before?" asked Bush.
> "Yes."
> "Then how—? Oh, I suppose you've been studying." To Bush it was . . . strange that a man should read up beforehand and be prepared for conditions hitherto unknown.[71]

Some always took infinite pains to be successful, such as Lord Cochrane, who "before an attack . . . typically 'reconnoitred in person, took soundings and bearings, passed whole nights in the boats, his lead line and spy glass incessantly at work.'"[72] In fact, Cochrane was truly an original, taking these concepts even further. He "had a scientific bent inherited from his father leading to, among many other innovations, the use of smoke screens and various other ingenious deception and propaganda methods."[73]

Horatio Nelson was like this as well, although certainly not infallible. In fact, with all his wonderful awareness, it is almost amusing to learn that he confused the French ships *Jean Bart* and *Jean Barras,* "a mistake for which Nelson's better knowledge of the names of the members of the French Directory, than of France's naval history, must be held responsible."[74]

Nelson's private secretary, "Doctor" Scott, wrote later that the admiral "possessed the wisdom of the serpent with the innocence of the dove." His other secretary, Mr. John Scott, echoed these remarks: "I have met with no character in any degree equal to his Lordship; his penetration is quick, judgement clear, wisdom great, and his decisions correct."[75]

Nelson was a sophisticated collector, interrogator (he called interrogations "bringing people to the post"),[76] analyst, and disseminator. He was mostly limited by the primitive technology—as were they all. Even Lord Howe—another skillful intelligencer who knew fairly specifically where his enemy was—had to quarter the sea for eight full days before he found them and fought the Battle of the Glorious First of June.[77] Today, with radar, satellites, and aircraft, it would not even be a momentary question.

These were different times in another way. The spirit of chivalry in warfare was still very much alive. For example, after the disaster at Tenerife, and the loss of his arm to Spanish ordnance, Rear Admiral Nelson dictated "a letter to the humane and courteous commandant of the Canaries, begging His Excellency's acceptance of . . . a cask of English beer and a cheese. His Excellency replied, sending his best wishes for the admiral's recovery and a couple of flasks of finest Canary wine, whereupon the admiral gallantly offered to carry to Cadiz His Excellency's despatches for the Court of Spain—'thus making himself the herald of his own defeat.' "[78]

Just as strange to modern thinking, fifteen years later, was British Capt. Philip Broke's challenge to American Capt. James Lawrence for a ship duel. Trying to coax Lawrence, in the *Chesapeake,* out of Boston to fight his *Shannon,* Broke gave away considerable intelligence information in a letter to Lawrence: "As the *Chesapeake* appears now ready for sea," he began, "I request that you will do the favour to meet the *Shannon* with her, ship to ship, to try the fortune of our respective flags. . . ." He listed the armament and crew of the *Shannon,* carefully denied a rumor of a reinforcement of 150 men, and remarked that he was short of provisions and water. Finally, he reminded Lawrence that, as the greater might of the Royal Navy was gathering, it was now or never for such a duel, not for any personal ambitions but for "nobler motives."[79]

As the reader will see in the three naval-intelligence scenarios following this chapter, Lord Nelson's approach contrasts remarkably with Sir Hyde Parker's during the events leading to the great 1801 Battle of Copenhagen, where, ironically, Nelson was Parker's second in command. Nelson, in addition to his other aspects of genius, was masterful in his data gathering, analysis, exploitation, and all-around awareness of intelligence in general.

Having written that, nothing better demonstrates the difficulties of intelligence gathering and reconnaissance in those days of sail and slow communications than, prior to the 1798 Battle of the Nile, the complete failure of the greatest intelligence-oriented admiral of the age to intercept a convoy of four hundred troop transports and forty warships during its leisurely passage, across the whole length of the Mediterranean, from Toulon to Alexandria—with a stop enroute to capture Malta![80]

Nelson's intelligence difficulties during the long Nile campaign aside, it is no exaggeration to say that Sir Hyde was completely oblivious to intelligence at Copenhagen. Moreover, when Rear Admiral Linois's command dilemma is examined at the 1804 Battle of Pulo-Aur, the reader will certainly empathize with that intelligence-oriented commander's desperate need for information—and his inevitable operational failure when he could not get it.

There is no question that it was difficult for the commander to divide his attention between the huge responsibilities of the "line" commander and those of the "staff" intelligence officer. This would be flatly impossible today, with the complexities of modern war; it was barely possible in the late eighteenth century. The integration of intelligence with command decision making proved, at times, overwhelming for many commanders and it is therefore tempting to criticize them for neglecting one over the other. Yet this period saw this phenomenon in full force; Nelson, Wellington, Napoleon, and even Washington, to name a few, managed it very successfully.

In the final analysis, intelligence was but one of the many responsibilities competing for the commander's limited time, attention, and energy. If he did not address it, it did not get done.

8

A Naval Intelligence Occasion
Pulo-Aur, 14–16 February 1804

We are bred up to feel it a disgrace even to succeed by falsehood[,] . . .
that honesty is the best policy, and that truth always wins in the long
run. These pretty little sentiments do well for a child's copy-book,
but a man who acts on them had better sheathe his sword forever.

Sir Garnet Wolseley

TACTICAL DECEPTION WAS REASONABLY EASY DURING THE GREAT age of fighting sail, when extraordinary similarities existed in the design of both warships and merchant ships. Examples are legion; however, not much compares to the successes the huge, commercial British East India Company enjoyed against the French navy in the Indian Ocean.

The standard Company ship, commonly referred to as an "Indiaman," was typically around twelve to fourteen hundred tons and appeared virtually identical in lines and rigging to any of the smaller naval ships of the line. In fact, it is interesting to note that, at the 1801 Battle of Copenhagen, the ship of the line directly astern of Admiral Nelson's had been a Company merchant ship for many years before being bought into the navy (and even more interesting is that HMS *Glatton*'s captain, on that occasion, was the famous William Bligh).[1] In addition, until around 1810, the navies of the world had no standard patterns for exterior paint; it often was left to the taste and private funds of the captain. Moreover, except for officers, there was no standard uniform for personnel, so merchant and naval seamen, with few exceptions, dressed alike.

As a result, despite the East India Company's general procedure of embarking indifferent armament and small crews, their eight-hundred-ton ships could likewise pass for naval frigates even at fairly close quarters. The Company's ships tried to capitalize on these similarities whenever practical, knowing very well that running from every strange sail would, in fact, only advertise their true weak state as relatively defenseless merchantmen. Aggressive tactics, such as steering straight toward French warships or privateers (to say nothing of the pirates of various nationalities that infested eastern waters) often intimidated the pursuer while concealing the Indiaman's true nature.

The finest example of East India Company triumphs over the French navy occurred in February 1804. The Company's great, and unescorted, China Fleet—a collection of sixteen twelve-hundred-ton Indiamen bound for London and eleven "country-trade" ships bound for India—had sailed from Canton in late January. Aside from the value of the ships themselves, the fleet was worth eight million pounds sterling in tea, porcelain, silk, and other goods—a staggering amount for the time. As the fleet approached the Strait of Malacca, it encountered a powerful French squadron including a ship of the line, two frigates, a corvette, and a brig, all under the command of the experienced Rear Adm. Charles Alexandre Léon Durand de Linois. Admiral Linois had received intelligence of the fleet's movements from a spy in Canton; the specific source and details of this espionage-derived information are not clear, but it is important to realize that at this time the Dutch and the French had well-entrenched systems of intelligence and influence throughout the East

Indies. Therefore, Linois was lying in wait for the fleet at a point ideal for interception.

Upon observing the French, the Company's Commo. Nathaniel Dance, on board the Indiaman *Earl Camden,* formed his big ships into a traditional line of battle and ordered the three leading ships to fly the Royal Navy's blue ensign. Linois became concerned; the bold formation and the lack of panic that he observed in the British were markedly contrary to his expectations. Furthermore, his intelligence specified a twenty-four-ship convoy, but he now observed twenty-seven (plus a brig), three of which displayed Royal Navy flags and pennants.

Overnight Linois shadowed the British, attempting to determine the true situation. He later wrote that "if the bold front put on by the enemy in the daytime had been a ruse to conceal his weakness, he would have profited by the darkness to endeavour to conceal his escape, in that case I should have taken advantage of his maneuvers. But I soon became convinced that this security was not feigned; three of his ships constantly kept their lights up, and the fleet continued to lie to in order of battle throughout the night."[2]

The next day Linois decided to initiate action at long range. Commodore Dance, initially dismayed, tried to magnify his bluff. He directed the Indiamen to reverse course and assertively close with the approaching French—as if they really did have three Royal Navy ships of the line in the lead.

After forty-five minutes of ineffectual long-range gunfire from both sides, Admiral Linois became convinced that he was, in fact, engaging a superior force of warships and therefore broke off the attack and withdrew. Commodore Dance found one last twist to his hoax irresistible and ordered his ships to chase the French across the South China Sea for two hours. He then resumed his original course, observing that "a longer pursuit would carry us too far from the mouth of the Straits"—not wise "considering the immense property at stake." Indeed, to appreciate just what kind of money was involved here, we should reflect that the entire

Fig. 8-1 *Sir Nathaniel Dance.*
In command of the British East India Company's ship *Earl Camden,* Dance led the fleet of twenty-seven merchant ships that deceived and evaded French rear admiral Linois's naval squadron at the Battle of Pulo-Aur. Dance, who ultimately served the company for forty-five years (seventeen of those as a captain and commodore), was subsequently honored as a hero. King George III knighted him; he was given a pension of five hundred pounds per annum; the Bombay Insurance Society gave him five thousand pounds; and the company distributed fifty thousand pounds among his officers and men (Miller, *East Indiamen,* 155–35). The original painting is by Smith/Ackermann.
© *National Maritime Museum, London*

Fig. 8-2 *Battle of Pulo-Aur* (14–16 February 1804).
Fought between a French naval squadron, under Rear Adm. Charles Durand
de Linois, and a fleet of British East India Company merchant ships under
Commo. Nathaniel Dance, this action took place in the South China Sea, off
the Strait of Malacca, near the island of Pulo-Aur. The forty-five minutes of
actual fighting are depicted here, with the French lined up to the left and the
largest British ships (acting as bellicose as possible) on the right.
© *National Maritime Museum, London*

budget of the Royal Navy in 1793 was £3,971,915; in 1794, £5,325,332; in
1795, £6,315,523, and in 1796, £7,552,552.[3]

What, exactly, happened here? The East India Company's deceptions
included:

1. Ship design, sail plan, rigging, and exterior paint consistent
with warships.

2. Real gun ports as well as false "painted" gun ports where there
were no actual guns.

3. False, wooden "dummy" cannon that could be pointed out both
real and false gun ports.

4. Relatively inefficient and light "cannonade" guns versus naval

cannons or carronades. Visual examination through a telescope would not differentiate between types.

5. Deck cargo struck below consistent with warship appearance.

6. Seamen attired consistent with naval personnel.

7. Officers attired in coats consistent with Royal Navy uniforms.

8. Ships flying Royal Navy colors, and commissioning pennants, versus East India Company flags.

9. Confident and aggressive ship handling consistent with warships versus that of essentially defenseless merchant ships.

10. Rumors spread (possibly underscored by money passed in Canton) that the fleet included three Indiamen armed as 64-gun ships of the line; such rumors reached Linois via the local Batavian government as well as a Portuguese merchant ship.

11. A naval lieutenant (Mr. Fowler) present who may have supplied tactical instruction and advice to Commodore Dance. In addition, at least three of the company's captains present had previously served in the navy, including Capt. John Timmons of the *Royal George*. Captain Timmons contributed key tactical counsel and assertive leadership.[4]

A description of a cannonade, versus a standard naval cannon or carronade, might be useful here, so in the words of O'Brian's Capt. Jack Aubrey, "conceive of an unlucky bastard cross between [a true cannon and a carronade], something that weighs a mere twenty-eight hundredweight and jumps in the air and breaks its breeching every time you offer to fire it, and that will not strike true at five hundred yards, no not at fifty, and there you have your cannonade."[5]

How did the deception evolve in Linois's mind? Primarily, he was concerned that at least some of the ships he was facing were either bona-fide men-of-war or, possibly, Indiamen armed with significant numbers of effective, true naval cannon. The reader must remember that in case of damage Linois was operating at considerable distances from any reasonable shipyards available to him. He could expect only minor repairs and supplies at the Dutch colony of Batavia; he could expect only a little more from his administrative base at the Isle of France (very southeast in the Indian Ocean); moreover, for any truly significant repair or supply he would have to return all the way to France. In fact, Capt. James L. Grant of the British East India Company's ship *Brunswick,* who was a prisoner onboard Linois's flagship *Marengo* during the action, wrote later that Linois "often confessed to me that, not having any port open to him for resort to in case of an accident happening to his ships, and no possible means of replacing a mast, should he unfortunately lose one, he is under the absolute necessity of acting as a privateer, and that it is therefore impolitic for him to risk the chance of an action, even with an equal force."[6]

As a result, what the British might view as trifling battle damage (with major facilities in India) Linois had to view as unacceptable. O'Brian's analysis, again in the words of Jack Aubrey, underscores the point: "Linois is a year out of a dockyard and he is three thousand miles from the Isle of France: he is short of stores, and a single spar or fifty fathom of two-inch rope is of a hundred times more consequence to him than it is to us —I doubt there is a spare topmast in his whole squadron. In duty he must not risk grave damage: he must not press home his attack against a determined resistance."[7]

In addition, the reader must also remember that the job of commerce raiders is to destroy or capture commercial ships, not to fight warships. Indeed, it is not hard to think of many commerce raiders whose careers were cut spectacularly short by breaking this rule; the css *Alabama,* dkm *Bismarck,* and dkm *Graf Spee* come to mind, to name just a few.

Linois, therefore, was determined not to fight a sea battle, and although he had considerable intelligence as to the composition (and value) of the China Fleet, he was significantly worried that he was facing heavily armed ships as well: "At first merely suspicious, he eventually became convinced that this was the case. The first stage by which he reached this conclusion was attained on the 14th, when twenty-eight sail were counted from the masthead. The second stage was when Bruilhac [captain of the French frigate *Belle Poule*] reported that two of the English ships carried guns on two decks." An Indiaman would typically carry some armament on its upper decks only, even though its lower deck might well appear to have real or painted gunports. The lower-deck area would usually be used up by cargo storage or passenger cabins. However, if guns appeared to be run out and/or gunfire was observed from a lower deck, this would be convincing evidence that the ship really was a warship, or at least an Indiaman armed like a warship. "The third stage was gained as a result of the convoy's resolute aspect; and the fourth as a result of its confident behavior in the action. The final stage in the deception was reached when the English actually pursued him for two hours. That *tactical error* was justified in its *psychological* effect. Linois could not doubt the presence of an escort after that. He broke off the action from fear of being surrounded. It may well have been the pursuit which decided him not to renew it. . . . Linois was not defeated. He was deceived."[8]

In all fairness to Admiral Linois, and to emphasize what was written earlier (the French admiral had a difficult problem, the nature of which most commanders should wish they never have to face), his choices were extremely hard. He had good human intelligence, both in quality and quantity, from Canton, Batavia, and several intercepted ships just before the battle. Other than that, he was reliant on visual information through handmade telescopes, and, to give the British credit, they excelled at making him see what they wanted him to see. The only way he could clearly decide the issue was to approach very near the enemy, continue visual analysis, and to actually draw their fire. Drawing fire at close range would allow him to observe real-versus-false guns, as well as the quantity and quality of gunfire (judging the caliber of gunfire vis-à-vis sound—as well as judging caliber by shot coming on board his ships!), but "the disadvantage of this policy lay in the likelihood of being unable, through damage, to break off an engagement with a force found to be superior."[9] Linois erred on the side of caution, and who can say he was wrong considering the intelligence available to him? After all, many history books teach us to admire the boldness of the American Admiral Farragut at the Battle of Mobile Bay, who said "Damn the torpedoes [naval mines]; full speed ahead!" Most of us are not aware that just prior to that order the USS *Tecumseh* had struck a mine and sunk with all hands. What if more than that one ship had been lost—or his whole squadron? Would we be quite so impressed by Farragut's bold decisiveness then?

What were the results of Dance's extremely successful deception? Linois was castigated by many of his superiors, including Napoleon, who wrote, "The conduct of Admiral Linois is miserable. . . . Tell him that he showed a lack of moral courage—the courage I value most in a leader. . . . Also tell him that I hope he will have done something for the honour of the flag before he returns to France."[10] Unfortunately, this severe reproof did less to spur Linois to greater action than it did toward breaking his spirit.

Commodore Dance and his captains were showered with monetary and titular honors. Moreover, although this was a tactical deception involving a relatively few ships, the strategic implications cannot be stressed enough. Had the deception failed, or had Linois acted just a little more boldly upon the otherwise good intelligence he possessed, there is no question that the entire China Fleet would have been captured. The loss of eight million pounds would have undoubtedly broken the enormous East India Company, and quite possibly the insurance underwriters of Lloyd's along with it. The failure of either of these two key institutions would have caused devastation within the City—the financial center of London—and therefore within the British Empire. What detrimental effects this would have had on the British war effort are beyond this writer's competence to analyze, but O'Brian describes it elegantly: "A fleet worth [eight] million of money has been saved; and the country, to say nothing of the Company, would have been in a strange position if it had been lost."[11]

Suffice it to say that the British reaction can be encapsulated by the comments of Vice Adm. Peter Rainer, commander in chief of the East Indies Station, who heard of the outcome with a mixture of relief and astonishment. He referred to the "fortunate escape made by the China Fleet" as a "most extraordinary circumstance," which is a truly remarkable understatement even for a people famous for such things.

9

A Naval Intelligence Expedition

Copenhagen, 9 December 1800–2 April 1801

Was our fleet off Copenhagen, . . . the Danish Minister would seri-
ously reflect how he brought the fire of England on his master's fleet
and capital; but to keep [the fleet] out of sight is to seduce Denmark
into war. . . . I hate your pen-and-ink men; a fleet of British ships of
war are the best negotiators in Europe.

Lord Nelson

AFTER ALMOST NINE CONTINUOUS YEARS OF WARFARE IN EUROPE, the opening of the nineteenth century saw a shifting in the balance of power. France had conquered Austria once more, while Russia had effectively withdrawn from the war. Russia's unstable Czar Paul I had developed a bitter hostility toward Austria and Britain, while conceiving a solid admiration for Napoleon Bonaparte, the "first consul" of France. In addition, Paul was particularly angered by the refusal of Britain to yield to him possession of the Mediterranean island of Malta, which he felt was his due as titular grand master of the Maltese knights of St. John.

France's star was ascending as Britain's prestige and influence corre-spondingly declined. Moreover, the manipulative first consul of France, the mad czar of Russia, the mindless king of Denmark (and Norway),

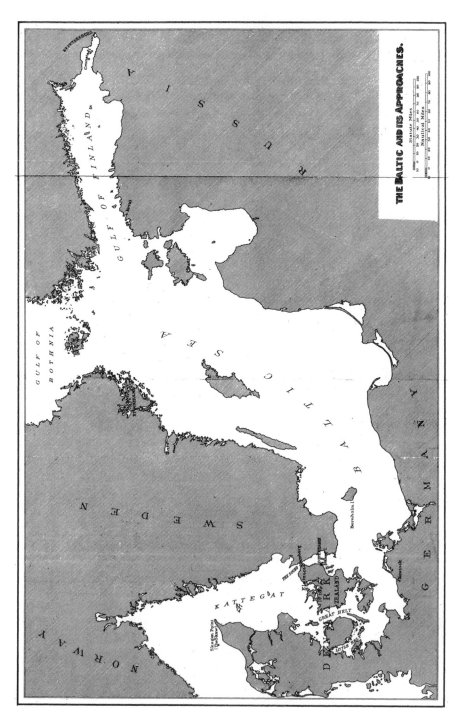

Map 9-1 The Baltic Sea and Its Approaches

the indecisive king of Prussia, and the unbalanced king of Sweden were about to precipitate a terrible crisis in northern Europe, adding a new threat to Britain as grave as had yet been faced since 1793:[1] "Towards the end of 1800 Bonaparte, playing upon the resentment of the Northern Powers at British interference with their trade, encouraged those States to revive the League of Armed Neutrality, which, comprising Russia, Sweden, Denmark, and Prussia, was pledged to resist the belligerent rights at sea claimed and enforced by Great Britain. The customary rights of search and seizure were boldly challenged. The neutral rights now proclaimed struck at the very foundations of British naval power."[2]

Britain had no routine naval presence in the Baltic; however, the British trade that flowed through this sea was essential, particularly with regard to materials for the navy. In addition, "between them the Armed Neutrals disposed of a fleet of well over a hundred sail of the line, twenty-four of which were immediately available. The Armed Neutrality threatened both to disrupt the blockade of France and to close the Baltic to British commerce, thereby depriving [the] country of Baltic grain and the timbers and naval stores which were vital to the Fleet."[3]

The passage of trade was crucial. So was the blockade; at this stage of the war it was practically the only weapon effectively working against France. In fact, prior to the much later invention and deployment of railway systems, one of the most effective weapons of sea power was the blockade of enemy ports: "The prevention of the transport of goods by sea meant over a large area the transport of goods at all."[4]

On or about 9 December 1800, the British secretary of state for the Foreign Office, William Wyndham (Baron Grenville), was informed —probably verbally from either the Swedish or Danish ministers in London—that the League of Armed Neutrality was reforming. Grenville immediately sent this intelligence to his envoys in Copenhagen, Berlin, and Vienna, writing them that the accuracy "cannot be doubted," and instructing them to seek out more information.[5] On 14 December it was confirmed that the Armed Neutrality agreement was signed and ratified by the aforementioned powers. Moreover, Russia simultaneously seized

Fig. 9-1 *Battle of Copenhagen; View from Amager.*
Looking northward across Nyeholm. Note the mast of the telegraph station, silhouetted in the very center of the image above the row of buildings along the waterfront. The painting was done by C. A. Lorentzen; the engraving was done by I. F. Clemens; the original is owned by the Frederiksborg Museum, Denmark.
© *National Maritime Museum, London*

three hundred British merchantmen that were in Russian ports, and sealed all warehoused British property in those ports.[6]

Britain just could not allow this threat to coalesce and build, which if allowed much time at all could be backed with more than fifty operational ships of the line. Denmark was the greatest immediate threat. Relative to Prussia, Russia, and Sweden, its navy was efficient; in addition, Denmark was strategically placed at the entry to the Baltic. Toward the end of December the British envoy in Copenhagen, William Drummond, sent intelligence to the Admiralty that "the Danes pretend they will have at least twenty ships-of-the-line ready before Spring. The number may be about fifteen[,] . . . with five frigates, three brigs, and two cutters."[7]

James Talbot, British chargé d'affaires in Stockholm, relayed the Swedish situation to Lord Grenville on 13 January 1801. He reported that there were "no batteries worth mentioning" along the coast of the

Skagerrak, and that "upon a great emergency" the Swedes perhaps could sortie eleven ships of the line—although several were old. On 16 January his intelligence dispatch reported that six Swedish ships of the line and several frigates were "immediately to be got ready" at Gothenburg, but "whether or no the number of good seamen necessary to man this Fleet are to be procured, I cannot pretend to say. . . . The government sailors for the most part have not been exercised since the Russian War [1789]."[8]

Meanwhile, the British government was having some concern with a complicating intelligence problem: the newspapers were publishing information that the government wished to remain secret. The nation's press was having great success keeping the British people, as well as foreign diplomats and agents, very much apprised as to what was going on, for

> the Press, and thus the people, was well informed . . . because it had good sources of news inside the Government itself and, perhaps more important, because influential people gossiped. Nor was there any form of voluntary or compulsory censorship to prevent the publication of secret information of use to the enemy. Politicians, admirals, and generals made their plans and sent off their orders marked "Secret"—and then all too often discussed them at dinner or in the drawing room after joining the ladies.
>
> It was almost impossible to launch a large-scale operation secretly against the enemy, so that surprise, the essential element of any attack, was almost always missing. The only thing that saved many expeditions from disaster was the fact that although the enemy had learned of British intentions, he had no chance—because of the blockade or the difficulties of transport—to make proper dispositions. Fortunately for Britain . . . other nations conducted their business in a similar way.[9]

On 5 January, the London *Times* reported, "The Public will learn, with great ſatisfaction, that Lord NELSON is about to be employed on a SECRET EXPEDITION, and will hoiſt his flag in the courſe of a very few days. . . . There is reaſon to believe his deſtination is to a diſtant quarter, where his Lordſhip's perſonal appearance alone would preponderate over the influence or the intrigues of any Court in Europe."[10]

This information was true enough, and sent reasonably clear mes-

Fig. 9-2 *The Battle of Copenhagen, 1801*
Painted by Nicholas Pocock (1740–1821) in 1806.
© *National Maritime Museum, London*

sages to British and foreign readers. On 6 January the government probably attempted to throw off the scent by causing the following to be
printed in the *Times:* "Vice Admiral Lord Nelson will hoist his flag in a
few days for the supposed purpose of proceeding with a squadron to the
Dardanelles, [perhaps] to chastise the insolence of the Russians in that
quarter."[11]

The *Times* also had this to say, on the sixth, commenting on Adm. Sir
Hyde Parker's recent marriage to an eighteen-year-old girl: "It is ſaid
that Sir HYDE PARKER has ſolicited his leave of abſence from his command to be extended, as it could make [his] honey-moon much too
ſhort, and the bliſs too tranſient."[12]

On the tenth there appeared more confusing reporting—either poor
speculation on the part of the *Times* or planted information by the government: "Lord KEITH is certainly coming home. It is believed Lord

NELSON will have a detachment from the Mediterranean Fleet placed under his command."[13] Then on 13 January the *Times* reported that "yefterday Lord NELSON took his leave of the Lords of the Admiralty, and this morning his Lordfhip will pofitively leave town to hoift his flag. We have reafon to know that his deftination is NOT for the Baltic."[14] On Thursday, 15 January, it reported, "Lord NELSON left Town on Tuefday morning for Plymouth, and will proceed immediately to the Mediterranean. . . . We are led to believe his Lordfhip will visit *Constantinople*. . . . Nor can the appearance of a British Fleet in the *Dardanelles* be without its effect upon that Power of the Baltic [Russia] whofe ambitions extend to *Byzantium*."[15]

It is interesting to note Nelson's reaction to these reports. In a letter to his friend, Hercules Ross, he wrote that "there is not the smallest foundation for the report of my going to the Mediterranean, nor of Lord Keith's coming home at present. I rather believe my destination is Northwards."[16]

During this time the Admiralty (under the Earl Spencer as first lord) was, of course, gathering intelligence, considering plans, and making preparations. They had received another intelligence report from envoy Drummond in early January: "Scarcely fifteen [Danish] sail of the line can be fitted out, although eighteen may be put in a condition to defend the Sound. All the frigates and small vessels are supposed to be in a state of readiness."[17] As noted earlier, Drummond's communications with London were almost always sent in cipher.

At this point the Admiralty was comfortable in its order of battle information concerning the Royal Danish Navy. In fact, intelligence was coming into the Admiralty from many different sources. Note this belated thanks from Adm. Lord St. Vincent to Lt. Gen. John G. Simcoe, in charge of the Western Command: "I am very much ashamed not to have thanked you for the important communication . . . of the state of Cronenberg and Copenhagen, when besieged by the King of Sweden. . . . You may rely on my care of it."[18]

Moreover, on 2 February, Nelson wrote to the newly appointed prime minister, Henry Addington, and described a conversation he had had with this same General Simcoe at Plymouth, wherein he had gained valuable information about Zealand and Copenhagen's fortifications. Nelson further commented that while he appreciated the intelligence, he did not disclose much information to Simcoe in return, not feeling at liberty to discuss that it was likely he would be soon employed there.[19]

In fact, events were picking up speed. On 13 January, upon receipt of a letter from the Danish foreign minister indicating a peaceful solution was all but impossible, the government of Prime Minister William Pitt moved for decisive action. King George endorsed his minister's alarm, writing on 15 January that he had long wished to bring the Armed Neutrality's threat to an issue, and that he had not "admired the constant attempt for above twenty years to avoid it. . . . If properly withstood, we must get the better, and truly, if we do not, the boasted power of Great Britain, as a maritime State, is entirely delusive. If this will not rouse men, we are fallen low indeed."[20]

With the king's concurrence, a secret war letter was sent out by the secretary of state for the Home Department, William Henry Cavendish-Bentinck (the third Duke of Portland). Addressed to "The Governors of All His Majesty's Possessions in the Mediterranean, North America, Cape of Good Hope, St. Helena, East Indies, West Indies," it read: "In the present state of affairs between this country and the Powers of Russia, Denmark and Sweden, His Majesty has judged it expedient that all Ships of War or vessels of any description belonging to those Powers . . . which are at present arrived, or which may arrive within the limits of your Government should be prevented from putting to sea until further orders."[21]

The secretary of state for War, Henry Dundas, required the Admiralty to order all captains "to detain and bring into the nearest port belonging to His Majesty all ships belonging to Russia, Denmark and Sweden 'which they may meet with at sea.'"[22] The secretary of state for Foreign Affairs, Lord Grenville, communicated the news to his envoys abroad.

The enciphered dispatch to Drummond, at Copenhagen, stated that as there was reason to believe that "measures may immediately be adopted in Denmark for laying an embargo on British property there, you are immediately . . . to destroy all your ciphers and secret papers." Drummond's reply had a twentieth-century ring about it: "I have destroyed all my secret letters; but, from the apparent omission of a cipher, I was thrown into some perplexity. Imagining, however, that your Lordship apprehended the forcible seizure of the archives I caused all the ciphers . . . to be burnt."[23]

The *Times* continued to be helpful; on Friday, 23 January, it reported: "We learn from the most refpectable authority, that Sir Hyde Parker is to have command of the Fleet deftined to act in the Baltic."[24] The following day it said, "Yefterday arrived the Mail from *Hamburgh.* . . . All the intelligence brought by it breathes the language of war and preparation in the *Baltic.* From the tone and tenor of the anfwer of the COURT OF COPENHAGEN to the categorical Memorial of Mr. DRUMMOND, there is no longer any room for hope from negociation and adjuftment."[25]

These newspaper articles actually gave Nelson himself the only information he had had for a few days as to what was going on. Another article two days later stated that "Captain DOMMETT will be Captain of the fleet deftined for the Baltic, under the orders of Sir HYDE PARKER."[26] Another, on the twenty-seventh, reported that Lord Nelson "is about to hoift his flag on board the *St. Jofeph* in the Channel Fleet, on which fervice he will continue till the opening of the Baltic . . . and act as fecond to Sir HYDE PARKER."[27] One more, on the twenty-eighth, read that the fleet "deftined for the Baltic will begin to be affembled next week. Sir HYDE PARKER and Lord NELSON are both going to Portfmouth to make the neceffary arrangements. Lord NELSON is to lead the [main body] into action."[28]

In fact, the government had taken further steps vis-à-vis decisive action. Previous newspaper speculation notwithstanding, they *were* going to send a fleet into the Baltic under the command of Admiral Parker.

The ships were to be drawn from the Channel Fleet blockading French ports. The risk that the French fleet, blockaded in Brest, would take advantage of this shift in forces and sortie was assessed as acceptable.[29]

Lord Nelson was designated as second in command, while Rear Adm. Thomas Graves and Rear Adm. Thomas Totty were the third and fourth flag officers to be deployed. The fleet included eighteen ships of the line and thirty-five smaller vessels, judged as a full admiral's command. Sir Hyde was selected because he had a fair reputation as an able administrator, because he had been involved in planning a similar expedition in 1781, and, of course, because of his seniority.[30] In Adm. Lord St. Vincent's opinion, Parker was best suited to engage in negotiation—he was certainly not "known as a fighting admiral but neither was it certain that there was to be any fighting."[31] In any event, if there were to be battle, St. Vincent thought that "Nelson will act the fighting part very well."[32]

The situation continued to gain complexity. On 22 January, Drummond forwarded the following intelligence to Lord Grenville: "I have very good reason to think that a proposal for an alliance between Russia and Holland has been made on the part of [Holland], and has been acceded to by the Emperor."[33]

Plans and preparations for the expedition accelerated, unaltered even by the major changes in the British government precipitated by the early February resignation of Prime Minister Pitt. The new administration of Henry Addington—which included Robert Banks Jenkinson (Baron Hawkesbury) as secretary of state for the Foreign Office and Adm. Sir John Jervis (the Earl of St. Vincent) as first lord of the Admiralty—saw the situation in the same light as did the old. They quickly dispatched the Hon. Nicholas Vansittart to Copenhagen ahead of the fleet, in the hope that diplomatic persuasion might turn Denmark from the league. They had some reason to think that his mission might meet with success, for they had recently received a secret "communication from Prince Charles of Hesse, intimating that the Danish Government might be detached from the Northern Coalition. . . . This communication from a brother-in-law of the King of Denmark appeared to the Government to be so important that they wished to avail themselves of it as speedily as possible."[34] As it turned out, this intelligence did not reflect the Danish government's real views at all; in actuality they were much more "truculent than conciliatory."[35]

By 12 February the Admiralty had developed a very detailed plan for the Baltic Fleet, including the following note from an Admiralty Board meeting showing due concern for operational security: "Sir Hyde Parker to hoist his flag when the *London* arrives at Spithead. . . . The squadron should not assemble, nor should any display of preparations be made until a very short time before it is to sail, that the expectation of it may not render the enemy more active in their preparations."[36]

Previously, on 22 January, another board meeting note had shown additional security precautions on the part of the Admiralty: "As there is reason to believe that the enemy have possession of both the private and public signals, it is judged proper to make an alteration in them."[37]

Meanwhile, the *Times* and other papers continued to publish mixtures of highly secret information and wild inaccuracies, such as, "Admirals Sir Hyde Parker and Lord Nelson are expected to sail immediately for the North Sea. . . . As we are doomed to fight our way to peace by victory, we anticipate, with the highest satisfaction, the new laurels which are preparing for our gallant seamen; and soon shall we see Lord Nelson lead the van into the harbour of Cronstadt, and serve the Russians as he did the French at Aboukir."[38]

In early February Nelson started to see the plan taking form. Writing to Lady Hamilton on the first, he told her that he had received "an order to hoist my flag in the *St. George,* as Lord Spencer says I must go forth as the Champion of England in the North."[39]

On 4 February, Nelson, on board the *San Josef,* wrote the following, demonstrating that the weather factor was always potentially disrupting to naval communications in this era: "It blows so very hard that I doubt if it will be possible to get a boat on shore [at times for two or three days together], either to receive or send letters, but if it moderates in time for the post of course mine shall go."[40]

By mid-February Nelson received official instructions; writing to Lady Hamilton on 19 February, he observed that he had just "got my orders to put myself under Sir Hyde Parker's orders, and suppose I shall be ordered to Portsmouth tomorrow or next day, & then I will try & get to London for 3 days."[41] In fact, he spent 24–26 February on leave in London, unnoticed by the press, which predicted twenty-four hours *after* his arrival that he was likely "to come to town before he sailed for the Baltic in order to attend councils and fix plans of campaign."[42]

In the next few days several bits of good fortune enhanced the intelligence ability of the fleet. First, the Rev. Alexander John Scott was recruited by Sir Hyde as his chaplain; they had sailed together earlier in a similar relationship which was to be successfully renewed at this time. As developed in chapter 7—and this is not the reason that Parker offered him the job—Scott was a scholar gifted in languages and he busily acted as a translator. Foreign newspapers and other materials were good sources of intelligence, which he well exploited.[43] To best prepare, Scott, on his own initiative, bought a Danish grammar and dictionary from a commercial bookseller. As Russian dictionaries were unobtainable, he luckily was given a copy of *Elemens de la Langue Russe* by a friend.[44]

Second, Capt. Nicholas Tomlinson, who had previously commanded a Russian ship of the line in the shoal and rocky waters of the Baltic, volunteered to serve without pay and to share his knowledge. Tomlinson provided charts, plans, memoranda, and key intelligence on the Baltic, the Russian mentality, and the state of the Russian fleet. A grateful Admiralty accepted this offer, for in the days before an organized intelligence office or a fully developed hydrographic department, such information was otherwise unavailable to the navy.[45]

Captains and masters of ships usually had to obtain their own charts rather than be issued official ones from the government. Here Nelson was assisted by his friend Alexander Davison, who privately purchased a number of charts for Nelson to use (Faden's at Charing Cross being one commercial source).[46]

St. Vincent brought another source to the attention of Sir Hyde, writing that a Mr. English had been superintendent of the arsenal at St. Petersburg for eight years: "He is ready to go all lengths with you; and if, after conversing with him, you are of opinion that he will be of use, order him to be received and well entertained by some good fellow of your Squadron."[47] Similarly, St. Vincent recommended Capt. Frederick Thesiger to Nelson, knowing that Nelson always valued any source of good intelligence. Thesiger also brought a wealth of experience, having commanded Russian ships against Sweden. Moreover, he spoke both Russian and Danish.[48] Nelson wrote the following to St. Vincent on 1 March:

> The wind was yesterday at S.S.W., which has prevented *Warrior, Defence,* and *Agincourt* from sailing. Time, my dear Lord, is our best Ally, and I hope we shall not give her up, as all our Allies have given us up.
>
> Our friend [Parker] here is a little nervous about dark nights and fields of ice, but we must brace up; these are not times for nervous systems. . . .
>
> I have not seen Captain Thesiger here, I shall receive him with much pleasure; if he is still in Town pray send word to him to meet me in the Downs or Yarmouth.[49]

Indeed Tomlinson, English, and Thesiger had gained their experience while on authorized, detached service with the Russian navy and government. This was reasonably common in this era. In fact, during a brief period of frustration Nelson himself had, years before, considered this option; a note in his wife's hand tells that "he once spoke of the Russian service."[50]

As it turns out, Parker essentially disregarded the valuable experience of these officers. This is partially due to his cautious nature, but it is also due to his apparent inability to ask advice of mere captains—and worse—captains who had taken leave from British service to sail under foreign flags. He is reported to have totally ignored Tomlinson's presence on board his flagship.[51]

Another insight into Parker's mindset can be gleaned from his first meeting with Nelson. In early March, Parker, Nelson, and Lt. Col. the Hon. William Stewart met at Parker's hotel. Stewart was the commander of the small military detachment that was to accompany the fleet, six hundred men of the Forty-ninth and Ninety-fifth Regiments.[52] While completely gracious to his visitors, Sir Hyde shortly withdrew to join his new wife; there had been, to Nelson's and Stewart's amazement, no discussion of a date for sailing, no reference to navigational issues, no interest in comparing charts, no remarks on any plan to attack the Danes or Russians, nor even any disclosure that there was the slightest interest in crossing the North Sea.[53] Nelson, apart from any personal considerations, was appalled for professional reasons: an important part of his own success in the past had been that he always made sure his subordinates had as much information as possible about his intentions and, when possible, gave them an insight into the way he thought.[54] Indeed, Nelson was dumbfounded. It was one thing for an admiral to disdain advice from a junior officer; it was quite another for a senior officer to withhold information and direction from key subordinates. "But," historian Carola Oman notes in her biography of Nelson, "he found himself, as days passed, ostentatiously excluded from conference."[55]

On 7 March he wrote to his friend, Capt. Sir Thomas Troubridge, who was currently a member of the Board of Admiralty:

> I was in hopes that Sir Hyde would have had a degree of confidence [in me] but no appearance of it. . . . I have . . . no other desire of knowing anything than that I may the better execute the service. . . . [Do] not say a word of it to Lord St. Vincent, for he may think me very impertinent in endeavouring to dive into the plans of my C.-in-C.; but, the water being clear, I can see bottom with half an eye.
>
> Poor [captain of the fleet] Dommett seemed in a pack of trouble. Get rid of us [order us to sail], dear friend, and we shall not be tempted to lay abed.[56]

Perhaps Sir Hyde felt that caution and deliberation were essential. Perhaps he was in no hurry to discuss his orders with his fire-eating subordinate, who, he may have feared, would likely press him for some

aggressively reckless action that could end in a disaster—and thus kept
him at a distance.[57] After all, as historian C. Northcote Parkinson commented, "It is no real advantage to have a known hero as one's second-
in-command."

Meanwhile, Sir Hyde had written to First Secretary Nepean asking
for the "private signals" issued the first day of the month. He further
wrote that since he had discovered the Admiralty had recently published "a new edition of Signal Books with all the corrections, I am to
beg you will order a few to be sent to me. . . . Do not forget a copy of the
chart of Lord Mulgrave's of the soundings &c. up to Copenhagen."
Nepean may have wondered why Parker was asking him to obtain the
chart, for Mulgrave's house in Harley Street was well within walking
distance of Parker's.[58]

On 4 March the *Times* reported that "the Baltic fleet will begin to be
affembled this day. The workmen in the Dock-yards work by candle-
light morning and evening to get the fhips ready for fea. Orders are
iffued to detain all Ruffians, Danes, and Swedes now ferving on board
any of his Majefty's fhips of war."[59] This was followed three days later
by news that "the fleet to which our caufe is confided will fail to-mor-
row from Yarmouth, if the wind permits. The Van will be led by the
CONQUEROR OF ABOUKIR [Nelson], to whofe immortal name every epithet
is detraction."[60]

On 12 March the fleet finally proceeded to sea, spurred on by a letter
from St. Vincent to Parker; the specific problem had been Parker's inability to analyze various issues relative to his professional reputation. He
had been intending to further delay sailing in order to attend a ball being
given by his new wife, but St. Vincent made the situation clear, writing
that he had "upon a consideration of the effect your continuance at
Yarmouth an hour after the wind would admit of your sailing would
produce, sent down a messenger purposely to convey to you my opinion,
as a private friend, that any delay in your sailing would do you irreparable injury."[61]

The *Times* next had the following to report: "The wind having changed to the Southward, we have reaſon to believe that the Fleet deſtined for the Baltic ſailed yeſterday from Yarmouth Roads. . . . Should the wind continue fair, we may expect some important intelligence from *Copenhagen* towards the latter end of next week. Never did a Fleet ſail from the ſhores of England with more juſt and animated preſages of victory. . . . The vigilance and activity of the late, as well as of the preſent Board of Admiralty upon this occaſion, are above all praiſe."[62]

By the sixteenth the news of the fleet's sailing had reached Copenhagen, where defensive measures were increased. As the fleet approached the Skagerrak in gale-force winds, dismal and freezing weather, and then remarkably thick fog, Sir Hyde lost confidence in his position. As a result, on 16 March, he ordered the hourly use of one of the era's most interesting "sensors," the deep-sea lead. This device, cast from the ship's side, was a weight attached to a long line. The weight had a cavity into which tallow could be placed. Therefore, when the lead was cast not only was the depth of water determined, but by examining the sample of the sea bottom stuck on the tallow, a pilot could confirm his position. Because the sea bottom varied from fine sand to coarse mud, and these areas were reasonably well plotted in the highly used sea lanes, an experienced navigator could—by the sight, smell (and taste) of the sample—correlate his position with courses steered, wind direction, experience, and his chart.[63]

Nelson was unhappy with the horrible visibility and weather, but even more so with Parker. In a letter to his friend Davison, dated the sixteenth, he wrote, "We have received much snow and sharp frost. I have not yet seen my Commander-in-Chief, and have had no official communication whatever. All I have gathered of our first plans, I disapprove most exceedingly; honour may arise from them, good cannot."[64]

On 17 March, HMS *Cruizer* was sent to reconnoiter, returning with the information that the British fleet was sixty miles off position. Definite news of the fleet's approach reached Copenhagen on 25 March, when the British finally arrived off the fishing village of Hornbæk. This confirmed a secondary source of news that had been transmitted by the Kronborg-Copenhagen telegraph discussed in chapter 3.[65]

In fact, negotiations had failed. Drummond's passport had been returned to him; Vansittart's mission had been for naught. The Danes were far too intimidated by the Russians to withdraw from the league. Indeed, they appeared actively hostile. Drummond had sorted out the embassy's archives, destroying some papers and packing the rest. He and the British consul at Elsinore, William Fenrick, left Danish territory on board the frigate that had brought Vansittart to Denmark.[66]

This ship, HMS *Blanche,* reached the fleet on 23 March. Drummond informed Sir Hyde of the situation, including his personal assessment of the state of Danish preparations. Unfortunately, Drummond, while an excellent diplomat, was a poor military analyst. More unfortunate, Parker took his information at face value as if it had come from a military expert. He was totally intimidated by what he heard, and so wrote the Admiralty, focused upon the "many additional Batteries at Cronenburgh [Kronborg] Castle, [and] also the number of Hulks and Batteries which have been placed and erected for the defence of the Arsenal at Copenhagen."[67] Moreover, Sir Hyde then discussed the situation with his civilian pilots, but not with the captain of the fleet nor with his subordinate flag officers. These pilots, with no enthusiasm for any possible approaching combat, fed Parker's misgivings as to the dangers of an attack.[68]

Parker began to base major decisions upon one man's assessment of the Danish defense. He did not take into account that Drummond was a layman, nor did he realize that he had other sources of information he could draw upon. Capt. Graham Hamond of the *Blanche* had spent three days at Kronborg and studied it very carefully. Lt. Thomas McCulloch had made the Kronborg-Copenhagen journey twice, with plenty of opportunity to observe the Danish fleet as well as the batteries defending the city. Moreover, both of these officers were not laymen and had made their observations with trained eyes. Yet Parker was content only to seek advice from a diplomat; asking the opinions of two inferior naval

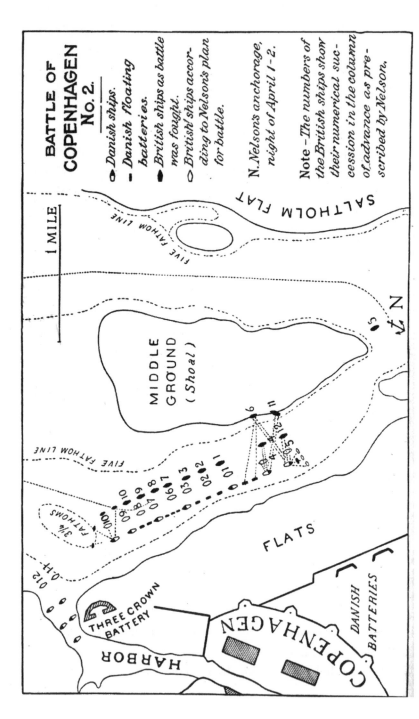

Fig. 9-3 *Battle of Copenhagen; Diagram.*
This illustration is gratefully borrowed from Capt. A. T. Mahan's classic book, *The Life of Nelson.*

officers apparently did not occur to him. He also missed an enormous intelligence-collection opportunity by sending the *Blanche* to Elsinore, versus Copenhagen, to take dispatches for Vansittart; Captain Hamond could have easily returned with detailed plottings of the Danish order of battle as well as the count and size of the batteries.[69]

However, Sir Hyde did finally signal Nelson to come aboard the flagship. "Now we are sure of fighting I am sent for," thought Nelson, "when it was a joke I was kept in the background."[70] There Parker, Nelson, and Vansittart met alone. Vansittart's views on the situation echoed Drummond's, for the same reasons. But now Nelson was given the opportunity to question Vansittart and later Drummond in detail, and in so doing was able to extract more precise intelligence about Copenhagen's defenses than either man realized he possessed.[71] Moreover, Parker gained a new appreciation for Nelson from these conferences. Indeed, it was clear that Sir Hyde had begun "to realize Nelson had a remarkable ability to pick the significant point from a welter of bewildering facts—or, as in this case, realize its omission."[72]

Nelson now thought he knew enough to proceed and was determined to get Parker into action. There had been considerable debate as to what was the safest passage to take; Nelson was indifferent, though he would have pressed through the Sound had he been in command. Colonel Stewart, in a report he wrote later on the campaign, saw it as follows: "The formidable reports which had been made by Mr. Vansittart, and by the Pilots whom we had brought with us . . . induced the Commander-in-Chief to prefer the circuitous passage by the Great Belt. Lord Nelson, who was impatient for action, was not much deterred by these alarming representations: his object was to go to Copenhagen, and he said 'Let it be by the Sound, by the Belt, or anyhow, only lose not an hour.'"[73]

Nevertheless, Nelson was this time more diplomatic in dealing with a superior officer than may be usually credited. He returned to the *St. George,* further evaluated the situation, and then drafted a long letter to Parker; he intended to send it across to the *London* the next day. It was a brilliant analysis and a precise, focused communication of the strategic issues. As it turned out he delivered it in person, reading the draft to Parker in "his high-pitched, nasal voice."[74] This is the essence:

> Not a moment should be lost in attacking the Enemy: they will every hour be stronger; we never shall be so good a match for them as at this moment. The only consideration is how to get at them with the least risk to our Ships. . . . On your decision depends, whether our Country shall be degraded in the eyes of Europe, or whether she shall rear her head higher than ever.
>
> I begin with supposing you are determined to enter by the Sound. . . . You are now above Cronenburg [Kronborg]; if you attack you must expect Ships crippled, and one or two lost; for the wind which carries you in will not bring out a cripple. This I call taking the bull by the horns. It will not, however, prevent the Revel [in the Gulf of Finland] Ships, or the Swedes, from joining the Danes; and to prevent this is absolutely necessary—and still to attack Copenhagen.
>
> One way is to pass Cronenburg and up the deepest Channel past the Middle Ground, and then down the King's Channel, to attack their Floating batteries, &c. This must prevent a junction between the Russians, Swedes and Danes, and may allow us to bombard Copenhagen.
>
> Should this be impracticable, the passage of the Belt could be accomplished in four or five days, and then the attack carried out and the junction of the Russians prevented.
>
> Supposing us through the Belt, would it not be possible either to go with the Fleet, or to detach ten Ships to Revel, to destroy the Russian Squadron? I see no great risk in such a detachment, leaving the remainder to do the business at Copenhagen.
>
> The measure may be thought bold, but I am of the opinion the boldest measures are the safest; and our Country demands a most vigorous exertion of her force, directed with judgement.[75]

Parker was convinced to press on. He continued to gain an appreciation for Nelson's "grasp of both the strategic and tactical situation . . . his remarkable ability to pinpoint . . . advantages and disadvantages, and his instinctive knowledge of when to accept and when to reject a great gamble."[76]

Nelson himself realized that Parker was looking at him in a new light; writing to Lady Hamilton, he remarked, "Sir Hyde Parker has by this time found out the worth of your Nelson and that he is a useful sort of man in a pinch. Therefore, if he has ever thought unkindly of me, I freely forgive him."[77]

Most likely at Nelson's suggestion, on the twenty-seventh Parker sent the *Cruizer* to examine several merchant ships that had come through the sound from Hamburg; they reported "consternation and confusion" at Copenhagen.[78] Nelson then sent the *Cruizer,* the *Blanche,* and two bomb (mortar) vessels close in to Kronborg. The *Cruizer*'s captain, James Brisbane, was able to report that the Danish batteries there were "of a low and weak construction," and that the enemy "appeared to be evidently under considerable alarm," unknowingly contradicting the information of Drummond and Vansittart.[79]

What no one in Denmark, nor in the British fleet, knew at this time was that on the night of the twenty-fourth Czar Paul had been strangled in his bed by some of his own nobles and officials in the Mikhaylovski Palace. This news, which would have radically altered the sequence of events, would be three weeks in getting to Copenhagen.

At this point Parker received a coincidental communication from the Danish crown prince; translated somewhat imperfectly by Reverend Scott, the tone and phraseology of this message nevertheless implied a new willingness to negotiate. Unfortunately, Parker did not recognize this change in attitude; moreover, he did not show the message to Nelson, who may have seen its significance. Nelson probably would have recognized the shift in the enemy's posture "and seen it as a chance to deal with the Danish Fleet quickly by diplomatic means while leaving the British Fleet undamaged to go straight on to deal with the Russians."[80]

At first the fleet proceeded toward the Great Belt, between the main Danish islands of Zealand and Fyn, which Parker had decided to use as his route to Copenhagen. However, when Robert Otway (the *London*'s captain) learned of this plan—thus far not having been included in the flag-level deliberations—he brought forth personal knowledge of that route which he had gained in previous Baltic operations. When he outlined the difficulties and dangers to Sir Hyde, the latter concluded that running past Kronborg presented a lesser risk.[81]

In anticipation of action in the shallow Danish waters, Nelson transferred his flag to HMS *Elephant,* captained by his old friend Thomas Foley, for it was smaller and of less draught than the *St. George.*

At 6:45 A.M., on 30 March, the fleet sailed past Elsinore and exchanged fire with "Hamlet's" Kronborg Castle, which Parker incorrectly interpreted as a declaration of war on the part of Denmark. Later that day the French ambassador in Copenhagen sent an intelligence report to French foreign minister Talleyrand in Paris: "The war between England and Denmark has broken out."[82]

Upon arrival off Copenhagen, the British found that the Danes had taken obvious practical measures and had removed all buoys, beacons, markers and other navigational aides from the area. These, of course, were reasonable and obvious tactics for the Danes to employ. On the larger scale, however, the modern Danes find great fault with their ancestors' strategic crisis management. A 1980 study found several problems with this campaign: the irresoluteness and uncertainty of the government, adverse pressure of time, inadequate preparation, a psychological factor best described as a hope that the danger would pass, and a fundamental lack of information on the intentions of the British (and Russians) as well as erroneous interpretation of the available information.[83]

In any event, as a result of this removal of buoys, nothing remained to indicate where the two key North and King's Channels lay. In addition, the British had no decent charts; furthermore, "few if any of the pilots agreed on any single fact about the area." As a result, feeling the responsibility incumbent upon themselves, Sir Hyde, Lord Nelson, Admiral Graves, and Colonel Stewart gathered together and, in Admiral Parker's words, personally "reconnoitered the enemy's line" at some significant risk.[84] Equally remarkable is the difference in analysis of the three admirals. Parker decided to go on with the attack, but with the concern that

the enemy's line "was found to be far more formidable than we had reason to expect."[85] He reported later to the Admiralty that, with admirals
Nelson and Graves, he reconnoitered "the formidable Line of Ships,
Radeaus, Pontoons, Galleys, Fire Ships and Gun-Boats, flanked and
supported extensive Batteries on the two Islands called the Crowns, the
largest of which was mounted with from fifty to seventy pieces of cannon. These were again commanded by two Ships of seventy guns, and a
large Frigate, in the inner Road of Copenhagen, and two sixty-four gun
Ships (without masts) were moored on the Flat."[86]

Graves was gloomy and decidedly against the attack, concerned that
they might be "playing a losing game, attacking stone walls." Nelson,
however, wrote to Lady Hamilton,

> We this morning passed the fancied tremendous fortress of Cronen-
> burg. . . . More powder and shot, I believe, never were thrown away,
> for not one shot struck a single ship of the British fleet. . . . The *Ele-*
> *phant* did not return a single shot. I hope to reserve them for a better
> occasion.
>
> I have just been reconnoitring the Danish line of defence. It looks
> formidable to those who are children at war, but to my judgment,
> with ten [ships] of the line I think I can annihilate them; at all events,
> I hope to be allowed to try.[87]

On board the *London,* Parker then dictated orders to various officers.
Essentially, Nelson was directed to take ten ships (two more added later)
to attack the enemy's line. Sir Hyde would hold the remainder of the fleet
in reserve a few miles away. Parker accompanied an additional reconnaissance mission; with admirals Nelson and Graves, and captains
Dommett and Otway, he "again reconnoitred the enemy's line, and determined on the mode of attack, the boats and launches fitting their carronades, &c."[88]

Later that night several ship captains and masters personally went out
on even more reconnaissance; it was a vital intelligence requirement to
know where there was forty, or four, feet of water, so these officers went

rowing around the "floating ice, with seamen busy with leadlines quietly passing back the depths they found. These were noted and bearings taken, using boat compasses lit by guttering candles and shielded with strips of canvas. Oars were muffled because any moment they expected to meet Danish guard boats rowing through the channels to prevent them carrying out just this sort of survey."[89] The British also laid down a considerable number of buoys to replace those removed by the Danes.

On the morning of the thirty-first, Parker called what was actually a council of war. This meeting consisted of himself, Nelson, Graves, Dommett, and several other captains. It would seem that he was still unsure as what to do; unable to personally analyze the situation, he required the three senior officers to give in writing their views on "the propriety of attacking the enemy." Graves was still opposed, but Nelson and Dommett were strongly in favor.[90]

At this point almost everything rested on Nelson's shoulders. Nelson observed that the Danish ships moored in a line probably revealed the western edge of the channel. Danish Commo. Olfert Fischer's defenses were not entirely well conceived; yet "the defenses that Fischer had managed to prepare in the time available were a little short of miraculous."[91]

Sir Hyde finally made the decision to attack. He gracefully offered Nelson more ships than Nelson had requested (which weakened Parker's position if hostile Russian or Swedish ships should appear). He then left the specific arrangements for the attack to Nelson's direction.

Many intelligence concerns remained unresolved: "From the *Elephant*'s position it was hard to distinguish the precise types of several of the Danish ships as one overlapped another. . . . It seemed that there were twenty Danish ships which Nelson had to attack with his twelve. The problem was to arrange the best permutation, since Danish floating batteries were scattered among the blockships, and Nelson did not make the mistake of underestimating their fire power or the difficulty of dealing with them because of their low profile."[92]

Moreover, by this time Nelson had lost all faith in both his British and the local pilots—as well as most of the charts he possessed. Nevertheless, he felt he knew enough to proceed. Working with several of his key captains, he established his plan of attack and line of battle and then drew up orders for the individual ships. Then the final drafts were handed to "six clerks, who had been waiting in the forward cabin with quills, ink, paper, sand boxes to blot the ink, and knives to keep the quills sharp. Copies of the complete orders were needed for each of the captains, with supplementary orders for certain ships."[93]

Despite his great acumen in intelligence and operational expertise, it cannot be assumed that Nelson made no mistakes. In fact, "he completely underestimated the Danish gunnery and the tenacity of the men serving the guns. . . . He had miscalculated the very nature of this particular battle for a brave and tenacious seafaring people like the Danes. . . . They were as desperate as men can only be when fighting for the direct safety of their families and homes."[94]

At 7:00 A.M., 2 April 1801, Nelson's temporary flagship, *Elephant,* hoisted the signal "The Captains of the Fleet are to come to the Admiral."[95] Each captain was given a copy of the "Orders for the Attack." Nelson then met with the civilian pilots (mostly mates of vessels which traded from Scottish and northern English ports to the Baltic),[96] who as a group were gloomy and effectively refused to take charge of the ships. The sailing master (a British naval warrant officer, as opposed to a hired civilian pilot) of HMS *Bellona,* Alexander Briarly, stepped forward and volunteered to lead the line. Briarly had fought with Nelson at the Nile, having been then the master of HMS *Audacious.* Nelson's comment later to St. Vincent was, "I have experienced in the Sound the misery of having the honor of our Country intrusted to Pilots, who have no thought than to keep the Ship clear of danger, and their own silly heads clear of shot. . . . Everybody knows what I must have suffered; and if any merit attaches itself to me, it was in combating the dangers of the shallows in defiance of the Pilots."[97]

Nelson seemingly never had very good luck with pilots. In fact, as a young frigate captain he had had the interesting experience of having his ship (HMS *Boreas*) run aground by a pilot even while in English waters.

That experience may have colored his opinion of pilots for the rest of his career.[98]

At 8 o'clock the *Elephant* hoisted the signals to "Prepare for Battle, and for anchoring, with springs on the anchors, and the end of the sheet cable taken in at the stern port."[99] Briarly can only be complimented on his skill, coolness, and highly developed sense of situational awareness; he successfully led the line based on the fleet's earlier reconnaissance and rebuoying of the channels, as well as adroitly utilizing some key landmarks he had previously noted, including a small red house, a mill, a church, and a wood.[100]

The rest, as the saying goes, is history. One could briefly note that Parker was totally unable to assess the progress of the battle—a fact which did not prevent him from hoisting his famous signal to "discontinue the action" at a critical point—as well as Nelson's much better battle-damage assessment, which convinced him to ignore that signal and achieve a monumental victory.

As mentioned earlier in the book, Nelson's famous disobedience of this order is the stuff of legend. He is reported to have reacted somewhat as follows: After having Parker's signal repeated to him twice, he shouted at the *Elephant*'s signal officer, Lt. Frederick Langford, "I told you to look out on the Danish commodore and let me know when he surrendered. Keep your eyes fixed on him [and not on HMS *London*]."[101] He then muttered, "Leave off action." He repeated, "Leave off action!" then added, with a shrug, "Now damn me if I do!" Next, turning to Captain Foley, he said, "You know, Foley, I have only one eye—and I have a right to be blind sometimes," and putting his small telescope to his blind eye, he exclaimed, "I really do not see the signal." A few moments later he was reported as saying bitterly, "Damn the signal. Keep mine for closer battle flying. That's the way I answer such signals! Nail mine to the mast!"[102] However, with that aside, the intelligence and communications aspects of this campaign basically ended as Nelson's ships assumed their stations across from the Danish line.

By the end of the day at least 1,000 Danes were killed or wounded, as well as about 950 Britons. One Danish ship was destroyed; the remainder of their line was disabled and captured (and, to be fair, most of the British ships were seriously damaged, and six were aground). Nelson later told the Danish crown prince that he had been in 105 engagements, but that the Copenhagen action had been the most severe.[103]

The Danes accepted a truce, initially conveyed by Captain Thesiger and enormously facilitated by his ability to speak Danish. As mentioned earlier, and at the time completely unknown to the combatants, Czar Paul I had been assassinated some weeks previously. With the publication of his death, and the Battle of Copenhagen, the League of Armed Neutrality effectively collapsed.

In the final analysis, Nelson's approach contrasts remarkably with Parker's during the events leading to April first. Lord Nelson, in addition to his other aspects of genius, was masterful in his data gathering, analysis, exploitation, strategic insight, and all-around awareness of intelligence information in general. To say that Sir Hyde was fundamentally oblivious to the value of intelligence would not be much of an exaggeration. In fact, Nelson towered above his superior in character, determination, fighting quality, situational awareness, and general superiority of judgment.[104]

10

A Naval Intelligence Campaign
The Nile, 29 March–1 August 1798

Nelson [faced] an astonishing array of possibilities. . . . The [enemy's] enormous force was . . . lost to sight; it was like having a man with homicidal tendencies and well armed at liberty in a crowded room full of furniture in pitch darkness.

C.S. Forester

You, Sir, are in search of the French fleet without any intelligence, or guidance, but that of your own judgment.

Captain Ball

THE YEAR 1798 WAS THE SIXTH YEAR OF THE WARS OF THE FRENCH Revolution. The position of the Royal Navy was relatively favorable; thus far the war had seen, among other things, the victorious Battle of the Glorious First of June, the temporary capture of the port of Toulon on the French mainland, the establishment and maintenance of a close blockade of the enemy coast, and the victorious Battles of Cape Saint Vincent and Camperdown. In general, there had been five years of active naval warfare that had polished the navy to a high grade of efficiency.

On the other hand, the strategic state of the war was far from comfortable for the British, owing, of course, to widespread French military achievements, but also to an apparent slowness to recognize the strong ideological nature of the war.[1] In previous conflicts the capture of the enemy's colonies and the disruption of commerce were very often the paramount keys to victory. Now, however, at least from France's viewpoint, the goals were decidedly different. Beyond any military defeat, the rulers of the French Republic hoped that England itself might be brought to a state of revolution: "It remains, fellow Citizens, to punish the perfidy ... of England, that has corrupted the Courts of Europe. It is in *London* that the misfortunes of Europe are planned; it is in *London* that we must end them."[2] Thus, when the British government concluded that the peace feelers which it had made during the summer of 1797 were doomed to failure "except on terms too humiliating to be considered, it at once turned its attention to the question of waging a distinctively offensive war, for effect in which co-operation was needed."[3]

In fact, on 30 March 1798, when the newly promoted Sir Horatio Nelson, Rear Admiral of the Blue, hoisted his flag on board HMS *Vanguard* at Spithead,

> England had been left quite without allies in her struggle with France. Austria, beaten into helplessness ... had made the peace France wanted; the Austrian Netherlands were ceded to France; French influence was acknowledged in Piedmont and by the Milanese; [and] the French frontier was advanced to the Rhine.
>
> The international situation was now that of the time of the American War of Independence; England was at war with France, the Netherlands and Spain.[4]

France had only one effective enemy in Europe: Great Britain.[5] Indeed, young Gen. Napoleon Bonaparte's Italian campaign had driven Austria out of the war, brought northern Italy under French domination, and precipitated the abandonment of the Mediterranean Sea by the British navy. This was in spite of the successful naval Battle of Cape St. Vincent in February 1797. Regardless, the Mediterranean had become flatly untenable due to the lack of hospitable ports—no allies, no harbors.

Adm. Sir John Jervis (Royal Navy Mediterranean commander in chief) was basing his forces in the last haven remaining open to him—even though it was actually outside the Mediterranean—the mouth of the Portuguese river Tagus in the vicinity of Lisbon. It was Jervis (Earl of St. Vincent, receiving his title from the name of his victory over the Spanish) who had made the decision to withdraw British naval forces from the Mediterranean. He felt that, at least temporarily, his first priorities were to blockade the Spanish in their major naval base at Cadiz while supporting the Portuguese in whatever ways he could.[6] However, during the early part of 1798, St. Vincent was very much occupied with the very real threat of losing even this last remaining station at Lisbon. In truth, tiny Portugal stood precariously alone, and under terrible pressures, as Britain's sole ally in France's virtual continental hegemony.

On 10 January, St. Vincent wrote to the First Lord of the Admiralty (George John, 2nd Earl Spencer) that he was constantly searching for the means to provide for his fleet, which he felt composed "a very considerable portion of the defence of the Empire, and to employ it advantageously [if] the Tagus ceases to be a *depôt* for the stores and provisions necessary for its support. Under all . . . circumstances, I cannot advise the continuance of the fleet in these seas, because the public will be led to expect what cannot be performed."[7]

Spencer could do very little besides send back encouragement. On 30 March he wrote to St. Vincent,

> It must evidently be right to maintain our situation on the coast of Portugal and [therefore] in the neighbourhood of the Cadiz fleet as long as we are able, and continue to seize any opportunity of disabling the force of Spain, which sooner or later must, I suppose, fall more completely than it even now is into the hands of France.
>
> Whatever suggestions your lordship may have to make on these topics . . . as far as our means can allow . . . I shall be happy to act upon them.

He did, however, have some good news to offer, as he was "very happy to send you Sir Horatio Nelson again . . . because I believe I cannot send you a more zealous, active, and approved officer. . . . If your lordship is

Fig. 10-1 *Battle of the Nile.*
This view shows the situation about 6:00 P.M. on 1 August 1798. HMS *Goliath,*
Capt. Thomas Foley (leading Nelson's line), is just rounding the head of
Bruey's fleet at anchor in Aboukir Bay. The original painting was done by
Nicholas Pocock.
© *National Maritime Museum, London*

as desirous to have him with you as he is to be with you, I am sure the
arrangement must be perfectly happy."[8]

Even as late as 6 April Spencer did not believe that the Portuguese
could hold out. In a letter to Lord Grenville (British secretary of state for
the Foreign Office), he wrote that the best plan might be to maintain, for
as long as possible, "our position between Lisbon and Cadiz, and when
we are excluded (which I conclude we soon shall be) from the Tagus, to
send Lord St. Vincent with the fleet he now has to sweep round the
Mediterranean and do all the mischief he can to the French navy there."[9]

St. Vincent faced an additional problem. Despite harsh realities that
seemed to dictate an even further westward withdrawal from the Tagus,
the British government's grand strategy demanded St. Vincent's actual
reentrance into the Mediterranean—in force and of a permanent nature.

For more than a year the Mediterranean had been decidedly a Franco-Spanish lake. Prime Minister William Pitt (Pitt the Younger) was hard at work to form a new coalition against the French, a plan that was dependent upon the attitude and cooperation of Austria. Because Austria was convinced that the earlier British withdrawal from the Mediterranean had ruined Austria's Italian campaign and brought things to a shambles, it was clear that unless a British fleet were sent back through the Straits of Gibraltar there was no hope of rallying Austria—or Russia —to renewed activity against the French. There was no help for it; from April on this became a burning foreign-policy priority. Pitt's government met decisively on 28 April, resolving on sending ships immediately to the Mediterranean.[10] Of course, the next question concerned where the necessary ships would come from without weakening required forces elsewhere. After all, the Admiralty could never lose sight that the main enemy fleet was at the northern French port of Brest, where it always retained the potential to sortie for attacks on distant British colonies, or to support an invasion of Ireland or Britain.[11]

As a result, on 29 April, Spencer "privately and confidentially" wrote St. Vincent that when St. Vincent became aware that the appearance of a "British squadron in the Mediterranean is a condition on which the fate of Europe may at this moment be stated to depend, you will not be surprised that we are disposed to strain every nerve and incur considerable hazard in effecting it."[12]

Naturally, the Mediterranean Sea was of some importance to Britain. In 1792 British trade in the region totaled £2.7 million. The land route to India (Alexandria to Suez) was important for the movement of official dispatches. The sea allowed military access to France's southern flank. Left unmolested and unthreatened, French Mediterranean forces could build up sufficient strength to break out in force and menace British operations anywhere in the world. Finally, as mentioned above, the Mediterranean presented a significant location to unite potential allied strength against the French.[13]

Moreover, if St. Vincent's situation were not already complicated enough, it had become apparent that the French were up to something fairly large scale in their Mediterranean operations. This was evident because

> the French-Italian coast was . . . alive with preparations. Ships of the line were refitting in numbers at Toulon; hundreds of transports were being made ready in every port from Marseilles to Leghorn; the Swiss confederacy had been plundered to provide money; thousands of troops lay in readiness on the coast. . . . Some tremendous stroke was being meditated; *but what it was could not be ascertained.*
>
> France could employ troops with effect (once she could get them there) in the West Indies, in Ireland [perhaps welcomed by Irish rebels], in Italy. Not merely that, but such was the state of her declared national doctrine [in effect, exporting the revolution] that all governments could be considered her enemies if it suited her; she could strike at an unoffending neutral if she wished, and no Frenchman in France would protest. . . . *Any point in the whole world, therefore, might be the objective of this armament.*[14]

By the middle of April officials in Whitehall had received intelligence that a French expedition to Ireland was in the works; whether it was related to the "Toulon Armament" was not clear.

At this time much of the information reaching London was from French newspapers. For example, the 27 March edition of *L'Echo* reported that five hundred seamen had been recently brought to Toulon for the navy, and that another eight hundred were shortly expected from Bordeaux. The 6 April edition of *Le Moniteur* mentioned that fourteen frigates and seventeen ships of the line were gathered in Toulon, and that some of the ships had troops and artillery on board for an amphibious campaign. Whitehall sent this last paper to St. Vincent, but not until the end of April.[15] Toulon (having been recovered from French royalist forces by Bonaparte and others in 1794) was perhaps the premier naval port in France's possession—and certainly was the most important Mediterranean naval base under any flag.

Indeed, some tremendous stroke was being meditated. The French Directory had developed a plan to employ their most able general; in truth, it had essentially been his own suggestion that sent the ball rolling. On 13 September 1797, Gen. Napoleon Bonaparte (then only twenty-nine years old) wrote to the French foreign minister, asking,

> [Why] do we not take possession of Malta? Four hundred Knights and 500 soldiers are all that form the garrison of Valletta. . . . With the islands of Sardinia, Malta and Corfu, we shall be masters of the whole Mediterranean.
>
> To go to Egypt [and] as soon as I have made England tremble for the safety of India, I shall return to Paris and give the [British] enemy its death-blow. . . . Turkey will welcome the expulsion of the Mamelukes.[16]

The Mamelukes were the members of a military order that were the de facto rulers of Egypt, under the nominal control of the Sublime Ottoman Porte, the sultan of Turkey.

Charles Maurice de Talleyrand, Bishop of Autun, was the French foreign minister. He assessed that the Porte had lost control of Egypt and, significantly, that the sultan currently received very little revenue from Egypt and therefore would not be overly provoked by its loss. His final arguments to the French Directory were persuasive; particularly in combination with the passionate and confident presentations of General Bonaparte.[17]

As a result, in March 1798, Napoleon was appointed to the command of the French Armeé d'Orient. After a lifelong attraction to "the lure and mystery of the East[,] . . . Bonaparte now saw himself as a second Alexander. He trusted in his destiny."[18] He was to seize the strategically crucial island of Malta, the "navel of the Sea," which was central to the east-west trade routes as well as those of the north and south between Europe and Africa. Then he was to lead "the land and sea forces under his command to Egypt and . . . drive the English from all their oriental possessions which he can reach[,] . . . and he will cause the isthmus of Suez to be cut through and he will take all necessary measures to ensure to the French Republic the free and exclusive possession of the Red Sea."[19] The conquest of Egypt was also to be used to create a base for an advance further east in order to destroy Britain's power in India. All the while, General Bonaparte was to pay scrupulous respect to the Moslem faith.[20]

Indeed, similar ideas had been entertained by earlier French governments for many years, including those of Francis I, Louis XIV, Louis XV, and Louis XVI. After all, even the term *Levant* is an old French one used to describe the countries of the eastern Mediterranean. A French officer, the Baron de Tott, thoroughly spied out the land around Suez in 1777 with such an aim; his musty reports proved very valuable to Napoleon and his planners in 1798.[21]

In many ways the plan logically fell in with French movements toward solidifying a position as the new great power of the Mediterranean. Royalist France had taken Corsica in 1768; Corfu had recently been absorbed in 1797. The seizure of Malta and then Egypt would complete this scenario very effectively.[22]

French operational security in this campaign was superior—quite admirable, in fact, for the time period. Even senior French naval officers were completely unaware of the expedition's final destination; rumors abounded in both the fleet and the army, naming Sicily, Portugal, Greece, and the Crimea.[23] And while it was impossible to hide the growing preparations of this "armament" with its extensive scale, the objectives certainly remained hidden from the British. French deception was elaborate. Napoleon's "public" assignment was commanding the army preparing to invade England, though he and the Directory had really abandoned that plan since "it is too great a chance [for the moment]. I [Bonaparte] will not hazard it. I would not thus sport with the fate of *la belle France* on the throw of a dice."[24] Make no mistake, Napoleon strongly wanted to invade Britain, but he felt France unready in 1798. He assessed that France did not have local superiority of the sea (indeed, much of the French navy was tightly blockaded in Brest), that there was insufficient funding, and that there were not enough French seamen with solid operational experience for such a project. In short, Bonaparte recommended postponement of an attack upon England while advocating aggressive movements in other areas.[25]

French activity tried to obscure any hint that the current invasion threat to Britain was diminished; to the last possible moment they proactively kept up the pretense of serious activity and intentions. Cover plans included the "preparation of raids on Ireland and Portugal, and on March 30 Bonaparte received an ostentatious order to take command . . . at Brest. These measures were designed to throw dust in the eyes of British intelligence, and so was the retention by the Toulon forces of the title 'Army of England' until April 12."[26]

As Oliver Warner notes in his book on the battle, "Even the spies who kept London informed of happenings on the Continent of Europe could not pierce the curtain of mystery which surrounded the Egyptian Venture."[27] But in late March, St. Vincent was informed by British consul general Udney (at Leghorn) that thirteen French and formerly Venetian ships of the line had passed from Corfu toward Toulon; additionally, he heard that a large body of French troops would shortly arrive at Genoa to be embarked.[28]

So, in the face of poor health complicated by the pressures of several huge operational problems, Adm. Lord St. Vincent sincerely welcomed the prospect of Rear Admiral Nelson at his side, Nelson having joined St. Vincent's fleet on 30 April, anchoring twelve miles east of Cadiz in twenty-one fathoms of water.[29] A man not generally prone to showing emotion in speech or in writing, St. Vincent nevertheless wrote Spencer on 1 May, "My Lord,—I do assure your lordship that the arrival of Admiral Nelson has given me new life. You could not have gratified me more than in sending him."[30]

Sir Horatio's letters to his wife, and to his friend the Duke of Clarence, give his initial impression: "We arrived here yesterday [23 April], in fourteen days from [England]. Lord St. Vincent is at sea off Cadiz. . . . I fear we shall have a dull campaign off Cadiz; and [St. Vincent's] force will not, I apprehend, admit of his detaching me up the Mediterranean, to endeavor to get hold of the French Squadron, now masters of that sea."[31]

This impression had not changed one week later, though by this time he had received secret orders from St. Vincent. St. Vincent had, actually, resolved "to send a small force off Toulon to make an armed reconnaissance of the area and to find out what it could about French preparations and intentions."[32] As St. Vincent expressed it to Spencer, Nelson's presence in the "Mediterranean is so very essential that I mean to put the *Orion* and *Alexander* under his command, with the addition of three or four frigates, and to send him away . . . to ascertain the real object of the preparations making by the French, which [intelligence reports indicate] is intended against Ireland."[33] The truth was that St. Vincent felt this mission so important and so difficult that he never considered entrusting it to his other, more senior flag officers. For his part, Nelson was very happy to be with St. Vincent again: "I joined the Fleet yesterday [1 May at Lisbon], and found Lord St. Vincent everything I wished him."[34]

Although Nelson felt comfortable discussing some aspects of the situation with his wife, he kept from her the details of his assignment, writing only that St. Vincent "is going to detach me with a small Squadron; not on any fighting expedition, therefore do not be surprised if it should be some little time before you hear from me again."[35]

Indeed, on 2 May, Nelson had received a very detailed "most secret" order from St. Vincent which, after reciting that St. Vincent had "received intelligence that a considerable Armament was preparing at Toulon, and a number of Transports collecting at Marseilles and Genoa, for an embarkation of troops, directed him [Nelson] to proceed . . . up the Mediterranean, and to endeavor to ascertain . . . the destination of that Expedition, which, according to some reports, was Sicily and Corfu, and according to others, Portugal or Ireland. . . . If the Enemy's Armament was coming down the Mediterranean, he was to take special care not to suffer it to pass the Straits before him, so as to impede his joining Lord St. Vincent in time to prevent a union between it and the Spanish Fleet in Cadiz Bay."[36]

The *Vanguard* subsequently arrived at Gibraltar on 4 May, where it discovered Rear Adm. Sir John Orde, and the seventy-four-gun ships of the line *Princess Royal, Orion, Majestic, Hector,* and *Alexander,* as well as several frigates.

Nelson was very properly caught up in the operational security of his mission, writing to St. Vincent on 6 May that he had disclosed to Admiral

Orde—a fellow British flag officer—only what was obvious: "Sir John Orde will know by his eye what Ships go with me, therefore I shall show him the list," and that "I do not believe that any person guesses my destination."[37]

Nelson's orders from St. Vincent were very much rooted in St. Vincent's orders from the Admiralty. Moreover, the intelligence problem was enormous; both sets of orders "offered an astonishing array of possibilities as to where [Napoleon's] thirty thousand men, thirteen ships of the line, and four hundred transports were likely to go."[38] The Admiralty's most-secret instructions to St. Vincent stressed that it was absolutely necessary that the armament "fitting at Toulon should be prevented from accomplishing its object, and that their Lordships had in consequence reinforced his Fleet with eight Sail of the Line and two Fire Ships": "Your Lordship is to lose no time in detaching from your Fleet a Squadron, consisting of twelve Sail of the Line, and a competent number of Frigates, under the command of some discreet Flag-Officer, into the Mediterranean, with instructions to him to proceed in quest of the said Armament; and on falling in with it, or any other Force belonging to the Enemy, to take or destroy it. Your Lordship is to direct the Commanding-Officer of the above-mentioned Squadron, to remain upon this service so long as the provisions of the said Squadron will last, or as long as he may be enabled to obtain supplies from any of the ports in the Mediterranean."[39]

A private and confidential letter, to Lord St. Vincent from Lord Spencer, went on to state the following—truly compounding the intelligence problem with its array of astonishing possibilities to which we have already referred:

> The armament at Toulon, Genoa, &c., is represented as being very extensive, and is very probably in the first instance intended for Naples. . . .
> This armament is in truth more likely to be destined either for Portugal or Ireland. . . . Whatever may be its destination, its defeat would surely be a great object for this country. . . .
> The circumstance of a British fleet being in the Mediterranean will

encourage the Austrians to act, and most probably divert the French force to a different destination from their present one.

. . . we are inclined to hope that you may find it practicable to send a detachment into the Mediterranean sufficiently strong to attain [our] end, and at the same time remain in a situation to watch with effect the fleet at Cadiz. . . .

I cannot . . . help feeling how much depends upon [this detachment's] success, and how absolutely necessary it is at this time to run some risk in order if possible to bring about a new system of affairs in Europe, which shall save us all from being overrun by the exorbitant power of France.[40]

In a subsequent letter to St. Vincent, dated 1 May, Spencer reiterated these earlier points and then went on to pass considerable information from a Captain Day, an observer who had been in Genoa. This and other intelligence from Genoa carried analysis that unstoppered casks ("4,000 casks of a very large size with ten iron hoops each, *without* any bung holes") were being bought by the French, which could be lashed to ships in order to reduce their draft for shallow-water operations.[41] This intelligence suggested the Levant as an additional possible target, but Spencer was skeptical; moreover, he felt it necessary to stress operational security. Analysis from Genoa held it "most probable that [the enemy] are destined either for the coast of Spain or Naples, or (though I can scarce believe it) for the Levant. . . . I need not recommend to you the utmost secrecy (more especially with respect to Portugal) of your intentions, as they might . . . be alarmed at the idea of any division of your fleet taking place."[42]

On 20 April Udney, the British consul general at Leghorn, had written Nelson:

With the same freedom and confidence, my dear Sir, which our long habits and your indulgence authorize, I will continue to give such information as I have collected . . . with my private ideas on the present situation of affairs, which, but to yourself alone, I would not presume to hazard.

It is ascertained that 40,000 men will be embarked in at least 400 sail of vessels under General Buonaparte; their destinations are daily circulated and varied, so that no certainty can be obtained; but from all I can learn, by well-founded intelligence, I am confident their first attempts will be on Malta, thence to invade Sicily, in order to secure that granary, and then Naples; in all which places they have by their emissaries secured a strong party.

What their other views afterwards may be with such an immense force, time will show: I am convinced, reflecting on the plan the late Empress of Russia attempted to put into execution, of getting possession of Egypt, that *Buonaparte will hereafter, and with more reason in his unbounded enterprises, pursue the same scheme of seizing and fortifying Alexandria, Cairo, and Suez* [emphasis added]. If France intends uniting with Tippoo Saib against our possessions in India, the danger of losing half an army in crossing the desert from Egypt would be no obstacle.[43]

Tippoo Sahib was the sultan of Mysore (in the south of the subcontinent) and was currently engaged in a series of wars by which he (and his father, Hyder Ali, before him) hoped to turn back the expansion of British influence in India. Tippoo was a Francophile, a soldier, an indomitable worker, a reformer, and an innovator. Defeated in 1792 and stripped of half his territories, he was determined to ultimately prevail against the British. Certainly the arrival of a French army, with the intention of supporting Tippoo, would immeasurably increase the odds for a new successful campaign against the British in India.[44]

Nelson sailed into the Mediterranean, at 6:00 P.M. on 8 May, with three ships of the line and three frigates. He waited until dark to sail so that no Spanish observers would see their eastward route. However, as the wind was light the squadron had to warp out of Gibraltar's harbor (rowing an anchor, via a ship's boat, out ahead of the ship; the anchor was dropped and then the ship hauled itself up to it, the process being repeated over and over as required). In fact, it was morning before the squadron could actually set sail, clearly in view of the Spanish fort at Cape Carnero, which fired shots in their direction.[45] The element of surprise was lost, although it does not appear the Spanish did much with the information.

In any event, Nelson now had an enormous problem to solve, "one involving ocean-wide strategy and immense political consequences, and the successful solution of *that* problem would bring about the immediate presentation of another, more *ordinary* problem, of [actually fighting and] winning [any] battle this success made possible."[46]

The assignment was also dangerous, difficult, and almost unparalleled; "he was in command of a fine squadron, with more responsibility and independence than most admirals with twice his seniority."[47] This was complicated by the inevitable second-guessing of the British public, an aggressive out-of-power political party, and two angry and embittered Mediterranean Fleet rear admirals who had been passed over for the command—all of whom would mercilessly condemn any mistakes or errors.

As discussed earlier, Nelson's first orders from St. Vincent, on 7 May 1798, were reasonably straightforward. Nelson took pains to pass along the full importance of the tasking in his own orders to his frigate captains: "It being of very great importance to obtain correct information of the destination of the large Fleet of the Enemy, and of the Fleet of Transports with troops, which is said to accompany them. . . . —You are therefore hereby directed to proceed to the Eastward, looking with proper caution into Barcelona, and from thence taking your station in a direct line between Saint Sebastian's and Toulon, endeavoring, by speaking of Vessels, to obtain the desired information, which, when got, you are to make all possible dispatch to the Commander-in-Chief off Cadiz."[48]

On the eleventh, St. Vincent sent out another order to Nelson, effectively recalling him, telling him to return to Gibraltar, reprovision, and then rejoin the fleet off Cadiz: "This Order was accompanied by a private Letter . . . in which Lord St. Vincent said, 'The Admiralty had at last discovered that it is necessary to provide a force to look after the French in the Mediterranean,' and that some Ships were expected from England, and added, 'You, and you only, can command the important service in contemplation; therefore make the best of your way down to me.' "[49]

Toward the end of the month St. Vincent, not waiting for Nelson's return, went ahead and sent after Nelson the detachment of ten additional ships of the line already mentioned. The British certainly were not above a little deception themselves as "the reinforcement from the Channel Fleet, under Sir Roger Curtis, joined St. Vincent off Cadiz on 24 May and changed places with the blockading squadron, the new ships being painted to imitate the old."[50]

Interestingly enough, this was a few years before the time when the majority of British ships were painted in the now-familiar black with yellow stripes down the rows of gun ports—the "Nelson checker." Five of these detached ships were basically yellow, with black and gold trim; two of them, the *Zealous* and the *Minotaur,* were bright red, with yellow and black trim. Captain Miller of the *Theseus* was particularly deception-minded with his paint scheme: he had his bulwark hammock cloths above the weather deck painted yellow to match the rest of the ship, giving the impression that the *Theseus* was a three decker instead of her actual two.[51]

Capt. Thomas Troubridge initially commanded the detachment of ten ships of the line, the fifty-gun *Leander,* and the cutter *Earl of St. Vincent.* On the morning of 27 May they entered the Mediterranean; however, Troubridge was immediately forced to send back the cutter as unseaworthy.[52]

Back in London, on 26 April, Lord Spencer had been shocked by reports that the French had up to seventeen ships of the line operational in the Mediterranean, for if the force were really what the last "accounts from Turin describe it, our detachment to the Mediterranean will be of no avail; for the whole of that plan proceeded on the supposition of their not having more than about ten sail of the line effective."[53] Seventeen turned out to be an exaggerated number, but as it was the French did have thirteen in their order of battle, some being quite large.

Knowing the tremendous reconnaissance challenge that Nelson faced, St. Vincent was irritated at not being able to send him more frigates. In May 1798, however, St. Vincent had to cope with the constant shortage of such ships—which remained a widespread problem for the entire war in all theaters. No different than other commanders during this time,

St. Vincent was extremely handicapped regarding the small number of frigates under his command. Theoretically possessing ten (plus seven other smaller ships), he had only five present at the beginning of May. Detaching three for Nelson's squadron was a major sacrifice.[54] The three given to Nelson were the *Emerald* (thirty-six guns, Capt. Thomas Waller), the *Terpsichore* (thirty-two, Capt. William Gage), and the *Bonne Citoyenne* (twenty). In a letter to Spencer, St. Vincent remarked, "I very much lament having no frigates to add, for Sir H. Nelson [already] has the whole [of my frigates] except the *Sea Horse* and the *Thalia*. The former must go to Lisbon for supplies, and the latter is taking a section of the ground about Cape Spartel, and two frigates are necessary to be [readily] within call of me."[55]

With the sending of the reinforcements, and the new orders, the die effectively was cast. Primitive communications being what they were, it would now be several months before St. Vincent—and Spencer—would learn whether their gamble was successful and whether their trust in Nelson was well placed. And Nelson's very "success or failure was to depend on his ability to guess and anticipate the thought of his adversary" —Napoleon Bonaparte, a man whom many consider the towering genius of his age.[56]

In the first few days of the reconnaissance part of the mission, sailing toward Toulon past Majorca and Minorca, Nelson gathered a few scraps of information from "speaking" merchant ships and, near Cape Sicié, from the capture of a French corvette out of Toulon. His principal aide at this time (for Capt. Edward Berry was primarily focused upon the details of commanding the *Vanguard*) was Lt. the Hon. Thomas Capel —only twenty years old and commissioned for less than a year. He served Nelson as his flag lieutenant, which is to say his signal officer and sole operational staff officer, but he was certainly no experienced, mature advisor. His other staff included only his secretary, John Campbell (whom Sir Horatio found lacking in energy), and his personal servant, Tom Allen. Nelson basically had an inadequate staff with really no solid officer to whom he could delegate flag-level issues.[57]

During 17–18 May, off Cape Sicié, Nelson wrote St. Vincent a careful intelligence report that gives clear insight as to his intelligence orientation including collection, multiple-source comparison, and analysis. His first real intelligence about enemy movements had come from the *Terpsichore* capturing the small six-gun French corvette *La Pierre:*

> From the general report of Vessels spoke, you will observe the *uniformity* of the reports—viz., that an expedition is preparing to sail from Toulon. We have *separately* examined the crew of the Corvette, and, from the whole, I believe the following may be depended on as near the truth—Buonaparte arrived at Toulon last Friday, and has examined the troops which are daily embarking in the numerous Transports; that Vessels with troops frequently arrive from Marseilles. . . . No one knows to what place the Armament is destined. Fifteen Sail of the Line are apparently ready for sea, but nineteen are in the harbour, and yet it is said only six Sail of the Line are to sail with the Transports now ready; that about 12,000 men are embarked; their cavalry arrived at Toulon, but I cannot learn that any are yet embarked. Reports say they are to sail in a few days, and others that they will not sail for a fortnight.
>
> The Admiral Brueys has his Flag in *L'Orient,* 120 guns; *Le Formidable* and *Spartanade,* of 80 guns, are also Flag-ships. The Venetian Ships are considered as very bad in every respect, but I do not learn that the Fleet is deficient in either men or stores.

Most important, the French objectives remained obscure—when would they sail and where were they bound? Though frustrated, Nelson felt obliged to add praise to their operational security: "They order their matters so well in France, that all is secret."[58]

On 20 May, Nelson's force was struck by a tremendous gale. The storm also happened to obscure the departure, from Toulon, of the French expedition's main body, which unseen passed by the British squadron only a few leagues distant.[59] The French force, shortly joined by convoys from Genoa, Corsica, and Civitavecchia, was comprised of thirteen ships of the line, seven frigates, and three hundred transport ships containing about thirty-eight thousand troops—as well as General Bonaparte. This fleet passed through the Gulf of Genoa and then headed south between Corsica and Italy. Admiral Brueys (Vice Adm. François Brueys d'Aigalliers) commanded the force at sea, though there can be no question that Napoleon was shaping events and making ultimate decisions.

The gale also caused Nelson's flagship to roll her foremast, main-topmast, and mizen-topmast overboard; several hours of desperate danger and remarkable seamanship saw the *Vanguard* towed away by the *Alexander* from probable wreckage upon a lee shore, mostly due to Captain Ball's refusal of Sir Horatio's order to cast off and ensure the *Alexander*'s safety: "I feel confident that I can bring [the *Vanguard*] in safe. I therefore must not, and by the help of Almighty God, *will not, leave you.*" (For a riveting, if fictional, description of a remarkably similar incident, see C. S. Forester's *Ship of the Line,* chapter 16, wherein Capt. Horatio Hornblower, commanding HMS *Sutherland,* saves his rear admiral on board HMS *Pluto*). In the shelter of Sardinia's San Pietro Bay, four days of strenuous efforts saw the *Vanguard* sufficiently repaired to proceed.

Nelson took the near disaster to heart, writing a remarkable letter to his wife on 24 May, which began by saying, "I ought not to call what has happened to the *Vanguard* by the cold name of accident: I believe firmly, that it was the Almighty's goodness, to check my consummate vanity. I hope it has made me a better Officer, as I feel confident it has made me a better Man. I kiss with all humility the rod."[60]

The final precipitate of the gale had been to separate Nelson from his scouting frigates. He was not initially alarmed at this, for he hoped that they soon would be found; on the twenty-seventh he set sail for a previously agreed-upon rendezvous. That same day the *Orion* captured a Spanish brig; it was retained as a prize with the idea that it could be used later as a dispatch vessel, small ships being at a premium.[61] Early on the twenty-eighth Nelson fell in with a merchantman out of Marseilles; this ship acquainted him as to the sailing of the French force on the twentieth. The speaking of another ship on 2 June generated further anxiety as she reported seeing—a few days earlier—eleven ships of the line supposedly English. Captain Saumarez in the *Orion* recorded that they were "at a loss what conjectures to put on this intelligence."[62] Nelson immediately pushed on to the rendezvous, desperate to reunite with his scouting force and to begin an organized search for the enemy. The third of June saw him reach the agreed point; however, there were no British frigates to be seen.

The fifth of June brought the brig *Mutine*, Cdr. Thomas Hardy, with both good news and bad. Captain Waller, of the frigate *Emerald*, had seen the *Vanguard's* masts go overboard before Nelson's ships of the line and frigates were separated during the gale. Believing that Nelson would have to return to a main base for repairs—if indeed the *Vanguard* survived the storm at all—the *Emerald* and the other frigates sailed for Gibraltar, far beyond Sir Horatio's ability to recall them. On 29 May, Capt. George Hope, in the frigate *Alcmene*, encountered the frigates. Hope, dispatched by St. Vincent to join Nelson, took command of the force. On 2 June, Hope had fallen in with Hardy in the *Mutine* and exchanged information. Hope made considerable efforts to locate Nelson, ultimately arriving at the Bay of Naples on 23 June; however, his attempts at finding Nelson were as fruitless as Nelson's attempts to find the French, with important consequences for the campaign.[63]

The good news was that the reinforcements sent out by St. Vincent, the ten ships of the line discussed earlier, were on their way looking for Nelson; these were the allegedly English ships reported on 2 June. On 11 June Nelson wrote to St. Vincent that the

> *Mutine*, Captain Hardy, joined me on the 5th, at daylight, with the flattering account of the honour you intended me of commanding such a Fleet. *Mutine* fell in with *Alcmene*, off Barcelona on the 2nd. Hope had taken all my Frigates off the rendezvous, on the presumption that the *Vanguard*, from her disabled state, must return to an arsenal. I joined dear Troubridge with the reinforcement of ten Sail of the Line, and the *Leander* on the 7th in the evening: it has been nearly calm ever since, which grieves me sorely.

The French have a long start, but I hope they will rendezvous in
Telamon bay, for the 12,000 men from Genoa in 100 Sail of Vessels,
escorted by a Frigate, had not put to sea on the 2nd, nor were all the
troops embarked.

You may be assured I will fight them the moment I can reach their
Fleet, be they at anchor, or under sail.[64]

The confidence in Nelson, bestowed by both Spencer and St. Vincent,
was remarkable. The men who controlled Britain's affairs at sea had
taken a great risk. Thirteen ships of the line was an enormous force—
almost unparalleled—to be given to a very junior rear admiral.

The moral courage shown by St. Vincent went even further, for
though the Spanish "made as if about to put out of Cadiz, and though a
concerted movement of United Irishmen threatened a new outbreak of
mutiny in the Fleet, the old Admiral never hesitated. On May 19th he
dispatched Hardy with Nelson's commission. On the 21st, [barely] waiting for the arrival of the promised reinforcements from England, he
sent his ten finest battleships and captains—the élite of the Fleet—under
Troubridge to join Nelson."[65]

Captain Troubridge was not only Nelson's close friend ("my hon-
oured acquaintance of twenty-five years standing") but he also held St.
Vincent's highest esteem—in some ways even more so than did Nelson.
St. Vincent had once written of Troubridge that he was "the ablest adviser
and best executive officer in His Majesty's Service"[66] and felt he was as
gifted a commander as Nelson.[67] Nelson more than agreed, writing that
he was the king's very best sea officer and that "I well know he is my
superior, and I so often want his advice and assistance."[68]

One of the captains not selected to join Nelson was Cuthbert
Collingwood, who was greatly mortified to be left out. In fact, this future
Mediterranean commander in chief was sorely aggravated at Lord
St. Vincent for overlooking the close relationship between Nelson and
himself; after all, "he knew our friendship; for many, many years we had
served together, lived together and all that ever happened to us strength-
ened the bond of our amity."[69]

Upon receiving his commission and Hardy's news on the fifth, Nelson immediately fanned out his three ships of the line to ensure meeting the reinforcements. On 7 June the *Vanguard* fell in with them. At the time neither the *Orion* nor the *Alexander* were in sight. Nelson felt he could not await their return, so with ten ships of the line he began his initial search for the French at sea. He tasked the *Leander* and the *Mutine* to find and redirect the others, which was accomplished by the tenth. So, at this point his command consisted of the following ships (number of guns follow ships' names):

Vanguard, 74	Capt. Edward Berry (flying the flag of Rear Adm. Sir Horatio Nelson)
Orion, 74	Capt. Sir James Saumarez
Culloden, 74	Capt. Thomas Troubridge
Bellerophon, 74	Capt. Henry D'Esterre Darby
Minotaur, 74	Capt. Thomas Louis
Defence, 74	Capt. John Peyton
Alexander, 74	Capt. Alexander John Ball
Zealous, 74	Capt. Samuel Hood
Audacious, 74	Capt. Davidge Gould
Goliath, 74	Capt. Thomas Foley
Majestic, 74	Capt. George Blagdon Westcott
Swiftsure, 74	Capt. Benjamin Hallowell
Theseus, 74	Capt. Ralph Willett Miller
Leander, 50	Capt. Thomas Boulden Thompson
Mutine, 16	Cdr. Thomas Masterman Hardy

In fact, the mission of Nelson's squadron was unusually narrow and specific: to locate and destroy Bonaparte's expedition. In modern terminology, it was much more of a task force than a fleet.[70] Moreover, it was a dangerous task force; most of the officers and crews had been hardened by five years of war, and although the *Majestic, Minotaur,* and the *Defence* had been involved in the great British fleet mutinies the year before, and the *Culloden* had experienced similar trouble in 1794, morale was generally high.[71] Coincidentally, the *Vanguard, Audacious, Bellerophon, Defence,*

Goliath, and *Zealous* were essentially sister ships, having been built to the same plans; the *Swiftsure* and *Theseus* were almost identical to the former group, having been built to slightly different plans by the same designer, Sir Thomas Slade.[72]

Sir Horatio was clearly stimulated by his new orders, which, again, profoundly altered his tasking. At first he had been limited to gaining intelligence of the French fleet's intentions; now he was directed to destroy the enemy regardless of their mission. St. Vincent's most-secret instructions, of 21 May, were to the point:

> I do hereby authorize and require You . . . to proceed . . . in quest of the Armament preparing by the Enemy at Toulon and Genoa, the object whereof appears to be, either an attack upon Naples and Sicily, the conveyance of an Army to some part of the Coast of Spain, for the purpose of marching towards Portugal, or to pass through the Straits, with the view of proceeding to Ireland. . . . On falling in with the said Armament, or any part thereof, you are to use your utmost endeavours to take, sink, burn, or destroy it.
>
> . . . you are perfectly justifiable in pursuing the French Squadron to any part of the Mediterranean, Adriatic, Morea, Archipelago, or even into the Black Sea, should its destination be any of those parts; and thoroughly sensible of your zeal, enterprise, and capacity, at the head of a Squadron of Ships so well appointed, manned, and commanded, I have the utmost confidence in the success of your operations.
>
> It is hardly necessary to instruct you to open a correspondence with his Majesty's Ministers at every Court in Italy, at Vienna, and Constantinople, and the different Consuls on the Coasts of the seas you are to operate in. Those of Algier and Tunis are absent from their Posts, and not likely to resume them.

This last was a very important point, for as already seen, diplomatic information was a principal source of intelligence. Regardless of the British naval withdrawals from the Mediterranean, British embassies still operated in Constantinople, Turin, Florence, and Naples—with that of Neapolitan ambassador Sir William Hamilton being the most significant. Additionally, there were nine British consulates throughout the rest of Italy, as well as in Malta, Morocco, Algiers, Tripoli, Tunis, and Egypt. Nelson's main problem here was neither the quality nor quantity of diplomatic information, but rather the difficulty in maintaining communications while at sea.[73] And, with sea communications in mind, St. Vincent's next remarks were significant as well: "You will see the necessity of my being informed of your movements from time to time. A good Sparonara or Felucca with faithful people on board, if to be found, will serve for an Advice-boat during the summer months. When I have a Cutter to spare, you shall have her."[74]

Nelson was unable to comb the seas for intelligence. Profoundly hampered by his lack of scouting vessels, as well as communications vessels (St. Vincent's so called advice-boats), he well realized his enormous intelligence problem. "During this miserable period of suspense and embarrassment, occasioned and prolonged beyond all reason or necessity by the want of lookout ships,"[75] neither the Admiralty nor St. Vincent were much help; their several orders pointed to a dozen possible destinations for the enemy force.

Remarkably, as poor of a sea commander as he was, Napoleon had initially ensured that *his* expedition was well prepared with small vessels: "It is indispensable to have with the squadron the greatest attainable number of corvettes and despatch vessels. Send orders to all the ports for all such to join the fleet."[76]

As noted above, St. Vincent's orders to Nelson envisaged attacks on, or the conveyance of forces to, Naples, Sicily, Portugal, Spain, Ireland, the Morea (the Greek Peloponnesus, which is the southern peninsula of the Greek mainland), the Greek islands, the Adriatic, the Black Sea, or —for that matter—any part of the Mediterranean. Nelson had to make the right choice out of this mess, "with only his native wits to help him, aided by what he knew of weather conditions in the Mediterranean, and by *any casual scraps* of information he *might* pick up *after* setting his course in what might be the *wrong* direction."[77]

There was no obvious objective for the hostile force; General Bonaparte had few open enemies. It was almost unthinkable that he would fling his thirty thousand men upon a province of unoffending, neutral Turkey. The apparent probability was that he would head for Sicily.[78] "Being entirely without intelligence as to the real object of the French, there was nothing to do but to follow upon their track, with eyes open for indications.[79] All that the Rear-Admiral had to guide him was the single fact that the Toulon fleet had quitted Toulon with a north-west wind."[80]

Nelson initially set course for Naples in search of news, believing that the French had passed south between Corsica and the Italian mainland. He swept around the north of Corsica and down the Italian coast. His destination, Naples, was then the second largest city in Europe (after Paris), and the Kingdom of Naples and Sicily comprised almost the entire southern half of Italy. He well knew that, ever since Bonaparte's successful 1796–97 campaigns subjugated northern Italy to France, the Neapolitans realistically dreaded further French military operations directed against them.

On 12 June, Nelson wrote Sir William Hamilton, British ambassador to Naples, in search of various kinds of information. Even though he had read two recent letters from de facto Neapolitan prime minister Gen. Sir John Acton, he still was vague about what

> co-operation is intended by the Court of Naples, [so he wished] to know perfectly what is to be expected, that I may regulate my movements accordingly, and beg clear answers to the following questions and requisitions:—
>
> Are the Ports of Naples and Sicily open to his Majesty's Fleet? Have the Governors orders for our free admission? And for us to be supplied with whatever we may want?

As mentioned earlier, supply was critical; Nelson brought no supply organization with him, nor was there already one present for British forces. So, without tapping into some sort of supply system—the Neapolitan/Sicilian being the obvious one—he could not remain in the Mediterranean for more than a few months. Contemporary warships rarely carried food for more than six months, and at that it was often marginal, being mostly salted provisions, not fresh. In fact, by 1 August the *Vanguard*'s surgeon, Michael Jefferson, would have eight active cases of ulcerated legs, strongly indicating the close proximity of scurvy, generally preventable by eating fresh fruits and vegetables.[81]

Nelson's letter continued:

> If it is convenient, I much wish for [the loan of some Neapolitan frigates] and other fast-sailing Vessels, for, by a *fatality*, all mine have left me.
>
> I want information of the French Fleet; for I hope they have passed Naples.
>
> I want good Pilots—say six or eight, for the Coast of Sicily, the Adriatic, or for whatever place the Enemy's Fleet may be at.[82]

That same day he sent the *Mutine* to look into Telamon Bay (Talamone, western Tuscany, south of Elba) thinking it "a probable place for the rendezvous of a large Fleet."[83] He passed Elba on the thirteenth; then he "spoke a Tunisian cruiser, who reported he had spoke a Greek, on the 10th, who told him, that on the 4th, he had passed through the French Fleet, of about 200 Sail, as he thought, off the N.W. end of Sicily, steering to the eastward. Am in anxious expectation of meeting with Dispatch-boats, Neapolitan cruisers, &c., with letters for me from Naples giving me information."[84]

On the fifteenth Nelson wrote directly to Lord Spencer, attempting to update the Admiralty as to events and speculating on the prospect of the French moving against Egypt and India:

> I take the liberty of acquainting you that Captain Troubridge joined on the 7th, but it was the 12th before we passed Cape Corse. . . . The last account I had of the French Fleet, was from a Tunisian Cruizer, who saw them on the 4th, off Trapani, in Sicily, steering to the eastward.
>
> If they pass Sicily, I shall believe they are going on their scheme of possessing Alexandria, and getting troops to India—a plan concerted with Tippoo Saib, by no means so difficult as might at first view be imagined; but be they bound to the Antipodes, your Lordship may rely that I will not lose a moment in bringing them to Action, and

endeavour to destroy their Transports. I shall send Capt. Troubridge on shore to talk with General Acton, and I hope the King of Naples will send me some Frigates; for mine parted company on the 20th of May, and have not joined me since.[85]

Coincidentally, London's worry about India was already on the rise. As early as January, Capt. Sir William Sidney Smith, a prisoner of war in France (and one of the most colorful British naval officers of the period), sent a secret message to Lord Grenville hinting that the French Directory was contemplating the disruption of Egypt and British trade in the Levant. Smith later reinforced this concern subsequent to his escape and return to England.[86] Additionally, London gained possession of a letter, sometime in May, from the distinguished French geologist and mineralogist Gratet de Dolomieu (himself a knight of Malta, who later gave his name to the mineral dolomite and to the Dolomite Mountains). Penned in early April, it gave this worrisome intelligence:

> The object of this grand voyage is not known. . . . What is certain is that they are going to embark at Toulon and Genoa, and that they are probably part of the military expedition which is in preparation. It is also certain that they have an immense amount of printing equipment, books, instruments, chemical apparatus which suggests a very long absence. Among the books one notices above everything travels to the Levant, Egypt, Persia, India, Turkey, the Black Sea, the Caspian, the travels of Anacharsis in Greece. They are taking a dozen geographical engineers, military engineers, mathematicians, astronomers, chemists, doctors, artists and naturalists of every sort; two professors of Arabic, Persian and Turkish, and all have gone on board without knowing where they are going.
>
> Guesses baffle everyone. Some say a conquest in Egypt and cutting the Isthmus of Suez is contemplated in order to undermine English commerce with India[,] . . . others again suppose that English possessions in India are to be attacked by land. . . . What is certain is that [Bonaparte] is the chief promoter of the enterprise, and that he takes a lively interest in it.[87]

In fact, Napoleon did take a remarkable collection of scholars, including

Dolomieu, to Egypt. He had in mind, for the future, banishing "from the life of France that atmosphere of boorish ignorance by which the Terrorists of the Revolution had rendered themselves odious."[88]

It is not clear who became privy to the contents of Dolomieu's letter; it certainly was not transmitted to the Mediterranean fleet in even an abridged form, and it may have even been initially discredited for, after all, Dolomieu may have been a knight of Malta, but he was also French.[89] Moreover, it does not appear that this information was particularly known by the secretary of state for War, Henry Dundas. Dundas was also president of the East India Board and is said to have been the dominant voice of that organization since 1784, when he first became a member. On 9 June, Dundas wrote Spencer the following, with no indication of any possession of specific information or of any well-founded alarm: "Did the instructions to Lord St. Vincent mention that Egypt might be in the contemplation of Bonaparte's expedition? It may be whimsical, but I cannot help having a fancy of my own on that subject." A few days later he again wrote Spencer: "My dear Lord, —India has occupied my thoughts all night. . . . If the plan of the French is to go by the Red Sea, it is demonstrable that a small active squadron at the mouth of the Red Sea is fatal to their project. That squadron coming an hour too late is good for nothing. It is *impossible* that any other service can be equally pressing, nor is there another on which so much may turn."[90]

Dundas was agitated enough to send a warning to the Rt. Hon. the Marquess Wellesley, governor general of India (and the future Duke of Wellington's elder brother). Lord Spencer additionally took the precaution of sending a parallel message to Vice Adm. Peter Rainier, the naval commander in chief on the British East Indies station.[91]

From 15 to 18 June, Nelson stood off Naples, hoping for supplies, information, the loan of scouting vessels, and the loan of pilots. He again begged Ambassador Hamilton for help not only in writing but also in the persons of Captains Troubridge and Hardy, who were to represent his views, obtain information, and beg for Neapolitan frigates—"Troubridge will say everything I could put in a ream of paper:"[92] "I have only to observe, in my present state, if I meet the Enemy at Sea, the Convoy will get off, for want of Frigates. Although I hope the best [I am] prepared for the worst. . . . My distress for Frigates is extreme; but I cannot help myself, and no one will help me. But, thank God, I am not apt to feel difficulties." He certainly did feel them; what he no doubt meant was that they did not discourage him.[93] In fact, over and over, with increasing despair, "Nelson lamented his lack of frigates. Nothing else could scout and communicate as swiftly and efficiently; without them, like a gamekeeper probing a wood on a pitch-black night, his only aids were reason, instinct and familiarity with his ground."[94]

Nelson further complained to Hamilton about Neapolitan foreign policy: "On the arrival of [our] King's Fleet I find plenty of good will towards us, with every hatred towards the French; but no assistance for us—no hostility to the French. On the contrary, the French Minister is allowed to send off Vessels to inform [his] Fleet of my arrival, force, and destination, that instead of surprising them, they may be prepared." The Neapolitans maintained they were at peace with the French Republic, and "therefore, could afford us no assistance in Ships, but that, *under the rose,* they would give us the use of their Ports, and sincerely wished us well, but did not give me the smallest information of what was, or likely to be, the . . . destination of the French."[95]

On 17 June, Hamilton sent Nelson the intelligence he possessed respecting the enemy; both "then and later, Hamilton showed himself active" and worthy of Nelson's confidence:[96]

> The first division of the Toulon armament had arrived off Trapani in Sicily on the 5th of June, and had been there joined, on the 7th, by the second division, making sixteen sail of the line, Venetian and French; —that Buonaparte was on board the *Sans Culotte;* that ten frigates . . . had been also seen, with about 280 transports. . . . An officer had landed [claiming] that Buonaparte had desired him to say, *The approach of the French fleet need not give any uneasiness to his Sicilian majesty, with whom the republic was in perfect peace, and that the armament he commanded, had another object, not Sicily.* . . . Accounts had also been received, that Buonaparte was off Malta with twenty-four ships of the

line, and 80,000 men. . . . The Maltese were all under arms, and preparing a vigorous defence.[97]

In addition, on 17 June, Nelson's messengers Troubridge and Hardy returned with a verbal report that the French were at Malta. What was not discussed was a conversation between General Acton and the French ambassador, Monsieur Garrat, who "had assured [Acton] that the grand expedition from Toulon . . . was really destined for Egypt, that they were to establish a colony and build a city on the spot where stood ancient Berenice."

Neither Hamilton nor Acton passed this information to Nelson in writing, nor did they tell Troubridge. Acton may have been undecided whether to openly oppose the French or to continue fostering a neutral image. Hamilton felt the story unbelievable and that it was disinformation meant to mislead the British while calming the Neapolitans. Of course, it was true enough; had it actually been relayed to Nelson, the results would surely have been momentous.[98]

As it was, Nelson's force immediately ran down the coast of Sicily after sending the brig *Transfer*—found at Naples—to St. Vincent with dispatches. To port they saw the fishing village of Scylla, to starboard the whirlpool of Charybdis. (Although Charybdis was no longer quite the aquatic terror of Homer's day, as late as 1824 a successor to the Mediterranean command wrote, "I have seen several men-of-war, and even a 74-gun ship, whirled round on its surface."[99]) Passing the Straits of Messina on 22 June, the British squadron received intelligence from speaking a Genoese brig which had sailed from Malta the day before: "The [brig's] Master reported that Malta surrendered on Friday the 15th of June, and that on Saturday, the 16th, the whole French Fleet left it, as was supposed, for Sicily: that a French garrison was left in the Town, and French colours flying."[100]

Bonaparte's forces effectively secured Malta during the period of 10–12 June. There had been no vigorous defense (actually, there had hardly even been a token defense), and the conquest was remarkably easy, even though the ruling Knights of St. John had earlier received a warning from their ambassador in Austria: "The formidable expedition now preparing at Toulon is intended for the capture of Malta and Egypt. I have this information from the Secretary of M. Treilhard, one of the French Republican Ministers. . . . You will most assuredly be attacked. . . . The fortress of Malta is impregnable, or at least capable of resisting a three months siege. The honour of Your Eminence, and the preservation of the Order, are at stake, and if you surrender without making any defence, you will be dishonoured in the eyes of Europe."[101]

Dishonored they were, but it might not be fair to judge them too harshly. Their best intelligence made it clear that the godless, revolutionary French were at large in the Mediterranean, unopposed and extremely powerful. Had they known that a strong, English, and conservatively Christian, fleet was as close as the Italian mainland they might have shown stiffer resistance.

Indeed, Napoleon—with far better sources of intelligence—did not know that the British squadron had grown from three to thirteen ships of the line and that it was only one hundred miles away. Had the knights held out for even a few days Nelson might have been able to relieve them.[102] As it was, an observer on the island commented that "Malta had never seen such an enormous fleet in its waters. For miles around the sea was covered with ships of every size. Their masts looked like a huge forest."[103]

After spending a busy six days reorganizing the island's administration and economy, and leaving a small garrison, General Bonaparte and the bulk of his forces sailed away on the nineteenth. In a matter of days he had accomplished what the Grande Turke, Sultan Suleiman the Magnificent, had failed to do over three hundred years earlier. Stymied after a siege of several months, Suleiman had had to return to the East in defeat. Flushed with victory, Napoleon moved east with eager anticipation of further conquest.

The intelligence the British garnered from the Genoese brig contained a crucial inaccuracy: a salient item was either unheard or mistranslated.[104] The information was substantially, but not quite, correct.[105] The French had left Malta only three days earlier, not six. Had Nelson interviewed the brig's captain himself, "he might have found out more, for he was a shrewd questioner, and his intellect was sharpened by anxiety, and by constant dwelling upon the elements of the intricate problem before him; but the vessel had been boarded by the *Mutine,* three hours before, and was now beyond recall."[106]

Actually, throughout the campaign, Nelson obtained extensive information from ships met at sea. Although chasing and detaining neutral and enemy vessels was difficult for a task force without frigates, there were at least forty-one ships and boats stopped between 8 May and 1 August. Nelson was desperate for information and promoted this activity, though he wanted minimal interference with the squadron's progress. Of course, after a ship was detained and its master questioned, the next requirement was for translation and analysis of any information obtained. Translation was challenging: Spanish, French, Italian, German, Arabic, Greek, Swedish, Turkish, and Ragusan were all needed during this campaign, and though many British officers and seamen spoke foreign languages, mistakes and misunderstandings were problematic.[107]

Something did go awry with the intelligence obtained from the Genoese brig, but Nelson had to use it as best he could, analyzing and correlating it with the other information he had. He had no way of knowing the truth and, in any event, had to act upon what information he possessed. He disclosed his analysis and reasoning to St. Vincent in a letter dated 29 June:

> I could not get to Malta till [the wind] moderated, and then I might get no better information. Thus situated I had to make use of my judgement. . . . I recalled all the circumstances of the Armament before me, 40,000 troops in 280 Transports, many hundred pieces of artillery, waggons, draught-horses, cavalry, artificers, naturalists, astronomers, mathematicians, &c. . . . The Armament could not be necessary for [merely] taking possession of Malta.

The Neapolitan Ministers considered Naples and Sicily as safe . . . any place to the westward, I could not think their destination, for at this season the westerly winds so strongly prevail . . . that I conceive it almost impossible to get a Fleet . . . to the westward.

It then became the serious question, where are they gone? (Here I had deeply to regret my want of Frigates, and I desire it may be understood, that *if one-half the Frigates your Lordship had ordered under my command had been with me, that I could not have wanted information of the French Fleet* [emphasis added].)

Upon their whole proceedings, together with such information as I have been able to collect, it appeared clear to me, that either they were destined to assist the rebel Pacha and to overthrow the present Government of Turkey, *or to settle a Colony in Egypt, and to open a trade to India by way of the Red Sea* [emphasis added]. . . . Three weeks, at this season, is a common passage to the Malabar Coast, when our India possessions would be in great danger.[108]

Simultaneous to the sighting of the Genoese brig early on 22 June, the British had also sighted the sails of four frigates to the east-southeast. More important, the French—for that was who they were—had sighted the British squadron in turn. Thus, Bonaparte and Brueys learned that the Royal Navy was back in the Mediterranean in force, and as a result they decided to slightly alter their course to obscure their real objective and, with any luck, throw Nelson off the scent.[109] Nelson did not stop to chase the French frigates, fearing he would be drawn off from the primary threat. He was certain that they could not be part of the French main fleet, for his best information indicated that it had left Malta *six* days before and thus should be much too far away for any possibility of visual sighting. Of course these ships were, in fact, scouts of Bonaparte's great fleet, and thus Nelson experienced the first of three close encounters narrowly missing the enemy. Fortunately, he was going to have several more opportunities before the campaign was over.

Totally unaware of this misfortune, and although not generally a proponent of councils of war, Nelson called together Captains Saumarez, Troubridge, Ball, Darby, and Berry and posed the question:

Do you think we had better stand for Malta, steer for Sicily, or push on to Alexandria? Saumarez gave his opinion in writing, from which may be seen how one inaccuracy in the intercepted intelligence (that the French were bound for Sicily), was offset by another (that Bonaparte had left Malta as early as the 16th):

'The French fleet having left Malta six [in reality only three] days ago, had their destination been the island of Sicily, there is reason to presume we should have obtained information of it yesterday off Syracuse, or the day before coming through the Pharo of Messina. Under all circumstances I think it most conducive to the good of His Majesty's service to make the best of our way for Alexandria, as the only means of saving our possessions in India should the French Armament be destined for that country.'[110]

For some time the popular view has been that Nelson often brought all his captains together on board the flagship, much reinforced by Captain Berry's often-quoted statement that throughout the cruise it had been Nelson's practice, "whenever the weather and circumstances would permit, to have his captains on board the *Vanguard* where he would fully develop to them his own ideas of the different and best modes of attack. . . . With the masterly ideas of their admiral therefore on the subject of naval tactics, every one of the captains of his squadron was most thoroughly acquainted."[111]

However, Nelson actually brought his captains together only in ones and twos, and aside from this occasion, apparently never had more than five together at one time between 10 June and 1 August. In reality, five of the captains—Gould, Louis, Miller, Peyton, and Westcott—do not seem to have been called over even once. "Despite the legend of the 'Band of Brothers,' Nelson appears remote and isolated throughout the campaign," writes Brian Lavery.[112] Sir Horatio's future campaigns would see more inspiration and bonding with subordinates than did this one; yet here even Sir James Saumarez—not always very happy with Nelson's leadership—was extremely impressed by Nelson's determination and single-minded focus.

The captains' conference of 22 June was fateful; all, including Nelson, were in agreement. Thus, finally deducing General Bonaparte's true destination—without any real confirmation—from what was a paucity of clues, Nelson boldly acted upon this strategic insight: "With the stake nothing less than the future of the world, he at once set course for Alexandria."[113] In another way he was bold as well, for the British navy historically had very little experience operating in the eastern Mediterranean.[114] But Nelson

> therefore determined, with the opinion of those Captains in whom I place great confidence, to go to Alexandria; and if that place, or any other part of Egypt was their destination, I hoped to arrive [with] time enough to frustrate their plans.
>
> The only objection I can fancy . . . is, 'you should not have gone on such a long voyage without more certain information of the Enemy's destination:' my answer is ready—*who was I to get it from?*
>
> The Governments of Naples and Sicily either knew not, or chose to keep me in ignorance. Was I to wait patiently till I heard certain accounts? If Egypt was their object, before I could hear of them they would have been in India. To do nothing, I felt, was disgraceful: therefore I made use of my understanding, and by it I ought to stand or fall.
>
> [Nevertheless] however erroneous my judgment may be, I feel conscious of my honest intentions, which I hope will bear me up under the greatest misfortune that could happen to me as an Officer—that of your Lordship [St. Vincent] thinking me wrong.[115]

A fair wind took the British to Alexandria; seven hundred miles in six days. "The chase was on," Ernle Bradford writes. "But the hounds that pursued were deprived of their eyes [frigates]. They had only their sense of smell (their deductive intelligence) to rely on as to the direction taken by the hunted."[116]

A few ships spoken had no news of the French, and they saw precious few ships in the empty pre–Suez Canal mideastern sea. Moreover, Admiral Brueys had been seizing and holding any ship he sighted during the voyage, "thus imposing a news blackout on the Eastern Mediterranean."[117] Captain Saumarez confessed to his journal that they were crowding sail for Alexandria; at present it is very doubtful whether we shall fall in with them at all, as we are proceeding upon the merest conjecture only, and not on any positive information.

Some days must now elapse before we can be relieved of our cruel suspense, and if at the end of our journey we find we are upon a wrong scent, our embarrassment will be great indeed. Fortunately, I only act here *en second;* but did the chief responsibility rest with me, I fear it would be more than my too irritable nerves could bear.[118]

En route, Nelson had composed two letters to George Baldwin, British consul at Alexandria. In them he attempted to both acquaint Baldwin with his analysis as well as query him for information. On 26 June Nelson sent them forward to Alexandria, via Commander Hardy in the *Mutine:*

I think [the French] object is, to possess themselves of some Port in Egypt, and to fix themselves at the head of the Red Sea, in order to get a formidable Army into India; and, in concert with Tippoo Saib, drive us, if possible, from India. . . .

I am most exceedingly anxious to know from you if any reports of preparations have been made in Egypt for them; or any Vessels prepared in the Red Sea, to carry them to India, where, from the prevailing winds at this season, they would soon arrive; or any other information you would be good enough to give me, I shall hold myself much obliged.

Pray do not detain the *Mutine* [my only scouting vessel] for I am in a fever at not finding the French.[119]

Hardy was not able to deliver the letters, nor gain any information, as Baldwin was on a leave of absence. The Egyptian commandant of Alexandria received Hardy with disbelief: "It is impossible that the French should come to our country. They have no business here and we are not at war with them."[120]

For several days "not a hundred miles separated the rival forces, making for the same destination."[121] In fact, on the night of 22 June the fleets passed very close to one another: "The British line of battle, swift, compact, and intent, passed unknowingly through the converging track of the French expedition."[122] With no sensors other than the human eye and ear, the darkness and thick weather prevented any contact, though some French later reported that they had heard ships' bells (and minute guns firing in the mist) not their own. "Had Nelson possessed a scouting line of frigates, he must surely have fallen in with them."[123] Had he even allowed a more-dispersed formation of his ships of the line—a daylight coverage of two hundred miles width was theoretically possible—detection may have ensued; but, hoping and expecting to encounter the enemy at any time he maintained a rigid policy of concentration—he wanted the captains to be in the tightest formation possible, "and on no account *whatever* to risk the separation of their ships. . . . It is very necessary in fine weather in the Mediterranean for the ships of the squadron to keep as close together as possible, for the winds are often so variable and in contrary directions in the space of four or five miles, that an opportunity of bringing the enemy to battle may be lost."[124]

As it was, dawn on the twenty-third saw the fleets beyond mutual sight for they were, in fact, on divergent courses; Bonaparte had ordered Brueys initially to head toward Crete in order to mislead any vessels they may have passed: "Had the horizon of the British fleet been enlarged by flanking frigates, chasing on either side, the immunity of the French from detection could scarcely have continued."[125] In fact, had the fleets seen each other and fought, "the world might . . . have witnessed a more colossal disaster on the sea than the defeat of the Armada. Nelson's plans were made. Two-thirds of his fleet was to have kept the French ships of the line occupied, while the other third dashed in among the helpless transports. . . . The crowded transports must have been sunk or burned in dozens, for a sailing fleet can not scatter to the four quarters of the compass."[126]

Had they engaged in combat, the entire history of nineteenth-century Europe (if not the world) would have been far different: "General Buonaparte would have [been killed] or ended his career, in all probability, in 1798 as a prisoner of war in England—or Naples, if he were unlucky."[127] And not just General Bonaparte; along with him were many of the most talented generals in France's service, no small number of whom would, during the next seventeen years, lead armies and some would even carry field marshal's batons in the Napoleonic Empire: Berthier, Marmont, Lannes, Murat, Desaix, Reynier, Caffarelli, Andreossy, Junot, Davout, Dumas, and Kléber.[128]

Napoleon, in a practical spirit of interservice cooperation (very unusual in those days), assigned his troops to augment the warships' gun crews.[129] These now-mixed crews were exercised every morning in naval gun drill. Some French historians maintain that with thousands of combat-experienced soldiers onboard the French ships, who would have helped the seamen man the guns, the outcome would have been favorable to the French; but "in view of the strength of British gunnery (shortly to be demonstrated)," as historian Ernest Jenkins remarks, "this seems doubt-ful." Regardless, it did not come to pass, and joins the myriad of things in history's long list of "what-ifs."[130]

Arrival at Alexandria, on the twenty-eighth, found no French nor any sign of them. "Nelson bore the blow unflinchingly, although with annoyance" and unspeakable chagrin:[131] "I stretched the Fleet over to the Coast of Asia, and have passed close to the southern side of Candia [Crete], but without seeing one Vessel in our route; therefore to this day I am without the smallest information of the French Fleet since their leaving Malta. . . . I have again to deeply regret my want of Frigates, *to which I shall ever attribute my ignorance of the situation of the French Fleet*" [emphasis added].[132]

Nelson, empty-handed at Alexandria, did not know that he had run past the French and gotten there ahead of them. He had done just the opposite of what "Bonaparte and Brueys had done a month before. They had waited for the Civita Vecchia convoy when it was really *ahead* of them; *he* had hurried after the French fleet when it was really *astern* of him."[133]

Nelson remained fundamentally sure that his analysis had been cor-rect; nevertheless, he did fall victim to the anxious worry that he had mis-judged, and that Sicily had been Bonaparte's true destination after all:

It is an old saying, 'the Devil's children have the Devil's luck.' I cannot find, or to this moment learn, beyond vague conjecture where the French Fleet are gone to. All my ill fortune, hitherto, has proceeded from want of Frigates.

From [Alexandria] I stretched over [400 miles of empty sea] to the Coast of Caramania [an area of Turkey including the Taurus Mountains down to the coast], where not meeting a Vessel that could give me information, I became distressed for the Kingdom of [Naples and Sicily], and having gone a round of 600 leagues at this season of the year . . . with an expedition incredible, here I am as ignorant of the situation of the Enemy as I was twenty-seven days ago.[134]

As already mentioned, Nelson's intuition and analysis had been correct. The French had had a three-day head start but, with a force so much larger than Nelson's their progress was significantly slower—almost half the speed—and they had made a slight detour to the north. Moreover, having "started in pursuit of Brueys with a three weeks' handicap (counting from Bonaparte's departure from Toulon on 19 May to Troubridge's juncture on 7 June) and supposing that he [Nelson] had left the vicinity of Malta six days (instead of only three) after the French, he did not realize that he might have outstripped them."[135]

Ironically, had Sir Horatio briefly loitered off Alexandria, even a mere twenty-five hours, he would have had the French expedition sail into his arms (or rather arm, for he had lost his right arm in combat a year before during his unsuccessful attack on Tenerife). As it turned out, the Armeé d'Orient disembarked four miles west at Marabout. Here an earlier intelligence failure—that of Sir John Acton and Sir William Hamilton—was crucial in not passing to Nelson the French envoy's remarks about Bonaparte's Egyptian intentions. With that information Nelson might have remained the few hours that would have ensured contact. Here also a scouting force of frigates would have probably detected the French. "Once more, cruelly crippled by his lack of frigates, Nelson had [just] missed an epoch-making victory."[136]

For their part the French had good reason to believe that they had almost been caught. Note the following in a letter from Admiral Brueys to French Minister of the Marine Bruix:

> Citizen Minister: Previously to our arrival off the old port of Alexandria, I had despatched the *Juno* to bring [our] consul on board. Citizen Magallon arrived on the first of July, and informed us, that an English squadron had appeared . . . off the port of Alexandria on the 28th of June, that they had detached a brig to the town, and that, on its return, they had made sail to the N.E.
>
> The commander-in-chief, Buonaparte, desired to be put on shore immediately: I, therefore, came to anchor on the coast, and, during the night, succeeded in landing 6000 men. . . . Not the slightest opposition was made to our descent.[137]

As stated earlier, it did not seriously impress Nelson that he could have passed by the French; furthermore, he feared that he might have misanalyzed, and the French had gone to Sicily after all. Sir Horatio's nerves were frayed to such a degree that he could not tolerate inactivity. Berry observed that Nelson's "anxious and active mind . . . would not permit him to rest a moment in the same place."[138] Loitering was not an option for him; Caesar Augustus's motto, *Festina Lente* (hasten slowly), was certainly not Admiral Nelson's.[139] Without delay the British fleet rushed back to the westward, past Crete (three hundred miles of empty sea), and then back to Sicily (seven hundred miles of more empty sea), doing "with his fleet the exploring duty that frigates should have done."[140] On 30 June, Nelson "proceeded for the coast of Caramania, steering along the south side of Candia, and thence back to Sicily, and anchored at Syracuse on the 20th of July, where the Squadron . . . watered and obtained fresh provisions, &c."[141]

Having not found the French, Nelson was exasperated and his confidence was shaken. He asked his captains to sign statements supporting the decision to go to Alexandria, while writing to St. Vincent "that I am before your Lordship's judgement and if under all circumstances it is decided that I am wrong, I ought for the sake of our country to be superseded."[142]

Nevertheless, he remained quite resolute. Driving on in the blazing July Mediterranean heat—the pitch very tacky in the deck seams—Nelson examined the intelligence problem over and over. He had time enough to do this, for his specific duties during the campaign were narrowly defined. He had no daily regimen nor specific tasks to accomplish. Of course, he was always concerned about overall supply issues, and he had to compose infrequent reports to superiors and handle occasional correspondence external to the squadron. But these duties were not overly time consuming, which allowed him considerable opportunity to remain focused upon the collection, collation, and analysis of intelligence. And, in those days before radios, faxes, aircraft reconnaissance, aircraft delivery, spy satellites, and satellite downlinks, the information flow was manageable. Intelligence came in at a slow rate, with a piece of correspondence or a detained merchant ship appearing on an average of only once every other day. Yet this was a two-edged sword, for Sir Horatio thus had time and more to brood over what needed to be done and what he did not know, and to grow obsessed over what was going wrong.

The modern reader, in our age of worldwide instantaneous information exchange, truly has a difficult time imagining the communications problem inherent to those days. Nelson occasionally found the means to send correspondence to St. Vincent at Lisbon or to the Admiralty in London. All that was required was the chance encounter of some sort of vessel that could be used to carry dispatches; that was the hard part, for at least St. Vincent and the Admiralty remained in known locations for such a vessel to find. In between such opportunities all he could do was write letters and pile them on his desk (or maintain a running diary-style letter) until forwarding became possible. Nelson refers to this situation, on 12 June, in a long letter to St. Vincent, which actually was written over four days: "As I see no immediate prospect of [dispatching] a Letter, I shall continue my private one in form of a Diary."[143]

Such communications difficulties were nothing, however, in comparison to those faced by anyone trying to *send* messages to an at-sea commander. Such people, whether in this case Lord Spencer, Lord St. Vincent, or even Ambassador Hamilton, had the same problems Nelson had in obtaining suitable dispatch vessels; but while they themselves remained in fixed locations Nelson was cruising up and down the Mediterranean, his position from week to week virtually unknown. All that a potential correspondent could do is send one or more copies of his message in one or more dispatch vessels (if available), hoping that at least one copy would reach the intended recipient, and even if that were successful, any time-critical information was usually doomed to be out-of-date upon receipt. (A perfect example of this, though fictional, is the attempt in 1810 of now–Rear Adm. Sir Thomas Troubridge to contact Capt. Horatio Hornblower, on independent operations on the coast of Latin America, to inform him that Britain was no longer at war with Spain and to require him to refrain from hostilities against the Spanish. Troubridge's letter "was marked 'Copy No. 2.' . . . Other copies had been distributed to other parts of the Spanish possessions to ensure that [Hornblower] received one." But it was too late—not knowing of the alliance Horn-blower had already captured the largest Spanish ship in the area, the *Natividad,* and had substantially aided local rebels fighting against Span-ish authority).[144]

The reality of the Nile campaign was that over a several-month period Nelson dispatched a considerable number of letters, personal and official, that for the most part reached their intended recipients—eventually. However, during this same time Nelson *received* virtually no informa-tion from his superiors or his political advisors; the main exception to this being the few occasions he passed by Naples and communicated with Hamilton.

Thus, the modern reader has to be flatly amazed by the sheer isola-tion of a commander in Nelson's position, as Nelson "believed that his failure would be a national disaster and the responsibility weighed very heavily. . . . He was almost completely out of contact with higher author-ity for several months and forced to make every decision on his own. . . . By the end of June he was showing clear signs of exhaustion."[145]

His own summary of the situation is telling: "I have this comfort, that I have no fault to accuse myself of. This bears me up, and this only. What a situation I am placed in! As yet, I can learn nothing of the Enemy; therefore I have no conjecture but that they are gone to Syria, and at Cyprus I hope to hear of them."[146] From Syracuse he wrote to Lady Nelson, on 20 July, "I have not been able to find the French Fleet, to my great mortification. . . . We have been off Malta, to Alexandria in Egypt, Syria, into Asia, and are returned here without success: however, no person will say that it has been for the want of activity. . . . It would have been my delight to have tried Buonaparte on a wind, for he commands the Fleet, as well as the Army."[147]

For his part, Napoleon did not particularly fear a fleet action and did not quite understand the nervousness of his admirals. Battle-scarred though he was, he had never seen the staggering destructive power of a British ship of the line in action.[148] To be fair, his previous personal contact with the Royal Navy caused him to have less respect for it than did some of his countrymen; after all, he saw it forced from the port of Toulon in the fall of 1793 largely because of his own vigorous efforts as commander of artillery (he captured a key position which dominated both the inner and outer harbors) which earned him promotion to brigadier general.[149] However, fearful or not, when Admiral Brueys suggested that four ships of the line and three frigates be detached to look for the temporarily missing convoy from Civitavecchia, the general became cautious and refused: "If, 24-hours after this separation, ten English ships of the line are signaled, I will have only nine ships of the line instead of thirteen."[150]

Although transparent to the majority of his subordinates, Sir Horatio's personal frustration was overwhelming. Nerves strung to the breaking point, "Nelson's anguish at the apparent failure of his pursuit was . . . expressed in a letter written to Troubridge several years later: 'Do not fret at anything. I wish I never had, but my return to Syracuse in 1798 broke my heart.'"[151]

Certain that the French were neither at Corfu nor westward of Sicily,

based upon having spoken several vessels prior to anchoring at Syracuse,
Nelson was able to learn nothing concrete at Sicily:

> Yesterday [19 July] I arrived here, where I can learn no more than
> vague conjecture that the French are gone to the eastward. Every
> moment I have to regret [my] Frigates having left me, to which must
> be attributed my ignorance of the movements of the Enemy.
>
> We are watering, and getting such refreshments as the place affords,
> and shall get to sea by the 25th. It is my intention to get into the Mouth
> of the [Greek] Archipelago, where, if the Enemy are gone towards
> Constantinople, we shall hear of them directly: if I get no information
> there, to go to Cyprus, when, if they are in Syria or Egypt, I must hear
> of them. . . . We have a report that on the 1st of July, the French were
> seen off Candia.[152]

Nelson's force did depart on 25 July, bound for the Greek peninsula; he
was sure "that some authentic intelligence might possibly be obtained in"
that region.[153] His mood was a little improved, writing that the instant
that the "wind comes off the land [we] shall go out of this delightful harbour where our present wants have been most amply supplied. . . . Surely
watering at the Fountain of Arethusa, we must have victory."[154]

His official letters contained a different message, complaining of the
squadron's treatment—"the King's Flag is insulted at every Friendly
Port we look at."[155] These negative remarks were pure disinformation;
Nelson was certain that his letters sent outside naval channels were being
opened, and he therefore wanted the French to believe the Neapolitans
were not being particularly helpful.[156]

Nelson was certain that the French could not possibly be west of Italy,
due to the significant absence of news combined with what he knew
were the past weather conditions in that area. His plan was to press on
for Cyprus, then Syria, and again Egypt if he had no luck at the Peloponnesus or at Constantinople.[157]

Even at this late date conflicting and incorrect intelligence was still
appearing in London. At the end of July, Dundas was apprised that a
short-run goal of material gain was the French plan, not territorial

expansion nor disruption of British trade: "Bonaparte is not bound for Alexandria but Constantinople and this is the opinion of the best informed circles in Paris, founded on the knowledge they have of the character of the government, [which seeks] for plunder wherever it is to be found. . . . The robbery of all the factories in the Levant and the spoils of the Porte will be a considerable object to them."[158]

However, the long campaign was almost over. An extract from the *Vanguard*'s journal relates the final sequence of events as the long chase —nearly eight-weeks' duration—came to a close:

> From Syracuse the Squadron proceeded with all expedition to the Morea. . . . On the 28th of July, being near the Morea, the *Culloden* was sent into the Gulf of Coron [the modern Messenia, an inlet of the Ionian Sea] for intelligence, and on her return, the next day, she brought . . . information that the Enemy's Fleet had been seen steering to the S.E. from Candia about four weeks before.
>
> The *Alexander,* Captain Ball, on the same day obtained similar intelligence from a Vessel passing close to the Fleet, and [the admiral] immediately bore up, under all sail, for Alexandria.
>
> At seven in the evening, of the 31st of July [having rushed almost 500 miles in three days], the Admiral made the signal for the Fleet to close, and early in the morning of the 1st of August, the *Alexander* and *Swiftsure* were sent ahead to look out.

The empty French transports were observed at Alexandria, but *not* the battle fleet. Fearing that they had again guessed wrongly, Captain Saumarez wrote that "despondency nearly took possession of my mind, and I do not recollect ever to have felt so utterly hopeless or out of spirits as when we sat down to [luncheon]."[159] What Nelson thought is unrecorded, but must have been pitiable. However, "at 4, Pharos Tower S.W. distant four or five leagues, the *Zealous* made the signal for the French Fleet, sixteen Sail of the Line. At 5, bore up for the French Fleet."[160]

In truth, the French warships were resting at anchor in the Bay of Aboukir. Nelson shortly sat down to a good dinner "after many anxious days during which he never spared himself, seldom sleeping and eating little food."[161] Arising from dinner, Nelson exclaimed, "Before this time tomorrow, I shall have gained a Peerage, or Westminster Abbey," referring to the possibilities of receiving high reward—or of being killed. Captain Berry later wrote that "the utmost joy seemed to animate every breast on board the Squadron, at sight of the Enemy."[162]

At the time Berry asked Nelson, "If we succeed, what will the world say?" "There is no *if* in the case," replied Sir Horatio, "that we *shall* succeed is certain; who will *live* to tell the story is a very different question."[163]

Nelson later told a story on himself regarding his feelings upon viewing the enemy: "When I saw them I could not help popping my head every now and then out of the window . . . and once when I was observing their position I heard two seamen quartered at a gun near me, talking, and one said to the other 'Damn them, look at them, there they are, Jack, and if we don't beat them, they will beat us.' I knew what stuff I had under me, so I went into the attack with only a few ships, perfectly sure that the others would follow me, although it was nearly dark and they might have had every excuse for not doing it."[164]

The French warships were indeed caught. But neither General Bonaparte, the French army, nor the fleet of transport ships were present at Aboukir. After landing four miles west of Alexandria on and after 1 July, the army had marched 150 miles south to Cairo across the baking desert. Defeating Mameluke cavalry at Shubrakhit on the thirteenth, and a larger Mameluke army at Giza on the twenty-first—the famous Battle of the Pyramids—Napoleon triumphantly entered the Egyptian capital on the twenty-second. It appeared everything was working in Bonaparte's favor, fulfilling his proclamation of a month before: "Soldiers —You are going to undertake a conquest whose effects on civilization will be incalculable. You will strike the surest and most painful stroke possible against England until you can deal her the final death blow. . . . Destiny is with us."[165]

Monsieur Jaubert, commissary of the French fleet, reflected upon the situation on 8 July: "The English fleet has played with ill luck on its side: first, it missed us on the coast of Sardinia; next, it missed a convoy of fifty-seven sail coming from Civita Vecchia, with 7,000 troops of the Army of Italy on board. It did not arrive at Malta until five days after we had left it; and it arrived at Alexandria two days too soon to meet with us. It is to be presumed that it is gone to Alexandretta [in the Gulf of Iskenderun in the extreme north-east corner of the Mediterranean], under an idea that the army is to be disembarked there for the conquest of India. We shall certainly meet it at last; but we are now moored in such a manner as to bid defiance to a force more than double our own."[166]

Having landed the army, Admiral Brueys wanted to return to France. However, prior to leaving Alexandria, Bonaparte had ordered him to loiter in Egyptian waters and not to return just yet. Brueys felt that the mouth of Alexandria's harbor was too shallow for his largest warships (particularly the 120-gun *L'Orient*), so he moved his squadron fifteen miles east to Aboukir Bay, anchoring there on 8 July. Brueys wrote,

> On the 7th of July, having satisfied myself that our ships of war could not get into the port for want of a sufficient depth of water at the entrance . . . stood off with the thirteen sail of the line, and the three frigates, with an intent of mooring in the road of Bequieres, or Aboukir. . . . I arrived there in the afternoon, and formed a line of battle. . . . This position is the strongest we could possibly take in an open road[,] . . . the result of many laborious and painful experiments.
>
> I have heard nothing further of the English. They are gone . . . and this is my private opinion, they have not so many as fourteen sail of the line, and not finding that they had a superior number, they did not consider it wise to measure themselves against us.[167]

Aboukir Bay appears as a semicircular indentation sixteen miles across in the shoreline of Egypt, facing northwest just to the west of the Rosetta mouth of the Nile River. Toward the northeast of the bay was a chain of islands, rocks, and shoals which formed a natural breakwater; here Admiral Brueys anchored his ships in a line of battle. Not having accurate charts, Brueys left considerable room for his ships to swing at their anchors; in fact, he was much farther from the actual location of the shoals than he might have been, which weakened his defensive position.

This proved to be a terrible mistake, for as it happened it allowed the British room to pass around the head of the French line, between the line and the shore, and between the individual French ships. In his defense, one can only remark that Brueys was sure that ignorance of the shoals would intimidate and restrain the British. They were slightly intimidated but, as Berry later described him, Nelson was "a seaman determined on attack."

Admiral Brueys might have saved himself if he had had his frigates at sea; with advanced warning of Nelson's approach he may have significantly rearranged his defenses, organized his command and fought at sea (with surely better results), or even escaped entirely. Sir Horatio's lack of intelligence throughout this entire campaign was largely due to the absence of scouting "eyes." Ironically, Brueys had four frigates with him at Aboukir but failed to use them at just the most critical time. Of course, across the abyss of two hundred years it is easy to be judgmental. The French fleet's acute shortage of provisions and water may well have precluded the frigates' ability to sortie; certainly with hundreds of their men on shore, desperately trying to keep pace with the fleet's enormous consumption of water and stores, each French ship's combat readiness was truly impaired.

Having previously thought about such a scenario and having thoroughly discussed this possibility with some of his captains during the long chase, Nelson chose to attack immediately. This was in spite of having no pilots knowledgeable of the bay, no charts (Nelson had a recently captured rough sketch of the bay; Captain Foley had a recently published French atlas, *Bellin's Collection,* which contained a good illustration of Aboukir; Captain Hood had a very incorrect English atlas), and in spite of the setting sun (nighttime sea combat was more the exception rather than the rule in those days). The concept of neither fleet having any accurate charts can only be a marvel for the modern reader in the information age, but the truth is that no proper survey of the Egyptian coast existed in 1798.[168] The contrast to our modern way of war is startling; for example, in 1990–91 over two thousand tons of high-quality maps (117 million map sheets) were delivered to coalition forces in the theater during Operation Desert Storm.[169]

Three of Nelson's ships of the line, *Swiftsure, Alexander,* and *Culloden,* were not immediately present; however, "the enemy was in sight; he must be given no chance to make special preparations, or to slip away again in the night."[170] (The *Swiftsure* and the *Alexander* were a dozen miles to leeward, doing the missing frigates' duty by reconnoitering Alexandria.) The French deployment presented formidable obstacles, but "it instantly struck [Nelson's] eager and penetrating mind, that where there was room for an Enemy's Ship to swing, *there was room for one of ours to anchor.*"[171]

The battle began at 6:31 P.M., 1 August 1798. By 8:30 thirteen British ships of the line had engaged thirteen of the French. As darkness fell they had sailed into the bay: "They had no chart of the locality, but sounding as they came, they swung out past the dangerous ridge of rocks which runs out from Aboukir Island under the sea, came up again on the enemy's side of it, and fell with crushing violence upon his helpless van. It is hard to decide which to admire the more, the seamanship or the daring of that entry into action in unknown shoals, in growing darkness, with the guns of the enemy loaded and waiting for them."[172]

Brueys had expected any attack to first fall on his fleet's rear, but once the battle began the French center and rear could do nothing but await their destruction in turn, subsequent to the initial destruction of the van (the leading division of the formation). It probably seemed to the French that Nelson's intelligence was uncanny as he went directly for the weakest part of their line. But Nelson really had no way of knowing that the van ships had dangerously reduced crews, or that the *Guerrier, Conquérant,* and *Peuple Souverain* were all fifty-some years old—and that the *Conquérant* had on board only 18-pounder cannon instead of the normal 36-pounders.[173] The wind—always a deciding factor with sailing ships—no doubt drove his decision. It was blowing straight down the line, favoring and facilitating the British attack while preventing any reordering or concentration of the French. Admiral Brueys was killed, while his flagship caught fire and subsequently blew up with an appalling detonation, the shock of which momentarily stupefied both fleets and caused a pause in the fighting. (The great tragedy of *L'Orient*'s destruction contains an enormous list of immeasurable material and human loss, not the least of which are the deaths of Commodore Casabianca and his ten-year-old son, subject of Felicia Hemans's famous poem "Casabianca": "The boy stood on the burning deck / Whence all but him had fled.")

The battle effectively ended at eleven o'clock, when two French ships of the line and two frigates cut their cables and stood out to sea, briefly pursued by HMS *Zealous*. The details of the fighting—and they are very interesting—may be found in any number of fine studies more focused upon tactics than upon intelligence issues. Suffice it to say that Nelson, his captains, and his crews most certainly did solve that "more ordinary problem" of fighting and beating the enemy, but only because Nelson had been able to previously solve his immense, primary problem of finding the enemy:

> *Vanguard,* off the Mouth of the Nile, 3rd August, 1798
>
> My Lord [St. Vincent],
> Almighty God has blessed his Majesty's Arms in the late Battle, by a great Victory over the Fleet of the Enemy, who I attacked at sunset on the 1st of August, off the Mouth of the Nile. The Enemy were moored in a strong Line of Battle . . . flanked by numerous Gunboats, four Frigates, and a Battery of Guns and Mortars on an Island in their Van; but nothing could withstand the Squadron your Lordship did me the honour to place under my command. Their high state of discipline is well known to you, and with the judgment of the Captains, together with their valour, and that of the Officers and Men of every description, it was absolutely irresistible. Could anything from my pen add to the character of the Captains, I would write it with pleasure, but that is impossible. . . .
>
> > Horatio Nelson.[174]

The French fleet suffered two ships of the line burned and nine more captured, with over three thousand casualties; the British, though very materially damaged and absorbing one thousand casualties, lost no ships.

It proved to be a dangerous encounter for the leadership of both sides; the dead numbered one admiral and three captains, while the wounded counted two admirals (including Nelson) and nine captains.

The Battle of the Nile was, arguably, the most decisive naval engagement of the great age of sail; in fact, the victory was effectively unparalleled in history. The Spanish Armada lost only two-thirds of its force while a fair-sized Turkish fleet survived Lepanto. Indeed, only a few subsequent battles, including Trafalgar, Tsushima, and, perhaps, Midway, can be compared to the Nile as examples of "the annihilation of one fleet by another of approximately equal [or inferior] material force."[175]

Nelson, only thirty-nine-years old and a junior rear admiral, had regained the command of the Mediterranean Sea for Great Britain. General Bonaparte and the Armeé d'Orient were cut off from France, terminating the Indian campaign and, in addition, preventing their return home:

> Most damaging was the blow suffered by French prestige. . . . Elsewhere in Europe Nelson's achievement undoubtedly hastened the formation of the Second Coalition. Between September 1798 and February the following year, Turkey, Naples, Russia and Austria joined forces with Great Britain and Portugal.
>
> Although in the long run the formation of this coalition was destined to prove to Bonaparte's personal advantage, providing him with the opportunity of increasing his reputation and of overthrowing the Directory, and thus dooming Europe to a further sixteen years of almost continuous war, its immediate effect was to presage disaster for France in Germany, Switzerland and North Italy.[176]

The victory directly answered Prime Minister Pitt's hopes of rallying key countries to renewed activity against the French. It became an extremely potent factor in remolding international opinion and attitude.[177]

For several days after the battle the British squadron stayed in Aboukir Bay, immersed in the business of burying the dead, organizing prisoners, making critical repairs, and generally recovering from the action.

Sir Horatio was personally occupied in recuperating from his wound (he had been grazed across the forehead by a piece of scrap iron fired from a French cannon, causing a shocking though superficial laceration; significantly, it apparently gave him a concussion as well, from which he took some time to recover). During this time he focused—as well as he could —upon his own reports and correspondence; in addition, he became preoccupied with some captured French documents.

On 8 August a packet of intercepted dispatches, bound for Paris, was passed to Nelson. These were shortly augmented by a similarly captured package bound for General Bonaparte from France; on 22 August HMS *Alcmene* captured the French gunboat *La Legére* off Alexandria: "We could not prevent the Dispatches for Buonaparte from being thrown overboard, which was however perceived by John Taylor and James Harding . . . who, at the risk of their lives . . . dashed overboard, and saved the whole of them. Both men were most fortunately picked up by the Boat that was sent after them, and I conceive it my duty to make known the very spirited conduct they showed on this occasion for the good of the service."[178]

The contemplation of all these documents gave Nelson another opportunity to exercise his skills as an intelligence analyst. He had this material translated and then studied it very carefully. Nelson realized that he possessed information that could be used (defensively and offensively) with great effect if promptly disseminated to the right parties.

He immediately wrote to Sir William Hamilton, giving him the bottom-line analysis that Bonaparte's "army is in a scrape, and will not get out of it."[179] Lack of provisions, the effects of the intense heat, and shortage of potable water were apparent. He then wrote to the governor of Bombay, providing a synopsis of the Nile campaign, including Napoleon's expressed intentions of taking Suez and Damietta as well as warning of the ultimate design on Bombay. In addition to this warning, he related that the French were hard pressed for various provisions, including "stores, artillery, things for their hospital, &c." This letter was entrusted to Lt. Thomas Duval, who was to travel by Alexandria, Aleppo, and Basra overland to Bombay. Nelson further wrote Lord Spencer and Mr. Dundas, apprising them of the situation and offering to pay Duval's expenses if neither the government nor the East India Company would, "for as an Englishman, I shall be proud that it has been in my power to be the means of putting our Settlements [in India] on their guard."[180] As dire as the French army's situation appeared, if access to Indian waters were not controlled, Nelson felt Tippoo Sahib might still be measurably reinforced via the Red Sea.[181]

Despite his concerns for continued French motions toward India, Nelson wrote the British minister at Florence, "I have little doubt but that the Army will be destroyed by plague, pestilence, and Famine, and battle and murder, which that it may soon be, God grant." To Francis James Jackson, Esq. (British ambassador at Constantinople), Lord Minto (Nelson's friend and British envoy extraordinary), and Adm. Lord St. Vincent, he most strongly suggested that if the Ottoman "Grand Signior [the Porte himself] will but trot an army into Syria, Buonaparte's career is finished."[182] Finally, on 7 September he wrote again to Hamilton in Naples: "I have sent an express to Constantinople, and requested Mr. Jackson to urge the Grand Signior, by every regard for his own preservation, to send an Army into Syria and his Fleet . . . to destroy Alexandria, and all the stores in it. . . . I will do my duty in representing the importance of the business, and if our Allies will not assist in completing what has been so gloriously begun, it is not my fault, and too late they will repent it."[183]

For his part, General Bonaparte made a good outward show upon hearing the news of his fleet's destruction. Speaking to his officers, he rallied their sagging spirits: "Come, come, gentlemen, our fate lies in our own hands. Much is required of us. Let us see that we accomplish it. Seas of which we are no longer master separate us from home; but no ocean divides Africa from Asia. In the past Egypt was a powerful kingdom: it lies with us to re-create its ancient glories, and to augment them by science and industry. Let us establish ourselves here, and we may change the face of the East, and add our names to those of the ancients."[184]

As it turned out, Napoleon inspected Suez and even ordered the construction of a flotilla to use in the Red Sea for moving the army toward India; however, he soon abandoned the project as impracticable. He then invaded Syria, in early 1799, to preempt an impending Turkish attack.

The French defeated the Turks at Jaffa (7 March 1799) and then approached the stronghold of Acre. The defenders (including a group of British seamen under the previously mentioned Commo. Sir William Sidney Smith) held out through more than nine aggressive attacks, ultimately forcing the plague-beset French back across the Sinai Desert toward Egypt. There, in July, Bonaparte fought and destroyed a second Turkish army (at the land Battle of Aboukir).

Napoleon then, in great secrecy, abandoned his army and sailed for France on 18 August 1799, determined to help the Republic ward off the assaults of the allied Second Coalition. By 11 November, his political star soaring, he was swept to power in the *coup d'état de Brumaire* and found himself sharing control of France with two other men. In a few more months he maneuvered himself into the position of First Consul, and as such became the de facto ruler of France.

In any event, the news of Nelson's battle of the Nile caused profound joy in London. That news, however, took a remarkably long time in its arrival—two months. In fact, it took until 4 September for the news to even reach Naples. Nelson's duplicate dispatches, sent via Naples, took sixty-one days to reach England.[185]

In the absence of good news, criticism had filled the void. Ministers, naval officers, and newspapers speculated on Nelson's inability to bring the French to battle. "It is a remarkable circumstance," one paper suggested to its readers, "that a fleet of nearly 400 sail, covering a space of so many leagues, should have been able to elude the knowledge of our fleet for such a long space of time."[186] On 8 August, another leading daily paper wrote, "At no period of the war have public affairs been more critically situated than they are at the present moment. But we are sorry to say, that to whatever point we direct our attention, there is much to lament and little to console us!"[187]

Admiral Goodall, a friend and supporter of Nelson, was asked, "What is your favourite hero about? The French fleet has passed under his nose!"[188] At one point Prime Minister Pitt had to write, "The account of Bonaparte's arrival at Alexandria is, I am afraid, true; but it gives us no particulars, and leaves us in entire suspense as to Nelson."[189] Official worry in London had been palpable as the long summer wore on; the British public was nervous as well. Among other issues, "it was known that Bonaparte was at large and that Nelson had failed to find him. He might by now be in Naples or he might be sailing towards Ireland. All that was certain was than Nelson had missed him: had bungled his mission. There were demands for his recall and for the resignation of the Ministers who had appointed him."[190]

With no solid information as late as 21 August, Lord Spencer wrote to Lord St. Vincent, hoping for success for Nelson "notwithstanding the report which has this day reached us of Bonaparte's having landed at Alexandria on the 7th or 8th of July . . . am very anxious to hear again from you, as we have no accounts of Nelson that can be depended upon since his being on the 21st of June off Cape Passaro."[191]

On 27 August, Dundas wrote to Lord Spencer, "I am always in hopes we shall hear of Nelson doing something brilliant with regard to the fleet."[192] For his part, Spencer tried to console Dundas, writing, "I am anxiously expecting the next Hamburg mail, because I think it will bring a resolution of all our doubts. . . . I have quite persuaded myself that there has been [a naval] action, and I feel very confident that the result of it is favourable to us."[193]

Lord Grenville, writing to Lord Spencer on 9 September, attached no ill-feeling toward Sir Horatio's apparent failure to find the French fleet; as a matter of fact, as he was negotiating with Russia concerning a renewal of the coalition against France, he said, "It is a great consolation to me to see that . . . although it may be very doubtful whether [Nelson] can do anything at Alexandria [against Bonaparte's army] without land forces, [his very] presence in those seas is absolutely necessary to give encouragement to the Porte, and indeed to Russia herself."[194]

However, Secretary of War Dundas was of another mood entirely. On 16 September he unhappily wrote Spencer that he had "not spirits enough on the subject of the late accounts from Sir Horatio Nelson to say a word on that business. I must in charity presume when he tells his own story he will be able to give a good reason for his leaving Alexandria after he had got there in so auspicious a manner."[195]

On that same date Spencer wrote to St. Vincent, indicating that he had recently heard some intriguing rumors from the Mediterranean. Such was his caution, however, that he could not allow himself to give "full credit to the very extravagant reports which had been propagated almost all over Europe of the decisive victory said to have been obtained by Sir Horatio Nelson."[196]

A week later Spencer wrote Dundas,

> As to Sir Horatio Nelson, I hope he will have a pretty good story to tell at least. His missing the French both going and returning was certainly very unfortunate
> —but we must not be too ready to censure him for leaving Alexandria when he was there, till we know the exact state of the intelligence which he received on his arrival there.[197]

However, two days later Spencer was writing Dundas again, with the first real information of Nelson's overwhelming victory: "The situation of the war in the Mediterranean will be so much affected by the truth or falsehood of the accounts which are transcribed to us through the French papers of an action in the Bay of Bequieres, that till we are quite sure what that event has been, it will be impossible to form any judgment of the best plan of operation to adopt."[198] *Béguieres,* or *Bequieres,* briefly puzzled Whitehall experts, until it was realized that these were the old-French forms of the Arabic "Al-Bekir."

In truth, from this point on, information came streaming into London on what was—in St. Vincent's words—"the almost incredible and stupendous victory which Rear-Admiral Sir Horatio Nelson and his gallant train of heroes has under the blessing of God obtained over the Toulon squadron." The rejoicing that burst forth as a result is hard to imagine now, even though slight hints of the incredible enthusiasm roused in England can still be detected today. Horatio Nelson had won a permanent heroic place in the British national heart.[199]

Nevertheless, it could well have been otherwise. It was a remarkable case of all is well that ends well: "Nelson's fruitless return to Syracuse had caused the utmost dissatisfaction. Even experienced naval officers had suspected Nelson of some serious fault. Had the French fleet . . . escaped back to Toulon, Nelson's recall and ruin would certainly have followed, and he might well have been lost to history."[200]

Thus ended this remarkable campaign, in which the actual fighting was almost anticlimactic. From the outset Nelson was confident of victory in combat; his overwhelming problem throughout was his intelligence problem—the one which broke his heart: "I will *fight* the French fleet the moment I can *find* them."

THE ENTIRE CAMPAIGN proved to be one of the most fascinating examples of the problems of naval warfare and strategic intelligence in the age of sail.[201] For nothing comes to mind that could possibly better demonstrate "the difficulties of naval intelligence gathering and reconnaissance in those days of sail and slow communications: the complete failure of the greatest admiral of the age to intercept a convoy of 400 troop transports during its leisurely passage, across the whole length of the Mediterranean Sea, from Toulon to Alexandria."[202]

Conclusion

*[The wars] abounded in supremely important lessons for the . . .
twentieth century. Problems of blockade; the right use of Intelligence; defence against invasion; the conduct of conjoint operations;
. . . —on all these, and others besides, much light is shed by the history of the French Revolutionary and Napoleonic Wars.*

Prof. G. J. Marcus

*The wars demonstrated the use of intelligence, but did little to insti-
tutionalize it.*

Prof. Michael Herman

L ONG BEFORE THE CLOSE OF THE EIGHTEENTH CENTURY MANY
nation-states, including England, had institutionalized diplomatic
information systems, developed cryptography and cryptanalysis, established networks of spies and informers, arranged for clandestine mail
opening, and created infrastructures to record, distribute, and file the
resulting information. In fact, "until almost the middle of the seventeenth
century, none of the three great Western powers [England, France and
Spain] possessed diplomatic archives as orderly and usable as those of

the Florentines and Venetians two hundred years before."[1] In England, "the most important function vested in the Secretaries of State in the seventeenth century was the management of 'the intelligence.' The term denoted not only the provision of extraordinary information concerning enemy countries or domestic plotters, but also a regular, settled supply of every kind of news from abroad."[2]

This mass of information contained varying degrees of *sensitive* material, or *secret intelligence*. As we look back in history, secret intelligence was not particularly differentiated from any other forms of governmental information; governments—certainly including the English—generally regarded all information as proprietary. Prior to the "emergence of private newspapers and press freedom, governments tended to see all information as their property, secret to some extent; the distinction between information 'in the public domain' and 'classified' official information is a modern one." In fact, "the present-day *London Gazette* was founded . . . to disseminate home and overseas news of every kind *for* government."[3]

Eighteenth-century intelligence remained organizationally centered in the diplomatic establishment, with an embassy and consular network of overseas correspondents. This was well-supplemented by a vibrant program of espionage, postal interception, cryptanalysis, and foreign-trade analysis. There were rudimentary efforts, by other organizations, to get into the intelligence business; indeed, by midcentury the Admiralty was itself sharply focused on French and Spanish bases regarding naval preparations and operations. Nevertheless, outside of the diplomatic structure, "other information collection and handling was largely *ad hoc,* without permanent institutions."[4] "Rather than there being any sharp break between diplomatic and intelligence material, the two were closely intertwined, a situation that owed much to the absence, with the exception of the [post office] deciphering branch, of any espionage institutions or establishment."[5]

Moreover, there is one other enormous difference between the eighteenth-century national-level intelligence operation and that which we find today: "Nowhere was the control of collection and the evaluation of results a specialized activity, separated from policy-making and action. For kings and ministers 'intelligence' in all its aspects was part of statecraft, inseparable from the exercise of power."[6]

The Admiralty, due in no small degree to its own efforts, was clearly involved in the flow of intelligence information. Because the first lord was at the cabinet level—and the first secretary was a high minister— the Royal Navy was continuously privy to national-level intelligence from the diplomatic, postal, and trade sources, information that was passed to the fleet as individual first lords, first professional lords, and first secretaries saw fit. This was, of course, a two-way channel as information from overseas naval commanders in chief and from detached ships moved to the Admiralty. Not only did the first lord and the first secretary share this intelligence with their fellow ministers, but quite often admirals deployed around the world would correspond directly with various ministers external to the Admiralty—not excluding the prime minister.

Without doubt, the collection, assessment, dissemination, and use of intelligence information was present throughout the fleet. Equally clear is that, subordinate to the Admiralty at whatever operational level one cares to consider, the most senior officer present on a given station was de facto the local premier intelligence officer. No other person had the time, availability, access to information, responsibility, qualifications, experience, or overview. Finally, no senior officer had anything resembling adequate staff support to even partially share such important responsibilities: "For centuries the *rudimentary* headquarters of generals sufficed for handling information in war, and the same applied even more to war at sea. . . . Organizing and using intelligence was a very *personal* matter, like other aspects of generalship; there was no standard wartime organization, and no perpetuation of wartime experience in peacetime. Eighteenth-century intelligence was still set in a military framework described by one writer as the 'stone age of command,'[7] slowly changing but still in transition through the Napoleonic Wars."[8]

Indeed, as the French Revolutionary Wars began, British governmental processes struggled to meet the challenge. For the first several years, in particular, there were formidable problems "in the vital areas of intelligence and planning. Departmental arrangements and staff-work were mediocre, co-operation between different arms virtually non-existent. . . . And good intelligence, in both London and the theatres, was conspicuous by its absence."[9]

In the last analysis, it may have not made a great deal of difference had there been a significantly better beginning. Even when there was good intelligence, all too often not a lot could be done with it in the era of goose-quill pens. Intelligence triumphs could only rarely be turned into military or naval victories: "Eighteenth-century states did not have the responsiveness—in both a bureaucratic and communications sense—to translate intelligence into action."[10] And, in spite of the firm opinion of Frederick the Great, superior intelligence could rarely overcome superior forces. "In general," note Keith Neilson and B. J. C. McKercher, "the military and naval establishments of the eighteenth century lacked the [ability] to exploit intelligence rapidly enough to be decisive. What ultimately mattered were the talents of commanders—their strategic, operational, and tactical skills; their leadership; and the fighting quality of their troops. These, together with what Clausewitz termed the elements of friction—chance and the fog of war—usually decided the outcome. Perhaps these matters still remain decisive in war today."[11]

While fundamentally true, Neilson and McKercher might be altogether too pessimistic. There has been some evidence, in the previous pages, of a reasonable amount of successful intelligence exploitation during this period.

Nevertheless, it is very hard to draw many practical lessons, or applications, for our modern age from methodology and technology two hundred years old; after all, theirs was not only another time, another system, and another navy, but also another world. Still, naval philosopher Rear Adm. Alfred Thayer Mahan insisted that "there are certain teachings in the school of history which remain constant, and being, therefore, of universal application, can be elevated to the rank of general principles." So, "it is not therefore a vain expectation, as many think, to look for useful lessons in the history of sailing-ships. . . . [It is] impossible to cite their experiences or modes of action as tactical precedents to be followed. But a precedent is different from and less valuable than a principle."[12]

THIS BOOK WAS NEVER INTENDED to be a biography, nor in any way a comprehensive analysis, of Horatio Nelson. If it had been, much found between its covers would have had to go, while another three to four hundred pages would need to be inserted. If nothing else, the three-year campaign of Trafalgar would have needed central attention, for it certainly was a campaign bursting with intelligence issues and incidents; indeed, a reasonable intelligence study of Trafalgar demands its own book.

Having written that, Nelson's dominance in this book is certainly acknowledged. It could hardly be otherwise: Nelson dominates the entire period, while thousands of his letters are readily accessible for evidentiary documentation. Above all, Horatio Nelson was a superb intelligence officer, and even if there had been another admiral as good at it as he was, there truly was no one else on his level regarding the translation of intelligence information into at-sea command decisions.

Without belaboring the point—and still avoiding comprehensive analysis—a few more words about Nelson are in order. The reader has already been exposed to many attributes that made Admiral Nelson unique (St. Vincent himself always acknowledged that "there is only one Nelson"). It may be useful to parade several other evaluations as to his abilities, skills, and character.

Lord Hood, perhaps the greatest English admiral of the American Revolutionary War period, personally saw in the young Captain Nelson an officer who was clearly both a sound and original thinker.[13]

Prof. G. J. Marcus saw, in his study of the older Captain Nelson, characteristic qualities of "instant decision, unfailing resource, unshakeable tenacity of purpose, brilliant tactical insight, swift and audacious action —combined with [an] all-consuming, over-mastering urge towards victory."[14]

Prof. Arthur Bryant and Rear Adm. A. T. Mahan both believed that the foundation of Nelson's ever-present readiness for battle was his "minute imaginative attention to detail: the sure hall-mark of a great leader. 'No man was ever better served than Nelson by the inspiration of the hour; no man ever counted less on it.'"[15] C. S. Forester certainly agreed, believing him "uniquely superior in his untiring patience and his extreme attention to the details of organization."[16]

As an admiral and as the commander in chief in the Mediterranean, Nelson's abilities for operational readiness and logistical legerdemain were spectacularly displayed: "He was always troubled by the danger which threatens every blockading fleet—that it may be attacked at its 'average moment' by the enemy at his 'selected moment.' He had to keep his forces massed and ready for instant action. For a period of nearly two years he did so, beginning . . . with every ship in bad order. During those two years the squadron as a body never saw the inside of a port. At the end of those two years the whole force at a moment's notice went off across the Atlantic and back again with a battle imminent at any moment. The achievement stands as nearly the greatest, and by far the least known, of all Nelson's claims to fame."[17]

Lord Nelson's professional reputation reached a remarkable pinnacle in the last few months of the Trafalgar campaign. During his short leave in August–September 1805, the government received him with considerable deference. On top of a spectacular career, his recent performance as commander in chief Mediterranean had riveted their attention. "The uncanny way in which Nelson had divined his enemy's movements had impressed them deeply, and he was called upon repeatedly for his opinions and advice" in many subject areas.[18]

Forester also crystallizes a point generally popular among the admiral's biographers. Nelson almost always evidenced a sincere willingness to be pleased, which was certainly "not a decided characteristic of the naval officer of that or any other age." Anything under his command—whether crew, ship, squadron, or fleet—generally received nothing but praise. Unquestionably this was the root cause of the popularity, cooperation, inspiration, and devotion that he always found in and from his sub-ordinates. This was in remarkable contrast to, say, Wellington; whereas Nelson was loved, the Iron Duke's successes were more based in respect-ful dislike, if not fear.[19] Prof. Brian Lavery elaborates on this issue: "Nelson must take full credit for his tactical instinct and more impor-tant, for the initiative he gave to his captains, the leadership which made them aware that they would be backed up and encouraged to find any weakness in the enemy position. In a navy where many admirals were too old to absorb new ideas, or were bound by the cautious tactics and practices of an earlier generation, Nelson was a truly innovative figure."[20]

It must be emphasized, however, that he was also—despite his popu-larity and despite the cooperation and devotion of his subordinates—very much a "man alone." C. S. Forester particularly emphasized this concept with his Horatio Hornblower series. Most naval commanders of this age were just so, bearing enormous individual responsibility, physi-cal solitude, and mental isolation, to a degree that is unparalleled today in any walk of life. "Nelson, despite the legendary 'Band of Brothers,' was very much alone," particularly during the three months of the Nile campaign and the three years leading to Trafalgar.[21]

Slight of stature, frequently seasick, and often otherwise ill, he was nevertheless incredibly tough, both physically and mentally. He liked combat. Any man who had been in over a hundred actions, and who had been severely wounded three times, was remarkably brave to still relish walking shot-torn decks amid tremendous death and destruction—"mind you," he said at Copenhagen, "I would not be elsewhere for thou-sands."

He was very hard. He was always focused upon not just the defeat but the annihilation of the enemy's fleets, without too much apparent regret for the huge numbers of dead and wounded sailors (theirs and his) that went along with it. Taking this a little further, Jan Morris, biographer of Adm. Lord Jackie Fisher, makes this interesting comment: "It seems to me . . . that Nelson was organically ruthless, as against *ad hoc*—profes-sionally and in private life. [For example,] he was not merely *faithless,* but *heartless* toward his wife: 'opened by mistake by Lord Nelson,' was written on one of her letters, returned to her from far away, 'but unread.'"[22]

C. Northcote Parkinson heavily underscored two telling points. The first, already emphasized here, is that though Nelson's stature is such that the entire period is referred to as his "age," in fact the period saw tremendous naval activity—and naval intelligence activity—for ten full years after his death. The second point summarizes Nelson's key to success, even though this passage was meant to describe some other notable commanders as well:

> Books on naval history must tend to concentrate on battles, ignoring other aspects and events. Readers are given a diagram and told a story of tactical brilliance. They are spared an account of the process by which the fleet was fitted, recruited, provisioned, disciplined, inspected, encouraged and inspired.
>
> It is a fact, nevertheless, that the Commander-in-Chief's orders and example on the day of battle may matter *less* than the work he has done over the previous months or years.[23]

Nelson was the quintessential master, whether one considers preparation or the actual day of decision. In 1805, his decision to return the Mediterranean Fleet to Europe—after the extremely bold gamble to follow French Admiral Villeneuve to the West Indies in the first place—was a model of extraordinary operational readiness and flexibility. It was also a model of brilliant intelligence analysis translated into action. In fact, C. S. Forester may have had the last word on Nelson as intelligence analyst: "It is hard to decide which to admire most: the accuracy of the deduction, the self-confidence which believed in it, or the force of mind with which he brought himself to [expose] England's most valuable colonial possessions solely on deductions made from a series of individually inconclusive facts."[24]

LIKE HORATIO NELSON HIMSELF, the incredible challenges of communication with quill pens and speaking trumpets have long ago disappeared. The enormous frustrations of gathering information without benefit of satellite imagery, aerial reconnaissance, photography, or electronics can hardly be imagined. Indeed,

> the hazardous difficulties of handling a fleet under canvas have passed beyond our conception. The difference in the character of the ships is so enormous that the modern naval man must feel that the time has come for the great sea officers of the past to be laid in the temple of august memories.
>
> Those who from the heat of Trafalgar sank together in the cool depths of the ocean would gaze with amazed eyes at the engines of our strife. All passes, all changes: the animosity of peoples, the handling of fleets, the forms of ships; even the sea itself seems to wear a different and diminished aspect from the sea of Nelson's day.[25]

It might also be stressed that their low technology actually simplified some things, for "in the days of the sailing ship, when weapons and ship designs were common property for all navies, the discipline and efficiency of the officers and crews, and the strategic disposition of the ship concentrations were the determining factors in naval warfare."[26]

Still, there remains an undeniable constant whether we consider operations in 1801, 2001, or 2201. Aside from the quality and quantity of forces, and irrespective of the fundamental talent and leadership of the commander, what often matters very profoundly is how that commander uses, ignores, or misuses available intelligence.

The admiral may be standing on a wooden deck, estimating the enemy's position himself with a brass telescope, while personally writing dispatches with a quill pen and blotter. The admiral, on the other hand, may be standing upon a steel deck, receiving an all-source briefing from an experienced, career intelligence officer, while viewing an electronic graphic displaying the tactical situation. Or the admiral may even be ergonomically seated on the bridge of a starship, viewing a multimedia intelligence analysis—produced by a "conscious" computer system with terabyte memory and running at billions of instructions per second, while simultaneously teleconferencing the analysis (and his orders) to his fleet dispersed about a solar system.

Whatever the specific case, in the final analysis the degree to which the naval commander uses, or fails to use, available intelligence in the decision-making process is crucial. Indeed, the commander's possession and use of intelligence have been decisive in history, they are decisive now, and they will be decisive in the future.

APPENDIX 1

The British Cabinet (Closet), (Typical 1793–1815)

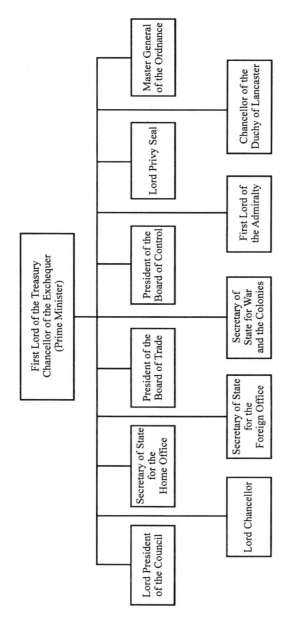

Cook and Stevenson, 15–18, 26.

APPENDIX 2

British Government Key Officials, 1793–1815

The names of government officials are taken from three sources: Cook and Stevenson, *British Historical Facts,* Sainty, *Admiralty Officials,* and Lavery, *Nelson's Navy.*

The King

George III (r. 1760–1811)
George IV (prince regent, 1811–20; king, 1820–30)

Prime Minister

The prime minister, or premier, was not really an office as it is known today. Generally a given administration was headed by a minister who personally held an important office, such as first lord of the treasury, or chancellor of the exchequer (Cook and Stevenson, *British Historical Facts,* 27).

Rt. Hon. William Pitt (1783–1801)
Henry Addington, first Viscount Sidmouth (1801–4)
Rt. Hon. William Pitt (1804–6)
William Wyndham, Baron Grenville (1806–7)
William Henry Cavendish-Bentinck, third Duke of Portland (1807–9)
Rt. Hon. Spencer Perceval (1809–12)
Robert Banks Jenkinson, second Earl of Liverpool (1812–27)

Secretary of State for War and the Colonies

Rt. Hon. Henry Dundas (later first Viscount Melville) (1794–1801)
Robert Hobart, fourth Earl of Buckinghamshire (1801–4)
John Jeffries Pratt, second Earl Camden (1804–5)
Robert Stewart, Viscount Castlereagh (1805–6)
Rt. Hon. William Windham (1806–7)
Robert Stewart, Viscount Castlereagh (1807–1809)
Robert Banks Jenkinson, second Earl of Liverpool (1809–12)
Henry Bathurst, third Earl Bathurst (1812–27)

Secretary of State for the Home Department

William Wyndham, Baron Grenville (1789–90)
Rt. Hon. Henry Dundas (1791–94)
William Henry Cavendish-Bentinck, third Duke of Portland (1794–1801)
Thomas, Baron Pelham (later second Earl of Chichester) (1801–3)
Rt. Hon. Charles Philip Yorke (1803–4)
Robert Jenkinson, Baron Hawkesbury (later second Earl of Liverpool) (1804–6)
George John Spencer, second Earl Spencer (1806–7)
Robert Banks Jenkinson, second Earl of Liverpool (1807–9)
Rt. Hon. Richard Ryder (1809–12)
Henry Addington, first Viscount Sidmouth (1812–22)

Secretary of State for Foreign Affairs

William Wyndham, Baron Grenville (1791–1801)
Robert Jenkinson, Baron Hawkesbury (later second Earl of Liverpool) (1801–4)
Dudley Ryder, first Earl of Harrowby (1804–5)
Gen. Sir Henry Phipps (later first Earl of Mulgrave) (1805–6)
Rt. Hon. Charles James Fox (1806)
Charles Grey, second Earl Grey (1806–7)
Rt. Hon. George Canning (1807–9)
Henry Bathurst, third Earl Bathurst (1809)
Richard Colley, Marquess Wellesley (1809–12)
Robert Stewart, Viscount Castlereagh (1812–22)

First Lord of the Admiralty

Col. (later Gen.) John Pitt, second Earl of Chatham (1788–94)
George John Spencer, second Earl Spencer (1794–1801)
Adm. Sir John Jervis, Earl of St. Vincent (1801–4)
Henry Dundas, first Viscount Melville (1804–5)
Adm. Sir Charles Middleton, Lord Barham (1805–6)
Charles Grey, Viscount Howick (later second Earl Grey) (1806)
Rt. Hon. Thomas Grenville (1806–7)
Gen. Sir Henry Phipps (later first Earl of Mulgrave) (1807–10)
Rt. Hon. Charles Philip Yorke (1810–12)
Robert Saunders Dundas, second Viscount Melville (1812–27)

First Secretary of the Admiralty

Sir Philip Stephens (1763–95)
Sir Evan Nepean (1795–1804)
William Marsden (1804–07)
Rt. Hon. William Wellesley-Pole (later third Earl of Mornington) (1807–9)
John Wilson Croker (1809–30)

Commander in Chief, Mediterranean Fleet

Vice Adm. Sir Samuel Hood (1793–94)
Rear Adm. Henry Hotham (1795)
Adm. Lord St. Vincent (1795–99)
Vice Adm. Lord Keith (1799–1803)
Vice Adm. Lord Nelson (1803–5)
Vice Adm. Lord Collingwood (1805–10)
Adm. Sir Charles Cotton (1810–11)
Vice Adm. Sir Edward Pellew (1811–14)
Rear Adm. Sir Charles Vinicombe Penrose (1814–15)
Adm. Sir Edward Pellew (1815–16)
Rear Adm. Sir Charles Vinicombe Penrose (1816–19)

APPENDIX 3

Secret Interceptions Distribution List, c. 1775

Although of a time period slightly earlier than the specific focus of this book, the following is representative of the "secrets" access list governing the distribution of interceptions by HM Post Office. During the period 1770–75 the Earl of Rochford was the secretary of state for the Southern Department; his undersecretary, Francis Willes, kept this list to control the circulation of documents. The list was established, and modified, by the king.

Information in this appendix is taken from Ellis, *Post Office,* 152–53, unless otherwise noted.

Hanoverian Box (German interceptions and Hanoverian dispatches, via the Hanoverian minister at St. James's Palace):

Lord Rochford (secretary of state for the Southern Department)
Earl of Suffolk (secretary of state for the Northern Department)

"Secrets" (British interceptions and most-confidential dispatches and reports):

Lord Rochford
Earl of Suffolk
Lord North (in effect the prime minister as first lord of the Treasury) (Cook and Stevenson, *British Historical Facts,* 27)

Common Correspondence (ordinary dispatches and reports, passed to the same ministers and then to members of the "efficient" cabinet):

Lord Rochford
Earl of Suffolk
Lord North
Earl Bathurst (lord chancellor) (Cook and Stevenson, *British Historical Facts,* 27)
Earl Gower (lord president of the Council) (ibid.)
Earl of Dartmouth (secretary of state for the Colonial Department)
Earl of Sandwich (first lord of the Admiralty)

APPENDIX 4

British Naval Administration, c. 1800

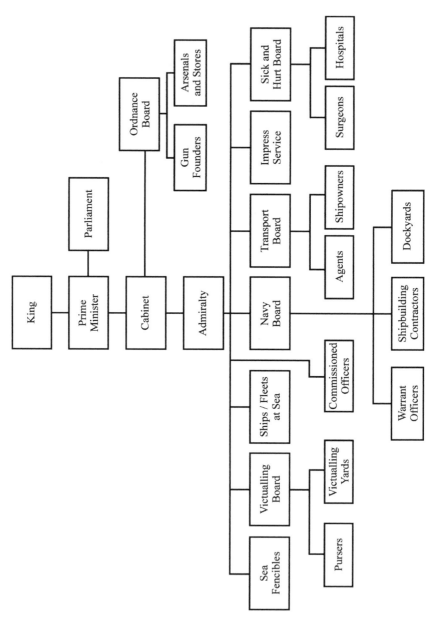

APPENDIX 5

The Naval Strategy of the War from the British Perspective

This summary, except where noted, has been extracted from Capt. Geoffrey Bennett's superb book *Nelson the Commander,* 86–87.

Britain's strategy was conditioned by her island structure and her consequent dependence on the sea. Bishop Adam de Moleyns spelled its essence as far back as 1436: "Kepe then the sea that is the walle of England."

This is a little different than the "wooden walls" of old England, as Anthony Price articulates so well, "for the truth was that, whatever Shakespeare among others might say in misunderstanding history, the 'moat defensive' of the sea, which was supposed to serve England 'in the office of a wall,' was only as good as its defending navy made it. It had failed to stop innumerable invaders in the past, most recently only a century before in 1688 [when William of Orange landed in Torbay, subsequently forcing James II to flee]. Until the age of railways and better communications on land, a would-be invader could actually transport an invasion force faster by sea than any defender could move defensive forces by land to resist an attack. The sea was not a moat, but a highway" (Price, *Eyes of the Fleet,* 12).

Nevertheless, Bacon added the rest in 1625: "He that commands the sea is at great liberty, and may take as much and as little of the war as he will."

The prime objective was the greatest danger, the enemy's battle fleet. In the time of Queen Elizabeth I Spain's was opposed only when it came so close to England as the Channel. In the Dutch Wars [First, 1652–54; Second, 1665–67; Third, 1672–73], when the chief threat was to the North Sea and the Channel, the British waited in their own waters until the enemy was reported to have left harbor—usually only in the summer months.

But something more was needed in the eighteenth century, when France's and Spain's geographical positions laid the Atlantic, the Mediterranean, and seas yet further afield, open to forays by their fleets, something which stronger ship construction made possible. The strategy of close blockade was then evolved by the elder Pitt [Prime Minister William Pitt, first Earl of Chatham, 1708–78, father of Pitt the Younger, who was prime minister at the time of Trafalgar] and Lord Anson [Adm. Lord George Anson, first lord of the Admiralty, 1757–62] for use in the Seven Years War (1756–63); neutralizing the enemy's fleets, until an opportunity arose to destroy them, by maintaining battle fleets of sufficient size off each of his principal ports, to ensure, so far as possible, that his ships did not put to sea without being brought to action.

And thus [at the end of the century] did Britain's storm-tossed ships stand—off Brest, Rochefort, Ferrol and Cadiz, as well as Toulon—between Napoleon and his dream of French dominion of the world.

Though close blockade was the keystone of Britain's defence against invasion, enabling Lord St. Vincent to declare to Parliament in 1803: "My Lords, I do not say the [French] cannot come. I only say they cannot come *by sea,*" other stones completed the arch of maritime control. Seaborne trade, vital for the conduct of any war, in part for the raw materials which it brought . . . in part for the wealth that it provided . . . had to be protected against attack by enemy cruisers and privateers, which an Act of 1708 made the first charge on Britain's naval resources. Merchant vessels were sailed in escorted convoys, since, to quote Dryden: "Your convoy makes the dangerous way secure." Nelson was thus tediously employed during his first months [1781, as captain of] the *Albemarle.* For a like reason, enemy seaborne trade was curtailed by sending British cruisers to range the trade routes to capture his merchantmen wherever they might be found, as Nelson was employed during his first months [1793, as captain of] the *Agamemnon.*

British squadrons were needed overseas, to find and destroy those of the enemy, as Rodney did in the West Indies just before the *Albemarle* joined Hood's force in those waters, and as Hughes tried so hard to do against Suffren in the Indian Ocean, highway for the rich treasures of the East [Adm. George Brydges, Lord Rodney, 1718–92; Rear Adm. Sir Edward Hughes, 1720–94; and Pierre-André de Suffren de Saint-Tropez, 1729–88, were all effective commanders during the American Revolutionary War].

Britain's warships were required to support her army and those of her allies, as Nelson did his best to support the Austrians in northern Italy—and, as Trafalgar made it possible, after his death, for Wellington to liberate Spain in a campaign that contributed so much to Napoleon's eventual downfall.

Britain also used her sea power to land military forces on enemy held territory. As Admiral of the Fleet Lord Fisher expressed it a century later: "The British Army should be used as a projectile to be fired by the Navy." . . . Finally, the British Fleet had to prevent the enemy from doing likewise or, if he managed to effect a landing, to ensure that he did not exploit it, as Nelson did when . . . Napoleon tried to extend France's empire to the Middle-East.

France and her allies could pursue a different naval strategy in the eighteenth century because they were Continental powers, by no means dependent on the sea, except to sustain their colonies. Mahan coined one name for it, the "fleet in being"; the French another, the *guerre de course.* Except for squadrons sent to

East and West Indian waters to dispute Britain's command of these areas (as when Suffren went to the Indian Ocean and D'Estaing and de Grasse to the Caribbean) [Vice Adm. Jean Baptiste Charles Henri Hector, Comte d'Estaing, 1729–94, and François Joseph Paul, Comte de Grasse, 1722–88, were additional commanders of the American Revolutionary War] France, Spain and the Netherlands kept their battle fleets within such ports as Brest, Cadiz, the Texel and Toulon, where they were safe from attack but were a constant threat to Britain's interests in Home waters and in the Mediterranean. These were seldom sent to sea except for a specific operation, as when Villaret Joyeuse [Vice Adm. Louis Thomas, Comte Villaret de Joyeuse, 1748–1812] was ordered out of Brest in 1794 to meet and bring in a valuable homebound convoy (and suffered defeat by Howe at the Glorious First of June) [Admiral of the Fleet Richard, Earl Howe, 1726–99, had a remarkable naval career, including a substantial personal contribution to at-sea signaling systems], as when Brueys was ordered to escort Buonaparte's Armée d'Orient from Toulon to Alexandria in 1798 (which doomed him to destruction at the Nile), and when Villeneuve and Gravina were ordered from Toulon and Cadiz to join with Ganteaume from Brest in 1805 to gain command of the Channel for the twelve hours that Napoleon needed for his invasion of England. [Vice Adm. Pierre Charles Jean Baptiste Sylvestre de Villeneuve, 1763–1806, defeated by Nelson at Trafalgar, later allegedly committed suicide in disgrace; Adm. Don Carlos, Duke of Gravina, commanding the Spanish at Trafalgar, later died of wounds received during that battle; Vice Adm. Honoré Joseph Antoine, Comte Ganteaume, 1755–1818.] Moreover, in all such cases, France's admirals were strictly enjoined to evade action, so far as possible, with any substantial enemy force, in sharp contrast to Britain's belief in engaging the enemy whenever opportunity offered.

This "fleet in being" strategy may be termed defensive: not so the *guerre de course*. Against Britain's maritime trade French privateers roamed the oceans. Powerful frigate-sized vessels, operating singly or in pairs, were a match for ships of their own size and could use their greater speed to escape if they chanced to meet an enemy ship-of-the-line. Britain's answer was the convoy system. Even so, many merchantmen sailed independently and were taken in prize. Indeed, such shipping was [very] vulnerable to attack [even] in the Channel, where France could employ numerous privateers smaller than frigates.

APPENDIX 6

An Overview of the War of the French Revolution and the Napoleonic War, 1792–1815

Essentially the War of the French Revolution was an effort, at least from the view of France's opponents, to contain the French Revolution. The Napoleonic War, however, was an effort to defeat Napoleon's attempt to unite continental Europe under his personal control, as well as to interfere with the attempt to build up French maritime strength (John B. Hattendorf, "The Royal Navy During the War of the French Revolution and the Napoleonic War," in King, Hattendorf, and Estes, *Sea of Words*, 30–31).

The passages below are extracted from Prof. David G. Chandler's marvelous *Dictionary of the Napoleonic Wars*, 96–98:

The First Coalition

On 26 June 1792, Austria and Prussia formed the First Coalition. Major motives were distaste for developing French republicanism, anxiety for the Bourbon royal family, the presence of growing numbers of émigrés, and the French declaration of war against the King of Hungary and Bohemia (the secondary titles of the Austrian emperor) on 20 April 1792. After the execution of Louis XVI in January 1793 Great Britain joined the coalition, followed by Spain in March. Russia, Holland, Naples, and Tuscany were loosely associated, but contributed little. The effectiveness of French armies began to tell, and in February 1795 Tuscany made peace with France. The same April Prussia left the alliance, the new Batavian Republic (Holland) joined France (16 May), and Spain also left the war on 19 August. Sardinia and Piedmont made peace with France in May 1796. Bonaparte's conquest of North Italy and limited French successes on the Rhine led to Austria signing the preliminaries of Leoben (18 April 1797), and the First Coalition finally collapsed on 17 October 1797, when Austria signed the Peace of Campo Formio. Lack of coordination, scarcity of common interests, and the problems of Poland—together with French energy and martial skill—were the main causes of failure.

The Second Coalition

French actions in Switzerland, Italy, and on the Rhine, and her ambitions in the Middle East, led Britain, Austria, Russia, Naples, and Turkey to form the Second Coalition, completed on 22 June 1799. Activity centered on Sardinia, Rome, and Egypt in 1798; the next year fighting spread to Naples, Syria, the Rhine, North Italy, Switzerland, and Holland—with Russian forces joining the Austrians and British in the last two theaters. Early French reverses gave way to successes—and then Bonaparte returned from Egypt. The *coup d'état de Brumaire* led to the Consulate, and in 1800 French counteroffensives on the Rhine and in North Italy (the Marengo campaign) led to substantial Austrian setbacks, culminating in victory at Hohenlinden on 3 December. Russia had made peace with France on 8 October, and that autumn the Armed Neutrality of the North against Britain took effect. On 9 February 1801 Austria and France signed a treaty; this left only Britain in the war, but the Peace of Amiens (signed on 25 March 1802) brought a short period of general peace.

The Third Coalition

The Enghien affair, Britain's wish to recover Hanover (seized by France in 1803), and a desire to restrict French expansionism led to the Third Coalition, formed on 11 April 1805 [and this marked the transition from the French Revolutionary War to the Napoleonic War]. Great Britain, Austria, Russia, and Sweden were members, with some German princes. The loss of the battles of Ulm and Austerlitz—and operations in North Italy around Caldiero—doomed the Coalition to failure in its turn; an Austro-French armistice was signed on 6 December, and 20 days later came the Peace of Pressburg. William Pitt's death was hastened by the news of this new collapse, largely due to weak coordination, poor planning, and to the proven genius of Napoleon.

The Fourth Coalition

Friction with Prussia over Hanover, a series of Russo-Prussian treaties, and an agreement with Great Britain led to the formation of the Fourth Coalition, effective 6 October 1806. The campaign of October–November ruined Prussia militarily (Jena-Auerstädt), but neither Prussia nor Russia made peace. The French occupation of Warsaw led in early 1807 to the bitter Winter Campaign of Eylau, in which Napoleon received his first serious check in battle, but in the following spring the French victory of Friedland led to the conference and Treaty of Tilset. Prussia was dismembered, Russia became an ally of France, and Napoleon's power and repute appeared at their zenith. Once again Britain was left the sole opponent to Napoleon.

The Fifth Coalition

Growing disillusion with life in a French-dominated Europe and the transfer of French troops to Spain led Austria to seek a new British Alliance, and on 9 April 1809 the Fifth Coalition came into being. The Danube Campaign of April–July, with associated Italian operations, followed, but at Abensberg-Eckmühl Napoleon regained the initiative. After the great French victory of Wagram Austria sought an armistice. The British expedition to Walcheren failed, and on 14 October Austria and France signed the Treaty of Vienna. Britain was again alone, but her armies were permanently in Portugal from April 1809, and the "Spanish Ulcer" would soon be exercising its long-term ill effects on France.

The Sixth Coalition

Following Napoleon's invasion of Russia in June 1812, Russia and Great Britain formed the nucleus of what became the Sixth Coalition. Spain and Portugal acceded, and after the subsequent French retreat into Poland, Prussia left Napoleon's alliance and joined the Coalition. Following the battles of Lützen and Bautzen and the armistice of 1813, Austria also joined the alliance, followed by Sweden and numbers of German states. The French were driven west of the Rhine after Leipzig, and the Allies invaded French soil early in 1814. On 9 March 1814 the Treaty of Chaumont bound the Allies together most effectively, with common undertakings and aims, and the triumphant outcome of the Campaign of France led to Napoleon's first abdication and the restoration of the Bourbons.

The Seventh Coalition

The Allies were meeting at the Congress of Vienna when Napoleon returned to France from Elba. On 25 March 1815 the Seventh Coalition was formed—all signatories of the Sixth becoming parties to the new agreement. The Allies promised 500,000 men, backed by British money, to bring about Napoleon's final downfall. The Waterloo campaign followed, and on 22 June 1815 Napoleon again abdicated. Allied armies poured into France in July, and with Napoleon's departure for exile on St. Helena, the need for military coalitions against France came to an end.

NOTES

Chapter 1. The British National Intelligence Effort

[1] Ernest R. May, in Hitchcock, *Intelligence Revolution,* 72.

[2] Cobban, "British Secret Service," 232.

[3] Polmar and Allen, *Spy Book,* 382–83.

[4] Washington to Col. Elias Dayton, 26 July 1777, in Fitzpatrick, *Writings of George Washington* 8:478–89.

[5] Richings, *Espionage,* 14–15.

[6] Cobban, *Ambassadors and Secret Agents,* 110.

[7] Ibid., 17.

[8] 22 Geo. III. 82, xxv, as quoted in Cobban, "British Secret Service," 232–33.

[9] *Report from the Committee on Accounts Relating to His Majesty's Civil List,* 15 March 1802, 208, as quoted in Cobban, "British Secret Service," 233.

[10] Cobban, "British Secret Service," 237, 248.

[11] Parkinson, *Britannia Rules,* 78.

[12] Andrew, *Secret Service,* 2; Brooke, *King George III,* 210.

[13] Matheson, *Life of Henry Dundas,* 228.

[14] Furber, *Henry Dundas,* 90.

[15] Sherwig, *Guineas and Gunpowder,* 162–63.

[16] Ibid., 195.

[17] Flayhart, *Counterpoint to Trafalgar,* 19.

[18] Cf. Foreign Office 37/6, 25 February 1785, as quoted in Cobban, "British Secret Service," 237.

[19] Cobban, "British Secret Service," 237.

[20] Cobban, *Ambassadors and Secret Agents,* 17.

[21] George III, *Correspondence,* vol. 5, no. 3669.

[22] Andrew, *Secret Service,* 5.

[23] Public Record Office, Audit Office 1/2121, Roll 5, and Audit Office 3/949, as quoted in Mitchell, *Underground War,* 257.

[24] Andrew, *President's Eyes Only,* 11.

[25] Legg, *British Diplomatic Instructions,* 306.

[26] Cobban, "British Secret Service," 238–47.

[27] Hall, *British Strategy in the Napoleonic War,* 48.

[28] O'Brian, *Fortune of War,* 177.

[29] Richings, *Espionage,* 64.

[30] This agency is detailed in Cobban, *Ambassadors and Secret Agents.*

[31] Cobban, "British Secret Service," 238–54.

[32] Thompson and Padover, *Secret Diplomacy,* 198.

[33] Ehrman, *Younger Pitt,* 649.

[34] To Trevor, 25 June 1795, in the *Correspondence of William Wickham* 1:108, as quoted in Ehrman, *Younger Pitt,* 581.

[35] Andrew, *Secret Service,* 3.

[36] Thompson and Padover, *Secret Diplomacy,* 202.

[37] Ehrman, *Younger Pitt,* 587.

[38] Black, "Mid-Eighteenth-Century Crisis," 221.

[39] Oman, *Nelson,* 664.

[40] Public Record Office G.D. 30/8/164, Oakes to Pitt, 27 November 1782, as quoted in Cobban, "British Secret Service," 248.

[41] Hall, *British Strategy in the Napoleonic War,* 48.

[42] Oman, *Nelson,* 14–19.

[43] Glover, *Britain at Bay,* 51–52.

[44] Matheson, *Life of Henry Dundas,* 267.

[45] Cobban, "British Secret Service," 243–44.

[46] British Museum Additional Manuscript 28060, folios 313–17, 13 April 1785, as quoted in Cobban, "British Secret Service," 243.

[47] Hall, *British Strategy in the Napoleonic War,* 48.

[48] Deacon, *British Secret Service,* 93.

[49] Hall, *British Strategy in the Napoleonic War,* 48.

[50] Oman, *Nelson,* 601.

[51] Burges, *Selections from the Letters,* 131–32.

[52] Deacon, *British Secret Service,* 97.

[53] Thompson and Padover, *Secret Diplomacy,* 197–98.

[54] Ibid., 190.

[55] Durant and Durant, *Age of Napoleon,* 250.

[56] Thompson and Padover, *Secret Diplomacy,* 203.

[57] Brig. Gen. Sir James Edmonds, "Leakages," *Army Quarterly,* October 1953, 84, as quoted in Glover, *Britain at Bay,* 51.

[58] Atherton, *Top Secret,* 7; Rose, *Napoleonic Studies,* 153–65.

[59] British Museum Additional Manuscript 34441, folios 395–6, as quoted in Cobban, *Ambassadors and Secret Agents,* 18.

[60] Cochrane, *Autobiography* 1:195.

[61] Nelson, *Dispatches and Letters* 6:402.

[62] O'Brian, *Mauritius Command,* 43.

[63] O'Brian, *Commodore,* 186.

[64] Spencer, *George, 2nd Earl Spencer* 2:213.

[65] Thompson and Padover, *Secret Diplomacy,* 197.

[66] Isaac Chauncey to Secretary of the Navy Paul Hamilton, as quoted in Dudley, *Naval War of 1812,* 314.

[67] For additional detail, study not only more of Cobban but also Mitchell, *Underground War.*

[68] Ellis, *Post Office,* vii–viii.

[69] Ehrman, *Younger Pitt,* 484.

[70] MacIntosh, *The British Cabinet,* 37–38.

[71] Ellis, *Post Office,* viii.

[72] Marcus, *Age of Nelson,* 290.

[73] Pope, *Great Gamble,* 119–20.

[74] Home Office Papers, Public Record Office 33/1, Freeling to Rose, 13 July 1791, as quoted in Ellis, *Post Office,* 61.

[75] "Observations 1793": The Postmaster General's observations on the report of 1788, General Post Office, E.C.1., folio 10, as quoted in Ellis, *Post Office,* 61.

[76] Historical Manuscripts Commission, Abergavenny Manuscript, 23; Lord Walsingham's Papers, General Post Office, E.C.1., 2, folios 42, 52; Home Office Papers, Public Record Office, 42/213, Postmaster General to Portland, 1 Sept. 1798, as quoted in Ellis, *Post Office,* 61.

[77] George III, *Correspondence,* vol. 2, no. 1092; vol. 6, nos. 4475 and 4507.

[78] Ellis, *Post Office,* 62–63.

[79] Black, "Mid-Eighteenth-Century Crisis," 212.

[80] *Politische Correspondenz* 11:294, 193, as quoted in Black, "Mid-Eighteenth-Century Crisis," 225.

[81] Ellis, *Post Office,* 63.

[82] Foreign Office Papers, Public Record Office 83/5, 5 August 1765; Grenville Papers, iii, 81; C. S. Parker, *The Life and Letters of Sir James Graham* (London: J. Murray, 1907), 1:444, as quoted in Ellis, *Post Office,* 63.

[83] Home Office Papers, Public Record Office 42/208, 28 April 1792; 79/1, 6 February 1812, as quoted in Ellis, *Post Office,* 63.

[84] State Papers, Public Record Office 35/31, folio 147, as quoted in Ellis, *Post Office,* 64.

[85] Colonial Office Papers, Public Record Office 5/135, Todd to Knox, 5 June 1776; Colonial Office Papers, Public Record Office 5/134-7, as quoted in Ellis, *Post Office,* 65; Butler, *Dr. Franklin Postmaster General,* 150.

[86] Ellis, *Post Office,* 65–67.

[87] Ibid., 68.

[88] British Museum Additional Manuscripts 38357, folio 36, as quoted in Ellis, *Post Office,* 69.

[89] George III, *Correspondence,* vol. 3, no. 1345.

[90] Ellis, *Post Office,* 69.

[91] British Museum Additional Manuscripts 32731, folios 7–11, as quoted in Ellis, *Post Office,* 69.

[92] Andrew, *Her Majesty's Secret Service,* 3.

[93] *Bland Burges Papers* 47:6, as quoted in Black, "Mid-Eighteenth-Century Crisis," 213.

[94] R. Sedgwick, *Letters from George III to Lord Bute 1756–66* (London: Macmillan, 1939), 210, as quoted in Ellis, *Post Office,* 70; Furber, *Henry Dundas,* 282–83, 298.

[95] Richard, Duke of Buckingham, *Memoirs of the Court and Cabinets of George III* (London: Hurst and Blackett, 1853–55), 1:117; Colonial Office Papers, Public Record Office 5/40, pt. iii, as quoted in Ellis, *Post Office,* 70. Black, in "Mid-Eighteenth-Century Crisis," believes that more intercepts were preserved than Ellis thinks.

[96] Matheson, *Life of Henry Dundas,* 234.

[97] Andrew, *President's Eyes Only,* 107.

[98] George III, *Correspondence,* vol. 5, no. 2942.

[99] British Museum Additional Manuscript 34414, folios 18, 265; 32845, folio 389; 35413, folios 245–46, 255; and 24321, folios 24–28. Home Office Papers, Public Record Office 42/207, Maddison to Nepean, 31 December 1790; 42/213, Under-Secretary to Freeling, 29 March 1798. Historical Manuscripts Commission, Abergavenny Manuscript, 39–40, all as quoted in Ellis, *Post Office,* 70.

[100] Ellis, *Post Office,* 71.

[101] Foreign Office Papers, Public Record Office 83/5, Bode to Hammond, 5 November 1801, as quoted in Ellis, *Post Office,* 71.

[102] Fitzpatrick, *Secret Service under Pitt,* 31.

[103] George III, *Correspondence,* vol. 4, no. 2359; emphasis added.

[104] Ellis, *Post Office,* 72.

[105] Ibid., 72–73.

[106] Ibid., 139.

[107] Ibid., 73.

[108] Castlereagh, *Correspondence* 1:272–93, 2:96–99.

[109] Ibid. 3:371.

[110] Ibid. 1:272–93, 2:96–99.

[111] Matheson, *Life of Henry Dundas,* 255.

[112] Richings, *Espionage,* 260–66; Nelson, *Dispatches and Letters* 5:42.

[113] Richelson, *Century of Spies,* 174.

[114] Thompson and Padover, *Secret Diplomacy,* 204, 238.

[115] Ellis, *Post Office,* 75; Pope, *Great Gamble,* 120. See also, for example, Nelson, *Dispatches and Letters* 4:279; "Mrs. Thompson's friend" is Nelson himself.

[116] British Museum Additional Manuscript 32731, folio 8, as quoted in Ellis, *Post Office,* 75.

[117] British Museum Additional Manuscript 35413, folios 247–48, as quoted in Ellis, *Post Office,* 76.

[118] Black, "Mid-Eighteenth-Century Crisis," 224.

[119] Thompson and Padover, *Secret Diplomacy,* 246–47.

[120] Haldane, *Hidden World,* 76.

[121] Thompson and Padover, *Secret Diplomacy,* 190.

[122] Ellis, *Post Office,* 76.

[123] Ibid., 76.

[124] Ibid., 77.

[125] Marcus, *Age of Nelson,* 289.

[126] Ibid., 401.

[127] Pope, *Life in Nelson's Navy,* 10, 237.

[128] Oman, *Nelson,* 100; Lavery, *Nelson and the Nile,* 29.

[129] George III, *Correspondence,* vol. 6, no. 4276, 331.

[130] Marcus, *Age of Nelson,* 402.

[131] Ellis, *Post Office,* 61.

[132] Admiralty 1/3993, 6 September 1809, as quoted in Marcus, *Age of Nelson,* 370.

[133] Keith, *Keith Papers* 3:233.

[134] Theodore Roosevelt, *The Naval Operations of the War between Great Britain and the United States, 1812–1815,* 247–48, as quoted in Marcus, *Age of Nelson,* 472.

[135] Ward and Gooch, *British Foreign Policy,* 333–34.

[136] Matheson, *Life of Henry Dundas,* 342.

Chapter 2. The Admiralty

[1] Rodger, *Wooden World,* 29.

[2] Morris, *Fisher's Face,* 239.

[3] Forester, *Age of Fighting Sail,* 128.

[4] Glover, *Britain at Bay,* 57.

[5] Matheson, *Life of Henry Dundas,* 338; Lavery, *Nelson's Navy,* 245–51.

[6] Parkinson, *Britannia Rules,* 6, 8.

[7] Nelson, *Dispatches and Letters* 3:25.

[8] Barham, *Charles, Lord Barham* 3:76–77.

[9] Ibid. 3:77–78.

[10] Parkinson, *Britannia Rules*, 8.

[11] Pope, *Life in Nelson's Navy*, 23.

[12] Parkinson, *Britannia Rules*, 8.

[13] Nelson, *Dispatches and Letters* 3:2.

[14] Lavery, *Nelson and the Nile*, 34.

[15] Ibid., 34.

[16] Nelson, *Dispatches and Letters* 5:429.

[17] Bennett, *Nelson the Commander*, 235.

[18] Pope, *Life in Nelson's Navy*, 32.

[19] Keith, *Keith Papers* 3:21.

[20] Gunther Rothenberg, in Neilson and McKertcher, *Go Spy the Land*, 109.

[21] Herman, *Intelligence Power*, 12.

[22] Andrew, *Secret Service*, 7.

[23] Herman, *Intelligence Power*, 16–17.

[24] George III, *Correspondence*, vol. 4, no. 2420.

[25] Ibid., no. 2748.

[26] Ibid., no. 2765.

[27] Rodger, *Insatiable Earl*, 209–10.

[28] Parkinson, *Britannia Rules*, 128.

[29] St. Vincent, *Letters of Admiral of the Fleet* 1:125–26.

[30] Ibid., 127.

[31] Ibid., 129.

[32] Ibid., 133.

[33] Ibid., 135–36.

[34] Ibid., 137.

[35] Ibid., 139–40.

[36] Ibid., 142.

[37] Ibid., 199.

[38] Lucien Bonaparte (1775–1840) by choice never really participated in the clan's political advancement. In fact, he effectively retired in 1804.

[39] St. Vincent, *Letters of Admiral of the Fleet* 1:199–200.

[40] Barham, *Charles, Lord Barham* 3:37–38.

[41] Ibid., 385.

[42] Ibid., 297.

[43] St. Vincent, *Letters of Admiral of the Fleet* 1:205.

[44] Katwijk is fifteen miles north of the Hague.

[45] Keith, *Keith Papers* 3:202.

[46] Spencer, *George, 2nd Earl Spencer,* 2:303–5.

[47] Marcus, *Age of Nelson,* 140.

[48] Melville (Dundas), as quoted in Matheson, *Life of Henry Dundas,* 336.

[49] Keith, *Keith Papers* 3:346–47.

[50] Ibid., 32.

[51] Rodger, *Wooden World,* 332.

[52] Renaut, *Secret Service de L'Amirauté Britannique,* 29–32. I am indebted to Monica McLean Scott for the translation.

[53] However, Renaut's fundamental claim is echoed by Herman, *Intelligence Power,* 14.

[54] Herman, *Intelligence Power,* 114.

[55] Deacon, *British Secret Service,* 101–3; Rowan and Deindorfer, *Secret Service,* 187–90.

[56] Robertson, *Secret Mission;* Deacon, *British Secret Service,* 103–6; Deacon, *Silent War,* 29–30; Marcus, *Age of Nelson,* 323; Thompson and Padover, *Secret Diplomacy,* 228–33.

[57] O'Brian, *Surgeon's Mate,* 324.

[58] Keith, *Keith Papers* 3:6.

[59] St. Vincent, *Letters of Admiral of the Fleet,* 2:398–401.

[60] Forester, *Captain Horatio Hornblower,* 421.

[61] Barham, *Charles, Lord Barham* 3:346, as found in Keith, *Keith Papers* 3:114.

[62] Keith, *Keith Papers* 3:243.

[63] Ibid., 237.

[64] Ibid., 21–22.

[65] Nelson, *Dispatches and Letters* 5:152–53.

[66] Ibid., 3:31.

[67] Ibid. 5:vi.

[68] Ibid. 6:493.

Chapter 3. Signals and Information Transmission

[1] Bennett, *Nelson the Commander,* 80–81.

[2] Ibid., 193.

[3] Price, *Eyes of the Fleet,* 162.

[4] Ibid., 80–81.

[5] Nelson, *Dispatches and Letters* 5:214.

[6] Ibid. 6:100.

[7] Ibid., 265.

[8] Ibid., 289.

[9] Zacharias, *Secret Missions,* 267.

[10] St. Vincent, *Letters of Admiral of the Fleet* 1:300.

[11] Forester, *Age of Fighting Sail,* 89.

[12] Pope, *Black Ship,* 23.

[13] Pope, *Life in Nelson's Navy,* 29–30.

[14] Henderson, *Frigates,* 78.

[15] O'Brian, *Wine-Dark Sea,* 11.

[16] O'Brian, *Reverse of the Medal,* 103.

[17] Forester, *Captain Horatio Hornblower,* 481.

[18] Nelson, *Dispatches and Letters* 5:373.

[19] O'Brian, *Far Side of the World,* 186.

[20] O'Brian, *Commodore,* 4.

[21] Nelson, *Dispatches and Letters* 6:184.

[22] Ibid., 308–9.

[23] Oman, *Nelson,* 302.

[24] Parkinson, *Britannia Rules,* 176.

[25] Henderson, *Frigates,* 126.

[26] Kent, *Beyond the Reef,* 257.

[27] Forester, *Hornblower and the "Hotspur,"* 86, 104.

[28] Nelson, *Dispatches and Letters* 5:201.

[29] Ibid. 6:247.

[30] Forester, *Age of Fighting Sail,* 32.

[31] Price, *Eyes of the Fleet,* 43.

[32] Bennett, *Nelson the Commander,* 81.

[33] Keith, *Keith Papers* 3:129.

[34] Public Record Office, Admiralty 1/415, as quoted in Glover, *Britain at Bay,* 165.

[35] Pope, *Great Gamble,* 170.

[36] Henderson, *Frigates,* 94.

[37] Marcus, *Age of Nelson,* 487.

[38] Gardiner, *British Admiralty,* 5–6.

[39] Keith, *Keith Papers* 3:389.

[40] *Times,* 29 January 1801, 2d.

[41] Pope, *Great Gamble,* plates after 84.

[42] Cochrane, *Autobiography* 1:288–89.

[43] Barham, *Charles, Lord Barham* 1:301.

[44] Ibid. 1:343–44.

[45] Ibid. 2:372–73.

[46] A signal code invented by Mahé de la Bourdonnais, around 1750, as found in Bourdé de Villehuet's *Le Manoeuvrier.* Bennett, *Nelson the Commander,* 84.

[47] Callender and Hinsley, *Naval Side of British History,* 173.

[48] Barham, *Charles, Lord Barham* 2:381.

[49] Nelson, *Dispatches and Letters* 3:230.

[50] Price, *Eyes of the Fleet,* 160.

[51] Keith, *Keith Papers* 2:325.

[52] Barrow, as quoted in Marcus, *Age of Nelson,* 268–69.

[53] Lavery, *Nelson's Navy,* 262.

[54] Pope, *Great Gamble,* 299–300.

[55] Marcus, *Age of Nelson,* 279.

[56] Hattendorf, in King, *Sea of Words,* 5.

[57] O'Brian, *Letter of Marque,* 102.

[58] Bennett, *Nelson the Commander,* 85.

[59] Marcus, *Age of Nelson,* 274–75.

[60] Lavery, *Nelson's Navy,* 262.

[61] Nelson, *Dispatches and Letters* 6:112.

[62] Pope, *Life in Nelson's Navy,* 208.

[63] Nelson, *Dispatches and Letters* 6:78.

[64] Ibid. 5:374.

[65] St. Vincent, *Letters of Admiral of the Fleet* 1:202.

[66] Henderson, *Frigates,* 15.

[67] Keith, *Keith Papers* 3:69.

[68] uss *United States* vs. hms *Macedonian;* uss *Constitution* vs. hms *Guerriere;* and uss *Constitution* vs. hms *Java.*

[69] Nelson, *Dispatches and Letters* 6:246.

[70] O'Brian, *Commodore,* 168.

[71] Marcus, *Age of Nelson,* 95.

[72] Nelson, *Dispatches and Letters* 5:258.

[73] Ibid., 162.

[74] Oman, *Nelson,* 381.

[75] Nelson, *Dispatches and Letters* 6:5–6.

[76] For greater insights into this process, particularly in this time period, consult Weber, *United States Diplomatic Codes,* as well as Thompson and Padover, *Secret Diplomacy.*

[77] Andrew, *President's Eyes Only,* 104.

[78] Weber, *United States Diplomatic Codes,* 17.

[79] Hamilton, *Hamilton and Nelson Papers* 1:205.

[80] Pope, *Great Gamble,* 103.

[81] Nelson, *Dispatches and Letters* 6:52.

[82] Ibid. 5:327–28.

[83] Ibid., 503.

[84] Ibid., 504.

85 St. Vincent, *Letters of Admiral of the Fleet* 2:185–86.
86 Paul Hamilton to Isaac Chauncey, 31 August 1812, in Dudley, *Naval War of 1812,* 300.
87 Spencer, *George, 2nd Earl Spencer* 3:180–81.
88 Forester, *Lord Nelson,* 201–2.
89 Price, *Eyes of the Fleet,* 53.
90 Ibid., 281.
91 Ibid., 89.
92 Hoche (1768–1797) rose from the ranks; having successfully worked internal-security operations against the Vendean rebels, he was nominated to command the army designated to invade Ireland.
93 Price, *Eyes of the Fleet,* 89.
94 Parkinson, *Britannia Rules,* 45.
95 Arthur, *Remaking of the English Navy,* 74.
96 St. Vincent, *Letters of Admiral of the Fleet* 1:70.

Chapter 4. Frigates: The Eyes of the Fleet

1 Price, *Eyes of the Fleet,* 4.
2 Oman, *Nelson,* 181.
3 Price, *Eyes of the Fleet,* 25.
4 Ibid., 91.
5 Ibid., 26–27.
6 Corbett, *Some Principles of Maritime Strategy,* 112.
7 Ibid., 111–12.
8 Nelson, *Dispatches and Letters* 5:467.
9 Ibid. 6:162.
10 O'Brian, *Hundred Days,* 274.
11 Price, *Eyes of the Fleet,* 282.
12 Corbett, *Some Principles of Maritime Strategy,* 106–7.
13 Nelson, *Dispatches and Letters* 3:98–99.
14 Price, *Eyes of the Fleet,* 92.
15 Nelson, *Dispatches and Letters* 3:43–44.
16 Ibid. 5:145.
17 Ibid., 283–84.
18 Ibid., 413.
19 Ibid. 6:269.
20 Ibid. 7:76.
21 Ibid., 76–77.
22 Ibid., 80–81.

23 Forester, *Lord Nelson,* 293–95.
24 Arthur, *Remaking of the English Navy,* 137.
25 Marcus, *Age of Nelson,* 357.
26 Keith, *Keith Papers* 3:349.
27 Marcus, *Age of Nelson,* 240.
28 Nelson, *Dispatches and Letters* 5:300–301.
29 Ibid., 394.
30 Ibid., 388.
31 Ibid. 6:35.
32 Marcus, *Age of Nelson,* 263.
33 Corbett, *Some Principles of Maritime Strategy,* 248.
34 Nelson, *Dispatches and Letters* 6:329.
35 Bennett, *Nelson the Commander,* 238–39.
36 Nelson, *Dispatches and Letters* 5:157–58.
37 Ibid., 161.
38 Price, *Eyes of the Fleet,* 201.

Chapter 5. Deception

1 Howard, *Strategic Deception,* ix.
2 Taken from Goldman, *Words of Warning,* and Elkins, *Resource Manager's Guide.*
3 Thomas, *Cochrane,* 188.
4 Cochrane, *Autobiography* 1:196, 272–74; Lloyd, *Lord Cochrane,* 44.
5 Cochrane, *Autobiography* 1:273–74.
6 Cochrane, *Autobiography* 1:101; Thomas, *Cochrane,* 62.
7 Forester, *Age of Fighting Sail,* 71.
8 Archibald, *Wooden Fighting Ship,* 80.
9 Parkinson, *War in the Eastern Seas,* 224, 430.
10 O'Brian, *Truelove,* 223.
11 O'Brian, *Nutmeg of Consolation,* 126–31.
12 Nelson, *Dispatches and Letters* 6:183.
13 Cochrane, *Autobiography* 1:100.
14 Marcus, *Age of Nelson,* 386.
15 Price, *Eyes of the Fleet,* 67.
16 Matheson, *Life of Henry Dundas,* 241.
17 W. James, *Naval History,* (1837) 1:268, as quoted in Marcus, *Age of Nelson,* 41.
18 Oman, *Nelson,* 51.
19 Cochrane, *Autobiography* 1:100, 128.
20 O'Brian, *Truelove,* 255.

21 William Crane to Paul Hamilton, in Dudley, *Naval War of 1812,* 209–10.
22 Cochrane, *Autobiography* 1:101.
23 Nelson, *Dispatches and Letters* 6:319.
24 Wilson, *Flags at Sea,* 84, 106, 111.
25 Price, *Eyes of the Fleet,* 263.
26 Cochrane, *Autobiography* 1:189–91.
27 Thomas, *Cochrane,* 130.
28 Price, *Eyes of the Fleet,* 95, 263.
29 O'Brian, *H.M.S. "Surprise,"* 297.
30 Ibid., 285.
31 Cochrane, *Autobiography* 1:178.
32 Mallalieu, *Extraordinary Seaman,* 42.
33 Cochrane, *Autobiography* 1:107.
34 Forester, *Age of Fighting Sail,* 114; Price, *Eyes of the Fleet,* 237.
35 Henderson, *Frigates,* 47–53.
36 Marcus, *Age of Nelson,* 272; Oman, *Nelson,* 615.
37 Corbett, *Campaign of Trafalgar,* 270; Glover, *Britain at Bay,* 82. Corbett identifies the ship as Swedish versus Danish.
38 Parkinson, *Britannia Rules,* 67; Price, *Eyes of the Fleet,* 156.
39 Marcus, *Age of Nelson,* 144.
40 Spencer, *George, 2nd Earl Spencer* 3:84–85.
41 Purser Henry Denison to Secretary of the Navy Hamilton, 11 November 1812, in Dudley, *Naval War of 1812,* 566.
42 Nelson, *Dispatches and Letters* 6:452.

Chapter 6. The Commander: Jack and Master of All Trades

1 Bennett, *Nelson the Commander,* 79.
2 Masefield, *Sea Life,* 56.
3 Ernest R. May, as quoted in Hitchcock, *Intelligence Revolution,* 72.
4 Rodger, *Wooden World,* 155.
5 Bennett, *Nelson the Commander,* 297.
6 From an 1857 manual, as quoted in Bennett, *Nelson the Commander,* 6.
7 O'Brian, *Ionian Mission,* 241–42.
8 Nathan R. Teitel, in Bligh, *Mutiny on Board H.M.S. "Bounty,"* 8.
9 Bennett, *Nelson the Commander,* 61.
10 Bligh, *Mutiny on Board H.M.S. "Bounty,"* 15.
11 Nelson, *Dispatches and Letters* 6:468.
12 Oman, *Nelson,* 573.

13 Bligh, *Mutiny on Board H.M.S. "Bounty,"* 15.

14 Bennett, *Nelson the Commander,* 6.

15 Lavery, *Nelson and the Nile,* 33.

16 Forester, *Captain Horatio Hornblower,* 16–17.

17 O'Brian, *Commodore,* 186.

18 Rodger, *Wooden World,* 259–60.

19 Ibid., 332.

20 Ibid., 335.

21 Forester, *Captain Horatio Hornblower,* 13.

22 King, *Harbours and High Seas,* 27.

23 Ibid., 27.

24 Keith, *Keith Papers* 3:217.

25 O'Brian, *Wine-Dark Sea,* 35–36.

26 Pope, *Great Gamble,* 503.

27 Nelson, *Dispatches and Letters* 5:169.

28 Ibid. 6:249–50.

29 Ibid. 5:273.

30 Parkinson, *Britannia Rules,* 82.

31 Nelson, *Dispatches and Letters* 5:284–85.

32 Bennett, *Nelson the Commander,* 6.

33 Collingwood, *Selection from the Public and Private Correspondence* 2:313.

34 Bennett, *Nelson the Commander,* 6.

35 Georges-Jacques Danton (1759–1794), French revolutionary leader ("We must dare, and dare again, and go on daring," in his 28 August 1792 speech to the Legislative Assembly); Charles Maurice de Talleyrand-Périgord (1754–1838), Napoleon's minister of foreign affairs ("Don't be eager").

36 Bennett, *Nelson the Commander,* 7.

37 Ibid., 7.

38 Marcus, *Age of Nelson,* 410.

39 Nelson, *Dispatches and Letters* 6:240–41.

40 Ibid. 5:248.

41 Forester, *Lord Nelson,* 216–18.

42 Oman, *Nelson,* 175.

43 Nelson, *Dispatches and Letters* 6:240–41.

44 Oman, *Nelson,* 54.

45 Ibid., 56.

46 Ibid., 533.

47 O'Brian, *Ionian Mission,* 113–14.

48 Oman, *Nelson,* 360–61.

49 Howarth, *Trafalgar,* 9.
50 Mackenzie, *Trafalgar Role,* 1–44.
51 Halloran, *Battle of Trafalgar,* I.
52 Nelson, *Dispatches and Letters* 7:60.
53 Oman, *Nelson,* 536.
54 Forester, *Lord Nelson,* 21.
55 Oman, *Nelson,* 664.
56 Bennett, *Nelson the Commander,* 293.
57 Oman, *Nelson,* 381.
58 Marcus, *Age of Nelson,* 345.
59 See this autobiography, *Sailor's Odyssey;* Warner's *Cunningham of Hyndhope;* and *Jane's Fighting Ships 1939.*
60 Oman, *Nelson,* 349.
61 Ibid., 387.
62 Ibid., 424.
63 Spencer, *George, 2nd Earl Spencer* 2:421.
64 Pope, *Black Ship,* 71.
65 Ibid., 81.
66 As quoted in Warner, *Command at Sea,* 101.
67 *World Book Encyclopedia* (Chicago: World Book, 1993), 15:235.
68 Nelson, *Dispatches and Letters* 3:99.
69 Burges, *Selections from the Letters,* 88–89.
70 Lavery, *Nelson and the Nile,* 110.
71 Ibid., 61.
72 Oman, *Nelson,* 591.
73 Bennett, *Nelson the Commander,* 69.
74 Lavery, *Nelson's Navy,* 252.
75 Oman, *Nelson,* 570.
76 Rodger, *Wooden World,* 19.
77 Nelson, *Dispatches and Letters* 6:118.
78 Forester, *Age of Fighting Sail,* 84.
79 Pope, *Great Gamble,* 195.
80 Lavery, *Nelson's Navy,* 251.
81 Pope, *Black Ship,* 15.
82 Pope, *Great Gamble,* 23.
83 Ibid., 23.
84 Ibid., 20.
85 Rodger, *Wooden World,* 17.
86 Pope, *Great Gamble,* 81.

[87] Forester, *Lord Nelson,* 43. Significantly, this was written in 1929.

[88] Pope, *Great Gamble,* 423.

[89] Bradford, *Nelson,* 274.

[90] O'Brian, *Ionian Mission,* 344.

[91] O'Brian, *Letter of Marque,* 50–51.

[92] Kent, *Flag Captain,* 128.

[93] Forester, *Captain Horatio Hornblower,* 109.

[94] Pope, *Black Ship,* 311.

[95] Oman, *Nelson,* 568.

[96] Ibid., 356–57.

[97] Forester, *Lord Nelson,* 278–79.

[98] Nelson, *Dispatches and Letters* 6:484.

[99] Forester, *Lord Nelson,* 293.

[100] Bennett, *Nelson the Commander,* 226.

[101] Marcus, *Age of Nelson,* 432.

[102] Oman, *Nelson,* 544.

[103] Nelson, *Dispatches and Letters* 5:318–19.

[104] Ibid. 6:188.

[105] Pope, *Great Gamble,* 150.

[106] Price, *Eyes of the Fleet,* 157–58.

[107] Pope, *Great Gamble,* 18.

Chapter 7. The Commander as Intelligence Officer

[1] Glover, *Britain at Bay,* 59.

[2] Keith, *Keith Papers* 3:198–99.

[3] Parkinson, *Britannia Rules,* 138.

[4] Oman, *Nelson,* 187.

[5] Ibid., 188.

[6] Keith, *Keith Papers* 2:378–79.

[7] Ibid. 3:120.

[8] Ibid., 119.

[9] Lord, *Dawn's Early Light,* 79.

[10] Keith, *Keith Papers* 3:256–57.

[11] Ibid., 241.

[12] Forester, *Lord Nelson,* 106–7.

[13] Nelson, *Dispatches and Letters* 6:469.

[14] Ibid. 7:55.

[15] Ibid., 49.

[16] Forester, *Lord Nelson,* 108.

[17] Nelson, *Dispatches and Letters* 6:475.

[18] Bainbridge's journal, on board the *Constitution,* as quoted in Dudley, *Naval War of 1812,* 644.

[19] Public Record Office, Admiralty 1/226, as quoted in Glover, *Britain at Bay,* 162.

[20] Pope, *Life in Nelson's Navy,* 103–4.

[21] Keith, *Keith Papers* 1:467.

[22] Price, *Eyes of the Fleet,* 204.

[23] Ibid., 202, 205, 207.

[24] Keith, *Keith Papers* 3:69.

[25] Ibid., 40–41.

[26] Public Record Office, Admiralty 1/224, as quoted in Glover, *Britain at Bay,* 163.

[27] Spencer, *George, 2nd Earl Spencer* 2:379.

[28] Keith, *Keith Papers* 2:173–74.

[29] Oman, *Nelson,* 539.

[30] Keith, *Keith Papers* 3:345.

[31] Bennett, *Nelson the Commander,* 243.

[32] Spencer, *George, 2nd Earl Spencer* 4:20.

[33] Kent, *Signal—Close Action!,* 15.

[34] Price, *Eyes of the Fleet,* 52. For a vivid example of this type of collection, albeit fictionalized, see Forester, *Hornblower and the "Hotspur,"* 55–60.

[35] Forester, *Hornblower and the "Hotspur,"* 58–59.

[36] Forester, *Commodore Hornblower,* 39–40.

[37] Nelson, *Dispatches and Letters* 5:428–29.

[38] Barham, *Charles, Lord Barham* 1:234.

[39] Keith, *Keith Papers* 1:322.

[40] Morris, *Fisher's Face,* 137.

[41] Nelson, *Dispatches and Letters* 6:192.

[42] Rodger, *Wooden World,* 325.

[43] Barnes, *George III and William Pitt,* 456.

[44] Matheson, *Life of Henry Dundas,* 345.

[45] Cochrane, *Autobiography* 1:239–40.

[46] Ibid., 284–85.

[47] Ibid., 261–62.

[48] Collingwood, as quoted in Lavery, *Nelson's Navy,* 253.

[49] Rodger, *Wooden World,* 8.

[50] Pope, *Black Ship,* 80.

[51] Lord, *Dawn's Early Light,* 44.

[52] Forester, *Commodore Hornblower,* 56–58.
[53] Oman, *Nelson,* 606; Scott, *Recollections,* 179–80. But Mackenzie, *Trafalgar Role,* does not show Estes or his colleagues listed on board on the day of battle.
[54] Scott, *Recollections,* 22–23, 33, 64, 73–75, 82, 97, 107, 109, 117–23, 128–33.
[55] Handel, *Masters of War,* 166.
[56] St. Vincent, *Letters of Admiral of the Fleet* 2:267.
[57] Ibid. 1:200.
[58] Oman, *Nelson,* 208.
[59] Spencer, *George, 2nd Earl Spencer* 2:187.
[60] Keith, *Keith Papers* 3:125.
[61] Ibid., 213–14.
[62] Oman, *Nelson,* 243.
[63] Ibid., 481.
[64] Bennett, *Nelson the Commander,* 242.
[65] Ibid., 244.
[66] Nelson, *Dispatches and Letters* 5:362.
[67] Ibid. 6:4–5.
[68] Oman, *Nelson,* 604.
[69] Nelson, *Dispatches and Letters* 7:2–3.
[70] Clausewitz, as quoted in Handel, *Masters of War,* 143.
[71] Forester, *Lieutenant Hornblower,* 65.
[72] E. P. Brenton, as quoted in Lloyd, *Lord Cochrane,* 40.
[73] Lloyd, *Lord Cochrane,* 10.
[74] Oman, *Nelson,* 164.
[75] Ibid., 534.
[76] Pope, *Great Gamble,* 262.
[77] Marcus, *Age of Nelson,* 33.
[78] Oman, *Nelson,* 250.
[79] Price, *Eyes of the Fleet,* 253.
[80] Ibid., 91.

Chapter 8. A Naval Intelligence Occasion

[1] Pope, *Great Gamble,* 226.
[2] Parkinson, *War in the Eastern Seas,* 226.
[3] Parliamentary Papers, 1868–69, 35:693–95, as quoted in Cook and Stevenson, *Facts,* 102.
[4] Parkinson, *War in the Eastern Seas,* 224, 430.
[5] O'Brian, *H.M.S. "Surprise,"* 280.

⁶ Quoted in Barham, *Charles, Lord Barham* 3:227.
⁷ O'Brian, *H.M.S. "Surprise,"* 303.
⁸ Parkinson, *War in the Eastern Seas,* 228–29.
⁹ Ibid., 230.
¹⁰ As quoted in Parkinson, *War in the Eastern Seas,* 234.
¹¹ O'Brian, *H.M.S. "Surprise,"* 333.

Chapter 9. A Naval Intelligence Expedition

¹ Forester, *Lord Nelson,* 240–41.
² Marcus, *Age of Nelson,* 171.
³ Ibid., 172.
⁴ Forester, *Lord Nelson,* 84.
⁵ Carysfort Papers, Elton Hall, as quoted in Pope, *Great Gamble,* 67.
⁶ Bradford, *Essential Hero,* 263; Mahan, *Life of Nelson* 2:62.
⁷ Public Record Office, Admiralty 3/144, Intelligence/Denmark 289, 30 December 1800, as quoted in Pope, *Great Gamble,* 74.
⁸ Public Record Office, Admiralty 1/4186, Talbot Dispatches, 13 and 16 January 1801, as quoted in Pope, *Great Gamble,* 91–92.
⁹ Pope, *Great Gamble,* 95.
¹⁰ *Times,* 5 January 1801, 2b.
¹¹ Pope, *Great Gamble,* 96.
¹² *Times,* 6 January 1801, 3a.
¹³ Ibid., 10 January 1801, 2a.
¹⁴ Ibid., 13 January 1801, 2d.
¹⁵ Ibid., 15 January 1801, 2c.
¹⁶ Nelson, *Dispatches and Letters* 4:280.
¹⁷ Public Record Office, Foreign Office 22/40, 9 January 1801, as quoted in Pope, *Great Gamble,* 97.
¹⁸ St. Vincent, *Letters of Admiral of the Fleet* 1:82.
¹⁹ See Nelson, *Dispatches and Letters* 4:282.
²⁰ Matheson, *Life of Henry Dundas,* 298.
²¹ Public Record Office, Admiralty 1/4186, State Letters, 14 January 1801, as quoted in Pope, *Great Gamble,* 105.
²² Public Record Office, Admiralty 1/4186, 15 January 1801, as quoted in Pope, *Great Gamble,* 105.
²³ Public Record Office, Foreign Office 22/40, no. 4, 15 January 1801, as quoted in Pope, *Great Gamble,* 105.
²⁴ *Times,* 23 January 1801, 2c.
²⁵ Ibid., 24 January 1801, 2a,b.

[26] Ibid., 26 January 1801, 2c.

[27] Ibid., 27 January 1801, 2c.

[28] Ibid., 28 February 1801, 3b.

[29] Bennett, *Nelson the Commander,* 186.

[30] Ibid., 186.

[31] Parkinson, *Britannia Rules,* 83.

[32] Bennett, *Nelson the Commander,* 186.

[33] Public Record Office, Foreign Office 22/40, Drummond-Grenville no. 5, 24 January 1801, as quoted in Pope, *Great Gamble,* 127.

[34] Nicholas Vansittart, M.P. (later first Baron Bexley), as quoted in Pope, *Great Gamble,* 147.

[35] Pope, *Great Gamble,* 148.

[36] Public Record Office, Admiralty 3/144, Minutes, 12 February 1801, as quoted in Pope, *Great Gamble,* 154.

[37] Public Record Office, Admiralty 3/144, Board Minutes (Rough), 22 January 1801, as quoted in Pope, *Great Gamble,* 123.

[38] Pope, *Great Gamble,* 171.

[39] Nelson, *Nelson's Letters,* 304.

[40] Ibid., 305.

[41] Ibid., 311.

[42] Oman, *Nelson,* 428.

[43] Pope, *Great Gamble,* 173.

[44] Ibid., 174.

[45] Ibid., 174–76.

[46] Ibid., 176, 179; Oman, *Nelson,* 430.

[47] St. Vincent, *Letters of Admiral of the Fleet* 1:83.

[48] Pope, *Great Gamble,* 177; Oman, *Nelson,* 434.

[49] Nelson, *Dispatches and Letters* 4:290.

[50] Oman, *Nelson,* 110.

[51] Pope, *Great Gamble,* 177–78.

[52] Oman, *Nelson,* 434.

[53] Pope, *Great Gamble,* 185–86.

[54] Ibid., 186.

[55] Oman, *Nelson,* 434.

[56] *Naval Miscellany,* vol. 2, 7 March 1801, as quoted in Pope, *Great Gamble,* 187.

[57] Hibbert, *Nelson,* 253; Mahan, *Life of Nelson* 2:67.

[58] Public Record Office, Admiralty 1/4, Admirals, Despatches, Baltic Fleet, f.Ha 8, as quoted in Pope, *Great Gamble,* 188.

[59] *Times,* 4 March 1801, 3a.

[60] Ibid., 7 March 1801, 2d.

[61] St. Vincent, *Letters of Admiral of the Fleet* 1:86.

[62] *Times,* 12 March 1801, 3b.

[63] Pope, *Great Gamble,* 235–36.

[64] Nelson, *Dispatches and Letters* 4:294.

[65] Rigsarkivet, Danish State Archives, synopsis of letters received by the crown prince and subsequent resolutions on them, 26 March 1801, as quoted in Pope, *Great Gamble,* 236, 253.

[66] Pope, *Great Gamble,* 247, 249.

[67] Parker, as quoted in St. Vincent, *Letters of Admiral of the Fleet* 1:63.

[68] Pope, *Great Gamble,* 261–62.

[69] Drummond, as quoted in Pope, *Great Gamble,* 274–75.

[70] Thomas J. Pettigrew, *Memoirs of the Life of Vice-Admiral Lord Viscount Nelson,* 2 vols. (London: T. & W. Boone, 1849), 1:448, as quoted in Oman, *Nelson,* 436.

[71] Pope, *Great Gamble,* 262–67.

[72] Ibid., 268.

[73] Lt. Col. Stewart, as quoted in St. Vincent, *Letters of Admiral of the Fleet* 1:65. Also found in Nelson, *Dispatches and Letters* 4:300.

[74] Pope, *Great Gamble,* 281.

[75] Bennett, *Nelson the Commander,* 188–89. The full texts can be found in Nelson, *Dispatches and Letters* 4:295–98, in Nelson, *Nelson's Letters,* 319–21, and in Clarke and M'Arthur, *Life and Services* 2:386–88.

[76] Pope, *Great Gamble,* 290.

[77] Hibbert, *Nelson,* 256–57.

[78] Nelson, Journal, as quoted in Pope, *Great Gamble,* 295.

[79] Brisbane's Report: Stewart's diary, Cumloden Papers, as quoted in Pope, *Great Gamble,* 297.

[80] Pope, *Great Gamble,* 298.

[81] Mahan, *Life of Nelson* 2:77.

[82] British Museum Additional Manuscript 41667D, Bourgoing to Talleyrand, 30 March 1801, as quoted in Pope, *Great Gamble,* 306.

[83] Borberg and Espersen, *Military Intelligence Service,* 9.

[84] Parker journal, as quoted in Pope, *Great Gamble,* 309.

[85] Sir Hyde Parker, "Journal.—Sir Hyde Parker, Knight, Admiral of the Blue.—Admirals' Journals, vol. 35," in Jackson, *Logs of the Great Sea Fights* 2:88.

[86] Parker, as quoted in Nelson, *Dispatches and Letters* 4:319.

[87] Hamilton, *Hamilton and Nelson Papers,* 2, no. 551, p. 132. Also found in Nelson, *Dispatches and Letters* 4:321.

[88] Parker, in Jackson, *Logs of the Great Sea Fights,* 89.

[89] Pope, *Great Gamble,* 313.

[90] Ibid., 316.

[91] Ibid., 330.

[92] Ibid., 347–48.

[93] Ibid., 348.

[94] Ibid., 352.

[95] Ibid., 355.

[96] Oman, *Nelson,* 444.

[97] Nelson, *Dispatches and Letters* 4:499–500.

[98] Forester, *Lord Nelson,* 62.

[99] Pope, *Great Gamble,* 357.

[100] Oman, *Nelson,* 455.

[101] Hibbert, *Nelson,* 261.

[102] Pope, *Great Gamble,* 410–11.

[103] Hibbert, *Nelson,* 265.

[104] Mahan, *Life of Nelson* 2:93.

Chapter 10. A Naval Intelligence Campaign

[1] Chandler, *Campaigns of Napoleon,* 208; Stokesbury, *Navy and Empire,* 184; Warner, *Battle of the Nile,* 23–24.

[2] Warner, *Battle of the Nile,* 24.

[3] Mahan, *Life of Nelson* 1:319.

[4] Forester, *Lord Nelson,* 165.

[5] Warner, *Battle of the Nile,* 23.

[6] Lavery, *Nelson and the Nile,* 37.

[7] Spencer, *George, 2nd Earl Spencer* 2:429–30.

[8] Ibid., 432–33.

[9] Ibid., 434.

[10] Windham, *Diary* (London, 1866), ed. Mrs. H. Baring, 2:392–94, as quoted in Lavery, *Nelson and the Nile,* 94.

[11] Lavery, *Nelson and the Nile,* 97.

[12] Spencer, *George, 2nd Earl Spencer* 2:438.

[13] Lavery, *Nelson and the Nile,* 36–37.

[14] Forester, *Lord Nelson,* 167.

[15] Public Record Office, Admiralty 1/6034, as quoted in Lavery, *Nelson and the Nile,* 35.

[16] Bennett, *Nelson the Commander,* 121–22; Lloyd, *Nile Campaign,* 10.

[17] Lavery, *Nelson and the Nile,* 14–15.

[18] Marcus, *Age of Nelson,* 126.

[19] Secret decree as quoted in Lloyd, *Nile Campaign,* 12.

[20] Bennett, *Nelson the Commander,* 122; Chandler, *Campaigns of Napoleon,* 212.

[21] Chandler, *Campaigns of Napoleon,* 210; Warner, *Battle of the Nile,* 24.

[22] Lavery, *Nelson and the Nile,* 12.

[23] Parkinson, *Britannia Rules,* 58; Lavery, *Nelson and the Nile,* 139.

[24] Howarth and Howarth, *Immortal Memory,* 186. Louis Bourrienne, *Memoirs of Napoleon Bonaparte* (London 1836), 1:115, as quoted in Lavery, *Nelson and the Nile,* 9.

[25] Lavery, *Nelson and the Nile,* 9.

[26] Chandler, *Campaigns of Napoleon,* 214–15.

[27] Warner, *Battle of the Nile,* 45.

[28] Public Record Office, Admiralty 1/397, as quoted in Lavery, *Nelson and the Nile,* 40.

[29] Lavery, *Nelson and the Nile,* 62.

[30] Spencer, *George, 2nd Earl Spencer* 2:441.

[31] Nelson, *Dispatches and Letters* 3:9–10.

[32] Lavery, *Nelson and the Nile,* 41.

[33] Spencer, *George, 2nd Earl Spencer* 2:441–42.

[34] Nelson, *Dispatches and Letters* 3:11.

[35] Ibid., 11–12.

[36] Ibid., 12.

[37] Ibid., 13.

[38] Forester, *Lord Nelson,* 173.

[39] Nelson, *Dispatches and Letters* 3:24.

[40] Spencer, *George, 2nd Earl Spencer* 2:438–40.

[41] Ibid., 445–46.

[42] Ibid., 445–46.

[43] Clarke and M'Arthur, *Life and Services* 2:76–77. Chandler, *Campaigns of Napoleon,* apparently identifies this correspondent as a Mr. Audry (p. 215).

[44] Lavery, *Nelson and the Nile,* 18.

[45] Public Record Office, Admiralty 51/1260, as quoted in Lavery, *Nelson and the Nile,* 65.

[46] Forester, *Lord Nelson,* 171.

[47] Lavery, *Nelson and the Nile,* 65; Forester, *Lord Nelson,* 168.

[48] Nelson, *Dispatches and Letters* 3:14.

[49] Ibid., 15.

[50] Parkinson, *Britannia Rules,* 59.

[51] Lavery, *Nelson and the Nile,* 109.

[52] Ibid., 105.

[53] Fortescue, *Correspondence of King George the Third* 4:178, quoted in Lavery, *Nelson and the Nile,* 99.

[54] *Mariner's Mirror* (1972) 58:282, as quoted in Lavery, *Nelson and the Nile,* 63.

[55] Spencer, *George, 2nd Earl Spencer* 2:446–47.

[56] Bryant, *Years of Endurance,* 239.

[57] Lavery, *Nelson and the Nile,* 50–51, 61, 152.

[58] Nelson, *Dispatches and Letters* 3:15–17.

[59] Captain Berry, as quoted in Nelson, *Dispatches and Letters* 3:17.

[60] Nelson, *Dispatches and Letters* 3:17–18.

[61] Lavery, *Nelson and the Nile,* 74.

[62] Mahan, *Life of Nelson* 1:325.

[63] Clarke and M'Arthur, *Life and Services* 2:94.

[64] Nelson, *Dispatches and Letters* 3:27–28.

[65] Bryant, *Years of Endurance,* 240.

[66] Oman, *Nelson,* 300.

[67] Howarth and Howarth, *Immortal Memory,* 188.

[68] Mahan, *Life of Nelson* 1:364; Nelson, *Dispatches and Letters* 3:30.

[69] Vice Adm. Cuthbert Collingwood, First Baron, *Private Correspondence of Admiral Lord Collingwood* (London: Navy Records Society, 1957), 90, as quoted in Lavery, *Nelson and the Nile,* 101.

[70] Lavery, *Nelson and the Nile,* 101.

[71] Ibid., 108, 113.

[72] Ibid., 109.

[73] Ibid., 117.

[74] Nelson, *Dispatches and Letters* 3:25–27.

[75] Mahan, *Life of Nelson* 1:327.

[76] *Correspondence de Napoleon* 4:79–80, as quoted in Mahan, *French Revolution* 1:259.

[77] Forester, *Lord Nelson,* 171–73.

[78] Ibid., 172.

[79] Mahan, *Life of Nelson* 1:328.

[80] Clowes, *Royal Navy* 4:354.

[81] Lavery, *Nelson and the Nile,* 116.

[82] Nelson, *Dispatches and Letters* 3:28–29.

[83] Ibid., 29.

[84] Ibid., 29–30.

[85] Ibid., 31.

[86] Oman, *Nelson,* 287.

[87] Lloyd, *Nile Campaign,* 12.

[88] Warner, *Battle of the Nile,* 28.

[89] Parkinson, *Britannia Rules,* 59.

[90] Spencer, *George, 2nd Earl Spencer* 2:448–49.

[91] Parkinson, *Britannia Rules,* 59.

[92] Oman, *Nelson,* 287.

[93] Mahan, *Life of Nelson* 1:328.

[94] Howarth and Howarth, *Immortal Memory,* 191.

[95] Nelson, *Dispatches and Letters* 3:32, 34, 35, 39. *Sub rosa,* the ancient custom of hanging a rose over the council table to indicate that all present were sworn to secrecy. It is probably connected with the legend that Cupid gave a rose to the god of silence (Harpocrates) to keep him from revealing the indiscretions of Venus.

[96] *Warner,* Battle of the Nile, 55.

[97] Clarke and M'Arthur, *Life and Services* 2:91–92.

[98] Public Record Office, Foreign Office 70/11, 29/5/98, as quoted in Lavery, *Nelson and the Nile,* 124–25.

[99] Bradford, *Essential Hero,* 180.

[100] Nelson, *Dispatches and Letters* 3:39.

[101] W. Hardman, *History of Malta* (1909) 13, as quoted in Lloyd, *Nile Campaign,* 15.

[102] Lavery, *Nelson and the Nile,* 87–88.

[103] Bradford, *Essential Hero,* 176.

[104] Ibid., 181.

[105] Bennett, *Nelson the Commander,* 125.

[106] Mahan, *Life of Nelson* 1:332.

[107] Lavery, *Nelson and the Nile,* 117–19.

[108] Nelson, *Dispatches and Letters* 3:39–40.

[109] Bradford, *Essential Hero,* 182; Warner, *Battle of the Nile,* 57.

[110] Bennett, *Nelson the Commander,* 125–26.

[111] Nelson, *Dispatches and Letters* 3:49.

[112] Lavery, *Nelson and the Nile,* 132, 155–56.

[113] Bryant, *Years of Endurance,* 243.

[114] Lavery, *Nelson and the Nile,* 126–27.

[115] Nelson, *Dispatches and Letters* 3:40–41.

[116] Bradford, *Essential Hero,* 184.

[117] Stokesbury, *Navy and Empire,* 192.

[118] Bennett, *Nelson the Commander,* 126; Mahan, *Life of Nelson* 1:336.

[119] Nelson, *Dispatches and Letters* 3:36–37.

[120] Herold, 57, as quoted in Lavery, *Nelson and the Nile,* 129.

[121] Warner, *Battle of the Nile*, 58.

[122] Bryant, *Years of Endurance*, 243.

[123] Stokesbury, *Navy and Empire*, 192.

[124] British Library Additional Manuscript 30260, as quoted in Lavery, *Nelson and the Nile*, 120.

[125] Mahan, *Life of Nelson* 1:338.

[126] Forester, *Lord Nelson*, 177.

[127] Henderson, *Frigates*, 1.

[128] Marcus, *Age of Nelson*, 127.

[129] Lavery, *Nelson and the Nile*, 79–80.

[130] Jenkins, *French Navy*, 228.

[131] Forester, *Lord Nelson*, 176.

[132] Nelson, *Dispatches and Letters* 3:42.

[133] Anderson, *Naval Wars in the Levant*, 357.

[134] Nelson, *Dispatches and Letters* 3:42–43.

[135] Bennett, *Nelson the Commander*, 127.

[136] Bryant, *Years of Endurance*, 245.

[137] Clarke and M'Arthur, *Life and Services* 2:105.

[138] Berry, 13, as quoted in Lavery, *Nelson and the Nile*, 129.

[139] Bradford, *Essential Hero*, 189.

[140] Mahan, *Life of Nelson*, 339–40.

[141] Nelson, *Dispatches and Letters* 3:42.

[142] Lavery, *Nelson and the Nile*, 131, 134; Nelson, *Dispatches and Letters* 3:41.

[143] Nelson, *Dispatches and Letters* 3:29.

[144] Forester, *Captain Horatio Hornblower*, 79.

[145] Lavery, *Nelson and the Nile*, 133–34.

[146] Nelson, *Dispatches and Letters* 3:44.

[147] Ibid., 44–45.

[148] Bryant, *Years of Endurance*, 244.

[149] Warner, *Battle of the Nile*, 23.

[150] La Jonquière 1:553, as quoted in Lavery, *Nelson and the Nile*, 80.

[151] Bennett, *Nelson the Commander*, 127.

[152] Nelson, *Dispatches and Letters* 3:45.

[153] Clarke and M'Arthur, *Life and Services* 2:103.

[154] Nelson, *Dispatches and Letters* 3:47.

[155] Ibid., 47.

[156] Lavery, *Nelson and the Nile*, 138.

[157] Nelson, *Dispatches and Letters* 3:46.

[158] Royal Commission on Historic Manuscripts, *Report on the Laing Manuscript* (1914), 2:661, as quoted in Lavery, *Nelson and the Nile*, 102–3.

159 Ross 1:215n., as quoted in Lavery, *Nelson and the Nile,* 167.
160 Nelson, *Dispatches and Letters* 3:48–49.
161 Bennett, *Nelson the Commander,* 128.
162 Nelson, *Dispatches and Letters* 3:49.
163 Bryant, *Years of Endurance,* 248.
164 Nelson, as quoted by Lord Fitzharris, son of the Earl of Malmesbury, from a meeting at Vienna in 1799, recounted in Lloyd, *Nile Campaign,* 55.
165 Lloyd, *Nile Campaign,* 58–59.
166 Clarke and M'Arthur, *Life and Services* 2:107.
167 Ibid., 105–7.
168 Parkinson, *Britannia Rules,* 62; Bennett, *Nelson the Commander,* 129, 131; Lavery, *Nelson and the Nile,* 171.
169 Maj. Gen. Jack Liede, USA (Ret.), in a Joint Military Intelligence College lecture, March 1997.
170 Forester, *Lord Nelson,* 182.
171 Nelson, *Dispatches and Letters* 3:50.
172 Forester, *Lord Nelson,* 183.
173 Lavery, *Nelson and the Nile,* 177.
174 Nelson, *Dispatches and Letters* 3:57.
175 Forester, *Lord Nelson,* 187.
176 Chandler, *Campaigns of Napoleon,* 217–19.
177 Forester, *Lord Nelson,* 193.
178 From Captain Hope's official letter, as printed in the *London Gazette* of 23 October 1798, as quoted in Nelson, *Dispatches and Letters* 3:117.
179 Nelson, *Dispatches and Letters* 3:95.
180 Ibid., 100.
181 Oman, *Nelson,* 304.
182 Nelson, *Dispatches and Letters* 3:113.
183 Ibid., 117.
184 Warner, *Battle of the Nile,* 133.
185 Oman, *Nelson,* 305.
186 Quoted in Hibbert, *Nelson,* 138.
187 Bryant, *Years of Endurance,* 259.
188 Bradford, *Essential Hero,* 186; Mahan, *Life of Nelson* 1:334.
189 Marcus, *Age of Nelson,* 138.
190 Bryant, *Years of Endurance,* 246.
191 Spencer, *George, 2nd Earl Spencer* 2:453.
192 Ibid., 454.
193 Ibid., 455–56.
194 Ibid., 459.

[195] Ibid., 462–63.
[196] Ibid., 459.
[197] Ibid., 469–70.
[198] Ibid., 470.
[199] Oman, *Nelson,* 294.
[200] Forester, *Lord Nelson,* 188.
[201] Stokesbury, *Navy and Empire,* 192.
[202] Price, *Eyes of the Fleet,* 91.

Conclusion

[1] Mattingly, *Renaissance Diplomacy,* 229.
[2] Fraser, *Intelligence of the Secretaries of State,* 1.
[3] Herman, *Intelligence Power,* 10–11.
[4] Ibid., 12–13.
[5] Black, "Mid-Eighteenth-Century Crisis," 223.
[6] Herman, *Intelligence Power,* 13.
[7] Van Creveld, *Command in War,* 17–57.
[8] Herman, *Intelligence Power,* 14.
[9] Ehrman, *Younger Pitt,* 342.
[10] Neilson and McKercher, *Go Spy the Land,* xii.
[11] Ibid., 111.
[12] Mahan, *Influence of Sea Power,* 1–2, 7.
[13] Forester, *Lord Nelson,* 51, 53.
[14] Marcus, *Age of Nelson,* 62–63.
[15] Bryant, *Years of Endurance,* 247.
[16] Forester, *Lord Nelson,* 14.
[17] Ibid., 284–85.
[18] Ibid., 317–18.
[19] Ibid., 49–50.
[20] Lavery, *Nelson and the Nile,* 180.
[21] Ibid., 5.
[22] Morris, *Fisher's Face,* 222.
[23] Parkinson, *Britannia Rules,* 21.
[24] Forester, *Lord Nelson,* 309–10.
[25] Bennett, *Nelson the Commander,* 297.
[26] Arthur, *Remaking of the English Navy,* 199.

BIBLIOGRAPHY

The historical study of naval intelligence, parallel to the history of military intelligence in general, is essentially rooted in the twentieth century; moreover, a remarkable number of books and articles—in fact a disproportionate number —dwell on the Second World War. Very few works develop any focus significantly farther back than the creation of the United States Office of Naval Intelligence in 1882, or the British Naval Intelligence Department in 1887. This is somewhat surprising, considering the continual concern for better understanding regarding the proper utilization of intelligence assets.

A review of military intelligence literature might almost suggest that intelligence has existed only since the late nineteenth century, as modern technology began to shape intelligence collection and dissemination. Technology's role in intelligence only intensified in the twentieth century, with a virtual revolution coming about during the Second World War. Technological advances were geometrically accelerated. In addition, there was enormous and unprecedented international cooperation in sharing intelligence. As Walter Hitchcock wrote in the preface to *The Intelligence Revolution: A Historical Perspective,* "[World War II] also caused an interrelated growth in organizational size, efficiency, and sophistication that helped gain the craft of intelligence an acceptance in operational circles that it had not previously enjoyed" (Hitchcock, *Intelligence Revolution,* v).

In regard to creating *Most Secret and Confidential,* several books have been of particular use, including both broad survey as well as specific focus. Indeed, if I may quote the author of the first of these volumes, "this book owes everything to other books, and to their authors, who have given this author such pleasure over [one third] a century." The first of these books is Anthony Price's *Eyes of the Fleet: A Popular History of Frigates and Frigate Captains, 1793–1815.* An award-winning author of nineteen espionage novels, Price presents a magnificent history full of valuable information and thoughtful insights. He particularly brings out the heavy responsibilities and problems of commanders in an age of primitive information and communication systems. The second work is Capt. Geoffrey Bennett's *Nelson the Commander.* Based on a wealth of archival research, Bennett offers a unique analysis of Nelson as a leader, manager, strategist, and tactician, as well as a picture of Nelson's place in the wars and his influence on subsequent history. The third is Kenneth Ellis's *Post Office in the Eighteenth Century: A Study in Administrative History.* The British Post Office was the center of communications controlling a fleet of packet vessels and an enormous propaganda and intelligence organ, serving as the government's eyes, ears, and mouthpiece. Ellis provides considerable information on intelligence, cryptography, cryptology, and secret-service funding—which is mostly drawn from primary sources only available to archival researchers in Britain. ("Great reliance was placed on intercepted material and there are many examples of the copies made during this period among the State Papers Foreign, which can be consulted at the Public Record Office at Chancery Lane" [Atherton, *Top Secret,* 7]). In fact, Ellis is the source on what was, in many ways, an enormous intelligence agency. The fourth work is Dudley Pope's exhaustive account of the Copenhagen campaign of 1801, *The Great Gamble.* Pope combines remarkable detail and smoothness of narration to make this a fine, scholarly history. He gives tremendous insights into the thought processes of Admirals Nelson and Parker, and, without writing a book on intelligence, he certainly weaves intelligence issues into many of its pages. Pope's book stands as the definitive account of this key campaign and battle. The fifth volume is Brian Lavery's *Nelson and the Nile;* in many ways it parallels Pope's work and is a remarkable contribution to the literature. It, in turn, is the definitive account of Nelson's Nile campaign—an intelligence campaign if there ever was one. The final work is C. S. Forester's *Lord Nelson,* which, along with his *Age of Fighting Sail,* is absolutely required reading for the individual interested in this era. It is safe to write that *Most Secret and Confidential* would not exist without Forester's influence, which certainly encompasses the fictional *Horatio Hornblower* series.

I have quoted very heavily from Bennett, Ellis, Forester, Lavery, Pope, and Price, thereby, in many cases, disclosing the original, primary sources they used in their research. I did this to reveal that ideas and conclusions are not always those of the secondary authors, but very often are from an archival source painstakingly located and drawn upon by such eminent historians.

A number of other books were certainly invaluable as well. Representative of the survey are Rowan and Deindorfer (*Secret Service: Thirty-Three Centuries of Espionage*) and Neilson and McKercher (*Go Spy the Land: Military Intelligence in History*). In the latter, Gunther Rothenberg writes, "In the second half of the eighteenth century every court and camp swarmed with spies, agents, and informants, but there were no permanent military intelligence organizations and few records were kept." Christopher Andrew goes on, writing that "Britain's two most celebrated commanders at the turn of the century, Arthur Wellesley (later first Duke of Wellington) and Horatio (later Viscount) Nelson, were [effectively] ... their own intelligence officers" (Andrew, "The Nature of Military Intelligence," in Neilson and McKercher, eds., *Go Spy the Land,* 2).

In addition, Deacon (*A History of the British Secret Service* and *Silent War: A History of Western Naval Intelligence*) and Richings (*Espionage: The Story of the Secret Service of the English Crown*) are generally insightful. Other specific works include Robertson (*Narrative of a Secret Mission to the Danish Islands in 1808*) and Cobban ("British Secret Service in France, 1784–1792"). Cobban tell us that most British information-collection efforts were very naval in orientation, as the intelligence "received by the Foreign Office [as well as the Home Dept.], with very few exceptions [was] directed to one object—intelligence about the situation and distribution of the French Navy" (Cobban, "British Secret Service," 248). Another extraordinarily useful work was Thompson and Padover (*Secret Diplomacy: Espionage and Cryptography, 1500–1815*).

It must be emphasized, however, that while useful for culling bits and pieces of data, none of the above (not even Deacon's *Silent War: A History of Western Naval Intelligence*) really do more than touch upon naval intelligence during the Age of Nelson.

A clear "analysis of British maritime strategy as a whole, including its maritime, power-projection, and continental components is Stokesbury (*Navy and Empire*)" (Robin Ranger, "Anglo-French Wars: 1689–1815," in Gray and Barnett, eds., *Seapower and Strategy,* 185). Additional and essential naval histories include Oman (*Nelson*), Pope (*Life in Nelson's Navy* and *The Black Ship*), Corbett (*Some Principles of Maritime Strategy* and *The Campaign of Trafalgar*), Mahan (*The Influence of Sea Power upon History, The Life of Nelson,* and *The Influence of Sea Power upon the French Revolution and Empire*), Lavery (*Nelson's Navy* and *Nelson and the Nile*), Rodger (*The Wooden World: An Anatomy of the Georgian Navy*), and Parkinson (*Britannia Rules: The Classic Age of Naval History, 1793–1815* and *War in the Eastern Seas, 1793–1815*).

Regarding essential background, Cook and Stevenson (*British Historical Facts, 1760–1830*), Chandler (*Dictionary of the Napoleonic Wars*), and Bryant (*The Years of Endurance*) were truly indispensable.

Again, most secondary works have no essential intelligence focus. The story has to be pieced together from data points discovered here and there. Marcus (*The Age of Nelson*) is an exception (as well as being an outstanding single account). Along with Marcus (particularly in *The Campaign of Trafalgar*), Corbett is essentially unique in seriously addressing "intelligence" by name both in text and index.

As a result, the challenge was to gather, synthesize, and analyze information from many diverse sources, delineating whatever patterns and consistencies that were exposed. Then I attempted to draw relevant conclusions about the nature of naval intelligence, and its impact upon command decision making, during this specific period.

Less evident, but fundamental to general knowledge, detail, and "atmosphere," were the fictional works of C. S. Forester, Alexander Kent, Dudley Pope, and Patrick O'Brian (there are others as well, but these are the premier). Led by Forester, these gentlemen "did for Nelson's navy what Clancy did for the modern U.S. Navy" (Ranger, 185). Each author spent a lifetime researching and writing on the age of Nelson. Kent is still busy writing; Forester died in 1966, Pope in 1997, and O'Brian in 2000. The distillation of their knowledge, even presented in fictional mode, gives any reader a feel for, and total immersion in, the era; not for nothing did Ernest Hemingway, for example, recommend Forester "to every literate I know." Professor John Bayley (Oxford) writes that "the Hornblower books were superb examples of their craft, and Forester remains unequaled for dynamism of narrative and precision of encounter: his single ship actions are surely the best ever described." Alone among the four, O'Brian presents the concept of a highly organized, fully staffed, and well-funded Admiralty intelligence apparatus for which one of his main characters (Dr. Maturin) actively functions as a key operative. However, unless he was privy to considerable information otherwise invisible to other historians and novelists, his naval-intelligence bureau by and large exists courtesy of O'Brian the gifted storyteller versus O'Brian the eminent historian—and a remarkable historian he was, too; as Dr. N. A. M. Rodger writes, "How far the modern naval officer stands from the world of [Nelson] no one can say with more authority than Patrick O'Brian."

To summarize, my dozen most-useful sources include Bennett, Cochrane, Cook and Stevenson, Ellis, Forester, Lavery, Marcus, Oman, Parkinson, Pope, Price, and Thompson and Padover. Of course, it goes without saying that my other "short list" must not be ignored—that is, the priceless treasures of primary sources discussed in the preface. Indeed, this book would not at all have its present form were it not for the published papers and/or autobiographical writings of Nelson, Cochrane, Collingwood, St. Vincent, Barham, Keith, Castlereagh, and George III, among others.

The fundamental nature of this book, historical analysis, inherently fell within the scope of traditional library and archive searching. Key to developing sources was access to the strong military, naval, and intelligence collections found in the U.S. Air Force Academy Cadet Library and the U.S. Defense Intelligence Agency's John T. Hughes Library. In addition, desk-top access to a variety of electronic informational databases, centered around the OCLC Firstsearch system, netted a remarkable bibliographic survey. Perhaps the most useful of these, due to the topic, was OCLC's WorldCat (a Firstsearch option), which delivers to the user instantaneous author, title, subject, and keyword searching to over thirty-eight million books and other documents. OCLC (formerly called the Online Computer Library Center), in Dublin, Ohio, is a nonprofit membership organization. More than nine thousand libraries contribute to and/or use information in the OCLC Online Union Catalog, the world's largest database of library bibliographic information. OCLC has participating libraries in over twenty-five countries and territories.

Assertive use of the national interlibrary loan system, in turn, physically delivered a quantity of important books not locally or otherwise readily available. Twenty-two libraries in thirteen U.S. states loaned me over fifty volumes—some extraordinarily rare and fragile—and for this aid I am truly grateful.

In fact, I feel obliged to borrow from Anthony Price just one more time, to recognize the panoply of invaluable sources—wherever found—that made this book possible: "To all these authors, and others unnamed, my admiration and thanks."

Primary Source Materials

Barham, Adm. Charles Middleton, Baron. *Letters and Papers of Charles, Lord Barham, Admiral of the Red Squadron, 1758–1813.* 3 vols. London: Navy Records Society, 1907.

Bligh, Vice Adm. William. *The Mutiny On Board H.M.S. "Bounty."* New York: Airmont, 1965.

Burges, Sir James Bland. *Selections from the Letters and Correspondence of Sir James Bland Burges, Bart., Sometime Under-Secretary of State for Foreign Affairs, with Notices of His Life.* Edited by James Hutton. London: John Murray, 1885.

Castlereagh, Robert Stewart, Viscount. *Memoirs and Correspondence of Viscount Castlereagh, 2nd Marquess of Londonderry.* 4 vols. Edited by Charles Vane, Marquess of Londonderry. London: Henry Colburn, 1848.

Cochrane, Capt. Lord Thomas, tenth Earl of Dundonald. *The Autobiography of a Seaman.* 2d ed. 2 vols. London: Richard Bentley, 1860–61.

Collingwood, Vice Adm. Cuthbert, 1st Baron. *A Selection from the Public and Private Correspondence of Vice-Admiral Lord Collingwood; interspersed with Memoirs of His Life.* 2d ed. 2 vols. London: J. Ridgway, 1828.

Corbett, Sir Julian S. *Fighting Instructions: 1530–1816.* London: Navy Records Society, 1905. Reprint, New York: Burt Franklin, 1967.

Cunningham, Andrew, Viscount. *Sailor's Odyssey.* New York: Dutton, 1951.

Dudley, William, ed. *The Naval War of 1812: A Documentary History.* Vol. 1. Washington, D.C.: U.S. Dept. of the Navy, Naval Historical Center, 1985.

Fitzpatrick, John C., ed. *The Writings of George Washington from the Original Manuscript Sources, 1745–1799.* Washington, D.C.: GPO, 1931–44.

George III, King of Great Britain. *The Correspondence of King George the Third from 1760 to December 1783, Printed from the Original Papers in the Royal Archives at Windsor Castle.* Arranged and edited by Sir John Fortescue. 6 vols. London: Macmillan, 1928.

Halloran, Laurence. *Battle of Trafalgar, A Poem. To Which is Added, a Selection of Fugitive Pieces. Chiefly Written at Sea.* London: Joyce Gold, 1806.

Hamilton, Sir William. *The Hamilton and Nelson Papers.* London: Printed for Private Circulation, 1893–94.

Jackson, Rear Adm. T. Sturges, ed. *Logs of the Great Sea Fights, 1794–1805.* 2 vols. London: Navy Records Society, 1900.

Keith, Adm. George Keith Elphinstone, Viscount. *The Keith Papers: Selected from the Letters and Papers of Admiral Viscount Keith.* 3 vols. London: Navy Records Society, 1927, 1955.

Legg, L. G. Wickham, ed. *British Diplomatic Instructions, 1689–1789.* Vol. 7, *France.* Part 4, 1745–1789. Camden 3d ser., vol. 49. London: Offices of the Royal Historical Society, 1934.

Nelson, Vice Adm. Horatio, Viscount, Duke of Bronté. *The Dispatches and Letters of Vice Admiral Lord Viscount Nelson.* Notes by Sir Nicholas H. Nicolas. 7 vols. London: Henry Colburn, 1844–46.

———. *Nelson's Letters.* Edited by Geoffrey Rawson. London: J. M. Dent & Sons, 1960.

Robertson, Rev. James. *Narrative of a Secret Mission to the Danish Islands in 1808.* Edited from the author's manuscript by Alexander C. Fraser. London: Longman, Green, Longman, Roberts, and Green, 1863.

St. Vincent, Adm. of the Fleet John Jervis, Earl of. *Letters of Admiral of the Fleet, the Earl of St. Vincent, whilst the First Lord of the Admiralty, 1801–1804.* 2 vols. London: Navy Records Society, 1922, 1927.

Scott, Rev. A. J. *Recollections of the Life of the Rev. A. J. Scott.* London: Saunders and Otley, 1842.

Spencer, George. *Private Papers of George, 2nd Earl Spencer: First Lord of the Admiralty, 1794–1801.* 4 vols. London: Navy Records Society, 1913, 1924.

Times (London). Film Editions. 1 Jan 1801 to 30 Jun 1801.

Secondary Source Materials

Anderson, R. C. *Naval Wars in the Levant, 1559–1853.* Princeton, N.J.: University Press, 1952.

Andrew, Christopher. *For the President's Eyes Only: Secret Intelligence and the American Presidency from Washington to Bush.* New York: HarperCollins, 1995.

————. *Secret Service: The Making of the British Intelligence Community.* London: Heinemann, 1985.

Archibald, E. H. H. *The Wooden Fighting Ship in the Royal Navy, A.D. 897–1860.* London: Blandford Press, 1968.

Arthur, Charles B. *The Remaking of the English Navy by Admiral St. Vincent— Key to the Victory Over Napoleon: The Great Unclaimed Naval Revolution (1795–1805).* Lanham, Md.: University Press of America, 1986.

Atherton, Louise. *Top Secret: An Interim Guide to Recent Releases of Intelligence Records at the Public Record Office.* London: H.M. Public Record Office, 1993.

Barnes, Donald G. *George III and William Pitt, 1783–1806: A New Interpretation Based upon a Study of their Unpublished Correspondence.* New York: Octagon Books, 1965.

Bennett, Capt. Geoffrey. *Nelson the Commander.* New York: Charles Scribner's Sons, 1972.

Black, Jeremy. "British Intelligence and the Mid-Eighteenth-Century Crisis." *Intelligence and National Security* 2, no. 2 (April 1987): 209–29.

Borberg, Preben, and Mogens Espersen. *Military Intelligence Service as Part of Crisis Management.* People and Defence Series. Copenhagen: Information and Welfare Services of the Danish Defence, 1980.

Bradford, Ernle. *Nelson: The Essential Hero.* New York: Harcourt Brace Jovanovich, 1977.

Brooke, John. *King George III.* New York: McGraw-Hill, 1972.

Bryant, Arthur. *The Years of Endurance, 1793–1802.* London: Collins, 1942.

Butler, Ruth L. *Doctor Franklin: Postmaster General.* Garden City, N.Y.: Doubleday, Doran, 1928.

Callender, Sir Geoffrey A. R., and F. H. Hinsley. *The Naval Side of British History, 1485–1945.* London: Christophers, 1952.

Chandler, David G. *The Campaigns of Napoleon.* New York: Macmillan, 1966.

————. *Dictionary of the Napoleonic Wars.* New York: Macmillan, 1979.

Clarke, Rev. James S., and John M'Arthur. *The Life and Services of Horatio Viscount Nelson . . . from His Lordship's Manuscripts.* 3 vols. London: Peter Jackson, Late Fisher, Son, & Company, 1840.

Clowes, William Laird. *The Royal Navy: A History from the Earliest Times to 1900.* Vol. 4. 1899. Reprint, London: Chatham, 1997.

Cobban, Alfred. *Ambassadors and Secret Agents: The Diplomacy of the First Earl of Malmesbury at the Hague.* London: Jonathan Cape, 1954.

————. "British Secret Service in France, 1784–1792." *English Historical Review* 69, no. 271 (April 1954): 226–61.

Colomb, Vice Adm. Philip H. *Naval Warfare: Its Ruling Principles and Practice Historically Treated.* 2 vols. 1891. Reprint, Annapolis: Naval Institute Press, 1990.

Cook, Chris, and John Stevenson. *British Historical Facts, 1760–1830.* Hamden, Conn.: Archon Books, 1980.

Corbett, Sir Julian S. *The Campaign of Trafalgar.* London: Longmans, Green, 1910.

————. *Some Principles of Maritime Strategy.* London: Longmans, Green, 1919.

Deacon, Richard. *History of the British Secret Service.* New York: Taplinger, 1969.

————. *The Silent War: A History of Western Naval Intelligence.* London: David & Charles, 1978.

Durant, Will, and Ariel Durant. *The Age of Napoleon.* New York: Simon & Schuster, 1975.

Ehrman, John. *The Younger Pitt: The Reluctant Transition.* Stanford, Calif.: Stanford University Press, 1983.

Elkins, Dan. *An Intelligence Resource Manager's Guide.* Washington, D.C.: Joint Military Intelligence Training Center, 1994.

Ellis, Kenneth. *The Post Office in the Eighteenth Century: A Study in Administrative History.* London: Oxford University Press, 1958.

Fitzpatrick, William J. *Secret Service Under Pitt.* London: Longmans, Green, 1892.

Flayhart, William H. *Counterpoint to Trafalgar: The Anglo-Russian Invasion of Naples, 1805–1806.* Columbia: Univ. of South Carolina Press, 1992.

Forester, C. S. *The Age of Fighting Sail: The Story of the Naval War of 1812.* Garden City, N.Y.: Doubleday, 1956.

————. *Captain Horatio Hornblower.* Boston: Little, Brown, 1939.

————. *Commodore Hornblower.* Boston: Little, Brown, 1945.

————. *Hornblower and the "Hotspur."* Boston: Little, Brown, 1962.

————. *Lieutenant Hornblower.* Boston: Little, Brown, 1952.

————. *Lord Nelson.* Indianapolis: Bobbs-Merrill, 1929.

Fraser, Peter. *The Intelligence of the Secretaries of State and their Monopolies of Licensed News, 1660–1668.* Cambridge: University Press, 1956.

Furber, Holden. *Henry Dundas: First Viscount Melville, 1742–1811.* London: Oxford University Press, 1931.

Gardiner, Leslie. *The British Admiralty.* Edinburgh: William Blackwood & Sons, 1968.

Glass, Robert R., and Phillip B. Davidson. *Intelligence Is for Commanders.* Harrisburg, Pa.: Military Service Publishing, 1948.

Glover, Richard. *Britain at Bay: Defence against Bonaparte, 1803–14.* New York: Barnes & Noble, 1973.

Goldman, Jan. *Words of Warning: A Glossary for Strategic Warning and Threat Management.* 2d ed. Washington, D.C.: Joint Military Intelligence College, 1996.

Gray, Colin S., and Roger W. Barnett, eds. *Seapower and Strategy.* Annapolis: Naval Institute Press, 1989.

Haldane, R. A. *The Hidden World.* New York: St. Martin's Press, 1976.

Hall, Christopher D. *British Strategy in the Napoleonic War, 1803–15.* Manchester: Manchester University Press, 1992.

Handel, Michael I. *Masters of War: Sun tzu, Clausewitz, and Jomini.* Portland, Ore.: Frank Cass, 1992.

Henderson, James. *The Frigates: An Account of the Lesser Warships of the Great French Wars, 1793–1815.* New York: Dodd, Mead, 1970.

Herman, Michael. *Intelligence Power in Peace and War.* Cambridge: Cambridge University Press, 1996.

Hibbert, Christopher. *Nelson: A Personal History.* Reading, Mass.: Addison-Wesley, 1994.

Hitchcock, Lt. Col. Walter T., ed. *The Intelligence Revolution: A Historical Perspective. Proceedings of the 13th Military History Symposium, U.S. Air Force Academy, Colorado Springs, Colorado, October 12–14, 1988.* Washington, D.C.: GPO, 1991.

Hoffman, Cdr. Lloyd. Untitled lecture presented at the U.S. Joint Military Intelligence College. Washington, D.C., 15 September 1996.

Howard, Sir Michael. *Strategic Deception in the Second World War.* New York: W. W. Norton, 1995.

Howarth, David. *Trafalgar: The Nelson Touch.* New York: Galahad, 1969.

Howarth, David, and Stephen Howarth. *Nelson: The Immortal Memory.* London: Conway Classics, 1997.

Jenkins, Ernest H. *A History of the French Navy from its Beginnings to the Present Day.* Annapolis: Naval Institute Press, 1973.

Jomini, Lt. Gen. Antoine Henri, Baron. *The Art of War.* 1838. Reprint, Novato, Calif.: Presidio, 1992.

Kent, Alexander. *Beyond the Reef.* London: Pan Books, 1993.

———. *The Flag Captain.* New York: Berkley, 1971.

———. *Signal-Close Action!* New York: Berkley, 1974.

King, Dean, with John B. Hattendorf. *Harbours and High Seas: An Atlas and Geographical Guide to the Aubrey-Maturin Novels of Patrick O'Brian.* New York: Henry Holt, 1996.

King, Dean, John B. Hattendorf, and J. Worth Estes. *A Sea of Words: A Lexicon and Companion for Patrick O'Brian's Seafaring Tales.* New York: Henry Holt, 1995.

Lavery, Brian. *Nelson and the Nile: The Naval War against Bonaparte 1798.* Annapolis: Naval Institute Press, 1998.

———. *Nelson's Navy: The Ships, Men and Organization, 1793–1815.* Annapolis: Naval Institute Press, 1989.

Lewis, Michael A. *A Social History of the Navy: 1793–1815.* London: Allen and Unwin, 1960.

Lloyd, Christopher. *Lord Cochrane; Seaman—Radical—Liberator; A Life of Thomas, Lord Cochrane, 10th Earl of Dundonald.* London: Longmans, Green, 1947.

———. *The Nile Campaign: Nelson and Napoleon in Egypt.* New York: Barnes & Noble, 1973.

Lord, Walter. *The Dawn's Early Light.* New York: W. W. Norton, 1972.

MacIntosh, John P. *The British Cabinet.* Toronto: University Press, 1962.

Mackenzie, Robert H. *The Trafalgar Roll: The Ships and the Officers.* Annapolis: Naval Institute Press, 1989. Originally published 1913.

Mahan, Rear Adm. Alfred T. *The Influence of Sea Power upon History, 1660–1783.* 12th ed. Boston: Little, Brown, 1890.

———. *The Influence of Sea Power upon the French Revolution and Empire, 1793–1812.* 9th ed. 2 vols. Boston: Little, Brown, 1898.

———. *The Life of Nelson: The Embodiment of the Sea Power of Great Britain.* 2d ed., rev. 2 vols. Boston: Little, Brown, 1900.

Mallalieu, J. P. W. *Extraordinary Seaman.* New York: Macmillan, 1958.

Marcus, G. J. *The Age of Nelson: The Royal Navy 1793–1815.* New York: Viking, 1971.

Masefield, John. *Sea Life in Nelson's Time.* New York: Macmillan, 1925.

Matheson, Cyril. *The Life of Henry Dundas, First Viscount Melville, 1742–1811.* London: Constable, 1933.

Mattingly, Garrett. *Renaissance Diplomacy.* Boston: Houghton Mifflin, 1955.

McMurtrie, Francis E., ed. *Jane's Fighting Ships 1939.* London: Sampson Low, Marston, 1939.

Miller, Russell. *The East Indiamen.* The Seafarers Series. Alexandria, Va.: Time-Life Books, 1980.

Mitchell, Harvey. *The Underground War Against Revolutionary France: The Missions of William Wickham, 1794–1800.* Oxford: Clarendon, 1965.

Morris, Jan. *Fisher's Face; or, Getting to Know the Admiral.* New York: Random House, 1995.

National Maritime Museum. *The Collections.* London: Scala Books, 1990.

Neilson, Keith, and B. J. C. McKercher, eds. *Go Spy the Land: Military Intelligence in History.* Westport, Conn.: Praeger, 1992.

O'Brian, Patrick. *The Commodore.* New York: W. W. Norton, 1996.

———. *The Far Side of the World.* New York: W. W. Norton, 1992.

———. *The Fortune of War.* New York: W. W. Norton, 1991.

———. *H.M.S. "Surprise."* New York: W. W. Norton, 1991.

———. *The Hundred Days.* New York: W. W. Norton, 1998.

———. *The Ionian Mission.* New York: W. W. Norton, 1992.

———. *The Letter of Marque.* New York: W. W. Norton, 1992.

———. *The Mauritius Command.* New York: W. W. Norton, 1991.

———. *The Nutmeg of Consolation.* New York: W. W. Norton, 1993.

———. *The Reverse of the Medal.* New York: W. W. Norton, 1992.

———. *The Surgeon's Mate.* New York: W. W. Norton, 1992.

———. *The Truelove.* New York: W. W. Norton, 1993.

———. *The Wine-Dark Sea.* New York: W. W. Norton, 1994.

Oman, Carola. *Nelson.* Garden City, N.Y.: Doubleday, 1946.

Parkinson, C. Northcote. *Britannia Rules: The Classic Age of Naval History, 1793–1815.* Gloucester, England: Alan Sutton, 1977.

———. *War in the Eastern Seas, 1793–1815.* London: Allen & Unwin, 1954.

Polmar, Norman, and Thomas B. Allen. *Spy Book: The Encyclopedia of Espionage.* New York: Random House, 1997.

Pope, Dudley. *The Black Ship.* New York: Henry Holt, 1998.

———. *The Great Gamble.* New York: Simon and Schuster, 1972.

———. *Life in Nelson's Navy.* London: Unwin Hyman, 1987.

Pratt, Fletcher. *Secret and Urgent: The Story of Codes and Ciphers.* Garden City, N.Y.: Blue Ribbon Books, 1939.

Price, Anthony. *The Eyes of the Fleet: A Popular History of Frigates and Frigate Captains, 1793–1815.* New York: W. W. Norton, 1996.

Renaut, Francis P. *Le Secret Service de L'Amirauté Britannique au Temps de la Guerre D'Amérique, 1776–1783, d'apres des Documents Retrouvés dans les Archives Britanniques.* Paris: Editions de Graouli, 1936.

Richelson, Jeffrey. *A Century of Spies.* New York: Oxford Univ. Press, 1995.

Richings, Mildred G. *Espionage: The Story of the Secret Service of the English Crown.* London: Hutchinson, 1934.

Rodger, N. A. M. *The Insatiable Earl: A Life of John Montagu, Fourth Earl of Sandwich, 1718–1792.* New York: W. W. Norton, 1993.

———. *The Wooden World: An Anatomy of the Georgian Navy.* Annapolis: Naval Institute Press, 1986.

Rose, J. Holland. *Napoleonic Studies.* London: George Bell and Sons, 1904.

Rowan, Richard W., and Robert G. Deindorfer. *Secret Service: Thirty-Three Centuries of Espionage.* New York: Hawthorn Books, 1967.

Sainty, J. C., comp. *Admiralty Officials, 1660–1870.* London: University of London, Institute of Historical Research, 1975.

Sherwig, John M. *Guineas and Gunpowder: British Foreign Aid in the Wars with France, 1793–1815.* Cambridge: Harvard University Press, 1969.

Stokesbury, James L. *Navy and Empire.* New York: William Morrow, 1983.

Thomas, Donald. *Cochrane: Britannia's Last Sea-King.* New York: Viking, 1978.

Thompson, James W., and Saul K. Padover. *Secret Diplomacy: Espionage and Cryptography, 1500–1815.* New York: Frederick Ungar, 1963.

Tracy, Nicholas. *Nelson's Battles: The Art of Victory in the Age of Sail.* Annapolis: Naval Institute Press, 1996.

Van Crevald, Martin L. *Command in War.* Cambridge: Harvard University Press, 1985.

Ward, A. W., and G. P. Gooch, eds. *The Cambridge History of British Foreign Policy, 1783–1919.* Vol. 1. New York: Octagon Books, 1970.

Warner, Oliver. *The Battle of the Nile*. New York: Macmillan, 1960.

———. *Command at Sea: Great Fighting Admirals from Hawke to Nimitz*. New York: St. Martin's Press, 1976.

———. *Cunningham of Hyndhope*. London: John Murray, 1967.

Weber, Ralph E. *United States Diplomatic Codes and Ciphers, 1775–1938*. Chicago: Precedent Publishing, 1979.

Wilson, Timothy. *Flags at Sea*. London: Her Majesty's Stationery Office, 1986.

Zacharias, Capt. Ellis M. *Secret Missions: The Story of an Intelligence Officer*. New York: G. P. Putnam's Sons, 1946.

INDEX

ABOUT THE AUTHOR

Steven E. Maffeo is associate director of libraries at the U.S. Air Force Academy in Colorado Springs. As a line librarian and an administrator, he has worked at several libraries including the University of Northern Colorado and the U.S. Naval War College. Mr. Maffeo has also maintained a parallel career in the naval reserve. After a short stint of navy active duty in 1972–74 and a brief time in the Colorado Army National Guard (Signal Corps), he enlisted in the Naval Reserve Intelligence Program (as an intelligence specialist third class) in 1979. Commissioned as an ensign (special duty intelligence) in 1981, he is now a commander and the executive officer of a large reserve intelligence unit (located at Buckley ANG Base in Aurora, Colorado) supporting the Joint Intelligence Center Pacific (headquartered in Pearl Harbor and Hickham AFB). His formal education includes an M.S. in strategic intelligence from the U.S. Joint Military Intelligence College in Washington, D.C.

Mr. Maffeo lives in Colorado Springs with his wife Rhonda and son Micah.